"From one of the most courageous voices for democracy in modern Africa comes this must-read book about the storied political landscape of Liberia, a nation whose historic founding holds surprising similarities to the United States."
— Bankole Thompson, Executive Board Member, Center for Racial Justice, Dillard University, USA

"Unputdownable!—A bold, breezy, matter-of-fact book detailing the fascinating failings and political odyssey of one of the world's most talented and accomplished footballers who, against all odds, transited to the tough politics of his country."
— Musikilu Mojeed, Editor-in-Chief, *Premium Times*, Nigeria

"Sieh's detailed account of George Weah's rise from school drop-out to internationally acclaimed football star and his impressive journey from the slums of Claratown/Monrovia to the Executive Mansion in Monrovia will thrill both football enthusiasts and political analysts alike. With his inside knowledge of government manipulations, frictions, fights, cheating, coalitions, the country's football club, and Weah's own rags-to-riches story, Sieh has created a world-class biographical picture of Liberia's troubling political transactions and the man at the center of them."
— Dr. Fred Van Der Kraijj, Historian, Researcher

D1287482

THE UNOFFICIAL BIOGRAPHY

GEORGE WEAH

RODNEY D. SIEH

The Story of Africa's
Footballer President

Rodney D. Sieh

George Weah: The Story of Africa's Footballer President

Copyright © 2023 by Rodney D. Sieh

First edition

Softcover ISBN: 979-8-9872227-1-3
Hardcover ISBN: 979-8-9872227-0-6
Electronic ISBN: 979-8-9872227-2-0

Cover Design | Patrick Knowles
Text Design | Kristy Twellmann Hill
Editors | Andrew Lockett & Paul Roberts

Publishing Support | TSPA The Self Publishing Agency, Inc.

For Sybil,
My darling mother, who is always watching over me.

TABLE OF CONTENTS

———

AUTHOR'S NOTE

———

L iberia's number one sport is football. In America, which has formative ties to Liberia, the sport is called soccer. Over the years of playing the "beautiful game", there have been many star performers and rare generational talents. There have been exciting and memorable performances. Some of the older generation of footballers speak of them with a glint in their eye, still finding the time to marvel and take in the game wherever it is played. They will tell their stories to whoever has the patience to listen. But no Liberian footballer has achieved global fame and recognition like George Tawlon "Oppong" Ousman Manneh Weah.

I am a fan of the game and have always been a huge fan of Oppong. The game came to offer Liberians more than just a pastime. For many like me, growing up in Liberia under the reign of Samuel Kanyon Doe, the 21st President of Africa's oldest republic, football was an escape from the horrors of the bloody 1980 coup d'état. This ended decades of rule by Liberians of American descent, who traced their ancestry to freeborn and formerly enslaved African Americans who immigrated to Liberia in the 19th century. The game of football became a therapy for the shocked and traumatized nation.

In the early hours of April 12, 1980, the sleeping nation was awakened to news that Master Sergeant Doe and a band of low-ranked military officers had overthrown the government of President William R. Tolbert. President Tolbert was assassinated in the Executive Mansion, sending the nation into a frenzy. Regarded as one of the most peaceful nations in the world, Liberia was rocked by a violent turn of events, mired by bloodshed, and the subsequent execution of thirteen members of Tolbert's Cabinet.

At age 29, Master Sergeant Doe was young and more than just an ardent fan of the game of football. He would form and captain his own team – the Executive Lions – and take to the field to play, but only with his designated referee, the Minister of Youth and Sports who was a former member of the Liberian military. Even those who opposed the rule of the Master Sergeant found it difficult to miss games involving the various local teams and especially, the Lone Stars, Liberia's National Soccer Team. This was a manifestation that football was a unifying tool for the country, and Master Sergeant Doe sought to use it, and invested in it, as such. He would lead attendance at Lone Star matches and position himself as the team's biggest cheerleader. He would wine and dine with the players and lauded each victory as a political one.

Doe's love for the game reaped dividends for Weah who played for Invincible Eleven (XI), arch-rival to Doe's supported Mighty Barrolle. But the attention to the game and associated investments by President Doe's government would lead to Lone Star's success and international scouts spotting Liberian talents. From the sandy beaches and gravel-patched pitches, one Liberian talent would rise to the pinnacle of the game. He conquered Europe where he later plied his trade and won the highest honours on offer from the sport. He achieved global superstardom. George Weah became known to the world as one of its best-ever football players.

The game came easily to Weah. Watching Oppong play, even at an early age, was like watching a magician at the peak of his wizardry powers. He played with a rhythm his peers would only ponder and imagine. Opposing teams and fans would jeer at him, but by the end of a game, would marvel and wish he was one of theirs. Oppong would cover the playing pitch, effortlessly zigzagging, "double-shoveling" and bamboozling opponents with his superior dribbling skills and cunning with the ball. Weah was a man transformed between the lines of a football field and transformed the sport for many young Liberian footballers.

Weah possessed skills rarely seen among his peers. And he delivered them with remarkable ease and muscle reflex. One could be excused for thinking Weah spent an inordinate number of hours practicing to achieve the level of muscle memory he needed to execute some of his dazzling movements. His was really a rare gift in the soccer arena.

His exploits took him to Cameroon where he signed with Tonnerre Yaoundé. He was in a different country but his exploits and talents remained unchanged. Weah played so well that the coach of the Cameroonian National Team, Claude Le Roy, would alert his friend, Arsène Wenger, head coach of AS Monaco, about the African gem plying his trade in Cameroon. George Weah had left Liberia for Cameroon and was being readied to leave Cameroon for Europe.

It didn't take long for Wenger to see what Le Roy and the rest of Africa had seen. In 1988, Weah moved to AS Monaco in France for just £12,000 from Tonnerre. Wenger even flew to Yaoundé, Cameroon, to see Weah in action before finally completing the transfer.

On his departure from Cameroon, Liberian soccer enthusiasts – very nearly the entire country – shifted their footballing interest from Cameroon to France. They followed Weah's exploits and seeming dominance of the beautiful game. Wherever he went, football became a new passion for many Liberians. They got to travel with Weah and even seemed to lend support to the team, city and country the Liberian footballing wizard would be playing for. When he played for Tonnerre, a number of Liberians who had never even heard of the club, became interested in their games and followed their results. It was commonplace to see stories of Tonnerre on back pages or in the sports column of the local dailies because Weah was playing for Tonnerre.

When George Weah moved to France, Tonnerre faded from the sports pages and from the minds of football-loving Liberians. A.S. Monaco was the new footballing interest. League 1 of the French Football Association League was the new source of international football interests. After all, that's where George Weah now was – the young dribbler from Gibraltar, a pot-hole-ridden slum in Monrovia, Liberia had made it to France, a national fantasy no one had imagined possible. The boy from the rocky and patchy field of the Antoinette Tubman Stadium was playing on cultured surfaces along with world stars and celebrated greats of the game. Weah of Liberia was playing in France, and by the blessings of his natural gifts. It was a story to fire not only the passion many Liberians have for football but to inspire a nation. Its throng of young footballers felt able to dream of what lay beyond their challenging circumstances.

And with this, to a nation seeking inspiration, George Weah represented more than just a soccer athlete. He represented the inspiration that dreams can come true too – even for Liberians.

It was a slower start for Oppong than many had actually thought. But although excited, Liberians were patient. Their trust in George was proved and assured in Cameroon. They prayed for his chance, and knew given a chance, he would again excel to rise above the rest.

Weah started behind in the French team alongside more accomplished and recognizable European footballing names like Glen Hoddle, Claude Puel and Mark Hateley. Notwithstanding the pedigree of his teammates, Weah knew reading between the lines, the game consisted of a team of eleven versus eleven, one football at a time, playing in a system he had yet to learn, and skills he knew that he was blessed to have. Overawed by his surroundings, he eased himself into the Monaco team and began to earn their confidence that grew during the practice sessions. He soon stood out at training sessions but showed a knack for not being too "systemic", and without much physical strength. But what he lacked, he more than made up for in his cunning on the ball, dribbling skills and knack for scoring goals. He soon got his chance – thanks to injury to star striker Mark Hateley. And George Weah of Europe was born.

In Monaco, Weah couldn't stop scoring goals. On most days, people like me would be glued to their radio sets to hear news about Weah's progress. Unable to afford satellite televisions, most relied on the radio to hear news about Weah. When Monaco would play on the weekends, there would be no rest until the results were heard. On many of these occasions, Weah made his way into the headlines. Liberians felt connected to AS Monaco through Weah. On many of these occasions, Weah made his way into the headlines. Liberians felt connected to AS Monaco through Weah.

His exploits in Monaco led him to win the African Footballer of the Year within one year of turning professional in 1989. Two years later, he won the Coupe de France with Monaco and helped the team reach the final of the European Cup Winners' Cup in 1992, scoring four goals in nine cup appearances.

By the end of 1992, Weah's exploits were visible for all to see, and when Paris Saint-Germain came calling, Monaco could not stand in the way. As

Weah transferred to Paris Saint-Germain (PSG), so did many Liberians who were basking in the joy of his dominant exploits.

Weah went on to play for PSG, from 1992–1995, winning the Coupe de France in 1993 and 1995, and the French League title in 1994.

The period saw Weah become the top scorer of the 1994–95 UEFA Champions League, with seven goals, after reaching the semi-finals with the club. A wonder goal against Bayern Munich on November 23, 1994, is forever etched in footballing folklore and memory.

The goal was a striker's mark of brilliance. Weah took the ball just outside the 18-yard box, flicked a pass to the Brazilian central midfielder, Valdo Candido Filho, and broke down the entire Bayern Munich defense, leaving the opponent's defenders falling by the wayside as he struck the ball in the upper left corner of the back of the net.

In Paris, Weah also reached the semi-finals of the 1992–93 UEFA Cup and the semi-finals of the 1993–94 European Cup Winners' Cup; scoring in total, sixteen goals in 25 European games, a feat that saw him win the African Footballer of the Year for the second time. Weah had dominated and conquered football in France. It was time to move on.

In 1995, Weah agreed to move to what many considered a tougher league, the League 1 - Serie A, the Italian League. Italians were and are still famous for their difficult defenses and tough-tackling tactics. George was warned. But he was unafraid and opted to defy the odds by taking his exploits to the tough Serie A league in Italy where he joined Italian giants, AC Milan.

Under Fabio Capello, Weah played alongside the legendary Roberto Baggio, Paolo Maldini, Franco Baresi, Dejan Savićević and Marco Simone. The team won the Italian league in 1996 with Weah finishing as top scorer for the team. Milan also won the title again in 1999.

At Milan, Weah also reached the 1998 Coppa Italia Final and finished as runner-up in the Supercoppa Italiana twice, in 1996 and 1999. Despite the team's dominance in the 1990s, Milan's fortune in Europe fell short with their best result coming in a quarter-final finish in the 1995–96 UEFA Cup.

Weah's individual performances for both PSG and Milan gained him global and iconic status, yet to be duplicated by any African footballer. In

1995, Weah was the recipient of several individual awards including the Ballon d'Or, the Onze d'Or and FIFA World Player of the Year, becoming the first and, currently, only native African player to win these awards.

Doe's investment in football also paid dividends for the likes of James Salinsa Debbah, James 'Bodywork' Karrow, Kelvin Sebwe, Joe Armstrong Nagbe, Christopher Wreh, Thomas Kojo, Jonathan "Boye Charles" Sogbie, Edward Zico Dixon, Mass Sarr Jr. and a host of others who saw an opening into Europe for football glory. The exploits and dominance of George Weah across Europe opened the doors for European teams and coaches to come looking for Liberian footballing talents which, previously, no one dared to seriously think existed.

For me and a lot of other admirers of the beautiful game, George Weah personified greatness, not just for himself but an entire country. Each trophy he hoisted and each goal he celebrated told the tale of a struggling country called Liberia. Each award and international accolade felt owned by every Liberian, especially those living in economically depressed communities and sprawling slums. One of them – their own – was conquering the world.

The waning years of Weah's football life took him to England where he signed for Chelsea toward the end of the 1999/2000 season and later for Manchester City in August 2000. Weah would float around in Marseille, and later Al Jazira, before finally hanging up his boots.

Weah's retirement from football would soon lead to rumours that he was interested in the Liberian Presidency. Former President Charles Taylor first touted the idea to laughter with many suggesting that then President Taylor was simply envious of Weah.

In mid-2005, Weah would make it official that he was contesting the Presidency.

I interviewed George Weah in a hotel in downtown Washington, DC., in the run-up to the 2005 Presidential elections. Although short on details, I found a man full of determination and hope in wanting to transform Liberia into a modern city. Although he would lose to the more experienced Harvard-trained Ellen Johnson Sirleaf later that year, Weah was unwavering in his quest for the Presidency. In 2011, largely dogged by criticisms about his educational background and thin political resumé, popular Weah ran next to the more politically experienced Ambassador Winston Tubman. They both lost to Ellen Johnson Sirleaf as she earned a second term.

In 2017, on his second try atop the Presidential ticket, Liberians rewarded Weah's contributions to the beautiful game, and perhaps his various efforts and attempts to lead the country, with the highest job in the land, the Presidency.

In spite of my admiration for Mr. Weah, we have often seen things differently. As an opposition leader, Mr. Weah often found my reports about his party, the Congress for Democratic Change, troublesome to his ambitions. The fallout from an interview I did with him for the *Daily Observer* newspaper, where I was an editor at the time, about his 2005 presidential bid raised issues about his French citizenship and a degree acquired from Parkwood University. It was one of dozens that the university listed as fake. This contributed to strained ties over the years.

As a journalist who has been jailed twice for exposing ills and speaking truth to power, and as an unrepentant voice of reason in a nation lingering in abject poverty, recurring abuse of resources and bad governance, I became intrigued by the uniqueness of George Weah's unconventional political appeal. He is a relatively unknown politician, riding on the back of a grass-roots movement and his own popularity. Thus, I felt obliged to dig deep into the persona of a man who mastered the game of football to become one of its greatest. What drove him to the decision to seek the Presidency? How did he come to it and why?

Like you, I was in awe of Weah at his peak of football greatness. While it is not unusual for celebrity athletes to venture into politics, in my view George Weah defied those odds. While there are a lot of question marks surrounding his style and approach to governance, often marred by lapses bearing similarities to many past leaders, this book, based on many interviews, extensive research and historical inputs will drive you closer to George Weah, the man, the footballer and the politician.

Having Mr. Weah's blessings to write this book would have been great but he did not agree and felt it wasn't the right time to tell his story. Thus, I have written an unauthorised version. It is based on interviews with former teammates, peers, political allies and nemeses. I have conducted lengthy research on a football career spanning nearly a decade and balanced it against a distinctly challenging political life. The latter is still under scrutiny and continues to be debated in the court of public opinion.

1

PROPHECY

June 1984

The rivalry between Mighty Barrolle and Invincible XI has always been one of the fiercest in Liberia's football history. The two sides dominated the sport for much of the late 1970s and the early 1980s.

Barrolle was famous for its red-coloured jerseys while IE made yellow the pride of its followers. On any game day – whether it was being played in the Antoinette Tubman Stadium in central Monrovia or in the Samuel K. Doe Sports Complex in Paynesville – fans of both sides showed up in patriotic solidarity with the team of their choice, displaying what they could find to show their love and devotion.

Although early in his career George played a couple of games for Barrolle, his heart was never there. George's ideal team was Invincible XI. However, initially, his ideal team never really wanted anything to do with him.

Alhaji Yaya Kamara, who many considered the "medicine man" of the club, was responsible for scouting and bringing up a lot of the young players in Liberia during those days. Alhaji recalls a rugged beginning for George, who had lots of skills but very little encouragement and opportunity. Simply put, George was a raw, untapped talent, waiting to be polished and unleashed. When the opportunity finally came knocking, George pounced on it, and never looked back.

For years, IE used Alhaji's home as a camp. On most days, players coming through the ranks called it a home. Located in the Jacob's Town belt of Gardnersville, a township on the outskirts of Liberia's capital, Monrovia, the home would later become an important passage for George's journey to football stardom.

"It's true, many of the great players who came through the team's ranks came through these doors," Alhaji recalls. "I have always been a strong supporter of the Invincible XI, from the time I lived on the Old Road – where I stayed before I built this house."[1]

Legendary football stars like the great Santos Maria, Sakpah Myers, Albert Nah, Joe Nagbe, Kai Jerbo and even James Salinsa Debbah all used Alhaji's home as a passageway to football greatness. "They all know me as someone who loves sport – and one who loves to see Liberian children rise up in whatever they decide to do."[2]

In those days, Alhaji was a successful businessman, using whatever he had to promote the players, sometimes pushing them beyond their limits and personal expectations. Alhaji had been a close friend of Lawrence Doe, the President of IE, but following Lawrence's exit, he became much closer to his successor, Archibald F. Bernard.

Recalling his first encounter with George, Alhaji says it was clear from the beginning that George was not in love with Barrolle and was only using the team as a stepping-stone to get to the team he really loved - IE.

Alhaji's first glimpse of George's talent came by way of a couple of matches between IE and Barrolle. Those two games, one played in Monrovia and the other in Buchanan, Grand Bassa County, were organized by the late Superintendent John Y. Kweku and featured top players from both teams, battling for bragging rights. Superintendent Kweku appointed by President Samuel Kanyon Doe, following the military coup of 1980, was an ardent lover and supporter of IE and would later become one of the first casualties of Liberia's long and bloody civil war.

As Director of the sports unit at the Ministry of National Defense during the Samuel Doe-led People's Redemption Council military government, Kweku was killed in an ambush when his team of bodyguards ventured into an area which was the centre of an intense battle between rebels from Charles Taylor's National Patriotic Front of Liberia and Prince Johnson's Independent

National Patriotic Front of Liberia in Palala, Bong County in 1990. Kweku and his men were traveling from the capital Monrovia when they were hit. Prince Y. Johnson, one of the warlords in Liberia's brutal civil war, would later claim responsibility for Kweku's death when he appeared before the Truth and Reconciliation Commission.

Ironically, Kweku was among the first group of emissaries that the late President Samuel Kanyon Doe had sent to Nimba County when the civil war started in 1989.

Not too long after he got to Nimba, Kweku was shot and killed, his legs severed in brutal fashion to the dismay of many, who at the time, were simply helpless to speak up or come to his aid.

The first game in Monrovia ended in a goalless draw with George featuring for Barrolle in one of the only couple of games he would play for the team. The second leg in Buchanan was won by IE 1–0 with George on the losing side after putting up a spirited performance despite only playing the final 20 minutes of the match. Those 20 minutes were enough to convince onlookers and some IE supporters that George had the potential to be something special. George had the prowl of a striker and the maturity beyond his years. There was something about the way he handled the ball, the way he dribbled past his opponents that was rare for his time and those on the opposing end of his exploits knew that George Weah had all the traits of greatness, even if he was a bit raw and unpolished. Prior to those matches, George had practiced many times with IE but got no attention. Playing for Barrolle was his way of trying to get the attention of the team he loved and admired the most.

Frustrated with the shunning from IE, George sought the intervention of some of Alhaji's close friends. "So, he found me through Kaddieyatu Diarrah."[3]

After that second game in Buchanan, Kaddieyatu, a short stout looking young woman who was considered the soul of IE, approached Alhaji about George who had worn the number 14 jersey for Barrolle during those two games. She said, "Mr. Kamara, that boy, number 14 who played for Barrolle, loves the team so much but he says any time he goes to IE officials, they shun him and turn him away."[4]

Kaddieyatu told Alhaji how George really wanted to play for IE, but no one was paying attention. "Since he doesn't know you, we felt we should let you know so you can speak to the team to allow him to join."[5]

Alhaji had seen his share of young promising players, eager to play but so often lacking the killer punch and the desire to press on and succeed. He reluctantly agreed. "I said OK, let him come. We want players; you tell him to come."[6]

After that game in Buchanan, Alhaji was sitting in his car when Kaddieyatu and another member of IE's technical team brought George over to him.

"Are you Mr. Kamara?" George inquired. George, then a shy and lanky young man, continued. "I want play for IE, but I don't know what I did to these people. Every time I go to practice, we play well together but after the practice, nobody can look at me. I've tried everything but no way. But Kaddieyatu tells me when I come to you, it will be alright."[7]

Alhaji remembers telling George, "Everything they told you is the truth." However, the old man still had his reservations and was a bit sceptical. "George, are you really serious to play? Are you ready to play for IE? Because for me, I'm always looking for people who want to be serious. So, if you're not serious, please do not waste my time."[8]

George pleaded. "Mr. Kamara, just give me that chance, you will see how well I will play."

And so, Alhaji agreed. "I said OK, today is Sunday, so we will not practice, Tuesday we will not practice but Wednesday, come to my house."[9]

It must have been around 2:00 – 2:30 p.m. on a Wednesday when George found his way to Alhaji's home. "He was here at my house and around 4:30, I took him to the IE practice ground on the airfield."[10] The airfield is less than a mile from Liberia's second main airport, the Spriggs Payne Airpor, named after James Spriggs Payne, who served as the fourth and eighth President of Liberia from 1868 to 1870 and from 1876 to 1878. He is remembered as the last President of the Republican party in Liberia. The airfield has always been a breeding ground for young talents. Most days you would find the best of the best footballers practicing, or a game taking place.

A stone's throw from the Airfield practice ground was the Ellen Mills Scarborough Junior High School, where George obtained his Junior High School certificate. It was on the Airfield that George had broken his first record in the high school league when he played for the Muslim Congress School by defeating the famous Wells Hairston High School.

As Alhaji and George arrived on the airfield for practice that Wednesday, Alhaji called the team's two coaches to make introductions. "I said, 'You know this man?' They said, 'Yes, he's always practicing with us here.'"

"From today," Alhaji told the coaches, "this is my son, please take care of him. He is the only person that I have ever recommended to you."[11]

In those days, Alhaji's words meant a lot, so his recommendation meant even more. But George still had to prove himself to the coaches and justify his inclusion on what was then a star-studded IE squad, especially as a lanky young striker looking to make his name.

The coaches said, "Sure Mr. Kamara, anything you say, we will do."[12]

That's how George became an IE player.

Alhaji left the Airfield practice ground and proceeded to Camp Johnson Road to meet Archie Bernard, the team's President, to inform him about the new recruit he had uncovered for IE. "I brought a new player to play for us," he said. "He played against us for Barrolle but came to me and said he wants to play for IE, that's the only team that he loves."[13]

Archie told Alhaji that he had no problem with George being brought on, but he too had reservations. "The only problem is, sometimes you spend your money on these boys but most times they are not serious."

Alhaji was insistent. "Please; let's try him. This time, it will be different."

Archie agreed. "Because you brought him, I believe he's someone we can bring up."[14]

James Salinsa Debbah, George's cousin who went on to become one of his fiercest rivals and a teammate on the national team, says he too was baffled when he faced George for the first time in an opposing jersey. They had played together briefly on Barrolle: "He played two games for Barrolle, and IE recruited him. The excuse he had – when I later asked him – was when his grandmother died, Barrolle people never showed up, he came up with that lame excuse and so he left and went to IE – and that's when the rivalry began."[15]

With George now firmly in IE, Alhaji's work was not yet done.

Alhaji recalls, "If I was someone who could run my mouth and said at the time that George would be somebody tomorrow, people would laugh at me. I never went to anyone to say make medicine or juju for the team, I will always say: pray for my team and the players."

On one such trip to a praying man, Alhaji says a prophecy was made about George. The praying man told Alhaji to call out the names of the players to him so that he could pray for them. "I will pray over them in the night and whatever God say to me I will reveal it in the morning,"[16] he said.

The prayer took place before George's first official game for IE.

The next morning, Alhaji visited the praying man who told him, "There was no need to make sacrifice. Just buy peanuts and small snacks and give it to children, but I see something in your team that I never saw before. Do you have any new person on your team?"[17]

The praying man went on to say, "The way God showed me. That man is a lucky man."

Pointing his fingers to the sky, Alhaji recalls, "I swear before anything, the praying man said George will be somebody tomorrow."[18]

The praying man had prayed three times and each time he prayed, he saw George standing tall over the rest of the players. He said, "The thing I'm telling you is not something small."[19] He then suggested to Alhaji that he should buy any living thing – chicken, goat, or sheep – big or small, the size wasn't important. There was only one catch. "Anybody tell you why you are buying the living animal, give it to the person. It can be anybody. That's the only thing you should do."[20]

So, Alhaji travelled all the way to Salala, Bong County, a district located in one of Liberia's most populous counties. There, Alhaji found a Mandingo medicine man in a small village in the area. The old man was renowned for curing major diseases and for making things happen for people looking for help. Among his many clients, according to Alhaji, was a son of Richard Henries, former speaker of the House of Representatives, and one of thirteen members of late President William R. Tolbert's government who was killed in the aftermath of the 1980 Military coup d'état, ending decades of Americano-Liberian rule. Henries' son had been sick for months and the family even sent him to America for help, but nothing could be done – until the

Mandingo old man cured him. "The liquor spoiled Mr. Henries' son's head. He had a drinking problem that hampered his life and his passion for living. It was that man who made the medicine for the boy to cure,"[21] Alhaji recalls.

Alhaji says his own wife's mother had an open mole, an acquired disease that occurs in adults who experience sudden fright or shock or who endure chronic adversity and stress. "Just like that, she turned crazy until the Mandingo man cured her."[22]

So, Alhaji went to a market in Salala and found a small sheep he purchased for US$25. "I bought the sheep and gave it to the man. From that day, I have never opened my mouth to tell George what I did because that's my way of doing things. But even after doing that, I wasn't sure how things would turn out."[23]

It didn't take long for things to unfold. But IE was in a state of uncertainty. The team had a lot of talents but lacked guidance. In actuality, IE was really in need of a coach to take the team over the top.

In next door Guinea, South African coach Mohammed Fernando Sithole was making waves and gaining traction as head coach of Horoya Football Club. But with Guinea going through a transition, Horoya was engulfed in a leadership problem of its own amid political uncertainty. President Ahmed Sekou Touré, head of state of Guinea since independence, had died on March 26, 1984. His Prime Minister, Louis Lansana Beavoqui, was named interim President, with pending elections to be held within 45 days. However, on April 3, 1984, hours before the Democratic Party of Guinea was to choose a new leader – who would have been the only candidate for President – Lansana Conté ousted the government, heading a military coup. Releasing 250 politician prisoners he encouraged some 200,000 Guinean exiles to return to the country. Just after the overthrow, the constitution of the country and National Assembly were put on ice. Political activity was forbidden. The new regime, a Military Committee of National Restoration was established with Conté at its head. On April 5, Lansana Conté became President of the Republic which he remained until his death in December 2008.

In the aftermath of the coup, Horoya's team leader, who was a member of Touré's government, lost his job. The official, according to Alhaji, had brought Sithole from South Africa to coach. With the country in crisis, Sithole was also out of a job.

With a new government in charge, the Soussou (So-so) people, a Mande ethnic group living primarily in Guinea and who were strong supporters of Horoya Football Club, did not want Sithole. They protested.

The Soussou are a patrilineal society, predominantly Muslim, who favor endogamous cross-cousin marriages with polygynous households. They are believed to have descended from the medieval era of slavery.

Alhaji recalls that, when word got out to IE that there was a good coach in Conakry now out of a job, a window of opportunity was opened for IE to pounce. "They said Sithole was going back to South Africa because the Soussou people don't want to see him."[24]

Alhaji then proceeded to inform IE's team President, Archie Bernard, about the possibility that a very good coach in neighbouring Guinea could be available. Archie was impressed but said he had a lot on his hands and could not make the trip to Guinea to bring Sithole. He said, "Mr. Kamara, you know anything you tell me I can do; but you know, I can't go to Conakry. If you able to go there, I will pay your way."[25]

So, Alhaji was tasked with the responsibility of traveling to Guinea to convince Sithole to come to Liberia where a top team with a lanky, untapped striker in George Weah, was in need of his services.

Archie purchased two tickets: a two-way ticket for Alhaji and a one-way ticket from Guinea to Liberia for Sithole. Alhaji boarded a Ghana Airways flight to Conakry.

When he arrived in Guinea, he had a fruitful discussion with Sithole who agreed to return to Liberia at the end of the month after tying up some loose ends.

In mid-April 1984, Sithole touched down in Monrovia on an early morning Ghana Airways flight. Alhaji wasted no time. At around 4:30 in the afternoon, he took the coach to the Airfield practice ground to observe the team's training session.

Alhaji said that afternoon, his heart turned on George and he was convinced that something special was in the making. "When we got there, none of the IE officials and players knew who Sithole was. I only told them I brought a friend to look at the practice."[26]

After more than 30 minutes watching the team in motion, Sithole called Alhaji to one side and asked, "That tall fella over there," referring to George, "Is he an old player or new player?"

"He's a new player. In fact, I'm the one who brought him to the team," Alhaji recalls, beaming with pride.

"That's a damn good player you've brought for the team there," replied Sithole. "Today, that's the kind of people the white people are looking for."[27]

Convinced that he had a future star on his hands, Sithole made a pact with Alhaji. "I give you four months – if IE agrees with my contract. In the fifth month, if some foreign clubs don't come and take George Weah and carry him, you should not pay me a cent. Make sure you keep him – and hold him tight. If the team really wants me to coach this team, keep that boy."[28]

The next day, Sithole and Alhaji were in Archie's office to seal the deal. But before leaving Archie's office, Sithole turned to Alhaji and told him to tell Archie about the scenario he had laid out.

"I told Archie that Sithole had said that if he was allowed to train George, he had the potential of being one of the key players in the world today. He was just lacking a little bit of speed."[29]

Alhaji again repeated Sithole's exact words, "If the team really wants me to coach this team, keep that boy."[30]

With a contract in hand, Sithole got down to business. As part of the contract, Sithole would live in Alhaji's house, frequented by most of the IE players. Sithole's first order of business was to work on George's fitness. So, the next day, when George arrived at Alhaji's house to meet Sithole face to face for the first time, he was instructed not to play any active football for one month. Everyday however, Sithole told George to run around Alhaji's house. "No football," he instructed, "just run around the house, thirty times a day."[31]

George loved the beautiful game. A month away from dribbling and outwitting defenders with his dazzling skills was a tough challenge but in the days that followed, he would soon come to see why his new coach, Sithole, demanded him to run around Alhaji's house. In those days, there were no treadmills, no modern bikes or weight rooms to train, just George using his raw power and strength to make an impression on his coach. Sithole turned to an old-school training method to get George to improve his fitness.

On one of those days, George had made some runs around the house – about 20 times – and decided to take a break on the corner of the house. He was breathing heavily. When Alhaji saw him taking a break, he asked him, "What's going on? Tired already?"

George, feeling the exercise was wearing him down replied, "Mr. Kamara, your man wants to kill me?"[32]. Equating the intense training and exercise to being killed was George's way of telling Sithole that the training was perhaps getting the better of him.

Alhaji scolded George for being lazy. I would tell him, "My man, get up. Look at Roger Milla today, look at Diego Maradona."[33] Those were the two players dominating football at that time.

Milla was the most dominant and popular footballer of his generation, scoring records with Cameroon and with French clubs Bastia, Valenciennes, Monaco Montpellier and Saint-Etienne. He defied age and still holds the records for being both the World Cup's oldest-ever player and its oldest-ever goal-scorer, having scored against Russia in 1994 at the remarkable age of 42 years and 39 days. In the 1990 World Cup, Milla, at age 38, was the centrepiece of the Indomitable Lions side that stole the show and shocked the world.

Maradona was an even more imposing presence in the game. Widely regarded as one of the greatest players in the history of football, he was one of the two joint winners of the FIFA Player of the 20th Century.

In drawing the comparison to Milla and Maradona, Alhaji attempted to show George that endless possibilities were awaiting him if he put in the work. Milla and Maradona never had their successes handed to them on a silver platter; they had to put in the work. For George, the fitness level would be key to him fulfilling his potential which, Sithole knew, was just around the corner.

When Coach Sithole saw Alhaji talking to George, he asked, "What is he saying?"

"The man says he's tired," replied Alhaji.

"He's tired? How many rounds has he run? Add another few laps on it. Let him keep running."[34]

Sithole told George later that day, "You see how people are running behind Milla and Maradona today? That's just how they will be running behind you tomorrow." Alhaji interrupted. "Those are the only two people the coach is using as example to describe what you could become tomorrow, George. He says you are one of the stars of tomorrow; but you just haven't reached your potential. So, do what the man tells you."[35]

So, George, Alhaji and Sithole went on and on for days like this and with each passing day, George's runs began to pay dividends as he slowly began to win the fitness battle. Coach Sithole took notice: he could see the difference, Weah's lanky frame made it easy for him to make runs, there was suddenly an extra bounce to Weah's game. Sithole could see the change in Weah's stamina: he was no longer breathing fast after a few runs around the house, and was no longer complaining about being tired. So, on the 30th day of the running exercise, Coach Sithole was satisfied and told George it was ok for him to resume training with the rest of the team.

George's first game for IE came in early May of 1984 against Horoya FC, Sithole's former team in Conakry. The eve of the game was marred by confusion and late President Samuel Doe was forced to fine IE's President Archie Bernard US$500 because he failed to bring order to the team's camp in Guinea over concerns that Sithole was too attached to Guinea. In fact, some forces in IE were against Sithole managing the team for the match because he had just come from Guinea, and they feared that he would have sympathy for IE's opponents. IE went on to lose the game 2–1 but George left his mark.

George's dribbling skills were on full display and his solo goal after he broke down Horoya's defense, made him an instant hit in Guinea after the match. A goal by his teammate, Ben Martin, was canceled as offside.

After the game, a mob of supporters thronged the IE's team bus to get a glimpse of the Number 14, George Weah. They had even coined a name for him: the "wizard dribbler" from Liberia.

Back in Monrovia and back at Alhaji's house in Jacob's Town, George sat on the floor, staring into the face of Sithole and declared, "Coach, from today, anything you tell me to do, I will do it."[36]

The excitement of hearing fans chanting his name in a foreign land gave George a glimpse of the endless possibilities which laid before him. He had gotten a taste of how hard work could lead to great things, how persistence and drive could propel him to greatness, just as Coach Sithole and Alhaji had been telling him..

Alhajij says, "George never slowed down after, in fact, he became even more determined. I was there to see him improve, to see him become the player that we wanted. In the end, the entire Liberia benefited from what he was able to accomplish on the football pitch."[37]

2

SITHOLE

———

George Telewoda, team manager during Weah's time with Invincible XI, looked back in awe watching Mohammed Fernando Sithole take George Weah under his wings. He had a way of getting to Weah and understanding him like no one could.

"To be frank, Sithole really made that boy when it comes to his physical training and all of that," Telewoda recalls. "So, he was the one person who really knew how to deal with George Weah when it comes to discipline and his physical training. On many nights, Weah would give up due to the intensity of the training but Sithole, the strong disciplinarian as he was, wouldn't allow him."[38]

If Arsène Wenger is credited for untapping George Weah's potential on the global stage, Sithole prepared him for that journey and was right behind Wenger in molding George Weah.

Ever fond of making a connection between his players, Sithole grew attached not just to Weah but many of the other players on IE as well. He named his daughter, Georgette, after George Weah, and his son, Joe, after another teammate of George, Joe Nagbe.

Upon reconnecting with Sithole's kids in 2018, Weah would share stories about Sithole's tutelage. Sithole's son, Joe recalls, "I remember Weah telling me that my dad would put him on his shoulder while running behind the team bus in training."[39] Joe was still a young man when his dad did his training drills with Weah.

Georgette says that Weah shared how he believed in her dad because her dad believed in him. "Weah told me once that he was amazed how this man from nowhere spotted that potential in him. If my dad had not come across him, he's not sure he would have exceeded to where he was in football. So, he always made reference to my father."[40]

Georgette's brother, Joe, recalls his father, as "a very loving man who was balanced with everybody – that's why Weah had this love and connection to him."[41]

Much of Sithole's work with George came early in the morning when everyone was asleep. Joe recalls, "My dad would wake him up in the morning to train before the other players arrive. Sometimes he would train four hours ahead of the rest of the team, before the actual training."[42]

Weah once told Sithole's kids how the training shaped his early start in football. Joe remembers Weah telling him years later how fond he was of his father. "Sithole's training was not easy training. By the time the training start, I was almost halfway exhausted but with consistency, I built that stamina to be able to play. That's how I was able to join IE and become a full player."[43]

Georgette recalls that her father's impact on Weah and the likes of Benedict Nyema, Boye Charles, Joe Nagbe and a host of other footballers, was key to helping promote the game in Liberia. "George Weah impacted that group, he helped to shape football in Liberia in a way that Liberians did not expect. Whenever there was a game, Liberians would gear up to watch the game because it was interesting to see the pattern that football took those days when my dad was around."[44]

Sithole's journey to Liberia was never planned. Telewoda recalls Sithole telling him once that he migrated from South Africa by way of Guinea. "Actually, from what he told me, he came with Miriam Makeba and from what I learned of him is that, at that time, Miriam was soliciting assistance from Ahmed Sékou Touré and Kwame Nkrumah for the anti-apartheid movement, and so she brought a lot of South Africans along with her."[45]

Makeba, the late South African singer and performer of fame was exiled in Guinea between 1968 and 1986.

President Touré had invited Makeba and made her an honorary citizen. The invitation jump-started a close, 25-year-long relationship between Makeba and Guinea. She also became a diplomat for Ghana and was appointed Guinea's official delegate to the United Nations in 1975; that year, she addressed the United Nations. During the 1970s, she went on a series of tours, travelling across five continents on behalf of the U.N., UNESCO and various movements against racism and discrimination.

In 2001, Makeba released *The Guinea Years*, a selection of recordings she made in Conakry, Guinea, during her time in exile.

While in Guinea with Makeba, Sithole, who was a technical football trainer back in South Africa, began assisting coaches for a couple of clubs, including Hafia and Horoya. Horoya, founded in 1975, won multiple football championships in Guinea and was crowned African Champions in 1978. Founded in 1951, Hafia, formerly known as Conakry II in the 1960s, won three titles under that name and 15 league titles overall, having dominated in 1960s and 70s. In the 1970s, Hafia FC dominated African football, winning the African Cup of Champions three times – 1972, 1975 and 1977 – and boasted several great footballers like Bengally Sylla, Abodulaye Keita, Cherif Souleymane, Petit Sory, Mamadou Aliou Keita, Mory Kone and Papa Camara.

A public spat with Camara was a key reason Sithole packed his bags from Guinea and moved to Liberia to coach IE. Telewoda recalls, "The Mandingo community, particularly Mr. Yaya Kamara, heard about the squabbles Sithole was having in Guinea and the problems Horoya was going through, and jumped at the opportunity to bring him to Liberia."[46]

According to Telewoda, Sithole stood out because he was a disciplinarian except that when he joined IE originally, he was seen mostly as a technical coach because of his ability to bring out the best in his players. "He should have been a physical coach. But more or less we used him because in Liberia at the time we didn't have certificated coaches. So, he was good with the discipline and the physical training because of what he learned from when he got drafted from whatever forces Miriam got him from."[47]

This is why Sithole took his training with Weah seriously. "He made sure Weah did what he was supposed to do and did not let anyone show sympathy for Weah because of the kind of skills he saw. The major problem

was, Weah just didn't have the stamina, he did not have the strength and
so we tried to work very hard on his energy level."[48]

Sithole was a family man. The daughter he had died while he was still
in South Africa. Georgette says her dad was the kind of person who would
love to take care of his children. "When he came to Liberia from Guinea,
he had lost his only child he had at the time, and our mom was able to
conceive for him and they had us. Until he met my mom, he was a very
unlucky person to combine with anybody to have children."[49] When the
civil war hit Liberia in 1989, Sithole managed to flee with his two children
to the Ivory Coast.

By 1999, nearly ten years later, and two years after Charles Taylor's
election as President, Sithole was invited to Liberia by Kekura Kamara, who
was a member of the public relations team of Weah to help plan a Reconciliation Conference. While in Liberia, Sithole fell ill and Kekura solicited
the help of Jonathan "Boye Charles" Sogbie, who was now playing football
at ASEC Mimosa in Abidjan, to assist in taking Sithole for treatment in
Abidjan. Jonathan was a top striker for the Liberian national team along
with Weah. Now playing football in the Ivory Coast, his help would be
crucial to what was about to unfold for Sithole.

The coach died in just a matter of days.

No one knew for sure what led to Sithole's death, not even his children,
Georgette and Joe. "Basically, he died from poison or alligator gut. That's
the story I heard from someone who was in Ivory Coast when I was there,"[50]
says Joe. The 'alligator gut' is a poison said to be induced into the wine or
other drinks of the unsuspecting victim by dipping the fingernail where a
small amount is placed. The unfortunate victim is supposed to die within
24 hours or less. While many theories were thrown around at the time of
Sithole's death, nothing was certain. "It wasn't like I knew what the historicity
of his illness was,"[51] says Jonathan, who was instrumental in helping with
Sithole's burial.

Georgette recalls a letter from her dad which suggested he knew time
was not on his side. "From what mom said, he wrote a letter saying that he
would like for us to be with our grandma in case of any eventuality because
he trusted our grandma. Shortly after, we heard he was poisoned, according

to what I heard. We were in Ivory Coast with him. So, when he died that's how they contacted our grandma."[52]

With Sithole gone, George Weah held on to one of the only few people who was as close to him as a father: George Telewoda.

Telewoda says he and George had a father-son relationship. Telewoda recalls, "We came to IE around the same time, and he took to me because I left Young Eagles and he left Barrolle and when he came over to IE, he and a guy called Lansannah Trawally and Alexander Cheneken. These guys were very young and what Sithole was trying to do was to blend the younger players with the older players; but George took to me, and it became a father-son relationship up to the war."[53]

As the war raged toward the capital, Monrovia, Weah wondered what was going on with Telewoda. Their relationship was on a high. So high that Telewoda says Weah "was able to get me a ticket and send it over – and when they drafted him to Cameroon, he tried to get me to go with him."[54]

Weah always felt attached to Telewoda and often thought of repaying his loyalty.

How is the relationship today? Telewoda says he and George have not spoken since his Senatorial elections in 2014. "During that period, he was at home, and I went there and – to this day I'm surprised but he never told me to my face what really happened – but he went off on me while we were at his house."[55]

Weah felt betrayed by Telewoda and was apparently upset that after all he had done for Telewoda, loyalty was not being repaid. Telewoda never saw Weah as a politician and never supported the idea of the football icon getting involved in politics. Telewoda would have been better off keeping his views to himself. So, when some political heavyweights like Ellen Johnson Sirleaf and others sought Weah's blessing to contest the 2005 elections, Telewoda was the emissary sent to win Weah over, and that was the decision from Telewoda that ended his relationship with Weah for good.

Weah and Telewoda had been through the trenches together. Seeing Telewoda on the other side of the aisle and not by his side when he began to flirt with the idea of jumping into politics, was just too much for Weah to bear. For Weah, Telewoda was now the enemy; he had crossed the line, he had burned the bridge that brought them together. The man with whom

Sithole had worked to groom one of the greatest world class footballers to ever grace the stage of the beautiful game was now an outcast for not believing in the political journey Weah was about to embark on. To Weah, this was a betrayal of the highest order.

3

OPPONG

——

Before the world came to know him as King George, George Weah was known simply as Oppong.

The Ashanti surname which originates from the Ashanti City-State became a household name during the rise of George. His exploits as a fancy dribbler with a knack for scoring goals made him the target of opposing defenders. But even before George's rise, the name belonged to a solid utility footballer named Charles Oppong. Oppong was a left-back and midfielder for both Asante Kotoko and the Ghana Black Stars.

For much of the 1980s, Charles Oppong made multiple trips to Monrovia as a member of either the Kotoko side, playing in the Confederation of African Football Champions league, or as a member of the Ghana Black Stars, playing in a World Cup or Africa Cup of Nations (AFCON) qualifiers.

"We played against Barrolle about nine games," recalls Charles. "IE, we played against them about seven games – all the time Kotoko would come to Liberia. Liberia was like our second home. We have many, many fans in Liberia, Ghanaians too who support us. The moment they hear Kotoko in Liberia against Barrolle or IE, everybody would show up at the stadium. The stadium was all the time jammed pack, supporting Barrolle or supporting Kotoko."[56]

It was in one of those Champions league games when Charles caught a glimpse of George. "I saw a young kid. I didn't know he was called George

Weah. But he could play – and he was giving us hell every time he touched the ball. I called him and said I can see you have potential, and I will take you as my brother. I love you so much. I wish you can come and join me in Kotoko. Then, he smiled at me. So, during the course of the game, we were talking about his potential."[57]

On any trip to Monrovia with the Black Stars, Charles would encourage George to avoid injuries but again, he always pitched the idea of George joining him in Kotoko. "Come and play for Asante Kotoko."[58] Again, George, didn't talk much and seemed concentrated on the match – but he always smiled back as a sign of respect for his opponent. So, after the game, Charles called George again and asked him if he was ready to come to Ghana to play for Kotoko. "He smiled and said, it's not possible – that's what he told me, that was my first time getting a detailed response from him."[59]

Before departing, Charles told George how impressed he was with his game. This time, George asked him for his name. "I said Charles Oppong. And I asked his name and he said he's George Weah."[60]

Charles grew up in a hard-knock neighbourhood in Kumasi, Ghana. Playing alongside Ghanaian greats Yaw Sam, Osei Kofi and Malik Jabir, he was a quick student and never gave up an opportunity to learn.

"I saw myself becoming a very good footballer and people would see me and say, 'Charles, you are so good why not try out for one of the teams in our area' – and I did."[61]

Charles would team up with the great Opoku Afriyie in the Division Two before heading off to college. Later, he played in the regionals, where scouts select players based on their academic credentials. It was the perfect setting for Charles to grow and where he would be recruited for the junior team of the Black Stars.

Word about Charles' exploits soon caught the eye of Ohene Djan, the former director of Sports under Kwame Nkrumah who was also Vice President of the Confederation of African Football. "So, Ohene picked me up from Kumasi and took me to a town almost ten miles from Accra, about eight players were selected and I was the small boy in between them."[62]

With the help of the former Kotoko player, Yaw Sam, Charles was offered a chance to learn the ropes. "Among all the players who were selected, I was a little boy at the time but when we got to camp, I was taken to a team called GIHOC Stars: Ghana Industrial Holding Corporation."[63]

After the first practice, Djan saw the leadership skills in Charles and made him captain. "Then I complained to the boss that I was the least of the players who were recruited, and the youngest, how could you choose me to be the captain?"[64]

Despite his apprehension, Djan assured Charles he was chosen because they saw something special. "I had the potential in me to be a leader. So, from that day, I made up my mind that I was a leader, so I had to play a leadership role. I was selected to the national team, the Black Stars. Can you imagine that? From elementary school, college to second division team to the Black Stars."[65]

In preparations for the 1978 Africa Cup of Nations (AFCON) tournament, Lt. Col. Ignatius Kutu Acheampong, Head of State at the time, sent the Black Stars to camp in Brazil where they spent three months. "Though I didn't play much at the time, I was always on the touch line, gaining a lot of experience from the national team. So, when the team needed me or if any defender got injured, I was the only person who was available. I could play all the defensive positions."[66]

When the Black Stars returned from Brazil, they beat Tunisia 3–0 in a friendly match and defeated the army team 4–0.

At the time, President Acheampong realised that he had to send the team back to Brazil, telling the administrators, "If these players stay in Ghana here before the Africa Cup of Nations, they will be spoiled. We have to send them back to Brazil."[67] So, the Black Stars were sent back to Brazil for another three months.

By the time the Black Stars returned to Ghana, it was almost a month before the start of AFCON tournament. The team was solid, rested, and prepared, and the results paid off. Ghana won every match at the 1978 Africa Cup of Nations (AFCON) and were crowned champions.

The Brazil experience for Ghana also paid dividends for Weah and Liberia. In 1986, President Samuel Doe used the same strategy, sending the national team, the Lone Stars, to Brazil for seven months. As with the experience of Charles Oppong and the Black Stars, George Weah and several other players polished their skills training in Brazil.

For Charles Oppong, George Weah was a gem from the very first moment he saw him kick a ball. "The moment I saw him, he touched my heart and I said he's my junior brother. Maybe the conversation I had with him was pleasing. Maybe it was my skills, or my leadership role but I think the way I talked to him, I appreciated him, I showed the love. In the old days, it wasn't all that common for someone to meet you and show you love. So, maybe, it may be that the way I talked to him, the way I considered him, the way we were talking throughout the game. Maybe he felt that I can be his senior brother. Maybe, I don't know how he adapted the name but the first time I saw him, I fell in love with his skills; and I knew he had the potential."[68]

It was not until years later that Charles realised George Weah, the kid whose football skills he fell in love with, had adopted his name. "I was in New York, the United States of America, preparing to go to Ghana for vacation. When I went to Ghana, my brother who resides in Sweden, came to meet me in Ghana and then he told me that, he has heard that George Weah, in an interview in Ghana had adopted my name. I said, 'Wow!' Then I started following Weah in European soccer and then I heard he was in Monaco. I said, 'Wow! Somebody adopted my name!' That was a credit to my name."[69]

4

CAMEROON

January 1987

When George Weah arrived at Cite Verté, a neighbourhood in Cameroon's capital Yaoundé on January 1, 1987, he was about to embark on a Herculean journey with the first division side, Tonnerre Kalara Club of Yaoundé. Most importantly, he had some very big shoes to fill.

The biggest of them all was Albert Roger Milla, one of the most recognizable football stars of the day and one whom Weah had been promised by Coach Sithole and Mr. Yaya Kamara he could surpass if he put in the work and developed his stamina.

Before moving to Tonnerre, Milla made his debut for Éclair de Douala at the age of 15, in the Cameroonian second division. Two years later, aged 17, he became the Cameroonian schools' high jump champion before playing for Leopard Douala and Tonnerre Yaoundé. At the time of Weah's arrival, Milla had made his mark on the global stage and was one of the first African players to play professional football and would go on to play in three World Cups for the Indomitable Lion of Cameroon.

Besides Milla, Weah was also encroaching on the territory of Théophile Abega Mbida. Abega was part of the Cameroon national football team, playing all three matches at the 1982 FIFA World Cup. He also captained his side to their first Africa Cup of Nations (AFCON) victory in 1984, where he scored a goal in the final. He was nicknamed "The Doctor" in tribute to his footballing intelligence.

Abega played club football for Canon Yaoundé where he won the 1978 and 1980 African Cup of Champions Clubs and the 1979 Cup Winners' Cup titles as well as four Cameroonian championships and five Cameroonian Cups. Later in his career, he moved to France to play for Toulouse before finishing in Switzerland with Vevey.

Following a collision with Zambian goalkeeper, Effort Chabala, at the 1986 Africa Cup of Nations (AFCON), Abega retired from football in 1987. He then went into politics, becoming the mayor of the sixth district of Yaoundé. In 2006, he was selected by the Confederation of African Football as one of the best 200 African football players of the last 50 years. Abega died of cardiac arrest at the Yaoundé General Hospital on November 15, 2012.

Tonnerre was both prominent and dominant in the 1980s, winning all of their five national championships as well as the National Cup.

Bessala Henriette, an 83-year-old food seller remembers the early days when Weah played for Tonnerre. "I saw him running around every morning with other young football players over there." Bessala points at a football pitch a hundred meters up a hill. Bessala is still confused as to why authorities have not named the field after Weah. "Weah so far is the most outstanding player who trained in that field, and I wonder why Cameroon authorities are hesitating to name the field after Weah."[70]

Bessala was Weah's neighbour 33 years ago when he came to Cameroon to play football. "Each time Weah scored, and his team won a match, neighbours will wait for Weah's return to celebrate." She remembers one evening she proposed a bottle of beer, but Weah told her, "Anyone who intends to be a good player should never take alcohol."[71]

Rejecting Bessala's offer was a bit harsh but George was focused. He knew that in order to be great, he had to be self-disciplined; he had to avoid all the side distractions standing in his way. Goalkeeper Dieudonné Nké, now the coach of UMS of Loum, one of Cameroon's elite football clubs, played with George in Cameroon in 1988. He says he still remembers the day Weah's extraordinary talent as a football player was discovered. "In 1987, after winning the cup of Cameroon and the Championship, Tonnerre Kalara football club of Yaoundé (TKC) travelled for an international tournament in Liberia to prepare for continental competitions. While in Liberia, we saw a boy playing excellent football. All the players of TKC were unanimous that George could provide a solution to their goal scoring worries."[72] Nké could not remember the name of the club TKC played against in Liberia but thinks that the soccer side was called Invincible XI. "Weah scored twice and after the game, Tonnerre's President army general Pierre Semengue ordered negotiations be opened to get Weah to join TKC."[73]

Semengue says George had other offers but did not hesitate to begin another football adventure in Cameroon. "We were told that Africa Sport of Abidjan had almost ended negotiations for Weah to play in Ivory Coast but to our greatest surprise, George Weah told us that he preferred to play in the country of his icon, Roger Milla. Our relationship with him was very cordial, any other player of TKC can testify."[74]

Semengue may have had his reasons why he thought George chose Cameroon, but George well-remembered the lessons and advice from Sithole and Alhaji. They knew. They saw the potential before George saw it in himself. Filling Roger Milla's shoes was a no-brainer for George. Fate had brought him this far and George was not about to let the opportunity of a lifetime slip away. Cameroon was his choice and Tonnerre the perfect vehicle to drive him to his next chapter.

In spite of his record talents, Weah spent most of his time in Cameroon in a one-bedroom apartment with some of his teammates. George kept his focus. Prior to signing with Tonnerre, he stayed in the home of the team's president General Pierre Semengue.

Dieudonné Nké, who played with Weah at Tonnerre recalls that when Weah first arrived in the team, he could barely speak any French, but quickly adapted. Tonnerre brought in a French tutor to help him learn the language and George slowly adapted to his new surroundings.

Kangsen Wakai, referring to a *Cameroon Tribune* article[75] quotes Nké as saying that Weah's progression and adaption were no different on the football field where it didn't take long for the rising Liberian star to impose himself on the team, alongside Ghanaian winger Koffi Abbrey. Tonnerre was the right fit for George. According to Nké, it was a team in which executives treated players like "extended family members"[76].

According to Wakai, prior to George's arrival in Yaoundé, Cameroon, the team was one of a handful in the Cameroon league that had known as much failure as it had triumph. "It was a team where players, mediocre and great, had come and gone; a team whose rivals, big and small, had emerged and disappeared. Meanwhile the game had undergone changes of its own. Tonnerre was a team whose history was as byzantine as the city and country, which would eventually claim ownership of the icons that would pass through its ranks. The likes of Ernest Ebongué, Roger Milla, Charles Toubé, Stephen Tataw, Rigobert Song, Jean Makoun, and Chadian great Japhet N'doram are just among a handful out of many. It is a history that is not only linked with the development of the game in the country, but whose subtexts provide edifying aspects of the territory's evolution from settler colony to nation-state."[77]

Wakai writes that when football was first introduced to the area that eventually became Cameroon, it was played mostly by European settlers in the metropolises of Douala and Yaoundé. "Like most social functions of the day, de jure and de facto segregation were the norm. In 1930 the wall that had prevented the races from playing collapsed when the then French governor of Douala, in commemoration of Bastille Day, decided to organise a desegregated friendly football game pitting the Douala team against the Yaoundé team. One of the more memorable moments from this historically significant match was the inclusion in the Douala team of a certain Tobias Mimboe aka Bayard aka the "wiper". According to legend, despite having lost the game, Bayard was jailed after the match by embarrassed colonial authorities for his flamboyant style of play and masterful dribbles against his white opponents, which in the authority's view had the potential of demystifying an order that thrived on the idea of its own impregnability."[78]

According to Wakai, legend also attributes the match for inspiring a certain Omgba Zing, an Ewondo who accompanied the Yaoundé team, to discover the area's first native football club on October 9th, 1930, at the home of a German settler in Mvog-Mbi. Zing's tenure as both captain and president of Canon Sportif de Yaoundé was brief, coming to an end in 1934 after a conflict with the Etons that put his ownership of the team into question.

In November of that same year, Wakai notes, Zing took his vision to the Mvog-Ada area of Yaoundé and founded Tonnerre Kalara Club (aka Tonnerre Yaoundé), jump-starting a crosstown rivalry which, could be argued, was partly responsible for the place football holds in the Cameroonian imagination. Wakai says, "Both teams are among a handful of teams that can claim credit for introducing some the game's great talents to the national and international stage. During Cameroon's first world cup finals in 1982, the year Biya became president, the team that represented Cameroon at the World Cup in Spain was made up of mostly players from both Yaoundé based rivals."[79]

By the time Weah made his debut with Tonnerre in the 1987 season, the team boasted an African Cup Winners' Cup (1975), three league titles, and two national cup titles which, according to Wakai, typify the belief that even if football was not born in Cameroon, then at the very least, a strand from the national gene pool was embedded in the modern game's DNA. "It is in this framing that Weah, in less than one season, would write his legend in not only the team's narrative, but the game's history in Cameroon. Scoring fourteen goals in just eighteen appearances, Weah did not stay long enough to see TKC win the national league and national cup titles. Yet in that time, his myth would echo from gully-filled fields in Sangmelima to dusty playgrounds in Maroua."[80]

Wakai says in those days, Weah was a marvel to watch. "Opposing defenders who encountered the striker in his playing days with the Cameroonian club are unlikely to forget how casually he untangled the ball during duels and how fast he flicked those feet that once ran bare in the slums of Monrovia. Who dares not remember the pace with which that sturdy physique sped past them as if it was the run of his life? In the memoirs of their playing days, their encounter with Weah will be printed in bold."[81]

Wakai recalls Weah as a power striker who blasted through defensive walls with ease. "It was his one-touch-and-strike approach in the eighteen-meter box and beyond, unleashing bullet-fast shots, that struck fear in the hearts of goalies he faced. And while he did not lack the inventiveness that has marked the styles of lethal marksmen like Roger Milla and Asamoah Gyan, it was Weah's ability to score from short, mid- and long range, which distinguished and continue to distinguish him from others before, during and after him."[82]

Wakai adds that it was not only Weah's precision, but rather an understanding of positioning during a play that made him an invaluable asset to his fellow offensive mates on Tonnerre. "Not every good striker is blessed with the combination of qualities that he possessed; the power to drive through defences, the focus for ball possession, and a willingness, at the risk of injury, to do whatever their body permitted in search of that goal. Whether it was on the rugged football terrains that characterised his Cameroonian chapter, or on the vaunted stages of European football, those who have watched Weah saw him dive almost recklessly headfirst between defenders, only to see the ball fly into the back of the net [for] moments later; they have seen him lift himself almost three feet high, legs crossed like scissors, then watched him whip a shot past a stunned goalie; their mouths have been left agape watching him run like a thoroughbred on a counter-attack, ball glued to his feet, and followed his every step until he released the ball with such force, the last thing they can remember is a shaking net. Those who listened to his games on radio have heard the likes of Zachary Nkou scream, 'Weah, Weah, Weah, goal!!!!!'[83]

George was blossoming into a fine striker and the Cameroonians knew it. When they saw an opportunity to wrestle him from his homeland with an offer of Cameroonian citizenship, Weah rejected it. "In those days, Liberia was virtually a state in name only. So, we offered him [Weah] Cameroonian citizenship, but he turned it down, insisting he wanted to remain Liberian. Because, I am a nationalist, I found that significant,"[84] General Semengue recalls.

General Semengue says, while in Cameroon, Weah quickly lived up to expectations. He scored two goals in his first match against the then legendary Cameroon elite soccer side Canon of Yaoundé. It was George's performance and rising popularity that prompted Semengue to suggest that Weah be called up to play for Cameroon's national team, the Indomitable Lions. "Today I can say without any fear of committing an error that Presidential destiny stopped him from playing for Cameroon. He should have been defending Cameroon in football pitches not thinking about politics in Liberia, his country of birth."[85]

George had his reasons for turning down the opportunity of a lifetime to play for Cameroon which, at the time, was one of the best and most consistent teams in African football, regularly qualifying for the FIFA World Cup, more than any other African team. Hell, George could have fulfilled his dreams of playing in the world cup had he naturalised and become a Cameroonian. But like General Semengue says, George not only had his reason, but he was loyal and patriotic to the land of his birth. He wasn't about to betray the Red, White and Blue with the star in the left hand corner, the national colours of Liberia.

One of Weah's fans is current TKC President, Dr. Achille Essomba Many. "When George Weah came to Cameroon, I was team doctor for TKC. Weah spent several weeks at General Pierre Semengue's residence. He was a committed footballer. You hardly saw him outside at late hours. At 6am he will get up for footing before going for training. Women love stars, but Weah showed little interest for women."[86] What Dr. Many did not know was that George was on a mission and he wasn't risking anything resembling a distraction to deter him from his quest. George's main priority was to improve his game and cement his legacy. George had put in the work from his days with Invincible XI in Liberia and the Liberian national team. He had heard the comparisons with the great Roger Milla and Diego Maradona from Alhaji and coach Sithole. Although still not quite the finished product, George was not about to fall prey to extracurricular activities and allow a few minutes of pleasure hamper his opportunity to fulfil his dreams.

George was rapidly becoming a student of the game and honing his football craft. He understood what it meant to score but he needed to aim higher. He wanted to prove that he belonged amongst the game's greats. Cameroon was just his latest step along the way, a journey that presented limited opportunities, but opportunities that he was willing to pounce on to the detriment of his opponents.

Weah's most outstanding performance in Cameroon was when he led TKC to win the 1988 Challenge Cup. Cameroon's President Paul Biya, was in the audience at the time. Biya had come to power just six years prior to George's arrival in Cameroon. The second longest-serving non-royal leader in the world and the oldest head of state in Africa, he came to power in 1982.

Essomba recalls that before the final, officials of French Ligue One side, AS Monaco, came to Cameroon to monitor Stephen Tataw, the captain of Tonnerre.

"Instead of following up Tataw, they were seduced by Weah's exceptional football talents. That is how Weah found his way to AS Monaco in 1988 after six months in Cameroon. He quickly became AS Monaco's top scorer,"[87] sports journalist and former team press officer of TKC, Hugo Bosso-keng, recalls.

Bossokeng remembers that George's extraordinary football talents attracted jealousy from some of his teammates. Theophile Abega who was Cameroon's Ballon d'Or complained that more attention was given to a foreign citizen.

"I encouraged him each time he sounded discouraged with comments made by Abega. I told him that his business was football, and he should forget comments made by his opponents. I am sure he was encouraged to do better as a player each time he listened to me,"[88] recalls the former Cam-eroonian national coach, Jean-Paul Akono.

Akono says Tataw got frustrated that AS Monaco opted for Weah when he was contacted before the Liberian. His frustration could be understood. After all, he had a somewhat decent football career. Playing as a right full back, Tataw captained the Cameroon national team at both the 1990 and the 1994 editions of the FIFA World Cup and later became the first player from Africa to play for a Japanese club. He played with Cammack of Kumba before joining Tonnerre from 1988 to 1991, and for Olympic Mvolye from 1992 to 1994. Although Tonnerre was one of Cameroon's leading clubs, it lacked basic facilities, playing on a baked earth pitch in a stadium with no showers or dressing rooms. In 1991, Tataw was reportedly earning £60-per-week. Weah's salary, although slightly higher at the time, triggered envy amongst some of his peers on the team.

By the time George left Cameroon, four matches short of the end of the 1987–1988 football season, he had recorded an impressive 14 goals in the 18 games he played for Tonnerre Kalara Club of Yaoundé.

Tataw, who was in the original plans to be recruited by the football scouts from Monaco, never came close to Weah's level. He had a few trial spells in England, first with Queens Park Rangers and Brighton & Hove Albion, both unsuccessful. In 1995, he joined Tosu Futures of Japan. While he was in Japan, he tried to guide his club to the J-League, the top division. But in 1997, Tosu Futures folded due to the withdrawal of its main sponsor. Tataw had hoped to play for Sagan Tosu, the new club in the city, but he did not agree to their terms and retired.

Despite his concerns over Weah, the two played well together and for Weah, Cameroon was a stepping-stone on the way to Europe's top clubs.

While he was in Cameroon, Weah's neighbour, Bessala Henriette, says, he was surprised their hero had forgotten his humble beginning. "He should have come here at least as a sign of gratitude to us. We received Weah, shared good moments with him, and ate with him. Why has he not visited us?"[89] More than 30 years after Weah set the city on fire with his electrifying football skills, his name still rings a bell at Cité Verte.

George Weah conquered Cameroon with ease, he was a threat to opposing defenders and was a gem to football fans. Even Roger Milla, whom Coaches Sithole and Alhaji once told George he could emulate one day, had become a fan, dubbing George, "the Black Diamond of Africa". With the football world lurking over his shoulders, George Weah had his sights set on the global stage and it was only a matter of time before he would move yet another step closer to achieving his ultimate quest.

5

MONACO

———

July 1, 1988

Timing is everything in life. The same applies to football. When George arrived in Monaco in the summer of 1988, the Arsène Wenger-coached team had too many strikers on the team.

George could not have had a better coach than Arsène Wenger whose tutelage helped him blossom into a clinical and prolific striker.

Wenger would later recall, in his book, *My Life … in Red and White*, that George struggled when he first arrived at Monaco and that the journey there was not an easy one. Wenger had asked a friend, Claude Le Roy, whether he had seen any strikers in Africa that could be an addition to his squad. Claude Le Roy was the then-head coach for the Cameroonian National Team, the Indomitable Lions. He had travelled to Monaco to see Wenger. Over lunch, Wenger says he confided in Le Roy that he had a concern about Mark Hateley getting injured. He wrote, "So, often I was looking for striker who might stand in for him. He immediately told me about a player at Tonnerre Yaoundé. When Claude got back to Cameroon, I would call him every Monday for several weeks and ask him for news about his promising striker. I sent Henri Biancheri to watch him play. He called me after the match. George had played with his hand in plaster, with a fracture. He hadn't done a lot, Henri told me, but when he received the ball, the crowd had responded enthusiastically and that was a good sign. I brought him over."[90]

Monaco paid £50,000 for George, 'chicken change' in today's transfer market. Once in Monaco, it took a while for George to adapt to a new system and a new style of play but an old ghost from his early days with IE would come back to haunt him.

In Monaco, Wenger found George disastrous at first. "Even the players laughed, but he was ready for work,"[91] Wenger told Arsenal Football Club website in February 2018. Wenger says he saw things in George Weah that were amazing, like his physical power and despite his size, he was agile. "He was heavy, so I made him lose weight and he worked very hard with me, sometimes in one v. one situations. We went on runs together and he became the player everybody knew afterwards. The transformation was absolutely unbelievable, it's one of the most spectacular I've seen. Many people said he was a Conference player, with no disrespect to the Conference league, but it's what people said."[92] In the United Kingdom, the Conference League was the name for the National League, the highest ranking and semi-professional league below the top four professional leagues. It was called the Alliance Premier League from 1979 until 1986, then the Football Conference League between 1986 and 2015. It is now called the Vanarama National League in line with its latest sponsorship deal.

So, this was George Weah's challenge. Once again, he had to prove that he belonged. Just as he did with Coach Sithole in Liberia and in Cameroon with Tonerre, Weah had to show Wenger and his new teammates that he had what it took to succeed in Monaco.

George was 23 years-old and Wenger recalls that, at his first training session, George made a pitiful impression, similar to what the South African coach from Guinea who was brought into coach IE had observed about George. "He wasn't physical at all. Everyone thought him hopeless and clumsy. He only spoke English and was very shy. It could only be him and me at first. Because when a coach chooses a man and gives him his debut, a very special relationship is established. He has to work hard to convince others and sometimes the player himself. And that work becomes a lesson in the art of stubbornness."[93]

So, Wenger took Weah running to gain fitness, just as Sithole had done back in Jacob's Town at Yaya Kamara's house, in Gardnersville, IE's training grounds. Wenger said George worked incredibly hard. "I took him running, we exercised together, just the two of us. Training makes men earn the respect of others. He was slender but made of solid stuff. He developed a technical finesse, an artistry that nobody would have expected of him. He was smart, powerful."[94]

It took a while for George to adapt, but Wenger says the Liberian striker was ambitious, talented and had a great hunger for work. It seemed like déjà vu for George. The determination to make use of every opportunity was a driving force. It brought back the memory of the time he scored his first goal for IE in Sierra Leone and the crowd chanted his name after the match.

Match after match, Wenger noticed that George was gaining in confidence. "At first, he used to get himself slaughtered in the penalty area and he said nothing. He just took it, he was amazing. I used to tell him, 'Come on, you can stay down, it's a penalty', but no, he would get back up on his feet. He was a man of absolute honesty, focused completely on the game. He was a part of the team for the 1988–89 season. I had him play against Valur of Reykjavik, he scored, and we qualified for the European Cup second round. And bit by bit, when he was paired with Glenn Hoddle, he became a real star, one of the best strikers in the world."[95]

Despite his impressions about George, Wenger had a dilemma. In those days, there was no European solidarity. So, many of the Englishmen and players from other European nations playing for Monaco at the time were considered as foreign players. Monaco already had Mark Hateley from the United Kingdom who was the team's top scorer when Weah arrived.

James Salinsa Debbah, who played alongside Weah for the Liberian national team, the Lone Star, recalls the dilemma he too faced when he joined Monaco shortly after Weah arrived. "If you came from England and came to play in France, you were considered a foreign player." Debbah was signed to Monaco three years after George's arrival at the club. "So, when I got there, I had to fight my way through too. They had George Weah. George had already established himself as the starting number 9; they had Jurgen Klinsmann from Germany, two Englishmen, Glenn Hoddle and Mark Hateley and the Ivorian, Youssouf Fofana."[96]

Youssouf would later prove to be a central figure in George's transition in Monaco. Youssouf was always kind to George, giving him guidance and taking him on rides to the "Mountain of Alaturbe" the practice field where Monaco trained.

Youssouf knew the terrain well. He began his footballing career with various youth academies in Paris, before joining the youth academy of RC Strasbourg Alsace before making his professional debut with Strasbourg and later AS Monaco.

With Youssouf helping him to get adjusted, George was able to adapt well. Weah got his break when Mark Hateley got hit with injury. Mark had made his mark on the global stage, playing at the highest level for Coventry, Chelsea, Liverpool and Aston Villa. In 1987, Mark teamed up with fellow Englishman, Glenn Hoddle, and the transfers paid instant dividends as Monaco won the French league title. All was going well for Mark until his form suffered a massive reverse thanks to a sickening injury clash with Galatasaray's goalkeeper in a European fixture. It was later revealed that Hatley had suffered a double dislocation of his ankle. Mark would undergo several operations and rehabs. In the season before Mark's injury, he was the club's top scorer with 14 goals to help Monaco win the title. But as the door closed on Mark, another opened for George.

George took advantage of Mark's absence. Even with Mark's injury, George had to work on his conditioning. He had to shed pounds and work extra hard. Like he did with Sithole back in Liberia, George underwent a massive transformation. He was playing above expectations and soon began to win over the coaches and players.

The transformation paid off; George scored 14 goals in just 23 games in his first season in Division 1. By the time Mark returned from injury, George was blooming into one of the world's finest. With Glenn providing the crosses, all George and Mark had to do was tap the ball in the goal. George became a menace for opposing defenders, torturing them throughout the French championship. In the following season, George helped Monaco reach the European Cup Winners' Cup Finals. The club also won the Coupe de France by winning the final 1–0 against Olympique de Marseille, led by Bernard Tapie and finished second place in the league.

The season did not end as Wenger had wanted as the club lost 2–0 to the German side Werder Bremen. But Monaco had put Europe and the world on notice that its generation of rising stars, led by George Weah, was a force. George had completed his most prolific season with Monaco, scoring 18 goals in 34 games and decided it was time to change gear.

As George grew in confidence, Wenger brought in a couple of his Liberia Lone Star team-mates to help him deal with the new environment. "He was very alone to begin with, then season after season, I brought over other Liberian players like the center-forward James Debbah in 1991 and the attacking midfielder Kelvin Sebwe in 1992. They formed a close-knit group which was invaluable."[97]

Wenger was proud of where George had reached. It was a long way from the tall, lanky shy kid who lacked confidence. George had arrived and in Wenger's own words, "Who would have predicted he would go on to do what he did?"[98]

George had paid his dues; the world had taken notice. In four seasons with Monaco, he won the African Footballer of the Year for the first time in 1989, Coupe de France in 1991, and he led Monaco to reach the final match of the European Cup Winners' Cup in 1992, scoring four goals in nine cup appearances. In total, George scored 66 times during his 149 appearances for Monaco in all competitions. Paris St. Germain took notice and signed George for US$7.6 million dollars.

In Paris, George continued his exploits, winning four domestic titles including the 1994 French league, 1993 and 1995 Coupe de France, and the 1995 Coupe de la Ligue. George also led PSG to the semi-finals of the 1992–93 UEFA Cup, and the semi-finals of the 1993–94 European Cup Winners' Cup, scoring 16 goals in 25 European games. That year, he won the African Footballer of the Year Award for the second time in his career.

During his successful period in Paris, George also led PSG to the UEFA Champions League semi-finals in 1994–95, scoring seven goals, making him the top scorer of the tournament. The Algerian great, Rabah Madjer is the only other African player to become the UEFA Champions League top scorer.

As he had done in Monaco, George paid his dues in Paris and in 1995, he was signed by AC Milan for $US8.4 million. Prior to the signing, sceptics were unsure that George would make it in the tough Italian league. But it didn't take long for George to become the toast of San Siro. In 1996, under Fabio Capello, he also finished the season as the club's top goal scorer. In

Milan, he formed a devastating attacking trio alongside Roberto Baggio and Dejan Savićević.

During his time with the club, George won the Serie A title once again in 1999 and reached the 1998 Coppa Italia final and finished as runner-up in the Supercoppa Italiana in 1996 and 1999.

George's biggest achievement with Milan came in 1995 when he became the first African and first black man to be crowned as the FIFA World Player of the Year with a total of 144 votes, followed by Jurgen Klinsmann with 108, Jari Litmanen, 67 and Alessandro Del Piero with 57. The Ballon d'Or started in 1956 with Blackpool player Stanley Matthews picking up the award. Every single winner has come from Brazil, Argentina or Europe. In winning the Ballon d'Or, George broke this tradition.

Wenger happened to be in Milan during the same time the award ceremony was taking place and was surprised when George called him to tell him he wanted him by his side to receive the FIFA World Best Footballer award. "I had no official invitation, and the security guards didn't want to allow me in. George had to intervene," Wenger recalls, "I can only imagine the expression on the face of those suspicious guards when I came back out after the ceremony with the Ballon d'Or trophy that Weah had given me! It's a wonderful memory. Perhaps the only time a player has brought a coach onstage, handing him his award."[99]

Wenger recalls that all the top coaches in the world were in attendance that day, including Fabio Capello and Marcello Lippi. "They were absolutely amazed that a player at his age (who was 28 at the time), was capable of that. He's just a remarkable person."[100]

But in the year after receiving the World Best award, George's impeccable football record would take a massive dent.

Weah had reached the pinnacle of greatness, accomplishing a feat which, until that Ballon d'Or moment, no one imagined possible. The gem from Africa had nowhere else to go but up, or so he thought.

The Jorge Costa moment would change George's life forever. In December 1996 Weah was handed a massive six-match European ban for his head-butt on the Porto defender. The UK's *Independent* reported: "Television pictures showed players from the two teams scuffling in the tunnel at the end of the game, which ended in a 1–1 draw. The match was littered with fouls and yellow cards."[101] George received a red card after attacking Costa in the tunnel at the Antas Stadium after the 1–1 Champions' League draw on November 20th. The incident left Costa with a broken nose. George claimed that Costa had racially abused him during both of Milan's games against the Portuguese side.

Until that incident, George had only received three yellow cards in UEFA competitions during the previous five years and was also granted a Fair Play Award by FIFA. The incident brought the issue of racism to the core of European football. Much of the sporting world appeared perplexed that Weah was being scorned and disciplined by the sporting body over a controversial headbutting incident to the detriment of his illustrious career.

In December 1996, *The New York Times* highlighted the racism aspect of the case, quoting then Liberian Sports Minister, Francois Massaquoi, who openly criticized the FIFA ruling as being biased. "Now that they are punishing Weah, what are they going to do with Costa, whose behavior against Weah was racist? Are they not going to punish him too because he is a white boy?"[102] Reports claimed that Massaquoi alleged UEFA took steps to ensure Weah would not be named as the world's best player again that year.

Rene Eberle, UEFA's Head of Competitions and Discipline Committee Secretary, said at the time there was simply no proof. "We cannot take action because there was no proof to warrant suspending Costa. It was quite clear Weah must have been provoked. What he did could even be seen as understandable, but there was no proof Costa made any such remarks. For alleged racist remarks we have no neutral witnesses. There is no confirmation from television, no confirmation from the UEFA observer and no confirmation from officials."[103]

Despite the ruling, Costa filed criminal charges against George over the incident. Costa told the Portuguese news agency, Lusa, that his decision to file a complaint with Portugal's investigative police was personal and totally unrelated to his team. His team, Porto, also came to his defense and filed a complaint to UEFA. Jose Carlos Esteves, Porto's club doctor at the time, was quoted by *The Independent* of London as saying that Costa, who was shown on television after the game with blood streaming from his nose, would have to undergo an X-ray to assess the damage.[104]

The six-match suspension put George's career on a temporary hold. Many football analysts said George's career was not the same after that, signaling the climax of the glory days of one of the best footballers of his generation.

For Weah, the incident tainted an illustrious career. Although the sport's governing body would bestow its Fair Play Award on him that year, Weah remained quiet on the matter. For Joao Havelange, FIFA's President at the time, "A reaction, provoked, cannot easily erase ten years of loyalty everywhere and in every competition,"[105] suggesting that FIFA was apparently unwilling to allow one of its greatest ambassadors of the game to be haunted by an ugly incident bearing interpretations of racism.

On January 11, 2000, George departed Milan for the English Premier League side, Chelsea, on a loan transfer until the end of the 1999–2000 English season.

In taking his exit from Milan, George declined a £1 million pay-off or golden handshake from Milan owner Silvio Berlusconi, declaring in a BBC interview that he did not deserve the payout. "Milan's President has been fair with my family. The only problems I had are between me and my coach. They gave me a free transfer, but he also wanted to give me money and I said didn't want it because I didn't work for it. He said, I still had a contract and was entitled to it, but I refused. I told him I wanted to be able to come back, look him in the face and shake his hand. I don't want us to have to avoid each other when we walk."[106]

Weah never fully explained what really went down between he and Coach Alberto Zaccheroni that led him to leave with a chip on his shoulders. But Zaccheroni, in an interview with coachesvoice.com suggests that Weah may have been unhappy when asked to play out of position. "I did not have a great relationship with George Weah. We respected each other, but we simply didn't see things the same way. He wanted to play as a number nine, but that summer Milan had signed Bierhoff. I had not asked the club to sign him – Capello had already signed him – so when I arrived and found him there, it was, of course, a nice surprise for me."[107]

Under Capello, who preceded Zaccheroni, Weah flourished. Now on the tail end of his career, new players were emerging and Bierhoff, the German, was on the rise.

Zaccheroni recalls, "Obviously, I could not ask Bierhoff to play on the flank, so I decided to deploy George on the left. There, he had 30 metres in front of him – and, with Andrés Guglielminpietro behind him, he didn't have to run after defenders. He wasn't keen on the new role, but he was very effective when cutting inside on his right foot."[108]

Like Weah, Bierhoff was a formidable aerial presence, finisher and target man able to lead the line.

Weah did not take Bierhoff's arrival well. As the German flourished, Weah saw his opportunities to score decrease.

Bierhoff had played under Zaccheroni at Udinense, another Italian top flight club, and it was there, that Bierhoff found success, winning his place in fame and in the German national team. In 1998, Bierhoff moved to Milan where he won Serie A contributing 19 goals to the campaign including a title-decider against Perugia. That season, he set a record of 15 headed goals – the most in any Serie A season – a record that still stands.

So, it was clear that Weah did not have a permanent place in Zaccheroni-led Milan and after scoring 46 goals in 114 appearances, it was time for Milan to close the curtain on one of its greatest ever footballers.

At Chelsea, George showed glimpses of his prime days, gaining traction with fans after scoring a smashing header against rivals Tottenham Hotspur on his debut. George also scored two crucial goals against Leicester City and Gillingham in Chelsea's victorious 1999–2000 Football Association's Challenge Cup.

But despite his FA Cup heroics, Chelsea did not make the move for George permanent, and, on August 1, 2000, he officially left Milan. He signed for newly promoted English Premier League side, Manchester City, on a free transfer for a two-year contract worth about £2.5m and weekly wages of £30,000.

He played 11 games in all competitions for City, but only started three games. Despite still exhibiting flashes of his footballing brilliance, George, now 33, was entering the twilight of his illustrious career and had lost the magic and the knack for scoring goals at will. Father Time, it seemed, was catching up with him, but George refused to believe that it was. He was living in a state of denial.

George had a rough time with City. In particular, he and club manager, Joe Royle, didn't get along because he saw very few opportunities to play. George Weah's mind believed he could, but the body would not let him. Contrary to what he really wanted to believe and hoped for, he had lost the magic. Upon signing for City, Weah was hopeful that he could get Royle's side into the UEFA league the following season. As ambitious as George's plan was, the reality was that City were newly promoted, challenging the big giants of the Premier League.

Maybe it was the wrong timing for George. Maybe it was the wrong team. The English league is a tough one, where teams fight like cats and dogs to remain in the top flight. For a newly promoted team like City, it was always going to be tough going up against the bigger teams of those days. And Weah, racing against time and age, had the Herculean task of leading the line in a league of new and younger players and a game that was moving faster than his legs and body could manage.

Playing his first match for City before the season commenced, George was a starting player in a testimonial for the Irish international and City rivals, Manchester United icon, Denis Irwin. Four minutes into the game, George received a poorly controlled pass and while trying to intercept the ball, forced Irwin out of the game after a tackle. It was a fluke tackle that left the Manchester United Irish legend's ankle encased in ice. Weah would offer Irwin a hand of apology, but the United man brushed him off in anger as he struggled in agony on the ground. The Irishman tried to play through the pain but in the 37th minute, Sir Alex Ferguson, United's coach, decided he had seen enough and took Irwin out of the game.

A woeful opening day performance by City followed as they lost 4–0 despite George being in the starting lineup.

In the entire 2000–2001 season, George only scored one goal for City. He did manage to score twice in the second leg of a League Cup tie against Gillingham.

The inconsistency was clear in George's next game. A poor performance prompted City manager Royle to pull him out of the game after 70 minutes. On October 16, realising it was not getting a return on its investment on George, City terminated his contract, just 10 weeks after he joined the club.

Eoin O'Callaghan, writing for the42.ie, wrote that manager Royle was less than enthusiastic about George's time at the club, declaring, "He brought some moments of magic with him, but it was always going to be a delicate situation with him."[109] For Royle, George was now a 34-year-old footballer who still yearned for first team football, unable to cope with the reality that his best years had passed him by. "I can understand that fully, but I have to do what I think is best for Manchester City. It is always regretful when things do not work out between club and player. George is a true professional who has a great stature throughout European football, and we wish him well,"[110] said Royle.

George accused Royle and City of disrespecting him, stating at the time, "I'm not upset just because I'm not playing. I do accept because of my age that I won't play all the games. But I will not accept being at a club where the manager names me in the team and then calls me five hours later to tell me that I am not in the team. In my opinion that is unprofessional and disrespectful and shows a lack of confidence in me. I was made to feel old and of no real use to the club. I felt I was being used for publicity to attract other players. I didn't come for the money. I respect the people I work with, and I expect the same in return. My reasons for leaving are the lack of respect, the lack of communication and the dishonesty shown to me by Joe Royle."[111]

It was déjà vu for George Weah. He had the same experience during his final months in AC Milan in Italy. It was the same reason Chelsea declined to sign him beyond his one-year after a free transfer from Milan. Both teams did not feel he still possessed the explosiveness that worried defenders, or the prowl for goals he once had. He was aging and the beautiful game was leaving him behind.

Following his time in England, Weah returned to France and had a spell at Marseille until May 2001. He later played for Al Jazira in the UAE Pro League, where he remained until his retirement as a player in 2003, at age 37. At his last club, Al Jazira, Weah played on a temporary basis.

Many other greats had been down this road. Roger Milla, the Cameroonian who also played for Tonnerre before venturing to Europe with the French Club Valenciennes and later AS Monaco, ended up in Réunion in the Indian Ocean where he played for JS Saint-Pierroise before returning to Tonnerre in Cameroon for four seasons. He eked out his playing days averaging more than a goal a game until 1996 with two clubs in Indonesia Pelita Jaya and Putra Samarinda, after the 1994 World Cup. Despite being capped 77 times for the national team, scoring 43 goals, Milla came face-to-face with reality that his days were numbered.

And so, it was for George Weah. It is tough for athletes playing in the twilight of their lives. It is often a bitter pill to swallow, a difficult scene to watch, especially for aging athletes, with Muhammad Ali and Mike Tyson the most recent examples of prime fighters who lost the killer instinct that instilled fears in their opponents. For Weah, on the tail end of his career, his love for the beautiful game was evident. It was time to begin looking at the next chapter. What was on the cards? What was he thinking?

In Cameroon, one of his idols, football legend Roger Milla, had become Roving Ambassador and an active militant of the ruling CPDM party in his native Douala III Sub-division. Milla's decision fuelled speculation that he had an ambition to run in municipal and legislative elections.

Milla never really gave the idea any real thought. Was Weah pondering following Milla's path into politics?

In the 1960s and 1970s, famous U.S. athletes like Ali, Kareem Abdul Jabbar, Jim Brown and others used their platforms to speak truth to power, to raise awareness about what was unfolding around them. As a footballer, and Ambassador for the United Nations, Weah used his platform to highlight the troubles in his homeland. Ironically, the best example of an athlete drawing the line from politics was Brazilian football legend, Pelé'.

Regarded as one of the greatest athletes of all time, and one of the most significant people of the 20th century, the football legend argues in a Netflix documentary film, *Pelé*, that he could have done more with his influence during the decades the country was under military rule.

Since making his professional debut as a striker with Santos FC at age 16, Pelé scored a world record of 1,279 during his professional career. Despite his success and influence, Pelé stayed away from politics. In the Netflix documentary, the Brazilian icon offered an explanation as to why he shied away from politics despite being investigated for possible left-wing sympathies in 1971 by the government of Emilo Garrastazu Medici's government. "I've been invited to participate in politics but honestly I've got no desire to get involved," Pelé said in an older interview clip used in the film. "Football already takes up most of my time and ultimately, I don't understand anything about politics."[112]

In Liberia, Weah's rise on the football pitch had given him immense popularity, so much so that echoes of politics began to surface as a possible next chapter, now that his best days as a footballer were far behind. But in Africa, politics can be a dangerous game. Rulers and leaders are often fearful of the rise and threats of a newcomer with a high profile and a populist aura which Weah possessed. The thought came with risks and perhaps Weah's disappointment at seeing the beautiful game leave him behind was about to prepare him for a new venture, one with lots of dangerous twists and turns and risks, it seemed, he was apparently willing to take.

6

HOUSE ON FIRE

———

Musa Massaquoi received a call from Abraham Kromah at about 2 a.m. on Monday, April 6, 1996. With bullets flying all over the capital, Monrovia, Musa was informed by his boss that the home of George Weah, the reigning FIFA World Footballer of the year, was being gutted by fire.

The day is remembered as one of the deadliest in Liberia's history, when Charles Taylor's National Patriotic Front of Liberia (NPFL) forces set Monrovia on fire, leaving hundreds of thousands of people fleeing for their lives.

For Musa, the order to react was clear but not without its own challenge. As he and his men proceeded to carry out the order, the fierce NPFL general, Benjamin Yeaten, and his men stood in the way.

Yeaten, dubbed "50", was an NPFL militia leader and mercenary who served as a deputy commander of the Armed Forces of Liberia (AFL) and director of the Special Security Service (SSS) during the Presidency of Charles Taylor.

He was notorious for committing war crimes and was one of Taylor's most trusted and loyal followers. In fact, he was considered the de facto leader of all of Taylor's armed forces and the second most powerful figure in the government.

With him was Jack the Rebel, another of Taylor's top fighters in the NPFL army. Jack was responsible for ensuring the President's private security and stability in the country.

The presence of both Yeaten and Jack the Rebel on the road leading to George's house made things quite difficult, Musa recalls. "It was like 2 o'clock in the morning. At the time, I was assigned with the Special Security Service (SSS) and assigned with Alhaji G.V. Kromah. I was in the service then and AB Kromah was just promoted to Chief of Staff in the Armed Forces of Liberia."[113]

Alhaji G.V. Kromah (aka AB or Abe Kromah) was a former journalist who became one of the warlords and leader of the United Liberation Movement for Democracy (ULIMO) faction during the Liberian civil war. Kromah (a moderate Muslin) had rose to the post of Director General of the Liberian Broadcasting System in1982, and Minister of Information in 1984 under President Samuel Doe. During the William R. Tolbert years, he served as Assistant Information Minister and before that, as a special assistant to the Vice-President. After a short period in exile, Kromah co-founded ULIMO: an armed resistance group that had pressured Charles Taylor to negotiate during attempts to locate a political solution to the Liberian conflict. In 1994, ULIMO split in two. Kromah was to lead the grouping known as ULIMO-K, that ran its operation from north-western Liberia, inside and near to, Lofa County. ULIMO-J, the other ethnic Krahn faction was led by General David Roosevelt Johnson, a former Customs Officer exiled in Sierra Leone where ULIMO was born.

So, when Musa received his orders to protect George's home that morning, he was unsure what to make of it – or what to do. "I asked Abe which one of George's homes were on fire," Musa recalls.

Abe Kromah told Massaquoi that the fire was at George's home on 9th Street. George's house was, by then, a refuge for many escaping the flying bullets. "Everybody who was around 9th, 10th and 11th Street used the place as a haven. The house was always very packed,"[114] Musa says.

Upon running into Yeaten and his men just around the Fish Market, a little over a mile from George's house, the feared general appeared determined that whatever was unfolding at George's home was on the orders of some higher-ups within the ranks of Taylor's NPFL.

Musa recalls, "I was moving toward the house with my group when Yeaten asked me, 'Where are you going?' I said, 'Ambassador Weah's house is on fire and my boss, AB Kromah, has instructed me to move there and put out the fire.'"[115] George had only a few months earlier been named as a Goodwill Ambassador for the United Nations International Children's Emergency Fund (UNICEF) and most Liberians began referring to him as Ambassador.

It was then that Musa says General Yeaten told him to stand down and forget about the operation and go back. Musa then took his radio and proceeded to call his boss, the Chief of Staff of the army, Abe Kromah. Musa tried his best to tell Abe that General Yeaten was preventing him from carrying out his orders, but Abe wasn't hearing it that day and began to rain insults on Musa, going as far as insulting his mother. "I gave you an order and you're telling me about Yeaten?"[116] Abe said, shouting in his loudest voice on the other end of the radio-phone.

So, as Musa and his boys proceeded to George's house, General Yeaten and his boys opened fire, and everyone ran for cover as an intense battle unfolded.

The raging battle at the scene of what used to be a fish market prevented Musa and his boys from proceeding to George's home. It was not until around 3am that morning that Musa and his men finally reached the house which was being gutted by fire.

There, General Yeaten and his troops had raped a lot of girls taking refuge on the property and gunshots could still be heard as Musa and his men tried to scope the area for Yeaten's men. Musa and his men moved down toward the beach behind the property to make sure none of General Yeaten's men were hiding or setting up an ambush.

"Because we did not have enough men with us at that time of the morning, we had to be sure," Musa recalls. "There were only three of us. So, when we finally arrived at the house, most of Yeaten's boys had jumped over the fence and escaped. George's room was filled with ashes and smoke."[117] Yeaten's men had a field day rummaging through whatever they got their hands on. George had made millions and was fond of expensive shoes and clothes. For Yeaten and his rebels, this was war. Yeaten's men took it upon themselves to take the shoes out of the boxes in George's bedroom to set up the fire.

Musa recalls, "You could see clothes and shoes all over the place, some burned, others still carrying brand name tags and not yet worn." [118] When Musa and his men saw what was going on, they immediately began to put out the fire. In the process, they managed to rescue several of the refugees who had taken refuge on the property.

It took Musa and his men at least two hours to bring the fire at George's home under control and by 5 a.m. that morning, calm was restored to George's home and the refugees taken to a safe haven on Alhaji Kromah's base. Like Weah's home, the Kromah base also was home to a lot of displaced people fleeing the fighting.

Back at George's home, Musa had managed to remove a fairly new Pajero jeep that Weah had only recently brought into the country and took it to the Kromah base for safe keeping.

The generator was left intact as were several other vehicles which Musa and his men managed to salvage and take to the compound of Alhaji Kromah.

In another part of town, word got out that a black Mercedes convertible belonging to George was seen in the vicinity of Mamba Point. Jones Blamo, then a Deputy Director at the National Security Agency, was designated along with another of his principal deputies, Paul Harris, to get the car which was parked in a parking lot of a home in Mamba Point and take the vehicle to Kromah base for safe keeping.

The mission was successful. Blamo managed to get the vehicle but while driving the car toward Congo Town where Kromah's base was located, they ran into Reginald Goodridge, the Minister of Information and chief spokesman for Taylor. Goodridge stopped Blamo and Harris from taking the vehicle. "I need it,"[119], he told the pair.

An intense argument ensued, nearly resulting in a scuffle. In the end, Blamo and Harris had to stand down.

Goodridge was a principal figure for Taylor. Both Taylor and Kromah's ULIMO-J had come to an arrangement and agreed to work as allies. This made it easy for the scuffle over George's black Mercedes convertible to end without any incident.

With the vehicle in Goodridge's hands, Blamo reluctantly agreed to let go. "We will monitor it – at least we have a trace of who has the car,"[120] he was heard saying.

Goodridge remembers the incident differently. He says President Taylor had asked him to get some rice from George Haddad, a popular Lebanese businessman in Monrovia. "Because George Haddad had been my friend for years, the President thought he would be the best person to help as a lot of displaced Liberians were in need of food. So, Taylor said, 'Why don't you go to George Haddad to negotiate for 500 bags of rice?' At the time there was no direct route between Congo Town and Monrovia."[121]

Goodridge says he was on his way to Haddad's office, in his vehicle which was designated MEDIA 1, while another friend, Mark Keshen, was riding with his boys. "We went to Red Light – all the way down Water Side around to where George Haddad still lives. And we negotiated successfully for the delivery of the rice."[122]

Goodridge says on the way back, driving down from the Mamba Point enclave where the French Embassy was located, he noticed maybe 20 to 30 cars lined up. There were some Nigerian troops taking cars. Among the cars, he saw George's black Mercedes convertible.

"I said, 'But Mike, let's wait. That's my friend George's car there.'" Goodridge went to the ECOMOG soldiers and told them, "That's George Weah's car."[123]

The ECOMOG was a West African multinational armed force established by the Economic Community of West African States, largely supported by personnel and resources of the Nigerian Armed Forces, with sub–battalion strength units contributed by other ECOWAS members – Ghana, Guinea, Sierra Leone, The Gambia, Liberia, Mali, Burkina Faso, Niger and others.

One of the ECOMOG soldiers responded: "Oh, the World Best."

"And that's how they released the car to me. They gave me the keys,"[124] Goodridge says. Then, Mark Keshen asked one of the guys to drive his jeep while he drove George's Benz to President Taylor's place.

According to Goodridge, Taylor said, "Wow Reggie my man, you raged hell with those guys. You took the boy's car from ECOMOG?"[125]

Goodridge explains that it was decided that at the appropriate time, the car would be sent to Abidjan. To his surprise, Goodridge recalls that on the BBC "Focus on Africa" program at 5 p.m., George proclaimed that Reginald Goodridge had burned his house – and stolen his car.

When BBC called him for comment, Goodridge politely told them, "I think he's ignorant. I was so upset. I said he was very ignorant for making that remark."[126]

According to Goodridge, three weeks later, Taylor made arrangement for men to take the Mercedes convertible to Danane, in Ivory Coast for George. Goodridge says George was seen in Abidjan driving the car and he is still waiting for an apology. "You would have thought that as a decent person, he would have called me – he had my number – he would have called me to make amends."[127]

Musa insists that Goodridge is not being truthful. "Goodridge lied. He had the convertible. He drove that car [until] April 6. The only reason he took the car was because of the relationship at the time because Kromah and Taylor had become close allies and so when the noise came about that's [when] Abe Kromah said, 'You leave it,' because we knew who had the car and it was traceable. So, that was how Goodridge took the car. He shouldn't lie on ECOMOG. Call Goodridge in front of me, Goodridge knows me. Goodridge knows the whole incident of the car. It's unfortunate that Jones Blamo died, Paul Harris died, but those are people who went for the car. We took the black Mercedes convertible; it was parked in Mamba Point."[128]

Looking back, Musa laments the risks he took to keep George's house from burning. "It was Abe Kromah's order that took me in the yard, and I went in that yard under bullets, managed to cut the fire off, rescue the people from there, get over to Congo Town and take them to safe haven."[129]

Musa says Abe did all he could for the people that were seeking refuge in George's house. "That yard, after the incident, was a place where we normally patrolled. We always patrolled that yard constantly to make sure nothing bad took place there because at the time, George was proudly flying the flag of Liberia, and we did not need anything to disturb him, so we should protect him. But it was Taylor's mandate, according to Yeaten, to burn the house down."[130]

Musa says to this day, he is still unsure why anyone wanted to burn down George's home. "At the time, none of us knew what was happening between Taylor and Weah." He believes Taylor was responsible because of what General Yeaten told him that day. "Yeaten told me to stand down, and when I called AB, he rained insults on me for not carrying out his orders to protect the property. Yeaten told me, 'This thing is bigger than you.'"[131]

Musa is still bewildered as to why Taylor's men would go into the compound of George Weah, set it on fire and rape women. "That house on April 6 was like an embassy, people were seeking refuge there and those guys moved in."[132]

Lewis Brown, who was President Taylor's National Security Advisor at the time, is unsure if the former President had a hand in the attack on George's home. "I don't know. What was obvious to many at the time was that the relationship between the two men was strained and not seemingly friendly."[133]

7

LET-DOWN

———

Monrovia, July 1, 2001

On the eve of the biggest game of their professional lives, George Weah and the Liberian Lone Stars thought they had it all locked up. They were on their way to the 2002 World Cup in South Korea and Japan. All they needed was to beat the Black Stars of Ghana and stamp their names in the history books. After all, they had beaten a star-studded, fully assembled Ghana 3–1 in the first leg in Accra on January 27, 2001.

Yes, Liberia had taken the wind out of Ghana's sails and the Ghanaians knew it. In fact, the Ghanaians were so convinced that they would lose in Liberia, they sent a third-tier team to Monrovia.

Although Liberia was without three of its top stars, James Salinsa Debbah, Jonathan "Boye Charles" Sogbie and No. 1 goalkeeper Louis Crayton, the team was not short of replacements. With George Weah leading the line, victory was assured – or so they thought. Placed in Group B that featured Nigeria, Sudan, Ghana and Sierra Leone, Liberia faced a Herculean task to qualify. But any team, in those days, featuring George Weah had a chance – and Liberia certainly did. If they succeeded, they would be amongst the smallest countries to ever reach the grandest stage. Liberia had been looking favourites for qualification – a history-defying first – and had they not lost their nerve and poise in the last three fixtures, the prize could have been theirs.

But ahead of the 2002 World Cup, Nigeria lurked. Unlike Liberia, Nigeria appeared composed and did all they could to exert pressure. All

George Weah and Liberia needed was to maintain their sanity and secure a win over the Black Stars to secure a world cup berth. Failure for Liberia would mean Weah was on the verge of becoming one of Africa's greatest players to miss out on the World Cup, joining a select group of world class footballers – Eric Cantona and David Ginola of France; Ian Rush and Ryan Giggs of Wales; Abedi Pele of Ghana and George Best of Northern Ireland. But George Weah had conquered the world and was confident that nothing was going to deny him a ticket to the World Cup.

After five games, Team Weah led the way with twelve points, the Nigerian Super Eagles followed with seven points and a disappointing Ghana had mustered a sole win and two draws in their matches. The Sudanese, on nine points, trailed the group leaders, Liberia. Only a historic triumph at the Samuel K. Doe Sports Complex in Monrovia stood in the way.

In the days leading to the big match against Ghana, it was clear that Liberia had its work cut out. They had to come through two games against Nigeria and the Black Stars unscathed and that would be enough for qualification. The Weah-led team held a three-point lead over Sudan, with a healthy goal difference to boot. Shocking Ghana with a 3–1 victory in Accra, the Lone Stars needed to avoid defeat against Nigeria and Ghana, and win against Sierra Leone. Nigeria helped themselves and Ghana winning their home fixture 2–0 against the Lone Stars. Liberia still had their fate in their own hands until they lost in Monrovia to Ghana's Black Stars, 2–1. Nigeria then had to beat Sudan which they managed easily 4–0 with goals from Jay-Jay Okocha and Yakubu (both later to become English Premier League stars) and one from Julius Aghahowa. With the last round of fixtures, the table had switched around. Nigeria led ahead of Liberia and Ghana, with two points between the top three. Sudan was already out of it.

With Nigeria flying high, Liberia needed some magic from Weah and a bit of luck in their final game of the qualifier. Also, some help from Ghana. Weah scored the lone goal in the team's final qualifying match in a 1–0 win against Sierra Leone. That was not enough.

Nigeria was in no mood for freebies at the Liberation Stadium, with three first-half goals from Victor Agali and a Tijani Babangida brace seeing the hosts race into a 3–0 half-time lead, en-route to topping the group.

Nigeria's resounding 3–0 thrashing of Ghana dashed Liberia's fading hopes; the final standings in the group had the Super Eagles of Nigeria on sixteen points, with Liberia tailing behind on fifteen points. A win here or there and Weah would have broken the curse and taken Liberia to the world cup. While there was a lot of blame to be shared, most of the players agree that the team shot itself in the foot, hours before the game kicked off.

Dionysius Sebwe grew up in a family of famous footballers. His brother, Kelvin Sebwe is still highly regarded as one of the best midfielders ever to emerge out of Liberia. Both grew up playing for the Black Stars football club before finding success in Europe and the United States Major League Soccer (MLS). At the time of the 2002 World Cup qualifiers, Dionysius was a central defender for the Kansas City Wizards in the MLS.

Looking back on the fateful game against the Black Stars, Dionysius says, the team simply let the country down. No excuses. It was a matter of do or die, it had come to just one game, one victory and Liberia would have been World Cup bound and Weah would have filled one of the few blind spots on his illustrious football career.

For Dionysius, the failure boiled down to one simple fact, the lack of leadership from Weah. "We did not go to the World Cup because of leadership failure. I came down from Kansas for the game and the other players came from Europe. Back then, we didn't have hotels, so we had to lodge at the 9th Street Sinkor residence of George Weah. I can't remember which room I was in, but the bottom line is we didn't have leadership because it turned out that we were all bigger than the coaches and the coaches were intimidated by us. You had all professionals in the team and the coaches never played professional football, so we got away with a lot of stuff."[134]

If the team had a coach with a high profile, it could have made the difference. "We needed someone to make sure no player left the camp. Most of the guys, including my brother, Kelvin, they fucking went out. They all went out that night. We got a major game and people were taking it for granted."[135] For Dionysius, the bulk of the team's problems rested with George. "He was our captain, coach player, Technical Director, he was everything. Every time he made decisions; nobody was there to tell him he was leading wrongly. I said, some of us are not going to take this shit."[136]

All along, George was so complacent and certain that Liberia had already qualified, he issued a mandate that any player who did not play in the preliminary qualifying rounds would not go with the team to the World Cup. So, it was surprising to Jonathan "Boye Charles" Sogbie that in the days leading to the crucial game against the Black Stars, George called a number of unfit players who were not playing active football in Europe – and not with any team.

Jonathan was unavailable for the match. He had just had surgery on his right hand and his team, Servette, had sent him to China with Chongqing Li Fan football club for six months. While Jonathan was in China, Mass Sarr Jr. and Thomas Kojo tried out for a team in South Korea but were not successful. Sarr and Kojo then received a try-out invitation from Chongqing Li Fan where Jonathan was playing. While on try-outs, George sent an invitation for them to come and play against Ghana. To this day, Jonathan believes that George – with whom he had a long, lingering beef – did not want him to go to the World Cup. So, by keeping him out of the qualifying rounds, George had a valid reason not to have him travel with the team. "George wanted to make that case. So, he sent for those people and they had not played in any of the preliminaries or the qualifying rounds, that's one of the reasons we lost that game."[137]

Eight days prior to the game against Ghana, the team's number one goalkeeper Louis Crayton nearly lost his eye.

Crayton and a group of players were in a vehicle belonging to Kolubah "Zizi" Roberts, one of the team's top strikers. Crayton was one of the grooms-men in Joe Nagbe's wedding. He sat in the front passenger seat of a Burgundy Prelude Honda Accord sports car driven by the little brother of Roberts.

The Honda Accord had been passed on from George Weah to Roberts. It was one of the first cars Weah rode around Monrovia whenever he returned home for international duty with the national team. Liberians had become fond of the license plate, Clar 14, in honour of his wife, Clar Weah.

Driving on the Congotown backroad right before Kaddieyatu Diarra's house, Crayton recalls that a sky-blue pickup truck, came out of nowhere, from the Boulevard Road close to the home of President Charles Taylor and ran into the Honda Accord, slamming the smaller car into a light pole on the main road.

The weight of the accident's impact dealt a major blow to Crayton. "After the car came to a halt, particles of glass went into my face but not in my eye," the former goalkeeper recalls. "My right shoulder was dislocated, I couldn't move my right shoulder, even to today's date, I still have pains due to the effect of the accident. There was just no way I could have played with that shoulder, the doctors did all they could but deep down, I felt it was a lost cause; I was in state of shock."[138]

Not too long after the crash, bystanders began to descend on the scene of the accident and soon it became clear that a couple of Lone Star players were involved in an accident. "I was bleeding from beneath my eye, but I could hear whispers from people on the scene, who recognized who I was,"[139] recalls Crayton.

Soon, news of the accident began to spread. George Gebro, a midfielder on the Lone Star, was also part of the convoy of cars carrying players to the wedding. His vehicle was right behind the Honda Accord carrying Crayton. Crayton believes Gebro may have spread the news about the crash to officials of the government. It didn't take long before radio newscasts began reporting the grim news that the nation's reliable goalie was unlikely to be fit to face the Black Stars of Ghana because he was involved in a freak car accident.

A red ambulance arrived on the scene and took Crayton and the driver to the John F. Kennedy Medical Hospital. When President Charles Taylor got wind of the accident, he dispatched a few of his aides to the hospital to check on the status of Crayton.

Crayton was a reliable goalkeeper, he had followed a long line of goal-keeping greats like Pewu Bestman, Boye Cooper, Zeogar Wilson, Momo "Wall" Blamo and Wreh Brapoh. With a major game on the line, his right shoulders and bleeding eyes put him out of contention to start in goal just when Liberia, within striking distance of a World Cup berth, needed him the most.

With Crayton out, the task of manning the posts for the match was handed to Anthony Tokpah. Louis and a few of the other players were on their way to the wedding of Joe Nagbe, one of the team's veterans. Louis had started his career playing for St. Joseph's Warriors, one of the top-tier teams in Liberia those days, then had spells at four Swiss clubs: Lucerne, Grasshoppers Zurich, FC Schaffhausen and Wangen Bei Olten from

1997–2001. Crayton continued in Swiss football with YF Juventus (2001–2002) before time at Zug (2002–2003).

Louis made his international debut for Liberia at the 2000 Africa Cup of Nations qualifying match against Tunisia, then went on to represent Liberia 36 times.

So, his presence between the goalposts was always a good thing for Liberia.

Looking back on the day, Louis is still unsure whether his presence would have made a difference. "There's a deep story behind this whole thing – from my perspective. I don't know if my presence would have made a difference because, you know, there's a saying that 'be not deceived, God is not mocked. For whatever a man soweth, so shall he reap' – something like that."[140]

Prior to the match, Louis said the team had a routine. "We had a practice of carrying out this routine whilst we were on camp. All the time we would have a little devotion and before we went on to play and it came to a point in time where we started winning and things started going our way and everybody forgot the routine, forgot what got us where we had reached."[141]

In fact, in the hours before the game, Kolubah "Zizi" Roberts, one of the top players on the team, refused to play in the defence.

According to Louis, Zizi declared to the rest of the team that the game was a historical one and he wanted to score. So, he was not playing in the defence. Zizi and George were engaged in a serious shouting match within hearing distance of the rest of the team, stirring a big confusion in the camp ahead of the game.

Zizi knew his worth, but the timing of his decision proved costly for the team. In 1996, Roberts aged 17, embarked on his professional career going on to play for eight different teams in Liberia, the USA, Switzerland, Greece and Italy. His great promise had been recognised when he signed for AC Milan in 1998 a year later but Roberts never played an official match for the team, appearing only at friendly competitions such as the Copa Centenário de Belo Horizonte and going on loans to some minor teams such as Ravenna and Monza. Even so, he had been an important player for the Lone Stars, playing 31 games and scoring 9 goals. He was named the Liberian Soccer Player of the Year in 2003.

Like Dionysius and Jonathan, Louis says, the blame for the team's loss fell on the captain, George Weah. "Our people got a saying that the fish doesn't get rotten from the tail, it gets rotten from the head. We weren't disciplined. I don't know if my presence in that goal would have made a difference, we just weren't disciplined. So, I cannot say too, this is the will of God to move me out of the team so that I would not be part of it because I was seriously intervening on behalf of my teammates because we weren't disciplined."[142]

There was just too much confusion in the team's camp prior to the game. "Oh yes!" says Louis. "Players felt big headed that they had reached their zenith and wouldn't listen to anybody. People were making remarks in rude fashion toward the coach, then there was also a lot of noise over the money that FIFA was going to give Liberia if the team had qualified."[143]

He recalls that the team officials were already dividing money before they even qualified. "As the saying goes, the baby ain't born yet, the eyes big. Too many things, there were so much confusion going on behind the scenes of that particular game, so many things happened. So, I don't think my presence would have made any difference because after all, the goals that they scored on us. I don't see any difference that I would have done but the whole thing, it was a mess, man! Trust me, it was a mess."[144]

Mess aside, maybe it was a blessing in disguise that Liberia never made it for a date in the group of death. "The fact is, if we would have gone to the World Cup in 2002, the group Nigeria was in, we would have been in that group with Argentina, England and Sweden."[145]

For some of the players like Dionysius Sebwe, missing out of the World Cup meant lost opportunities for many of the players to showcase their skills and secure possible contracts. But Louis says most of the players on the team were already aging. "I don't know if four games to the World Cup or three games to the World Cup would have made an impact in anyone's career because at that time, everyone that was on that team were already over our thirties. So, I don't see how much difference that it was going to make in playing three games in the World Cup. We would have played three games. How many people would have seen us to have made a difference? I've seen friends of mine that played for Togo that went to the World Cup in Germany in 2006 and when they left the World Cup, it didn't make a difference for them."

At the time, the average age on the Lone Star's team in 2002 was at least 35. "We were not young, we were not kids on that team, we were grown men. So, I don't see how much of a difference it would have made."[146]

Louis says the game against Ghana was lost because the team was ill-disciplined. "Some people asked me, 'How come you guys attended a wedding two days before a such a big game?' No! The wedding was eight days. I always tried to clarify that the wedding was not two days before the game, the wedding was eight days before the game."[147]

Louis recalls that George never had any strict rules. "He would say, 'We are all professionals. You know what we're supposed to do. Just make sure you go and enjoy yourselves and come back in time for the game.'"[148]

Sadly, Louis says, everyone went clubbing: everyone forgot what was at stake, what needed to be done.

Despite his injury, Louis says he became a distraction for the team, stemming from some money he received from President Charles Taylor to assist with his injury. "George and others got mad at me because when I had the accident, President Charles Taylor had sent for me and gave me US$10,000. He said, 'Louis, help yourself with this money when you go back to Switzerland to go to the hospital.'"[149]

To his surprise, Louis said, his teammates – including George – took offence. "Weah, the captain, was not concerned about what had happened to me. He wanted to know how much money Charles Taylor gave me. So, when I came back to the camp I didn't tell him."

He asked, "Did Charles Taylor give you anything?"

I replied, "Charles Taylor said he will see me after the game."[150]

Louis' decision not to tell George and the rest of the team how much he had received from President Taylor sent the camp into frenzy.

What made matters worse is that President Taylor had told Edwin Snowe, who was the then-head of the Liberia Football Association. President Taylor had asked Snowe whether Louis told him about the US$10,000 given to him to help with treating his injury. Snowe told the President that he was not aware. Louis says instead of Snowe coming to him to ask, he went straight to George and told him about the US$10,000 President Taylor had given him.

"So, I became a laughing-stock on the camp," Louis recalls. "They were calling me a Judas, calling me a hypocrite, that I'm fake, I'm pretentious. So, I told Snowe, 'But why didn't you come to me and ask?'"[151]

According to Louis, Snowe later came to him and acknowledged that he should have come to him first to ask about the money from the President, instead of going to George directly. Amid the confusion, an angry Louis stormed the camp telling George to his face. "So, I said, 'First of all, the money that Charles Taylor gave me for my injury, what did you all want me to do? Divide it with you people?'"[152] Louis says the money was not even half of what was required to treat him when he returned to his team in Switzerland.

Although he never got to play the game against Ghana due to injury, Jonathan "Boye Charles" Sogbie says had he done so, things may have ended differently. "If I had been on that team, on that camp, I would have insisted, I would have made some noise that nobody should take part in any wedding, that nobody should go anywhere until that game was over. Saturday night is not far from Sunday. What do we lose?"[153]

Liberians did not take the national team's failure to qualify for the world cup lightly. Much of the blame fell on George. The pressure and the blame prompted George to call it quits on the national team. His decision came after Liberian fans hurled objects, as well as abuse, at him after the game.

Liberia was banking on George to lead the team to the 2002 Africa Cup of Nations Finals in Mali, a 'sort of' consolation prize for missing out on the World Cup.

Speaking to Monrovian local radio station DC101, George said, "I am finished. I am resigning after the Freetown game, and they can bring in new people to take them to the African Cup. I will not play with them anymore and I will not coach any more. I will not have anybody insult my mother. For that reason, I will never be part of the Liberian team. I am going to leave Liberia and go to the States and live my life."[154]

Amid the insults, some angry fans even went as far as suggesting that George had compromised the game. Dionysius says he too heard the rumours but really didn't think that played a role in the team's failure to qualify for the World Cup. "I heard things were happening but to be honest, I had no proof. I didn't think anything was going to happen in terms of George intentionally trying to do stuff."[155] But he does however feel that leadership lapses played a major role. "For starters, the way the team was drawn. I was the best defender at the time, but he left me out. If you look at the record, I'm the only Liberian defender to play at the highest level. I'm not saying Sakpah Myers wasn't good – we all played for the national team, but they never played in Holland in the Dutch Premier league; George never helped me, nobody helped me. It was my performance that a scout saw and then took me to Europe."[156]

Dionysius says George had his own way of running the team and sometimes it led to problems and the game against Ghana was no exception. "Whether there were other reasons he was doing it, because I think I came in the second half. He had this thing where he would put people he wanted to put in the game. Sometimes when he tells me not to play on the team it was always because of some simple disagreement or maybe I wasn't buddy-buddy with him at that moment – and I didn't have time for that. So, that night, most of us didn't take the game seriously. I don't know whether it was that Liberian thing that we had already arrived, so, that seriousness just wasn't there. If I had to do it all over again, the approach would be different."[157]

When he tried to make suggestions, George would brush him off. "During camp, I was in college at the time. So, I was usually in my room reading, and George and others had problem with that: 'That man just like to be in the room, reading.'"[158] Dionysius was no brush over. He attended Park College where he played football. In March 1995, the Kansas City Wizards selected him in the 1996 MLS College draft. He also played for Orlando Sundogs, FC Utrecht and SC Heerenveen in Holland. Part of the problem was the division of the team. "On that team they had that European clique. So, if you were not part of that core group, then you're lost. The team was always drawn from Europe. Everybody else was added on and then we would practice. Even for me to get on that team, I had to justify myself."[159]

For Dionysius, it all came down to the lack of leadership. "If we had a good leader, things would have been different. I'm not saying George was bad. When it comes to football, motivation, inspirational, he was very talented, but leadership was not there. He had problems articulating to the guys he was trying to coach. He had it but it was just raw."[160]

The Liberian national team was not the same after the loss to Ghana. Although the team won the last game against Sierra Leone during the qualifiers, everyone seemed dejected. "Everybody was sad," Dionysius recalls. "I mean, we avoided each other, and we were just pissed. Everyone went into their own corner and said, 'We screwed up.' Everyone was in shock over the result. I don't think there was a meeting called. We never met as a group to say, 'Guys, you know how did we do?' There was nothing like that, only regrets and failed expectations."[161]

James Debbah did not play due to injury but even he, who had been George's strike partner for many years, was in shock after the loss to Black Stars of Ghana. "Up to now, I still ask that question to a lot of my colleagues. I still don't know what happened. People come up with conspiracy theories but if you put all the pieces to the puzzle – I was injured and did not play but the entire tournament, we played a 4-4-2 formation, and it was very effective. Against Black Stars, George changed the whole system to 3-5-2. It was something the players were not used to."[162]

Secondly, Dionysius says, Weah chose to feature players who had not been playing active football or played any of the qualifying games. According to Dionysius, Thomas Kojo, for example, had not played any of the games and was not match fit. Nevertheless, Weah had pencilled in Kojo as a right back to play against Ghana. Even more troubling for the team, according to Dionysius, Weah had made sure that Joe Nagbe, a natural midfielder, play in the defence. For Dionysius, Joe was simply not fast enough to go head-to-head with the fast-paced Ghana Black Stars attackers. To make matters worse, Weah substituted the only player who was of any threat to the Black Stars, Frank Seaton. To this day, Dionysius says he still gets chills over why Weah took Frank out of such a crucial match, when he was playing so well. "I always say it was complacency that beat us, but I can't defend it."[163]

A case in point for Dionysius was the decision by some of the senior players to attend Joe Nagbe's wedding on the eve of the big match. "How could you all attend a wedding at a major game like that. Zizi Roberts came from the club at 5 a.m. There were too many things. They didn't take the game serious at all. We were too complacent. Imagine if we had qualified for the World Cup, a lot of players would have gotten contracts. Our failure to qualify ruined a lot. For me, I was completely disappointed. It's like missing the Holy Grail, who wouldn't want to go to the World Cup? All we needed to do was beat Ghana Black Stars in Monrovia – after winning in Sierra Leone."[164]

Whether it was complacency or simply the fact that the Liberians over the years had become content with mediocrity, missing the World Cup shattered not just Liberia's hopes but Weah's as well. He had won everything there was to win. Now, all he needed was the exclamation point. It wasn't enough that he was the first African footballer to win the prestigious World Footballer and European Footballer of the Year. For Liberia, it would have hit home the point that amid the horrors of war and chaos, there was a shining light in a nation in turmoil and Weah, the powerful striker out of Gibraltar, had come so close but yet so far from achieving one last impossible and unimaginable feat, a World Cup berth.

8

MELTDOWN

———

B y the time the 2002 Africa Cup of Nations in Mali came around, George Weah had softened his heart and thought that he would never wear the red, white and blue colours for Liberia again.

At 35, Weah was on the tail-end of a successful football career and perhaps hoping that he still had one last kick in him to climax his career on a high. Retirement was on hold once more. He had missed out on going to the World Cup. But now, he had a chance to salvage that loss by winning the coveted Africa Cup of Nations on his second try, this time in Mali in 2002.

Placed in Group A with Nigeria, Mali and Algeria, the tournament marked a tall order for a team with so much promise yet often failing to fulfill its potential. The team drew 1–1 with Mali in its first game, another 2–2 draw with Algeria before falling 1–0 to Nigeria and bowing out.

The tournament in Mali marked Weah's swansong. The former World Footballer of the Year, and the best and most popular player from the continent of Africa, Weah had given everything in the sixteen years since he first wore Liberia's red, white and blue national colours. As he walked into a room of reporters after Liberia's exit from the tournament, echoes of violence back home ricocheted through his mind. Just as the final whistle was blowing at the end of the match against Nigeria, news agencies began reporting that thousands of displaced Liberians were fleeing toward Monrovia, the capital, after clashes between towns called Sawmill and Tubmanburg, sixty miles outside the capital.

Sawmill was home to about 10,000 people who had fled fighting since the middle of 2001 in northern Lofa County between rebels and President Charles Taylor's forces. The rebels, from a group called Liberians United for Reconciliation and Democracy, included fighters from factions in the civil war that had ripped apart the country.

Human rights groups had accused both sides of atrocities in a war declared over that month, which was closely linked to the brutal 10-year conflict in neighbouring Sierra Leone.

As news of Liberia's exit from the tournament became eclipsed by renewed fighting amongst rebels, a pensive Weah pondered his next move. "I'll be a businessman in future," Weah told journalists after the match. "I'll enjoy it. I'm not going back to Liberia again, not until there's a change of government. The people live in fear."[165]

Perhaps there was a lot of blame to go around as to why Liberia did not do well at the AFCON tournament in Mali in 2002. Besides the indiscipline in the team's camp and differences amongst Weah and his teammates, the strained ties between Weah and President Taylor was evidence that there was more beneath the surface. Weah's popularity was overshadowing an embattled dictator, struggling to keep rebels at bay.

The irony of it all is that Weah, whenever he faced daunting questions about his beef with President Taylor, dismissed any suggestion that he was interested in politics. While most Liberians wanted him for President, he would often quip, "I'm not a politician."[166]

In defeat, Weah was full of reflections and honest admissions that perhaps the Liberian Lone Star team was simply not ready to shine. "If I'm honest, we didn't deserve to qualify," Weah told journalists after the loss to Nigeria. "But the Lone Star has made great progress. I have had a great career, I've no regrets."[167]

Meltdowns had become a defining theme for Weah and his generation of footballers. The team had qualified for the 1996 AFCON tournament in South Africa but never made it past the first round. The tournament in Mali offered yet another unfulfilled promise. Amid the hopes and expectations of an entire nation, was an aging and declining team, mired in lingering feuds and disenchantments. As it was in South Africa of '96, the crux of the team's preparations centered on a major beef that had been years in the making.

George Weah and Jonathan "Boye Charles" Sogbie never really saw eye to eye. For starters, they both played the same positions, wing and cen-tre-forward. Many moons ago, the Lone Star began brewing the feud that would pose yet another heartbreak for supporters of the national team.

After a rugged upbringing, Jonathan paid his dues. Like George, he got his start with Invincible XI. After excelling for IE, Jonathan took his skills to ASEC Mimosa in the Ivory Coast, Lausanne Sport, Servette Geneve in Switzerland and in his later years, the Connecticut Wolves, Rhode Island Stingrays and Chongqing Lifan FC in China.

He and Weah first met in 1982, when Jonathan attended the St. Mary's High. At the time, Jonathan played for a local community team called Ashanti Kotoko in Logan Town. Playing alongside the late Thomas Freeman, Charles Barnabas and Dominic Brapoh – who all attended St. Mary's – Jon-athan was a rising star in the community.

So, on a sunny Saturday afternoon, Jonathan and his Kotoko boys travelled to George's doorstep, to play Young Survivors in Claratown.

Before the game, Jonathan recalls, there was just too much noise about a young lad called Oppong. "Then, they called him Oppong. I didn't even know his 'George Weah' name at the time."[168]

According to Jonathan, George came onto the pitch wearing a wig, looking like soul singer James Brown. "He was a very fancy player, dribbling and stuff like that. We beat them anyway: 1–0 in Claratown. And that was the first time I ever saw this guy or heard about him."[169]

Jonathan returned to Bong Mines where he spent most of his time with his family. "Those days, I went back to Bong Mines because that's where I lived. But we came to Monrovia because my father was transferred at the Bong Port and we were in Duala, Momo Town."[170] In Bong Mines, Jonathan played for a local team called Lofa Bridge. Once again, he and George Weah's paths were about to collide. George travelled to Bong Mines. At the time, he played for a team called Azariah.

Along with George was Joe Nagbe, a solid midfielder who would later go on to become one of the iconic footballers of the national team. George and Joe travelled all the way from Claratown to play for Azariah. At the time there was a serious competition between Azariah and Lofa Bridge. "We always beat them anyway," Jonathan recalls. "But this day, I remember specifically because he brought Joe and another player with him, and that game was tense, seriously tense. Everybody in Bong Mines were in attendance. We played and we beat them 3–0. Surprisingly, I scored all the three goals and so the competition began with the public and that's how that feud started to move forward."[171]

George returned to Monrovia and Jonathan stayed in Bong Mines.

At the time Jonathan had no idea what George had been up to or which team he was playing for. "I later learned that he played for Barrolle but that was around 1985–86."[172]

It was off season for the National Football League but the rivalry between Mighty Barrolle and Invincible XI was always something special. So was the rivalry between Jonathan and George. So, in late 1986, IE dispatched two of its coaches, the late Jallah Duncan and Bushwick Kennedy, to Bong Mines to recruit Jonathan "Boye Charles" Sogbie. "They came to Bong Mines to pick me up," says Sogbie, "but at the time they came, there was a tournament between LBS Falcon, NPA Anchors and Bong Range."[173] Prior to the start of the game between Bong Range United and NPA Anchors, the coaches from IE informed Jonathan that they had come to take him to Monrovia. "So, the first game was with Bong Range United and NPA Anchors. Now, when that game started, I was approached immediately that IE had come to take me to Monrovia to play against Mighty Barrolle on Sunday because it was on a Saturday."[174]

Just like that, Jonathan was on the verge of donning the yellow jersey of IE and team up with his old nemesis, George Weah. But first, Jonathan had some obligations.

Jonathan informed the coaches that his team was relying on him for the game and could not just leave them on their own. "I said, at the time, that I could not leave because this team depends on me. For me to leave, it means this team would be defeated. This means I have to play, and you come for me tomorrow morning."[175]

The coaches were not hearing it and insisted that Jonathan leave immediately for Monrovia. "They came with a taxi. I appealed to them and told them, let me try to score two goals and then I can leave the game, I'm sure we can defend two goals and then we can go to Monrovia and play against Barrolle."[176] The coaches granted Jonathan the permission to stay and play the game.

On the field, murmurs and chatters were in the air. Many could be heard in low tones, doubting whether Jonathan would make it with IE. Yes, he was a great young player in Bong Mines. But did he have the stuff to play on the national level? Can you believe it, Jonathan scored the two goals as promised in the first half and got in a taxi with the IE coaches and headed for Monrovia. Surprisingly, after Jonathan left the game, Bong Range lost 3–2. "Just what I was afraid of."[177]

On the way to Monrovia, the IE coaches kept bringing the game up. They were overly concerned that Jonathan was a bit cocky, overconfident in himself. "Some saw it as personal arrogance. But I was confident in my ability that I could have scored those two goals – and I did that."[178]

Upon arriving in Monrovia, Jonathan joined the rest of the IE team in Chocolate Factory, Jacob's Town at Mr. Kamara's home. Jonathan was introduced to the rest of the squad, many of whom he idolised, listening to live radio commentaries of IE vs. Barrolle games on the state-run Liberia Broadcasting Corporation. Standing in the same space as Robert Clarke, Ezekiel Doe, Isaiah Lincoln, Joe Nagbe, Tony Bracewell, George Weah, Simeon Mattar and other great players, Jonathan was in football heaven.

"I was personally interested in being with them than actually playing," Jonathan recalls. "When you are a kid and they put you amongst celebrities you tend to blend in like that. But it was more about meeting them and taking the news back to Bong Mines rather than just saying I played a nice game."[179]

At the time there were no smartphones or digital gadgets to take memorable pictures. So, Jonathan had to settle for Polaroid cameras.

In those days, jersey numbers were assigned to specific players and everyone in the dressing room had already picked up their jerseys. George, of course had his number 14. Jonathan looked around in amazement, wondering which jersey he would wear but only one was available that day. Thomas Weeks was a prominent player for IE in those days, but he was not playing that day and so his number 13 was available for Jonathan to wear.

"So, I went and pick up the number 13. I had no idea that the number 13 was for Thomas Weeks but at the time, Weeks had not come. Weeks was amongst the senior players but being an off-season game, he was sitting this one out. "When Weeks came and did not see his jersey, he said, 'Well, you can wear this number 13 jersey provided you play to impress me. If not, do not touch this uniform again.'"[180]

Jonathan was dumbfounded. "I didn't know whether I was going to perform well – and we were playing Mighty Barrolle. Imagine, IE playing Barrolle and I'm a new kid on the block appearing."[181] Jonathan took some time to get adjusted. He had not practiced with the team and being his first game, he did not want to disappoint.

At the time, George used to play the left wing and for this game, the coach had drawn up the play for Jonathan to play on the right and George on the left. Even though Jonathan was a striker, the team could not compromise Tony Bracewell's position for Jonathan. So, Jonathan was dispatched to the right. For about three to four minutes, Jonathan couldn't touch the ball.

George Harris played the ball from the centre all the way to the right side, then Jonathan trapped the ball and was facing an opposing Barrolle player, Frederick Cole. "I took the ball toward Cole full speed, and I stopped. And Cole also stopped, and I hit the ball on my left foot and pushed it forward, what they called the double shuffle. And I hit the ball and it went in front, passing Cole. I cut inside the field because you are most dangerous within the 18-yard box. I cut inside and Frederick could not touch me at the time. Without hesitation, I brought the ball back where Ezekiel Doe was placed. He pretended to want to kick, broke the ball and hit it toward the goal and that was the first goal."[182]

With one goal up, Jonathan began to feel confident in himself. "I started to say, this thing is not as difficult as I thought. I started to get adjusted to the game. Dominic Brapoh was on the Barrolle side, and he redeemed 1–1. In the second half, George Weah asked me to switch wing with him. He will go right, and I will go left."[183]

George went to the right side, dribbled opposing players and stalwart defender, William Gray, and walked in the goal. After George's goal, Jonathan said to himself that everything George Weah did, he had the ability to do.

"So, there's no point in passing ball to anybody else. So, the next ball that came to me I did exactly what George would do, and I scored, 3–1, I got the next ball, and I did the same, 4–1."[184]

The result marked the first time in the history of IE that the team had beaten Barrolle 4–1.

Jonathan stuck with the number 13 as his jersey number, one he wore throughout his play for IE and the national team, the Lone Star. The game marked the coming out party for Jonathan, and the birth of what would become a lifelong feud with George Weah.

Jonathan always saw George as a big player but claims that George always avoided the big games because he was afraid of being roughed up. "He was afraid of foul play and every time we had a major game, the guys would set for him because he likes to dribble and get by defenders. That's why he was called the wizard dribbler. So, he would always avoid Barrolle games and Cedar United and those kinds of things. Until I started to get used to those kinds of things."[185]

Jonathan says every time IE was set to play a team like Barrolle, George would find a way to avoid playing by making endless demands and setting conditions. "Either they didn't pay his school fees, or they didn't pay his rent. Someone was supposed to pay his rent, they didn't do it. At some point I would just get upset and say you don't want to play because we are playing Barrolle. So, if you don't want to play, don't come."[186]

Jonathan says George's rants and attitude began to get to him. "All the other games, the Cedar, the Sparrow, Oilers and others, he would dominate all the game but when it got to Barrolle, he got afraid."[187]

Things like that went on between George and Jonathan and eventually boiled over to the national team.

Jonathan can still remember his first call-up to the national team. "It was in 1988, I remember I was in school when I was announced together with Kelvin Sebwe who was playing for the Black Stars at the time. The late coach, Walter Pelham, had put the list out and everyone in my school were ecstatic. I didn't even hear the announcement until my schoolmates came and told me."[188]

In those days, the coaches would announce the team line-up on the 12 o'clock news.

James Debbah had been the team captain for much of the first few games for the national team, until George took over.

For Jonathan, George started to exert dominance. "If and when you did not agree with him on issues, or on any matter, he took it personal." Jonathan has always been a vocal person and he was not about to allow George to walk over him. "The captain is not the best person on the team because everybody cannot speak at the same time. The captain does not tell you what to do, the captain speaks for the team. He's a messenger. But with George, he felt that he was most popular and was a very good player on the team and he had the captain's armband – and the coaches listened to him and most times, I would let things slide for the sake of harmony to exist but when it became necessary, I spoke out."[189]

One of the first run-ins with George came in the build to a qualifier for the AFCON in 1996 which was scheduled to take place in South Africa. "I had an arthroscopy surgery on my knee where they put the tube in your leg, and they have a video on the screen. Liberia had to play Tunisia in Tunis and I sent in my excuse because I got injured in Italy while on camp with Servette. We were in training when I hurt my leg, but it was a minor operation – two weeks rest period. We lost that game 2–1 in Tunis and George thought that I did not want to play away from home and so, he would make sure that I was not going to play the next game at home. When that game came against Tunisia, the FA forwarded me an invitation which I honoured."[190]

Upon arrival in Monrovia for the return leg, a lot of noise was in the air that Jonathan would not be allowed to play on George's orders.

David Kotee was a die-hard supporter for IE and upon hearing the news that Jonathan would be omitted from the team, took to the airwaves on a local radio station, declaring, "Jonathan 'Boye Charles' Sogbie will play for Lone Star tomorrow. We, the Concerned Few of IE, will assemble on the football pitch and protest if Boye Charles is not in jersey."[191]

David was clear that there would be no game.

By the time the group assembled at the Samuel K. Doe Sports Complex to face Tunisia, the message had resonated, the threat of protest was heard and Jonathan was in his jersey to face Tunisia.

Prior to the game, something peculiar was unfolding, something that kept Jonathan in his tracks. "When we got on the field, the bus entered the field, George Weah who did not speak to me since the Friday when I arrived for the game, stood in the middle of the field, kicking the ball around and there was noise all around the stadium. Then he signalled to Mass Sarr Jr. and me."[192]

"Mass Sarr, Charlie, you come,"[193] Jonathan remembers George calling.

Jonathan said he felt insulted and very offended. "This was a staged act. We were not speaking, we had no conversation because you're the captain, you're in the middle of the field and calling us as if everything is fine. And Mass Sarr started to run toward him. I felt compelled to comply. So, I came as well, eager to hear what he had to say. This guy was in the middle of the field and just gesturing, showing his hands and saying absolutely nothing as if to say there was some kind of a system, we were supposed to play, and he was instructing Mass Sarr and myself what to do. And I'm looking at this guy and saying, 'What the hell are you doing? Who are you impressing here?' Anyway, we played the game and we won, 1–0. I was the lone goal scorer and we qualified for the Africa Cup of Nations in South Africa in 1996."[194]

Now that the national team, the Lone Stars, had qualified for the AFCON, backroom discussions were being held on which kits the team would wear. The options were many because George was a brand name. Would it be locally made? Adidas? Nike? Diodora? Puma? Jonathan said at the time, whoever was to bring the most money was the one the team would go with. With that in mind, Jonathan was approached by an agent, for Diodora in Italy, named Franchesco Franchescini from Napoli.

According to Jonathan, Franchescini came to Geneva, and they had a conversation regarding a possible sponsorship deal for the Liberian national team. "I flew to Italy and after the meeting with Franchescini. I asked him to come down to look at one of our games so we could arrange with the Liberia Football Association to finalise the deal."[195] Franchescini was offering US$250,000 for the two weeks that the team would be in South Africa, providing tool kits, bags, boots, jerseys and everything associated with team's participation in the tournament.

Jonathan thought the deal would be good, not in particular for those playing overseas but most for the local players. "I thought it was a good idea because most of the guys playing back home were struggling, the country was in a state of uncertainty, and we didn't have money. So, to get any money from anywhere would help, especially while we're gonna play anyway. So, we agreed, and we brought him down and we met with the late Willard Russell, who was the President of the FA at the time. He was working closely with Mr. Eddie Dunn, who is still around, he has a travel agency and was the former Chief of Protocol."[196]

In Monrovia, Eddie Dunn, Willard Russell, and Jonathan met with Franchescini and an agreement was reached. The FA agreed that the national team would wear Diodora with 10% going to Franchescini. But there was a catch. George Weah had to be consulted before the deal was finalised.

When the LFA and Diodora contacted George, he told them he could offer more than US$250,000 Diodora was offering.

They took the issue to Jonathan and his response was, "The more, the merrier."

Days later, Jonathan says he waited for the deal George was going to sign. "At the time George had a personal boots deal with Diodora. So, I was confident we could have gotten more. George never came back to us or the team until we got to South Africa, and they were introducing our game kits, only for me to see that we are using Diodora."[197]

Jonathan was in a state of bewilderment. "So, my question is, where is the deal – that was supposed to be more than US$250,000. I confronted Mr. Russell. I said George told me he could give more, that's why we did not take the deal I brought to the table. To have this jersey here it means we should have gotten more. Where is the contract? To date, I have not seen that contract, to date that contract does not exist. No Lone Star player got US$1."[198]

Jonathan asked Mr. Russell, "Why did you do this?"

Russell said, "My aim is to become the first FA President to get Liberia to the Africa Cup of Nations."[199]

"But that's not sufficient," said Jonathan. "That's a personal goal, desire. What about the general good? So, you put your interest above the interest of the team, of the country? To this date, I have not seen that contract and I believe that contract was signed. In order to use that jersey, there must have been an agreement, George Weah has not produced that contract."[200]

Jonathan says whenever the national team played in other team's uniforms like Diodora and others, the players were compensated. "But when we were playing with Weah Sports, the Liberian government paid George Weah for us to wear his jersey when he should have paid us because we were promoting his jersey – that was a disservice to the country."[201]

Even before the team went to South Africa for the AFCON tournament in 1996, the local players had to be prepared but the coaches were short on finances.

Coach Wilfred Tijani Lardner had made several attempts to reach George, but he came up short.

At the time, most of the starters played in Europe. The local guys like Jonah Sarwieh, Henry Gbeetoe, Alexander Cheneken Freeman and others were still in Monrovia and they too had to be prepared for the tournament because the league in Liberia is not as competitive to what we have in Europe. So, the team needed to have the necessary logistics. Jonathan says he knew George was in camp preparing for the Champions League which is probably why the coaches could not get him. They couldn't get George, so Coach Lardner turned to Jonathan.

There were few cellphones those days. So, Tijani would go to the local DHL office on Broad Street and use the phone of a guy called Abdullai to make the call to Switzerland. From Abdullai's phone, Coach Lardner called Jonathan. "So, I asked what was needed. All of the things they cited came up to about US$16,000. So, I told them I will send those things the following day by DHL."[202]

The things arrived in Liberia the following day and Tijani, in good faith, thought to present the items to the media. At the time, the popular sports daily, *Sports Chronicle* owned by the late T. Mohammed Winpea, carried a banner headline: "Like Weah, Jonathan 'Boye Charles' Sogbie Supports Lone Star."

For Jonathan, his effort to help the national team became an offence. "That was my crime. George Weah did not see that as complementary. He saw that as a competition, that I was trying to measure arms. So, George held that against me quietly. He's one of those people or persons who, when you carry news to him, he does not evaluate, he does not seek clarity, he assumes its true. And so, George held this thing against me, I didn't know."[203]

In Weah's defence, Zeogar Wilson, who was a member of the national team, would later write in a *FrontPageAfrica* newspaper op-ed how much of an asset Weah was to the national team. In fact, Wilson credits Weah with securing the contract with Diodora. According to Wilson, the contract with Diodora would have ended in 1996 but the sports apparel giant expressed the desire to renew his contract. Wilson wrote, "Weah would renew the contract under one condition; that Diodora signs a sponsorship contract with the National Team to supply jerseys and sporting equipment for the 1996 Africa Cup of Nations in addition to a cash contribution and it didn't matter if that would have reduced the cost of his renewal with Diodora."[204] Diodora agreed and George renewed his contract and, according to Wilson, Diodora provided the jerseys and sporting equipment for the competition plus $50,000 in cash for the Lone Star for the Africa Cup of Nations.

Wilson says George later contacted him at the Ministry of Youth and Sports and requested that he write the FIFA Undersecretary for Sports and request for sporting materials for Lone Star. "I said to him that FIFA would not deal with government at that level, don't you think?"

Weah responded, "Just kindly write the letter, Mr. Minister."[205]

Wilson says he did as requested. "George received a call from the Under-Secretary about my letter and to inquire whether he was aware, and George said, 'Yes.' Two weeks after the call, Diadora delivered over $100,000 worth of sporting equipment and jerseys to his home in Italy for the Lone Star."[206]

However, Jonathan's version was different and when the team arrived in South Africa for the 1996 tournament, Jonathan realised that he was about to feel the wrath of George. Liberia was placed in Group C along with Gabon, Zaire and Nigeria. Nigeria withdrew from the tournament, so their three matches in the group were cancelled, leaving behind Gabon, Zaire and Liberia to play for qualification to the next stage. At the time, a fully fit Jonathan "Boye Charles" Sogbie was destined to start for the national team. But in the first game against Gabon, Weah kept him on the bench.

Goals from Kelvin Sebwe and Mass Sarr saw Liberia edge Gabon 2–1.

In practice the next day, Jonathan found himself playing with the second team and not on the starting team. "So, I'm asking myself, what is the issue?"[207]

In a bid to motivate the second team, Jonathan promised each member of his side US$50 dollars if they could defeat the first team. "I told them, maybe they want to see some of you guys' strength. Let's play against the first team. But in any case, if we win this practice, every player gets US$50 from me. And those guys were motivated automatically, and we beat them 2–0. I'm not kidding. In that practice too, George was so upset, he slides Cheneken and twisted Cheneken's ankle. But the idea is we beat them 2–0. And I scored the two goals."[208]

At the end of the practice that day, Josiah Johnson realised that there was something fundamentally wrong. And so, he called a meeting on the 9th floor of the Holiday Inn Hotel in Durban. Josiah, a former Liberian national team player, manager and administrator, had been around the national team for years. He started his career with Youth Leaders before moving on to Connections where he made his international debut in 1958. Johnson then moved to Barrolle in 1959, staying there until 1971 when he began his coaching career. During his time with Barrolle, he trained with and worked for the Special Security Service, the Presidential security team. Johnson trained as a coach in West Germany and then became head coach of the national team, replacing the German coach, Bert Trautmann, in 1978. Josiah remained with the national team set-up to assist Trautmann and in the 1980s he moved into football administration, also serving as Deputy Minister of Sports.

With such pedigree and a knack for recounting old stories based on his experience, Johnson's knowledge of the game was crucial to a team lacking wisdom and experience. Josiah, like most of the administrators, was suspicious about Jonathan's absence from the team and his relegation to the second team without any explanation.

As Jonathan recalls it. "Josiah kicked off the meeting by telling the team that he was feeling tension in the team and was unhappy with what he had seen in practice and concerned as to why [I] did not play the game."[209]

Looking back, Jonathan says that prior to that team meeting, Josiah had conversations with the coaches and all of them expressed the same concerns – why one of the teams' top players sat on the bench against Gabon, and why he was playing on the second team in practice.

The irony of it all was that all the coaches reported to George. They had turned the team over to George and he called the shots.

Jonathan understood. "I knew that because you cannot teach what you don't know and what we were learning out there as professional footballers was even better than the coaches. So, they were just there to provide guidance, they relied on George."[210]

In the meeting, player after player and coach after coach, took turns explaining and expressing how they felt. One by one, without naming names, Jonathan's team-mates and officials said the same thing: that people were comparing themselves to George Weah. Jonathan recalls James Debbah, specifically, standing up and saying, "All the fingers are not equal even though you're small, the other person is big, but they are all fingers. So, if you're not the first on the team, it doesn't mean you're not on the team."[211]

Taking his turn, George said, when James Debbah was captain, he respected him, but now that he had become captain, others did not want to give him the same respect.

"Everybody said, 'some people, some people' without being specific," Jonathan recalls. "We are 32 in the room, 29 persons got up to speak and say, 'some people'. Who are we talking about?" So, Jonathan stood up to speak. "I said, almost everyone has spoken, who are we referring to as 'some people'? All of the people are here. Why don't you guys have the balls to look at me and say, Charlie, you cannot compare yourself to this man? Why are you referring to me as 'some people'? I am here. The room [became] so quiet. Although it was a carpeted room, if a pin had dropped, you would have heard the sound. There was an audible silence in that room."[212]

Jonathan went on to tell his coaches and teammates that when the team needed help and couldn't find George, they had called him. "Coach Tijani did not call James Debbah, even though James Debbah was in France and Debbah, even if he had the capacity, would not have contributed. He did not call Mass Sarr Jr. because he does not have the capacity. Kelvin Sebwe, Joe Nagbe, Mass Sarr Jr. and all of you guys were in France. He left your +33 numbers and dialed code +41 to talk to me in Switzerland. And today I provided all of those things that we needed, that's what got all these Jonah Sarwiehs and other local players here today. Why couldn't you people see my action as being complementary instead of competitive? What did I do wrong? Is it because I agree to love Liberia? Is that how I compare myself to George Weah? Even if George Weah is a millionaire, if he brings US$10, if you're able to bring US$1 why wouldn't you do that? Is it because you want to exploit him? So, how do you now have a voice to speak whenever something goes wrong? He who pays the piper, names the tune."[213] The room was in stunned silence as Jonathan made his case and his argument about how he was being treated.

To Jonathan's surprise, everybody saw reason with what he was saying but because it was George Weah, nobody said a thing. Nobody!

At the end of the day, Josiah stood up and said, "Let bygones be bygones."[214]

Jonathan did not understand the response but once again, for the sake of peace, he said, "Let bygones be bygones."[215]

Later that night, at approximately 11 o'clock, Jonathan was in his room with he heard a knock on his door. The late Boye Cooper, a bow-legged substitute goalie was sharing a room with Jonathan. In his prime, Boye, playing for Mighty Barrolle, was dubbed "Dino Zoff" after the famed Italian goalkeeper. He would die eight years later on the Oru Refugee Camp in Nigeria after a brief illness. Boye opened the door and told Jonathan, "It's the skipper."

Jonathan asked, "Who is the skipper?"

"The Ambassador," said Boye.

"Who's the Ambassador?"

"George Weah."[216]

Jonathan walked to the door and asked Boye to give them some privacy. He turned to George. "What's up?"

George replied clearly, "I misunderstood the thing you did for the team, but the way you explained today, now I get the picture."

Jonathan was furious. "So, why didn't you say this in the meeting this afternoon? Why did you come to my room this time of the night to explain to me alone, when you could have stood to say you are wrong in front of everyone? To be a man does not necessarily mean you have to be right all the time. When you are wrong, say I'm wrong and say sorry. Why come in the dark to apologise? I will get on the bus, and I will tell everybody on the bus that you came to apologise because you realise your mistake."[217]

True to his word, Jonathan told George in front of everyone on the bus, what had happened the night before. "I said the captain came to me to say he's sorry. And that's how I was considered to play the game against Zaire."[218]

After their 2–1 victory against Gabon, Liberia needed just a goal against Zaire to advance to the next round. Once again, Liberia would be denied. Goals from Roger Lukaku, father of Chelsea striker, Romelu Lukaku, and Samuel Essende saw Zaire beat Liberia 2–0 and send the team packing. Controversy again followed the game. After the match, there were some rumours that Jonathan did not pass the ball to George to score a late goal which would have seen Liberia advance to the knockout stage.

"It's true, I did not pass the ball for Weah to score, but it was not intentional," Jonathan says. "The first objective of a striker is to score. In the case of any impossibility, then you can pass. It was only on television after the game that I saw that George was behind me." Jonathan explains, "We had a corner kick. I was standing second post, Joe Nagbe was standing first post. George was in the middle and he would always be from that distance. So, as he's running, Joe will be coming around and I will go to first post. Cheneken kicked that ball and the momentum I carried, the ball went over me, and I went outside the field behind the goal and decided to pass around the other side to come to the second post. By that time the goalkeeper had the ball. Everybody including George went down. The goalkeeper did not see me. He bounced the ball and exposed it. Once you exposed that ball, it's in play and I came running from behind the second post and headed this ball to the first post with my back turned to the field. It's just me and the goalkeeper but it was at a close angle. At that time, George was running from the back of the field to assist but my first instant as a striker is to score. I didn't have time to break the ball and turn around waiting. So, I kicked the ball, it hit the post and went outside."[219]

Jonathan says it was later on, after the game, when he saw the replay on TV that he realised that George was behind him. "In fact, it would have been a big thing for me to make an assist for George to score. We wanted to win. Why wouldn't I pass the ball? So, it wasn't an intentional thing. But you know people are in these kinds of situations, perceptions become a reality. There is no reason I would not have given that ball because I wanted to win."[220]

Even after the game, the team was still in disarray. George had announced that no one was allowed to have guests in their room, not even family members. But to Jonathan's dismay, George and others invited seven girls to their rooms, the night before the game. "George Weah had his own personal bus, a white Volkswagen bus with seven girls inside. While we are on the seventh and eighth floor, those guys are downstairs in the night club in the bar. They would wait for everyone to go to bed, then they would go down and they would be in there with those girls till late."[221]

Jonathan said after the team took its exit from the tournament, everyone tried to shift blame about why the team lost or why it did not perform well and who was responsible. "The fact of the matter," says Jonathan, "is that we are not addressing the issue of people going to the club with women after everyone fall asleep and [partying] with them the night before the game. Why are we not talking about that? It's like everyone knew but no one was saying anything. Everyone knows the truth, no one wants the say the truth."[222]

George and Jonathan remain distant friends since their playing days, but tension is always in the air. Off the field, there were rumours that the beef between the pair stemmed from a situation over a woman, Thelma Bernard: sister of Archibald Bernard, a former President of IE. Thelma had taken over the team from her brother. Jonathan dismisses the notion that his and George's issue was the result of his affair with Thelma. "George and I never fought over Thelma Bernard. I went out with Thelma Bernard but me and George did not fight over her. If he has issue with that, I do not. Thelma Bernard was President of IE. She came to me and said she liked me. And me, being a Bong Mines Boy, I embraced her, and we had a good relationship. However, she was not going out with George or anyone at the time. If they had something in the past, I don't know. My disappointment in this brother is not based on vendetta or hatred, but on principle, always principle."[223]

Jonathan recalls a time when George actually commended him for stepping in to help the team when no one else offered to. "I remember one time we were going to Togo to play; we were at the airport in the Ivory Coast. I think it was Weasua Airplane. George had said he had spent too much money on the national team, and they were bringing five local players to join us for the game, but at that time I was in China nursing my injury. So, I'm there and he said we needed 1.5 million CFA to transport the other guys to and from Lome, Togo and he was asking for money. Kelvin Sebwe, James Debbah, Mass Sarr, nobody wanted to contribute. So, I stepped in. I said it might be too early, but I can bring you 1 million CFA tomorrow morning. Is that ok?"

George replied, "It is, thanks."

"By 10 a.m. the next morning, I gave him an envelope of 1 million CFA. He himself announced that to the rest of the team, telling them, 'You see, I'm talking about money business, and no one wants to pay, Boye Charles has come to the rescue, the man is not even playing our game.'"[224]

At the time, Jonathan says George was happy because he had supported his attitude. "It was good, but whenever I criticised his attitude, it was bad, that was bad."[225]

George Weah was on his way to something bigger and perhaps better. Captaining the national team and leading them to so many victories, heart-aches and defeats was prepping the football icon for what lay ahead. But leadership is more than just about leading a team, or a group. It requires having a thick skin and the ability to not be swayed by criticism or ruined by disappointments along the way.

In Boye Charles and James Debbah, George Weah had two peers who loved him. They owed their careers to him. If it wasn't for his exploits in Europe, they would never have been scouted to play professional football in Europe. But like Weah, they were also athletes and celebrities in their own rights. Like Weah, they too were confronting their own egotistic demons. It is often said that a leader who lacks a thick skin is paralysed by challenges or criticism.

In the eyes of many who played with him in the heydays of the Lone Star, Weah lacked a depth of tolerance to withstand criticism. That may have been the reason why he made sure Boye Charles was kept on the bench at times or why it had to be his way or no way at all. Whatever the reasons or whatever went through Weah's mind left an indelible mark on his peers about his persona. The cold truth of it all was that only a handful of his peers had the guts to tell him he was steering the team wrong. Those who cheered him on were simply grateful to be in that space and were just happy to be in the presence of the football great. The ones who stood up to be counted had to live with the reality that they would forever be in the doghouse.

9

AMBITION

___

July 1997

Jonathan Sogbie, alias "Boye Charles", didn't know what to expect when George Weah called and told him he would like for the both of them to fly to Monrovia together out of Geneva for a scheduled Africa Cup of Nations Qualifiers against Tanzania.

The pair had been through some stormy times together.

Jonathan played for Servette, a top tier team in Switzerland at the time while George was still playing for Paris Saint-Germain (PSG).

No one could ever put a finger on why the pair always seemed to be at loggerheads, but tension was always in the air when the two were in the same space. So, it was a bit of a surprise when George chose this trip to Monrovia to make a startling revelation to Jonathan.

"At the airport in Geneva, George hinted to me that he wanted to be President of Liberia," Jonathan recalls. As startled as he was, Jonathan told George, "It is a laudable thought, but it requires serious preparations because you will be making decisions that will affect the lives of unborn children that could lead the country. You know when doctors make mistakes, one or two persons die, when police commit a crime, maybe one person will die but when a politician makes a mistake, there's coup d'état and 250,000 people die – that's the Liberian scenario. This is not a child's play. You have to think about it, George – and you have to prepare yourself consequently."[226]

George told Jonathan that he was preparing.

It was not until February 14, 2005, eight years later, that Jonathan realised George was not dreaming out loud. "I was in the U.S. State of Rhode Island when I got a call from George telling me he was on his way for a fundraising dinner in his honour."

George said, "I'm coming to your place for a dinner. It's only US$20 a plate for people to come and see me speak to Liberians in Rhode Island in respect to what I told you in 1997."[227]

A stunned Jonathan took a long pause, before remembering their discussion eight years earlier, regarding George's quest for the Liberian Presidency. "Yes, I remember," said Jonathan, "but George, do you remember what I told you?"[228]

In fact, three years earlier, in 2002, George had confided in another former player, James Salinsa Debbah, about his intentions to contest the Presidency. James says George was pressed into running by Archibald Bernard, the former President of Invincible XI. "We were in Dubai, playing for Al Jazira Football Club. He and I were going for practice that day and the phone rang and I picked up the phone. Archie called and said he wanted to talk to George. I was driving but remember like it was yesterday. George and Archie talked for almost 1 hour and 40 minutes."[229]

Right after that phone call, George's mood changed. Archie would call at least two more times after that – and the discussion was pretty much the same. Archie kept admonishing George that he could be President.

Around the same time, Charles Walker Brumskine was on the verge of announcing his candidacy for the Presidency and thought it would be a good thing to reach out to two of the country's top footballers in George and James. James recalls Brumskine saying, "I think you all may have heard that I will be contesting the Presidency. But I want your support."[230] James said that George was sitting next to him, and he passed the phone over to George. Brumskine told George that he would be grateful if George could support his bid for the Presidency.

James says both he and George agreed that they would meet up with Brumskine when they returned to Monrovia, but George was not interested in any further discussions regarding support for Brumskine's bid for the Presidency.

Two days later, Archie called again to speak with George and from then, James says, it was clear George had made up his mind. After speaking with Archie, George turned to James and said, "Jimmy, we don't need to support guys like Brumskine again; we ourselves can be President."[231]

That was when it hit James. "President?" He looked at George but did not say a word. He just brushed it off.

But George insisted, "James, my man, don't you know you and I can be President? You, yourself, you don't know you can be President?"[232]

"Wow," said James. "I just brushed it off. But he had that ambition, he had that mentality."[233]

Sometime in October 2004, nearly a year before the Presidential elections in Liberia, George was being courted by everyone. Despite hanging up his boots and leaving the best of his football days behind, his popularity was still high. So, it was a no brainer for anyone with any kind of aspirations for politics to have Weah on board. And so, the discussions began. The first of such meetings took place in Minneapolis, Minnesota.

Samuel Kofi Woods, a noted lawyer and human rights activist recalls a series of important meetings that seemed to be going well – until it became clear that Weah had his own personal ambitions for the Presidency. Until then, no one saw it coming, except perhaps former President Charles Taylor, who told a circle of friends that Mr. Weah had Presidential ambitions. The relationship between the pair was difficult to decipher. The two were the most widely known personalities, Weah, a world-class footballer and Taylor, President at the time. Taylor was making national and international headlines for leading the Liberian war and winning the election to ostensibly end the years of fighting, and George Weah was relishing the national and international headlines for his international exploits in football. Looking back, both men seemed to want a little of what each other had. Taylor had political power which many thought he had gained by fear. Weah had popularity which many believed he had gained by talent and a story of rags to riches. Taylor wanted Weah's friendship and seemed to try to get it. He would have the protocol organised during dinners with the Lone Star so that George Weah would sit next to him and would have Weah paid more than any player or team official.

Weah would make public gestures to demonstrate that he was unhappy with the special treatment and advances even if he accepted them. He would appear to be sulking and unhappy. Initially, it came across as being the result of his lack of familiarity with the formal protocols. Over time, it became obvious that he was not interested in returning the warming up and friendly outreach of Taylor. The Liberian Presidency is one with big ears. Soon there were stories of dislike filtering to the President and Weah warming up to leading opposition figures flaunting the political values of his celebrity popularity with Liberians at home and abroad.

Combined with the various international and local reportage around Weah, Taylor concluded Weah was seeking the political power he had.

George had expressed fears for his life after attempts to burn down his home, accusing President Charles Taylor's government of targeting him with violence. The incident even prompted George to announce that he would quit international football after Liberia's campaign in the 2002 AFCON, telling the BBC in an interview that he would return to Monrovia only if there was a change of government.

George accused President Taylor at the time of jealously, viewing him as a potential political rival. "I don't want somebody to come and kill me because of my popularity. It's not safe, I don't want something to happen to me before my children grow up. If something happens to me, some people will cry for a week. But after that, it's my children who will suffer."[234] George said his good relations with former President Samuel Doe had possibly weighed heavily against him. "Doe was comfortable with my popularity. So, he helped me a lot to build up a team – but Taylor doesn't want to accept the fact that I am popular. He's jealous. He thinks I want to be President – I'm not a politician."[235]

With the benefit of hindsight, Mr. Lewis Brown, who was National Security Advisor to President Taylor, says the fact that the two individuals were the most known nationally and internationally, made political sense that they would either come together – President Taylor likely hoped this would happen initially – or else they would fall apart to become political adversaries.

Every known politician in the country at the time had been resoundingly defeated by Taylor on his way to being elected President on the first ballot.

According to Brown, Taylor believed he could defeat any of them again. However, Weah's celebrity offered something different. And it seemed that despite President Taylor's best efforts to befriend Weah, the latter's response was less than endearing.

Political opposition to President Taylor appeared to splinter at the time. Off and on, Weah would tilt his public comments to the opposition's perspective of the country. It seemed that the opposition viewed Weah as friendly and unthreatening to their own positions. Many of those in the opposition community believed Weah's celebrity status was helpful, thinking it would not transform into political power for himself because he was not a politician.

Explaining his decision to sever all links with the Liberian national team, Weah said he was sick of the political interference surrounding the team. "Football has gone into politics," he said, "and I don't want to be part of the politics. The President of Liberia is against us. The government is against us. I don't deserve that. I will resign as a player because I can't travel because of family problems. And as a technical director, I'm out. I'll play for the moment, but after the tournament, I'm finished."[236]

Weah was fearful that Taylor would kill him, hurt his family, and bring harm to him. The burning of his 9th Street home was the wake-up call he needed to put it all in perspective. After all, Weah had family, friends and relatives in Liberia he feared would be at risk if he continued to toe this line and be at loggerheads with President Taylor.

At this point in time, no one – apart from James and Jonathan – knew that George was harboring thoughts about becoming President. Woods himself had been approached and was heavily courted by key political players. "I was approached by people from the Brumskine camp and various camps to be a running mate. I was also approached by some of my friends to contest the 2005 elections,"[237] he says.

Woods recalls that Samuel Tweah, the current Finance Minister, James Kollie, a former Deputy Minister of Finance and a third person, Varney Kennedy, were part of those discussions. "They approached me and requested that I run to be President of Liberia. This was back around 2003. I told them that I had been in exile for several years and I did not think I was prepared to run as President."[238]

A few weeks later, Woods recalls, some of the same people who had approached him, made the same advances toward Weah, and had a discussion. "They had approached me earlier and they felt that I was important. They convened a meeting in Minnesota, and we had general discussions about the future of Liberia, and we agreed to meet in Florida."[239] Woods attended the meeting along with some colleagues and friends. "We went to Florida and met with Weah for two days. We had a good discussion. In fact, we had a very long discussion and some of those discussions were centred around the need to contest political power. Weah and I met. The both of us met together, alone, contrary to what people are saying, and landed on a note to continue the conversation. So, at that point we did not have a disagreement."[240]

Reality began to sink in later as the October 2005 General and Presidential elections drew nearer.

Woods recalls another meeting during which discussions concluded that Weah was in fact, interested and that he would be petitioned. "The fellas at the meeting said, 'Look, we cannot discuss anything about leadership here now. We want to promote democracy. It is important to get to Liberia, establish institutions and compete internally. That is the democratic process.' I don't think that was welcomed by some of those around, including Weah himself. So, we split and went our separate ways and since then we've never had a conversation in terms of merging or anything else. I don't recall any further discussion on that issue as far as I'm concerned."[241]

Woods had several meetings with Weah prior. "I want to say this because there is information floating around that I was one of the founders of the Congress for Democratic Change – that is not true. Let them not give me that credit because I don't deserve it and I was not one of the founders. I met George Weah prior to even him being petitioned or prior to the formation of the Congress for Democratic Change. We met, and even met in Florida at his house and others. We met there. Now, there are two persons who continue to work in this government that can relate."[242]

At that same time, lots of information floated around that it was Woods and Cllr. Jerome Verdier, a former head of Liberia's Truth and Reconciliation Commission, who initially put the idea of the Presidency into the head of Weah.

Woods says that was not the case. "I didn't know about Weah being petitioned. In fact, it was Weah who informed me that he was being petitioned and he asked me to join his team and I said, 'How well do you know me?' I asked him that question three times. 'You want me to be part of your team, do you know me politically?' All he said was, 'I've heard a lot about you, and I have a lot of respect for you.' I told him, 'Well, you need to know me politically and we need to get to know each other. I don't get in a political relationship just as a matter of power. There has to be a clear line on principles and values.' And we talked and that was it."

Woods recalls that was the bottom line. "We met in Florida, we disagreed on the approach and how he wanted to pursue it. I didn't go to him and Verdier did not go to Weah to tell him or encourage him to be President."[243]

Among the many key players in that October 2004 meeting in Minneapolis was James Kollie.

Samuel Woods and James Nyepan Verdier Jr. (Jerome's brother) may not have encouraged George's quest to be President but the aura that greeted the October meeting generated a lot of buzz.

On October 8, 2004, James Kollie received communication from Samuel D. Tweah, confirming that George would attend a political meeting the next day. According to James, the plan was to hold an honest and frank conversation with George regarding political thinking, and then solicit from him his thinking regarding the 2005 Presidential and General Elections.

Ahead of the October 9 meeting, Kollie and the other members of the group had held several meetings amongst themselves to prepare a presentation before meeting with George. One of those in attendance was George Yuoh, who was invited because he was frank and regarded as a straight shooter. James had contacted George Yuoh in a bid to gauge his thoughts about the group's intentions to work with George Weah in the ensuing 2005 elections. In that conversation, George Yuoh informed James that he was not a friend of George Weah but had several friends who were close to him. George Yuoh made it clear to James and others that they had to be mindful of George Weah. From what friends had told him, George Weah had a 'thin skin' and so that was something they needed to be aware of. George Yuoh's inclusion in the meeting was pertinent because he had only a few days earlier, on September 18, 2004, penned an article on *The Perspective's* website in which he said some positive things about George Weah, to the effect that the Liberia Football Association, headed by Izetta Wesley, had manipulated the rules to stop George Weah from contesting the Presidency of the LFA.

Kollie believes that the decision to deny George Weah from contesting the Football Association's Presidency by so-called political elites may have given rise to momentum that triggered the group's decision to encourage George Weah to seek the Liberian Presidency. "This momentum was needed because it made George Weah to favourably consider or entertain the idea of running for President. I think he was desperate at that point and so the idea of running for President made perfect sense. It might have been for the wrong reason but his frustration and our 'youth adventurism' became a match made in heaven."[244]

So, on Friday, October 8, members of the meeting's organisers, dressed in suits and ties, drove in separate vehicles to receive George Weah from the Minneapolis St. Paul International Airport. "We had rented a Lincoln Navigator and were prepared to rent a hotel for him because we wanted the meeting to be very serious by treating him as our official guest. But George Weah decided he stay at his friend's house,"[245] Kollie recalls.

George had informed the group that he was passing through Atlanta, Georgia, to pick up a female youth activist and would also be accompanied by his friend, Sylvester Williams (aka Careca) and another friend, Meapeh Gono. However, just before George Weah's arrival, a couple of potential setbacks emerged. First, James received an email from George Yuoh informing him that Patrick Chea, a good friend of George Weah, had informed him that Weah wanted his friends to manage the October 9th meeting. James later received another email from Abu Massaley, another of George Weah's friends, saying that Weah did not want the group to receive him at the airport.

Kollie was furious.

In a series of email exchanges, James raised serious objections to having the meeting with George Weah managed by his friends. "I insisted that they could attend the meeting if they wanted to but to be the ones to manage the meeting? I found that very offensive and insulting. However, George Yuoh was only delivering a message and so I couldn't do anything to him."[246]

Kollie was also frustrated and demoralised by the second request which demanded that the group turn over the Lincoln to George Weah's friends, who would then go to receive him from the airport. "We all began to wonder what was going on. But we decided to take it in strides. We were entering the game of the big boys and we needed to be able to withstand some shocks and maybe this was the first test."[247]

Despite the frustration, James and the others remained calm but concerned. But time was running out and the organisers were getting jittery. James didn't hear from Patrick Chea until around midnight when Patrick turned his phone on and called Samuel D. Tweah to inform him that George Weah was at his (Patrick's) house and if the group wanted to see him, they could drop by.

At this point, James became even more furious. "Are you kidding me?" he said. "If we want to see him?" He recalls, "We were the ones that invited him to Minnesota and so how can anyone ask if we want to see him? It became very troubling, confusing and shameful."[248]

Despite the setback, the group decided to not give up. Kollie and others got in their cars and drove to Patrick's house around midnight in hope of meeting with George Weah. There, they saw George Yuoh, Patrick Chea and a number of other folks. To the dismay of the group, George Weah did not even spend a minute with them. James recalls that less than a minute after the group entered the house, George Weah informed the group that he was going to bed. "It was Careca who came and sat with us for a few minutes. And then I recognised Meapeh Gono, the youth activist that accompanied Ambassador Weah from Atlanta."[249]

James had known Meapeh for years: their mothers were friends and James even tutored Meapeh and her brother Gabriel as their study class teacher after their cousin, Dr. J. Emmanuel Moore, left for studies in the US. After chatting with Meapeh and Careca, James and the others decided to go home, later acknowledging that the environment at Patrick's house felt very uncomfortable.

In Liberia, there is an old saying that if the Christmas will be good, you will know from the eve. The experience on the eve of the October 9, 2004 meeting was like a nightmare for James and the organisers. The eve, according to James was the worst day ever. "The shame, the frustration, the disgrace, the belittlement, the bewilderment, and you name it, were vexing and perplexing. We began to wonder as to what had really happened."[250]

Saturday, October 9th was met with much scepticism and low expectations. The group assembled at Kollie's house in the morning ahead of the big meeting with George Weah. Kollie and the others had a lot to talk about, a lot of questions to ask and so many queries regarding George's personality.

Kollie recalls, "Under our plan, we wanted a whole day of interaction and discussions so that we could establish whether there was a fit or not. We wanted to talk about what we were looking to achieve and what we thought were the impediments. We wanted to talk about the issue of 'thin skin' and the personal sacrifice that would be required to make the transition from the football field into the political arena. We were excited about discussing the political future of our country. We were idealistic in our approach as history now reveals."[251]

At around 2 p.m., Kollie and the group received the call that George Weah was ready to meet them, but there was a catch. They were informed that they needed to be quick as the Ambassador had other meetings. "For Heaven's sake, what is going on?"[252] James wondered.

Nevertheless, the group decided to prepare and work within the window they were given. What was supposed to be an all-day affair of interaction and discussions, turned out to be a moderated forum in which the Liberia National Congress (LNC) was given five minutes to make a statement. The forum was moderated by Stanley Ford, a friend of George Weah. James, like most of those in attendance, wasn't quite sure what to make of what was unfolding. "I am embarrassed and ashamed like hell but at the same time trying to understand and appreciate the dynamics. Things are moving really fast."[253]

Midway into the meeting, Samuel Tweah read a petition calling for George Weah to run for President. The petition came as a shock and dealt the first major contradiction. Until that meeting, diaspora Liberian communities across the U.S. had been critical of groups petitioning people without any serious conversations, yet there they were, repeating the same mistakes they had castigated others for and justifying their own ineptitude.

Later that day, Samuel Tweah informed the group that George Weah would be meeting with Samuel Kofi Woods at the home of Al Jerome Chede. Kollie and his group were told to assemble for that meeting. But first, James had some concerns. Woods had known of the effort by the group to meet with George Weah that weekend. So, many were taken aback that Woods had agreed to a separate meeting without telling the rest of the group. The meeting between Weah and Woods was part of the plan all along. In fact, James recalls, had the meeting with Weah gone as had been planned, they would have asked Weah to meet with Woods in furtherance of the combined political discovery.

Al Jerome had succeeded in arranging a meeting between Weah and Woods at his house, and Kollie took exception. "My problem with Kofi Woods was that we had agreed for the Liberian National Congress to arrange a meeting with Weah; if for any reason he managed to secure the meeting using another person, I thought we deserved the courtesy of being informed."[254]

Kollie ran into Woods at the meeting but never forgave him. "I counted it against him because I had tried to keep him informed along the way."[255]

The goal of a possible marriage between Woods and Weah, Kollie recalls, was to give the comfort needed to mitigate any perceived shortcomings of Weah. The group was confident that the pairing was destined for victory although it was unclear in what particular order and who would head the ticket.

Kollie recalls that Weah informed Woods that his (Weah's) people had already petitioned him to run for President. Weah went on to tell Woods that he had heard a lot of good things about Woods and that he (Weah) would be delighted if Woods could join him even though he was still holding consultation on the petition. Woods informed Weah that he took note of the request but thought that they should do more talking and build a relationship. At the end of the meeting, Woods requested that he, Tweah and Kollie find time for a follow up meeting.

Kollie said at the time, everyone thought that meeting ended well. "In fact, this was the only good news we had to report to our people: that the meeting with Ambassador Weah and Kofi Woods went very well. This made us to buy time with our members until we got to the bottom of the mess."[256]

On Sunday, October 10, 2004, Weah and his delegation left Minneapolis. Both Meapeh and Kollie exchanged numbers, promising to stay in touch. Meapeh promised James that she would call Kollie as soon as she returned to Atlanta. True to her word, Meapeh called Kollie upon her return and they both shared experiences about what had transpired in Minneapolis.

She told James that she had no idea he was part of the group arranging the meeting with George Weah. "I didn't know you were part of this group but what those guys said about you, the Ambassador did not even want to see you people. Those guys had said all kinds of terrible things about you people, especially Tweah. But anyway, I will talk to the Ambassador and inform him that I know you and that what those guys said were all lies. I will inform him that you are not that kind of person."[257]

On Monday, October 11, 2004, George called Tweah to compare notes, indicating that Meapeh had in fact spoken to George about her conversation with James.

Looking back, Kollie says, the same friends were the ones trumpeting the narrative that George's greatest weakness was that he had 'thin skin' and rather than help him, they exploited that weakness on that Friday night to turn Weah against the Minnesota group.

Kollie says he still believes that they should have made a turning point decision on that weekend. "In fact, several colleagues did but for some of us, we thought giving up would be a sign of weakness and so we decided that we will fight. We will not allow those calling themselves Friends of George Weah (FOGOW) to hijack this political process that we had begun. Many of them had castigated us for believing that it was possible. They never believed that George Weah could ever be seriously considered for anything in the field of politics."[258]

On Tuesday, October 12, Tweah and Kollie went to see Woods at his St. Paul's apartment. Kollie was clear in that meeting with Woods that those calling themselves FOGOW were playing dangerously and trying to undermine their efforts.

On Thursday, October 14, Tweah received a call from Weah that he (Tweah) and James should join him over the weekend because Woods and team would be coming to Fort Lauderdale, Florida, on Friday, October 15 for some political discussions. James had issues with the one-day notice but still made arrangements for travel. He was able to get two tickets for he and Tweah to travel to Florida. However, they were unable to get a flight for Friday. The earliest they could get to Florida was Saturday, October 16 around 1 p.m. in the afternoon.

Kollie says, up to the time he and Tweah arrived in Florida, Woods had not informed them that he had been invited to Florida. However, he had all his men informed and they were able to all get to Florida on Friday afternoon or evening which meant that they had sufficient time. The only person who got there about 2 a.m. on Saturday morning was Cllr. James Verdier. Other members of Woods' delegation were Calvin Dwuye, George Yuoh, and Tarnue Mawolo (now deceased). Patrick Chea (now deceased) was also in Florida for the meeting.

While Kollie and Tweah were busy hopping from one airport to another in a bid to get to Florida and participate in the discussions, their presence guaranteed that they were still major players in the political adventure.

As the groups convened in Florida that Saturday morning, discussions started between the two teams: Team Weah and Team Woods.

Weah and Woods met separately from the rest of the group in a bid to find time to bond and to build the chemistry. On the other side were the two teams: Team Weah had Meapeh Gono, Careca and Patrick Chea while Team Woods had James Verdier, Calvin Dwuye, Tarnue Mawolo and George Yuoh.

As the group started discussions, Team Weah proposed that it would be a good idea if Woods would honour Ambassador Weah's request to join him as his Vice running mate. Team Woods, represented by James Verdier, screamed that it is was ridiculous and impossible for Woods to run with Weah as Vice running mate because he didn't think that Weah was capable of being President.

Verdier's angst drew ire from Weah's group, and a shouting match ensued prompting Weah and Woods to intervene. The pair was successful in calming the two groups down and encouraged them to continue the conversation.

Egos were flying all over the place. No one appeared willing to give in, no one seemed eager to throw in the towel. For a moment in time, as it had always been with politics in Liberia, everyone felt they were on the side of right, and the other was wrong. James Verdier's angst was evident: he, Woods and the others had been played.

James had received a phone call from his friend and brother, Kofi Woods, who informed him about a planned meeting between him and Weah. Woods asked James to form a part of his team to the meeting.

Verdier recalls that at the time of the meeting, there were wild and open discussions about political parties and potential candidates for the legislative and Presidential elections scheduled for 2005. At the time, scores of Liberians were being paired idealistically as potential Presidential and Vice-Presidential candidates considering their shades of contributions to our national political history and their electability.

Verdier says Weah invited them to his home for dinner for what were informal discussions about everything relating to his quest for the Presidency. It was there, Verdier recalls, that Weah narrated that every penny he spent on the Liberian national team, the Lone Stars, during his playing days were reimbursed to him by either FIFA, LFA, the government of Liberia, or through sponsorship – Diodora, for example.

The meeting finally convened the next day in the same hotel where James and others were lodged. Weah sat next to James and the pair had some very personal, friendly and private conversations prior to the meeting. They knew each other casually and had interacted a couple times in Liberia while Weah was an active football player.

The crux of the meeting centred on organizing a team of young progressive and popular Liberians to contest the Presidential elections in Liberia. Woods had been a name mentioned in many circles, according to Weah. At some point during the meeting, Weah and his team orchestrated and announced a phone call, alleged to be from Liberia. Weah had to take the call outside of the meeting room with two of his team members. Upon his return to the meeting, Weah announced that the phone call was information that he had been petitioned by citizens in Liberia to contest the 2005 elections as a Presidential candidate and that he had gladly accepted.

James Verdier recalls that everyone on Woods team knew that it was a pre-emptive move to politically coerce and constrict discussion into an agreement for Mr. Woods to submit himself as Vice-Presidential running mate to Weah.

At this point, James rhetorically asked aloud, "So why did you invite us here? Did you invite us to tell us you have been petitioned or to discuss the formulation of a team that has yet to be accomplished?"[259]

A long and heated debate ensued amongst members of the two teams for about half an hour or more during which James said repeatedly, "I don't think Mr. Weah was a better first candidate than Mr. Woods, for many very obvious reasons, except being a football celebrity."[260]

After a short break, the meeting reconvened and Weah posed a direct question to James, "Counsellor, can you give two reasons why you think I am not qualified to run for the Presidency?"

James immediately replied, "I can give you five! Mr. Weah, you are incompetent at this time, because you are uneducated, you are inexperienced, you are half-baked and dangerous because of your ambition." [261]

Woods interrupted: "J.V., its ok."[262]

The meeting fell into disarray and technically broke down. Woods and Weah, the two principals, went alone into a separate meeting. They both agreed to continue to consult on the way forward.

The two groups went back into the second round of talks, with very little changed and the same shouting exchanges. Woods and his group felt baffled and made their voices clear. The bottom line is Woods' camp did not see the human rights activist agreeing to be Weah's running mate. For Woods and his supporters, Weah was not ready for prime time. Weah had conquered the game of football, but could he lead a nation emerging from war? This time, it was simply uncontrollable and both sides decided to end the talks. Both groups disengaged, agreeing that they would reconvene at some point in time.

During the break, Tweah was able to locate Calvin Dwuye's number and placed a call to him. He informed Calvin that he and James were en route to Florida and would be there in the next hour or so.

Team Woods had no idea Kollie and Tweah had been invited for the meeting between Woods and Weah. An angry James had planned to express himself to Woods once he arrived in Florida. James was unhappy that Woods had not been forthcoming even though he had done everything to be forthcoming with Woods.

Kollie and Tweah arrived in Florida greeted by a tense atmosphere. But after speaking with Woods and his guys and getting a proper briefing from both sides, it was clear that the quest for a pairing of Woods and Weah would not materialise. Kollie suggested that the discussion be abandoned because it was useless to continue.

Kollie's position was based on three cardinal points. The dismissal of Weah as head of ticket coming from James Verdier meant that it was Woods' position. If it had come from someone else then they could negotiate but for James Verdier, who was a cousin to Woods, it meant that the decision had Woods' blessing. The assertion that Weah was not prepared to be President but could be a Vice President did not make sense to Kollie at all because, according to Kollie, the Vice President could be President at any minute. If a Vice President could so openly covet the Presidency, then it was a bad idea to make that person Vice President because they could overthrow the President at any time.

On the basis of those three points, Kollie felt that there was no utility in continuing the conversation.

Despite the disagreement, the mood in Florida remained tense and awkward for the rest of that Saturday. Even though the groups had dinner together and later, went out to the club at Miami Beach, it was clear that the weekend resulted in a futile effort to form a ticket. At the club, Calvin tried his best to get Kollie and Tweah to resuscitate the talks. But Calvin had no idea that James was the main proponent calling for the talks to be abolished. Thus, the Weah-Woods discussions ended in Florida on Sunday, October 17, 2004, with no agreement.

After the departure of Team Woods from Florida, George asked Tweah and James to stay behind and spend an extra day. So, they changed their flights from Monday to Tuesday in a bid to hold discussions they missed out on in Minnesota.

For Kollie, those few hours spent in Florida with George after everyone had left turned out to have been the best ever. "We never ever had time to discuss anything serious again. We were either playing basketball or football and having some dinner or some other programs. It always worried me because my concern was that we were talking about the lives of 3.5 million people, and we could not find the time to discuss what we will do when the Liberian people entrust us with power? Well, sometimes my colleagues argued that we needed to play on George's turf sufficiently and then when he is comfortable, he will play on ours."[263]

Several days after the fateful Florida meeting, James Verdier received a phone call in Charlotte, NC, from Weah, asking if he had done anything to him that warranted his opposition to him contesting the Liberian Presidency.

James recalls, "I then used that occasion to inform Mr. Weah that I was one of his best fans even though he played for Invincible Eleven. But he had skilfully and proudly represented us as a country and a continent throughout the football world and we were very proud. I said, 'Use your fame and resources to support another popular candidate and become the King-maker. Then use this time to go to school, serve in another capacity, if offered, learn the Liberian bureaucracy and political system, before presenting yourself to the Liberian people for election.'"[264]

Unlike his brother James, Jerome Verdier was not a big fan of Weah. Like his brother, Jerome was a lawyer, and was the original organiser of the Congress for Democratic Change on whose back Weah rode into politics.

He was not part of the meetings in Florida, but he was an influential lawyer in Liberia. "I did all the paperwork, organised the organising committee and presided over the proceedings until the constitution for the party was adopted."[265] Like his brother, Jerome was also infuriated when the issue arose of Weah declaring his intention to contest as standard bearer of the CDC. "I heard about it and to his credit, he sent those interested to me for clarification or concurrence because I had earlier said it was an impressing move,"[266] recalls Jerome.

After consultations, he wanted to know why Weah, and his team insisted on pushing his name forward as a candidate for the Presidency. Weah had insisted that he got Jerome's blessing, but Jerome wasn't falling for the bait. It turned out that one of the key reasons for Weah announcing his quest so early was to raise money, a proposition Jerome believed at the time was wrong.

Jerome recalls, "My response was emphatic and categorical. This is wrong and the motive for money is wrong motive for pursuing a political action." In Jerome's view, "Money should never be the motive or driving force behind a political action. This is wrong and amounts to corruption of the process and objective."[267] He went on to emphasise that it was wrong also because the party was not yet registered and doing so was undemocratic. The proper thing to do was to wait until the party has been registered and declare its convention or congress for holding of elections. Only then would it be the time to make such declarations. "I went further to emphasise that the

National Elections Commission guidelines called for internal party democracy ... [since the influence] ... of money would be violation of that policy,
rule or regulation." [268]

To Jerome's surprise, not too long after the Florida gathering, he listened
to the Voice of America radio news program during which Weah announced
his intention to contest the election as standard bearer of the CDC.

The following morning after Weah's announcement on the VOA, Jerome
convened a meeting of the organising committee and asked if anyone had
heard what he had heard on the VOA. Most of those in attendance said
they did. "It was there and then that I tendered in my resignation and turned
over all documents to the party and said they should find another lawyer
to submit the papers to the probate court." [269]

Moments later, Jerome could not help but wonder why Weah was in a
rush to become President, and so soon after retiring from football. "All I
could think of was greed, corruption, lack of adherence to the rule of law
and bad governance. There was everything wrong about following rules and
regulations, the lack of discipline and personal, selfish interest over the good
of the party. Selfishness was written all over it and I hated it." [270]

George Weah and Jerome Verdier had a rather strange relationship. The
respect was mostly one-sided. Weah respected Jerome, mostly because he
came highly regarded as a promising lawyer with a lot of potential. They
had met for the first time sometime in 2004 at the residence of Ellen Johnson
Sirleaf. According to Jerome, Weah had sent someone to his office requesting
a meeting at Sirleaf's home. "I decided to go with them, only to be taken
to ... Sirleaf's house," says Jerome. "I asked George, 'You said you wanted
to see me, and I was brought here? What are you doing here?'" [271]

George told Jerome that this was Ellen Johnson Sirleaf's residence and
that she had sent for George to talk.

Jerome replied, "This is the old order, you don't want to be here." [272] He
turned his back on Weah and Sirleaf and walked away.

For Jerome, Sirleaf represented an old leadership that was passing away.
He felt that it was time for a new thinking, a new generation to prepare for
leadership. At the time, Jerome felt that the CDC was the way forward; it
was structured that way to appeal to the grass rooters.

What the Verdier brothers didn't know – or perhaps failed to understand – was what made many people apprehensive about George Weah's political ambition. He was a man lacking confidence in his new-found terrain of politics while gambling on his popularity to take him to the Presidency.

Weah was slowly but reluctantly becoming a student of his own version of populism, hoping to use politics to represent the interests of the grassroots base which saw him as a saviour against the so-called political elites. For that moment in time, it didn't matter what James and Jerome Verdier felt about him, or how things should be. It didn't matter how experienced he was or whether he was fit to lead a nation emerging from war. All that mattered was that Father Time had caught up with the former world class footballer. Now, George Weah needed a new venture, a new dimension to his game of life, a new meaning to his existence, something to keep him relevant now that the glory days were behind him.

10

DECISION

———

Weeks before George began testing the waters for the Liberian Presidency, momentum was building within his close inner circle that his mind was already made up – and there was no way he would be running second to anyone in the contest for the Presidency.

Perhaps this was the reason why the talks between he and Samuel Kofi Woods broke down in Minneapolis, Minnesota, and at his base in Miami Beach, Florida – and why no one close to his circle was willing to budge over who should head a ticket going into the October 2005 Presidential elections.

The trigger point for George's decision came on July 14, 2005, when the US international sports network ESPN announced that George had been selected as the recipient of the prestigious Arthur Ashe Courage Award for 2004, given to individuals whose contributions transcend sports.

James Kollie, who by now had become one of the strong advocates for a Weah Presidency, recalls that, "It was the ESPY airing that made us believe that it would be easier to sell George. The first meeting in Minneapolis took place on July 25, 2004, just seven days after the ESPN Arthur Ashe award."[273] The ESPYs award (Excellence in Sports Yearly) is an accolade presented to recognise "individual and team athletic achievement and other sports-related performance during the calendar year preceding a given award ceremony."[274]

George had conquered the world of football and was about to be the centre of attention on the global stage on a primetime US media market network. The award was presented at the 12th Annual ESPYs on Wednesday, July 14, 2004, at Hollywood's Kodak Theatre and televised on ESPN four days later on Sunday July 18 at 9 p.m. EST.

While the honour was aimed at celebrating George's football exploits, ESPN said the primary focus was on George's life off the field, highlighting his commitment to humanitarian projects all over Africa as an international soccer star. One example was how George had used his name and fame to take guns out of the hands of children to try to help save a generation devastated by war.

The event offered a perfect timing for George's still unannounced Presidential aspirations. He was now in good company, joining previous winners – boxer, Mohammed Ali; college basketball and coaching great, Jim Valvano; major league baseball umpire, Steve Palermo; sports journalist and author, Howard Cosell; multisport athlete, Loretta Claiborne; college coaching great, Dean Smith; tennis icon, Billie Jean King; Olympian Cathy Freeman, and Dave Sanders, a teacher who was killed during the infamous Columbine High School shooting.

George also had Arthur Ashe's name attached to his legacy. Ashe was a U.S. tennis legend and pioneering black sportsman who won three Grand Slam singles titles: Wimbledon, the Australian and the U.S. Open. As the first black player selected for the U.S. Davis Cup team (which he later went on to captain) and the only U.S. black male to win Grand Slams to this day, he reached the top of the game before retiring in 1980. Initially reticent about politics, later in his career he became a vocal civil rights advocate. When he contracted HIV-AIDS from a blood transfusion in 1982 he went public about his illness and campaigned for awareness about the disease and founded the Arthur Ashe Foundation for the Defeat of AIDS and the Arthur Ashe Institute for Urban Health. In 1993, he died of AIDs-related pneumonia. Later in the year Ashe posthumously received the Presidential Medal of Freedom from President Bill Clinton. As a role model for black sportsmen campaigning on political issues, there were few (Mohmmed Ali aside) more notable at the time.

Actor Denzel Washington was at the top of his game, awaiting the July 30 release of the hit Frank Sinatra remake, *The Manchurian Candidate*, and he was coming off the release of another hit, *Man on Fire*. Having the legendary actor introduce George for the Ashe award made the evening much more enthralling for the former world footballer of the year who was on the verge of transitioning into politics. Hosted by comedian and actor Jamie Foxx, the 2004 ESPY Awards brought out the stars, including Tom Cruise and a host of other athletes and entertainment celebrities.

Denzel was in his element during his introduction of George, drawing similarities between George and Ashe.

"When Arthur Ashe found fame, he did not close his eyes, he did not forget the many who could not share his fortune; when Arthur Ashe found fame, he used the equity of his celebrity to shine a light on ignorance and spark global understanding. Tonight, we honor another man who found fame and chose not to forget, another man who begs the world to see and to understand.

His name, like his country may not be well known on this side of the Atlantic but we're talking about a giant and his name is George Weah of Liberia.

George Weah is one of the greatest soccer players of our time – from a nation where chaos had been the rule and where children are born killers, spit upon, houses burned, risking death, over and over again, George Weah is nonetheless going home again, and again and again.

His relentless message of hope defies reason in an age of mindless terror and bottomless hatred. But this is a man born to be a striker, born to finish what he started. George Weah refuses to close his eyes – and George Weah will never, ever let us forget how much work there's left to do.

It began in 1980, with an assassination and violent coup d'état. The government in place for 133 years was overthrown – and for over two decades thereafter, Liberia was overcome by civil war.

Millions were displaced, the landscape was ravaged by poverty and disease, hundreds of thousands were killed, including nearly an entire generation of children, raped, drugged, beaten, and brainwashed to serve in a murderous campaign of warlords.

It was a light in Liberia that shined before and through the darkness, again that offered a way to forget the war and for one man, a way to rise above it all.

George Weah grew up here, abandoned by his parents, he was one of fourteen children, raised by his grandmother. The only education he ever received was in the angles and artistry of soccer, his only classroom, a dusty pitch near his home and he quickly progressed from student, to master of the game.

His people would come to call him King George, a title befitting the greatest player Africa ever produced. He rose to stardom at home and then internationally. In 1995, he became the only man ever to win the African, European and world player of the year award in the same year. Famous, rich, and revered, he was distanced from his embattled homeland by miles and stature. When he called from afar for UN intervention, the consequence was immediate and personal.

In 1997, at the height of the war, George Weah did come back, as a conquering hero. He supports the national team with US$2million of his own money. As a player and coach, he led the Lone Star within one win of a world cup berth in 2001, reviving the pride and hope that had been lost in Liberia for over a decade.

The war continued, still Weah did not retreat to the safety of his athletic life. The world's greatest striker stayed home and made peace his priority.

In December of 2003, a truce was declared – and Weah's effort in Liberia had extended to saving lives, he now continued his struggle to restore the country – one child at a time.

He came back because it was home, he stays because helping Liberia was now his life. Evil men had forced the children to act as weapons of war, an honorable man has invited them to serve as instruments of peace."[275]

ESPN had dedicated twelve minutes to George. What better way for a relatively unknown politician to get his feet wet on the biggest platform?

Ron Semiao, senior Vice President of ESPN Original Entertainment, described the George Weah story as remarkably inspiring. "He has taken the path less travelled and the profound impact of his commitment to international humanitarian causes is reminiscent of the way Arthur Ashe lived his life. They both used their exceptional sports talent as a springboard to help improve the lives of others."[276]

The world was sold on Weah, and he knew it. Flanked by two child soldiers, Princess Swaray and Hilson Hugo, Weah said that, while he had won many awards in his time, the Ashe award was his greatest achievement in life because it stood for true humanity. Swaray and Hugo had fought at age 11 and 12. "It was so devastating,"[277] Weah told the audience at the Kodak auditorium. "These kids are here today to say to you people that they are innocent, they are very sorry for the horrifying images you all saw during our Liberian civil war. All they want today is to be educated, reintegrated in society so they can be people tomorrow."[278]

The event was a brilliant showcase for Weah, who on April 7th, 1997, was named UNICEF Goodwill Ambassador based on his humanitarian work with the youth of Liberia during that country's most turbulent times.

"It was very difficult for me, coming from practice every day, watching television, Liberia on the news, people running away, people dying," Weah said in a featured package preceding his award from Denzel. "So, all I said to myself was, look, what can I do to better the situation in my country. I felt that Liberia is my country, and I must come back. By eating, living, and playing with them, you will know what is going on. This is reality, I can't run from reality. Every Liberian loves sports. I know sports can play a vital role in the peace process and sports can help to discipline the kids and unify them. Peace for Liberia, free education, disarm."[279]

It is not very often that an athlete makes the transition into politics. A few have done it, some successful; and others, not so successful. The most famous, Arnold Schwarzenegger, was a professional body builder who became the youngest person to be named Mr. Olympia, winning the title six straight years. He was elected governor of California in 2003. Former U.S. Senator Bill Bradley won an Olympic gold medal in 1964 and was played basketball for the New York Knicks (1967–1977) winning two championships in 1970 and 1973. Bradley was inducted into the Naismith Memorial Basketball Hall of Fame in 1983. He served in the U.S. Senate from 1979 to 1997 representing the state of New Jersey.

Emmanuel Dapidran Pacquiao Sr., the Filipino boxing legend regarded as one of the greatest professional boxers of all time, has been serving as a Senator of the Philippines since 2016 and previously as a representative of Sarangani's at-large congressional district, from 2010–2016. Former Governor Jesse "The Body" Ventura, a one-time pro-wrestler, was elected Governor of Minnesota for Ross Perot's Reform Party serving from 1999 to 2003. He was the Reform Party's only successful only candidate in terms of winning a major government office. Then, there was David Bing, a seven-time All-Star guard in the NBA who was eventually voted into the Basketball Hall of Fame. The Detroit Pistons legend was also the Rookie of The Year for the 1975–76 season. In 2009, he won a special election after former mayor of Detroit, Kwame Kilpatrick, resigned in disgrace. Bing won the scheduled election held six months later as well. Kevin Johnson, a three-time NBA All-Star and the 1988–89 winner of the Most Improved Player award, still holds the Phoenix Suns franchise record for assists, free throws made, and free throws attempted. He then served as 55th Mayor of Sacramento, California from 2008 to 2016.

During a radio interview on November 18, 2004, George Manneh Weah declared his run for the Presidency, laying to rest months of fevered speculation. "I will be a candidate in the Presidential election," he said. "I have no choice but to accept the people's request."[280] So, he was about to embark on a Herculean journey. In early 2005, he granted an interview to the *Daily Observer* newspaper during which he sought to convince voters and the international community that he was the right man to take Liberia out of a brutal civil war and transition the country to normalcy. "There is a pretty strong link between sports and politics and there's no way sports can shy away from politics,"[281] George told the newspaper.

As a matter of fact, George said he felt that the leadership role played in sports could also be played in the political arena. "It is true that I was very successful in my passion, which is football. And today I am into politics. I am quite optimistic that I will have a smooth transition because I will have respect for human rights and dignity."[282]

The newspaper pressed George on his leadership qualities, asking what set him apart from the other Presidential candidates in this race. "I have honesty," he replied, "the ability to attract people and my passion for helping Liberia and Liberians. I have been there for my people in the times when my people needed me and not even realising that I would be in a race for the Presidency. I've been there for them before, and I will be there for them again."[283]

George was clear about his intentions to contest and what he would do if elected. "We talk about what will happen in the first ninety days. We hope to address some of the basic necessities, including electricity for our people, sanitation problems, safe drinking water, food, shelter and all the things that are needed to keep our people happy. So, these are some of the things we are going to address."[284]

George was also mindful of the era of Charles Taylor and Samuel Doe, when rulers ruled with iron fists and clamped down on the media. He vowed to tread a different path. "I've fought for media institutions in the past and I would do so again. If you can recall some time back when the journalists were imprisoned, I intervened and I said that it was their right to express their views. The media have the right to speak out and address corrupt practices of government institutions. I also said to the media too that they need to be transparent and direct a correct flow of information so that our people can be aware of what is taking place."[285]

At the time of George's quest there were numerous concerns about his citizenship. "Well, because it is an election season, people will come out and say anything to gain an edge. A lot of people don't know what I do. Only those that are close to me know my abilities and my capabilities. Like the last time in Monrovia, there was a story in one of the papers with a photo of my passport with a number in it saying they had finally found Mr. Weah's French citizenship passport and they put in a Liberian passport number which was 002014. You know, I will be honest with you because I live an honest life and I don't want to cheat anybody. In the past when I played in Paris, of course I played under dual nationality."[286]

In August 2005, the National Elections Commission (NEC) cleared George to stand as a Presidential candidate, dismissing a complaint over his French citizenship.

Rivals even called for George to be disqualified from the race, saying he had adopted French citizenship whilst playing soccer in France from 1989 to 1999. But the elections commission disagreed. "The evidence addressed by the complainants is not sufficient to prove the dual nationality of... George Weah to render him ineligible to contest the 2005 elections as Presidential candidate,"[287] the NEC said in its ruling.

A content George slammed his accusers. "I am happy about the decision taken by the NEC because those people who brought this case against me did not know what they were talking about in the first place,"[288] he told reporters.

In the days leading to the elections, George's temperament was also an issue. His relationship with some of colleagues on the national team raised questions about his ability to unite a nation emerging from war. His national team strike partner James Salinsa Debbah aptly summed up the sentiments from most of the members of the team. "The background from which this man came from, he should have unified the people. He comes from a terrain that is appealing to all demographics – everybody will accept you for who you are. Look at the footballers. You can't unify your own group; how can you unify the country?"[289]

But George drummed the criticisms. "Those are just speculations and speculations are not true. When you talk of professionalism, most of the people around me and those who know me would tell you that I am a professional man. I know the issue has to do with the national team when I was the coach and as the technical director, I believed in results, and I am a professional person. I was building a national team based on results and not based on friendship or recommendation. So, if I put these players together and they did not perform to the best of their abilities, I had no choice but to rest them. So, other players felt that the 'ambassador doesn't like me', but that's not so. I know there's been a lot of news out there about me that I'm quick to get angry, but that's not so. And the whole thing came up from the Lone Star issue, which I've just explained. Anyone will tell you that Ambassador Weah tried to develop the minds of the players and tried to instill commitment and qualities."[290]

As in any political contest, the issues and accusations dominated George's Presidential quest and despite his peace role with UNICEF, there was some speculation that he was supporting one of the rebel factions in the civil war, the Movement for Democracy in Liberia (MODEL).

George took on his critics, declaring, "If I was really part of MODEL, as has been reported in the news, what about the people in Liberia that fought the war? They are there."[291]

Former U.S. First Lady, Michelle Obama, once said, "Don't ever make decisions based on fear. Make decisions based on hope and possibility. Make decisions based on what should happen, not what shouldn't."[292] Weah knew he was about to embark on an unfamiliar journey, a journey without the glittering lights of the San Siro Stadium in Italy, the Parc de Prince or the famed Monaco stadium where he made his name. He was embarking into a territory that would affect the lives of nearly five million people. This was no longer kiddies play, this was life.

Weah understood the implications of people's perception about his ties to MODEL. The interviewer had actually completed the interview when Weah asked him to sit down because he wanted to address the MODEL issue. For Weah, it was important to clear the air. Liberia's history demanded it. The former UNICEF ambassador was about to embark on a journey in a nation whose history had been punctuated by years of civil and social upheaval. Two devastating civil wars in a thirty-year span had killed scores of Liberians and sent many into exile. These were conflicts that saw warlords commit crimes with impunity in the absence of law and order. Men, women, and children were gunned down in their homes and villages, scores had been massacred and women and young girls raped in front of their families.

This is why it was important for Weah to distance himself from the civil war and its implications for the unchartered territory he was about to enter. "They can accuse me of joining them, not somebody from the outside. And even if I was supporting MODEL, don't you think I would put in the resources and today all of them will be at the ministry working? Don't you think I would seek for what I put in? Of course, if I did that and I can't work in the society then I would be a crazy man that I would put my resources in it and do everything to get it back. My professor said to me, you know Mr. Weah, you know you are a good man, and we respect you, but what I'm going to tell you is, 'Once you're into politics, people will try to find every dirty thing and put it on you. Whether it's true or not. So be prepared.' That's why I haven't said anything. The MODEL issue came up because I saw it in the news and it's not true."[293]

11

SPOILER

———

At the end of a series of marathon political meetings in Florida and the wonderful showcase at the ESPYs during which George Weah received the Arthur Ashe Award, it was clear that George Weah was running for President on his own – and on his own terms. Never mind what critics and his potential opponents thought about his qualifications for the job he was seeking, his education lapses, or their disdain about his plan to transition from a world class footballer to the Liberian Presidency.

George Weah had made up his mind that he was running for the Presidency and there was nothing anyone was going to do about it, nothing anyone would say that could sway him away from it. Win or lose, he was entering the Presidential race, to the dismay of many more experienced politicians and advocates who had been in the vanguard for change. Many of George's opponents were less popular and further away from connecting with the thousands of Liberians who had followed his football career.

After all, George was not in their league, he was not a politician but a footballer who had very little understanding about leadership, about governance, about what it required to lead a nation of nearly five million people emerging from a rugged civil war. His teammate, Jonathan "Boye Charles" Sogbie had earlier spelled it out to George in so many ways, hoping that the football icon would at least grasp the essence of what he was about to venture into. James Debbah, another teammate also raised concerns and questioned George's decision, his ambition and his quest for the Presidency. Simply put, George Weah had conquered the beautiful game of football, but for many of his critics, he wasn't quite ready, or perhaps not ready at all.

This is why very few of George's would-be opponents understood why he connected so well with the grassroots and those languishing at the bottom of the economic ladder, except for Varney Sherman. "One has to take into consideration that this guy took our base, this is the man that the population wanted. One man, one vote? Weah will win,"[294] Sherman recalls thinking at the time.

Prior to the elections, Sherman, a well-respected and notable lawyer, was highly regarded as the most wealthy of all the candidates in the election. Boasting the likes of Firestone, ArcelorMittal and other major corporations amongst his clientele, his financial portfolio was untouchable by more than a mile. He was a partner in his law firm, Sherman & Sherman, and was vocal in denouncing the government of the day for what he saw as non-enforcement of a hiring policy meant to favour Liberian citizens and businesses. In the 1980s, he was a part of Maxwell & Maxwell Law Firm as an associate, working as a consulting attorney and as a trial lawyer at a time when Liberia was in the throes of recovering from Samuel Kanyon Doe's 1980 coup.

By then, he returned home from America where he received a degree from the Harvard Law School. At Maxwell law firm, handled legal client affairs of numerous corporate clients of Maxwell & Maxwell including Citibank, BCCI and Chase Manhattan Bank as well as several construction and engineering businesses.

With his presence in the race now a foregone conclusion, Weah's next challenge was choosing the perfect running mate to offset his lapses, a more experienced person who would serve as a guide for Weah and show him the ropes.

Enter J. Rudolph Johnson, a former Foreign Minister, who Sherman, in hindsight, felt was a perfect decoy due to his experience in the foreign service and government.

Prior to picking Johnson, Weah had no idea who would be the Vice-Presidential candidate. All the top politicians available wanted him to be their Vice. James Kollie, who was part of the process to select the running mate, recalls that a few names with lesser political ambitions floated around. Among them was Saah Philip Joe, a former president of the Liberian Teachers Association and member of the House of Representatives. But many within Weah's circle were against the thought. "This would have been calamity. The fear of this scenario becoming a reality made the search for a credible and viable running mate even more pressing,"[295] says Kollie.

At one point, Kollie recalls, the search for a running mate was discussed during a June 2005 meeting at the airport in Washington, DC. "At that meeting, it was decided that we pick a woman as a Vice-Presidential candidate as a means to counter the female appeal of Madam. Johnson Sirleaf. Based on this, Weah placed a call to Judge Ash-Thompson to see if she could consider being his running mate. At that time, the Judge was Vice President at the University of Liberia and she asked if Weah could meet with her boss, Dr. Alhassan Conteh, and have a discussion with him."[296]

So, Weah and his team left the DC airport meeting with Judge Luvenia Ash-Thompson as the potential running mate. But there was just one problem. Weah and his team began to get buyer's remorse, fearing that Thompson would be the wrong fit for the largest grassroots political party because she was not considered to have a history with the grassroots movement.

It didn't help matters when Charles Walker Brumskine, another opposition candidate, decided to choose a woman, Amelia Ward, as his running mate. "We then rationalised that there was no reason to continue the pursuit of Judge Ash-Thompson as a female running mate; Thompson was no longer a strategic imperative,"[297] says Kollie.

During the process, Weah's advisors submitted the names of Dr. Walter Gwenigale, a noted health practitioner; John Morlu Sr., a financial counsellor for the government of Liberia and Ambassador J. Rudolph Johnson. From all indications, John Morlu was not prepared to relinquish his ambition and Dr. Gwenigale was clear with Kollie on the phone that it was not possible. Gwenigale was one of the top doctors in the country. A run for the presidency, if he had won, would definitely have been an end to his career.

With both Morlu and Gwenigale out of the picture, J. Rudolph Johnson was the last man standing. Interestingly, Johnson himself had his eyes set on the Presidency. So, Kollie decided to reach out to Johnson's political establishment in the U.S. and jumpstarted the negotiation. "I called his wife, Judge Gladys Johnson, and pleaded with her to talk with the

Ambassador to consider joining Weah as running mate. They gave me his Liberian contact and encouraged me to reach out to him. I did,"[298] Kollie recalls.

Kollie pitched the idea to Johnson that if he agreed to go along with being Vice President to Weah, he could actually be leading and mentoring a lot of the young people.

Kollie, along with Samuel Tweah, then arranged the first meeting between Weah and Johnson. Once again, Weah was faced with yet another older politician trying to play the age card. In their first meeting, Johnson argued that since he was older person and more experienced, it would be better if he went as head of the ticket and Weah went as his running mate.

Johnson's insistence on heading the ticket led to the talks breaking down. But Kollie was persuasive. "I received a call that Johnson had come with a different proposal than what was discussed. I called Johnson back and told him that we didn't have much to go back and forth. I told him that this moment was Weah's moment and that the country wanted him, and I needed him, Johnson, to support Weah's bid for the Presidency."[299] Johnson, with some reluctance, finally agreed and the second meeting was organised with Johnson officially accepting to go as running mate to Weah.

An elated Tweah immediately called Kollie to celebrate the news. George Weah had his Vice-Presidential candidate.

The election of 2005 itself marked a turning point for Liberia, a nation regarded as Africa's oldest since gaining independence in 1847, which was hoping to turn the corner with a transition from war to peace.

It had now been sixteen years since the civil war erupted when Charles Taylor's National Patriotic Front of Liberia launched an invasion on December 24, 1989. A total of seven major rebel groups had fought each other in the hope of forcefully gaining power. Among them were Charles Taylor's National Patriotic Front for Liberia (NPFL), Alhaji Kromah's ethnic Mandingo-based United Liberation Movement for Democracy in Liberia (ULIMO/Mandingo), a Krahn-based ULIMO splinter group led by Roosevelt Johnson (ULIMO/Krahn), an NPFL splinter group named the Central Revolutionary Council (CRC-NPFL) led by former Charles Taylor supporter Juconti Thomas ('Tom') Woewiyu, another Krahn-Sarpo-based group called the Liberia Peace Council (LPC) led by George Boley, the Lofa Defence Force

(LDF) headed by Francois Massaquoi, and the Armed Forces of Liberia (AFL), the Krahn-dominated army of the late President Samuel Doe.

Peace-keeping forces from the Economic Community of West African States' (ECOWAS) Ceasefire Monitoring Group (ECOMOG) forcibly intervened on August 24, 1990, in the wake of violent opposition from Charles Taylor's NPFL to separate the warring factions and to provide security for the Liberian capital, Monrovia. After nearly a decade of war, leaders of the main warring factions signed a new peace agreement on August 19, 1995, known as the Abuja Accord. USAID/OFSA succinctly summarised the situation at the time: "As Liberia's thirteenth peace agreement, it was viewed as a sincere effort to restore peace to the country and represented a reconciliation between long-time adversaries, the NFPL and ECOMOG, a consensus among West African States on Liberia, and direct involvement of faction leaders in implementing the accord – all essential factors to lasting peace. The Accord produced an ambitious disarmament, demobilisation and election schedule; however, Liberia's factions did not have the political will to implement the Accord's provisions."[300] A senseless civil war had killed thousands of Liberians and sent many into exile. Now, in October 2005, amid a poorly executed UN-backed Disarmament, Demobilization and Reintegration program aimed at disarming combatants of the civil war, many had turned in their guns and military gears for return to civilian life in hope of becoming normal again.

Normality, even by Liberian standards, could mean an opportunity to feel safe again, to feel decent and confident that, with the guns now silent, fathers and mothers could see their children again, diaspora Liberians who had fled to seek shelter in other countries around the world could return home, children would return to school and investors would once again see reason to return and invest in many of the country's rich natural mineral resources.

Amid the hope of a new Liberia, lay the fears of a nation aware of its history with notorious elections, a history going as far back as 1927 and the elections logged in *The Guinness Book of World Records* as the most fraudulent election ever reported in history. The Presidential election of 1927 saw Charles D. B. King of the True Whig Party secure a third team ahead of Thomas J. Faulkner of the People's Party. Yet the nature of the victory was spectacularly flawed. Somehow with a registered electorate of only 15,000, King amassed votes of 243,000 and Faulkner, 9,000. Worse still were the accusations Faulkner levelled at members of the True Whig Party government that they had used slave labour in Liberia and had sold slaves to Fernando Po, a Spanish Colony off Africa's west coast. In response, the League of Nations commissioned a report, the "International Commission of Inquiry into the Existence of Slavery and Forced Labor in the Republic of Liberia", notwithstanding the True Whig's Party refusals to recognise the allegations or to cooperate. The U.S. Government also suspended relations briefly as further pressure before an inconclusive report was published on September 8, 1930. The charges could not be proven but both King and his Vice President Allen Yancy were said to have profited from forced labour, which the report considered tantamount to slavery. Faced with this, Liberia's House of Representatives commenced an impeachment process against King, who promptly resigned. He was succeeded by Edwin J. Barclay of the True Whig Party. The unlucky Faulkner had another tilt at power losing the 1931 elections to Barclay who held the Presidency for the True Whigs until 1944, when William Tubman took over.

The trend of allegations involving election irregularities would surface again fifty-eight years later when Liberia, under Head of State, Samuel Kanyon Doe, held elections on October 15, 1985, marking the first elections since the April 12, 1980, military coup that brought Master Sergeant Doe to power.

The path to elections has been laid in 1984 when a new draft constitution was greenlighted after a referendum. A civilian and military Interim National Assembly led by Doe was to pave the way. When a ban on political parties was raised, four parties fought out the elections. Sadly, the process was affected by allegations of fraud, vote-rigging yet Samuel Kanyon Doe survived (officially at least) when he claimed 50.9% of the electoral tally, scraping home with the bare minimum of votes needed to avoid a runoff with Jackson F. Doe in second place.

Doe's NDPL won large majorities in both houses of the Legislature although many independent observers believed that the Liberia Action Party of Jackson F. Doe, who officially finished second, was the actual winner. It was later revealed that Samuel Doe had the ballots counted in a secret location by his handpicked staff. The period after the elections saw increased human rights abuses, corruption and ethnic tensions, ultimately leading to the start of what would become a brutal civil war in 1989 and Doe's overthrow and murder in 1990.

Until the coup on April 12, 1980, Liberia was ruled by one party, the True Whig Party (TWP), one of the oldest political parties in the world and the oldest in Africa. President William R. Tolbert was overthrown in a coup led by Master Sergeant Doe and a group of conspirators.

The TWP was in power from 1877, and was mostly composed of American-Liberians, who constituted less than one per cent of the population. President William V. S. Tubman ruled from 1947 until his death in a London clinic in 1971; and William R. Tolbert continued afterwards, winning the 1975 elections.

Upon seizing power, Doe declared that the group wanted to arrest Tolbert and when he resisted, he was shot dead. A counter-insurgency operation on April 16 was put down and Samuel Doe gained full control of the government. Doe's military People's Redemption Council (PRC) invoked martial law and took control of all legislative and executive powers. This led to numerous executions, rampant corruption, increasing rate of unemployment and deteriorating health conditions. At the U.N. General Assembly, the coup-makers announced that elections would possibly be held by 1983. Doe also built his image internationally by having border issues fixed with neighbouring countries and also promised a fair trial to the family of Tolbert.

During 1984, a new draft constitution was approved in a referendum, which provided for a 58-member civilian and military Interim National Assembly, headed by Doe as President.

The following years and two civil wars had not fully erased traditions of democracy in the country and by 2005, were once again high. For Varney Sherman, the weeks, months and years leading to October 2005 were crucial and marked the build-up of what was to follow, starting with the signing of the Accra Comprehensive Peace Accord. Sherman recalls, "We had gone to Accra for the Peace Conference and before we went, we had an agreement, considering that we put together what was called the Alliance of Political Parties, headed by our candidate, Cletus Wotorson, that the Liberian Action

Party would not put up a candidate, that is if those who collaborated with us would come up with a suitable candidate."[301]

As the civil conflict got worse, Sherman says the rebel factions – the Liberians United for Reconciliation and Democracy (LURD), and others – started coming closer to the capital. Sherman recalls, "All of us became aware that it would be difficult to have elections. Of course, ECOWAS invited all the parties of the conflict, political parties and civil society groups to Accra. In Accra, we agreed as the Liberian Action Party (LAP) and assumed that there were two possibilities coming out of that peace conference: One, the Laurent Kabila-style government where Charles Taylor would remain the head of government, political parties and others would come in – or alternatively, a new government that would pave the way for fresh elections."[302]

Laurent Kabila became the third President of the Democratic Republic of the Congo in 1997. Opposing Mobutu Sese Seko, the longstanding President of Zaire/Democratic Republic of Congo, Kabila overthrew him in the First Congo War (1996–1997) heading up the Alliance of Democratic Forces for the Liberation of Congo (ADFLC) which had backing from Uganda and Rwanda. Once installed he faced an awkward situation being indebted to foreign powers that had helped him achieve the Presidency. Taking the situation in hand, he demanded the departure of all foreign troops from the country to thwart coup attempts: the result however was the Second Congo War in which various rebel groups such as the Rally for Congolese Democracy (RCD) and the Movement for the Liberation of the Congo (MLC) now had the support of his erstwhile Rwanda and Uganda allies. On January 16, 2001, Kabila was assassinated by a bodyguard and succeeded shortly by his son, Joseph.

For some of the stakeholders deciding Liberia's future, the decision to adapt the Kabila-style scenario was a good route to take. But Sherman says it was agreed that Charles Gyude Bryant, who was head of his party, the Liberian Action Party (LAP), should put his hands up as head of the transition government because LAP had said it would not put up a candidate for the interim leadership and Bryant had no ambition to run for presidency in the future. "If they gave us a good candidate, people will support us so that we would not renege on our representation that we would not put up a candidate."[303]

Sherman explained that when he and his peers arrived in Accra, Ghana, to elect the chairman of the Transitional National government, LAP changed their minds because Ellen Johnson Sirleaf of the Unity Party wanted to be the Interim President while Charles Brumskine supported Harry Moniba, against the backdrop that Moniba was the legitimate person to succeed, given he was Doe's Vice President.

Sirleaf ran on LAP's ticket in the disputed 1985 General Elections for the Montserrado County Senatorial seat. Although she was declared the winner, she refused to accept the seat as the opposition alleged voting irregularities. Nearly a decade later, she contested the Presidency on the ticket of the Unity Party but lost to Charles Taylor, who amassed 468,443 votes for 59% to Sirleaf's 59,557 votes for 9.58% of the votes.

At the discussions surrounding the Accra Comprehensive Peace Accord, many were baffled over Sirleaf's decision to contest the interim Presidency.

For Sherman in particular, his party, LAP, had to do all it could to keep Sirleaf from winning the interim Presidency. "When it got that tough, I was called and we (LAP) won the election to chair the interim government, and Gyude Bryant chosen as Chairman of the NTGL [National Transition Government Liberia]."[304]

Sherman says the angst against Sirleaf was largely due to the way LAP was treated. "We had all agreed that we would only be committed to that proposition, that LAP would not put up a candidate. The theory was that Gyude Bryant would have done so well, that LAP would have flown into the Presidency. The hindsight was, we could show that we were not involved or associated with the war or any of the warring factions and we would be able to find a suitable candidate who we could support."[305]

Sherman says it was on that basis he was forced to step in. "The other reason I came in was that we came to the agreement that the only person who would have had the financial capacity either personally, or who could have raised the money, was Varney Sherman. Since I catered all the other bills, you take up the mantle to be the candidate and we could appeal to the younger generation, the professionals."[306]

In the final analysis, the decision to elect Bryant as interim government leader was simple: he was not the conventional politician but rather a businessman with really nothing to lose.

The formation of the interim government was part of the peace agreement to end the country's long-running civil war, which had ravaged since the Liberians United for Reconciliation and Democracy (LURD) rebelled against President Taylor in 1999. Bryant emerged as a chairman due to a reputation of political neutrality. Warring factions including LURD and the Movement of Democracy in Liberia (MODEL) found him acceptable. His background as a leading figure in the Episcopal Church of Liberia, an institution critical of the Doe and Taylor regimes, also seemed to look forward to a more democratic future.

Sherman's decision to push Bryant's chairmanship of the interim government also had its motive. Sherman had the wealth but also quietly had his eye set on the Presidency and knowing that the interim government was only a temporary process, the quest for the Presidency itself was in striking distance – and that's where he believed he could use his wealth to secure it.

Like Bryant, Sherman had not been in government. He had not been involved with any of the warring factions. So, heading into the 2005 elections, he was one of the frontrunners until George Weah entered the picture. Although wealthy, Sherman was considered by many to be out of sync with those languishing at the bottom of the economic ladder. He was far removed from the bottomless pit of those enduring poverty and was seen as someone who really didn't understand the plight of the poor. So, Weah's presence in the 2005 elections offered what Sherman and many of the other politicians lacked, a person to whom the people could relate to.

In hindsight, Sherman acknowledges that he and several members of the hierarchy of his party, LAP, came to the conclusion that Weah had ambushed their base. "These young, disenfranchised people, that was the base we had. We came to the conclusion that I had gone all over Liberia – and then Weah came and took our base and I personally thought that we had an obligation to that base, that was their choice, instead of Varney Sherman, it should be Weah."[307]

So, by the time the elections of 2005 came around, it was clear that despite their wealth of experience in governance and expertise, Weah's popularity had eclipsed them all.

As expected, Weah went on to perform well in the first round, emerging ahead with 28% of the vote while achieving first or second place in all of the fifteen political subdivisions with the exception of Lofa, and Margibi, where he came third by just 277 votes. He also took almost the entire southeast of the country, his stronghold that included Grand Gedeh with 88% of the votes cast, Grand Kru and River Gee with around 50%, and Sinoe and Nimba. Weah even came in second to Ambassador Winston Tubman in Tubman's stronghold of Maryland County by just 542 votes. Weah also captured Montserrado, containing heavily populated Monrovia.

True to Sherman's fears, Weah had the numbers.

Charles Brumskine, a former President Pro-Tempore of the Senate, running on the Liberty Party ticket, took smaller portions of the regional block of the central seaboard counties of Grand Bassa with 58% of the vote and Rivercess with 46%, and came second in Margibi. Brumskine came third nationwide with 14% of the vote. Winston Tubman took 9% of the Presidential vote, emerging ahead in Maryland, his home county; and Bong, his running mate, Jeremiah Sulunteh's home county, by more than 31,000 votes.

Sherman, running as the standard bearer of the four-party Coalition for the Transformation of Liberia (COTOL), was placed fifth out of 22 candidates, receiving 7.8% of the vote nationwide while winning his home county, Grand Cape Mount.

After a lacklustre performance, Sherman says, endorsing Weah was the easiest choice he had to make. "So, after the first round, I don't think Weah knew much about what we had planned or what we were thinking," he recalls. "He had approached me personally, actually asked me for my support. The other person who asked me for my support was Ellen Johnson Sirleaf."[308]

With both Sherman and Tubman deciding to endorse Weah – Brumskine having been decided against – Sherman says the two endorsements should have been sufficient to take Weah over the top but in the end, Sirleaf finished first with 59% of the vote to Weah's 41%, according to the National Elections Commission at the time.

Sherman recalls that part of his reasons for backing Weah in the second round was his choice for Vice President. "The plan was for Rudolph to assist with the day-to-day management of the government. So, I bought it! It was a fantastic idea. And I was thrilled with the idea and that was the environment under which we supported him."

Endorsement was key for the 2005 elections.

Sherman explains that he turned Ellen Johnson Sirleaf down for several reasons. "One, she sent people to me, she never offered to talk to me, that was the start of a situation where I could not rely on her commitment. The other thing is that in doing the debate, Ellen Johnson Sirleaf had brought in for lack of a better word, the disagreement we had in the build-up to the 1997 elections where instead of choosing Sirleaf, the party decided to select Cletus Wotorson. I was one of those who said that she was too late. We had asked her to be our candidate and she turned us down, so we decided on Cletus Wotorson. We went to the convention and endorsed Wotorson."[309]

On the day of that convention, Sherman says Sirleaf told the group that they should postpone the convention because she wanted to be a candidate. "We said, we couldn't do that, we told her she did not comply with the process, so we could not allow her to be the standard bearer. She gave us some very good reason, why she was now interested but we said we couldn't change."[310]

Sherman's beef with Sirleaf intensified during the Presidential debate leading to the 2005 elections. During the debate at the Centennial pavilion, the last question that the moderator asked was, "Is there a candidate who has a question for another candidate?"

Sherman says the only person who said yes was Ellen Johnson Sirleaf. She asked, "Cllr. Varney Sherman, 'What have you done for Liberia, that should be a reason why Liberians should vote for you?'"[311]

Sherman responded, "Before I tell you what I have done for Liberia, I first want to say, I was not a member of a warring faction, I never supported anybody to bring war to Liberia."[312]

The debate was over as the crowd roared into cheers. Sherman says Sirleaf fell into a trap of her own creation. Her plan to embarrass him had backfired. The reference to the war was a thorny issue for Sirleaf who, for most of her political life, had been dogged by how much role she played in helping Charles Taylor start the war in Liberia. Sirleaf had always admitted that she visited Mr. Charles Taylor, as rebel leader, behind the lines in Nimba County, but that he fooled her in believing his agenda of justice. While she had denied ever being a part of any rebel faction in the destruction of Liberia, she had gone on record, during an appearance before the Truth and

Reconciliation Commission in February 2009, admitting that she endorsed the rebellion against President Samuel Doe, describing the rebellion as "a people's movement". She also later admitted to being part of the Association for Constitutional Democracy in Liberia (ACDL) which gave support to the NPFL rebel group of Mr. Taylor.

According to Sirleaf, she sympathised with the NPFL because of its theory and at that point in time, she donated ten thousand U.S. dollars for humanitarian purposes. She told the TRC that she disassociated herself from the NPFL when she paid a visit to Gborplay in Nimba County in May of 1990. She recalls while in Gborplay, she saw things that did not show that the NPFL was a liberation group. She said if there was anything to apologise for, it would be her association with, and support for Charles Taylor.

Weah was not part of the debate, but his opponents were. The fact of the matter is, Weah could actually afford to sit on the sidelines and watch the other candidates duke it out.

Sherman never had to complete his answer. The question about the war had closed the debate. "I had brought in something that people never talked about in a debate: the fact that she supported Charles Taylor. And I assumed that I had not supported her, and she was successful, support would have been meaningless. But like I said, the most important thing is that George Weah actually came to me."[313]

Weah did not participate in the debate, there was Brumskine, Sherman, Ellen, Tubman.

According to Sherman, Weah was aware of his lapses, owing to his inability to effectively articulate and communicate, he never decided to participate in a debate where he knew he would be at a disadvantage. Weah however was impressed with Sherman's delivery.

To this day, Sherman believes Weah was cheated. "I still believe George Weah won that election. I'm so very convinced. But the international community did not buy it, they did not think he was the person to take our country out of the situation we were in into a more stable and acceptable form of governance and democracy. Simply put, he won, I'm so convinced up to this date."[314]

And so was Weah, who alleged that the election had been rigged through voter intimidation and ballot tampering. The footballer-turned politician even managed to convince his supporters to protest the results in the streets of Monrovia. Holding what he believed were fake ballots in his hands, Weah looked disappointed, disjointed. Despite his popularity, his hopes for the Presidency had been dashed, his votes tampered with, and no one was going to convince him otherwise. He had been cheated.

Despite Weah's objections to the election results, a number of African leaders called upon the followers of Weah to relinquish their hopes and courteously abide by the result, so that Sirleaf be President. Moreover the African Union had described the polls as "peaceful, transparent, and fair".[315]

What was most intriguing about the 2005 Presidential elections is that it exposed a lot of people who saw Weah as a pushover, an inept figurehead who could be easily swayed. The belief that his choice of Rudolph Johnson as Vice President was the perfect decoy presented Weah as someone who would lead as a ceremonial head of state, controlled by more experienced advisors.

It was Weah's first venture into the rugged jungle of politics. Far removed from the confines of a 130-yards football field, Weah finally found himself barricaded by a force he never anticipated. He had conquered the world of football, now he had to discover a way to study his new game, a game more complicated than he could ever imagine, a game so obtuse that it could drive the politically naïve and unprepared insane. But here he was, staring down a tunnel into an unfamiliar territory. It wasn't about kicking football at this point, it was about mastering the game of politics, and returning to the drawing board in a bid to give himself another shot at the elusive Presidency, bearing any further glitches or unforeseen and avoidable circumstances along the way.

12

BAD TIMING

———

June 2010

J ames Bestman came into George's life just when the football money was drying up.

Weah had made millions of dollars playing the beautiful game, but a series of investments and extravagant spending took its toll. Much of his money was put into a number of experimental projects like his radio station, Kings FM in Monrovia, and a commercial property near Fort Lauderdale. This building came with a zoning agreement so it could be used as a delicatessen or grocery store. It was bought for $460,000 with a mortgage in 2002.

Weah also had a property in Staten Island which he would later sell in 2005 and another property in Queens, New York.. The ownership of this was transferred to him in 1993 by his agent Alaji Sidibay during the time Weah was playing for Paris Saint-Germain.

While James was running the streets as an underground drug and money laundering kingpin, Weah was breaking down defences, and scoring goals and conquering the world as one of the most gifted talents of his generation. Toward the tail end of his professional football career, George frequented New York where he and James would hang out.

Everyone knew Bestman to be a drug kingpin with a track record a mile long. George was fully aware and knew Bestman at that level. In fact, in the 1990s just when the civil war was at its peak in Liberia, Bestman spent three and a half years in prison in a self-defence murder case in New York.

According to records from the Brooklyn Federal Court, Bestman testified that in 1991, that he sold drugs at an address listed as 160 Park Hill Avenue in Staten Island, New York with Anthony Christian, Harvey Christian and their brother James Christian, all of whom also sold drugs. Bestman had met Jason Quinn in the early 1990s and would see him around 55 Bowen Street with Anthony Christian and Harvey Christian.

Bestman, the court record states, pooled his money with the Christian brothers to buy drugs together from a supplier. "Significantly, Bestman testified that even back in 1991, Harvey Christian was a "natural leader" who would "recruit people to work for us", that is, to sell crack for the enterprise. Bestman identified another individual who sold crack with the Christian brothers from the early 1990s onward, including at 225 Park Hill and 240 Park Hill."[316]

The enterprise members, according to the court records, worked together at 160 Park Hill, a "freelance" building, where Bestman would use his speed to reach customers before rival drug dealers, while, at the same time, Anthony and Harvey Christian physically blocked the rival dealers. In 1992 or 1993, after Brian Humphreys and another drug dealer forced the enterprise out of 160 Park Hill, Bestman and the Christian brothers moved their operation to 225 Park Hill and 240 Park Hill Avenue.

The enterprise, according to court records, quickly came to "control" 240 Park Hill, meaning that the only people who would sell crack there were the enterprise workers. This is where Bestman ran into trouble. "The arrangement lasted for five or six months, beginning at the end of 1993, and involved the members buying guns and drugs together. The arrangement at 240 Park Hill ended in 1994, after Bestman shot and killed Erron Lewis, also known as '2 Cent', while protecting the enterprise's turf."[317]

Bestman was in jail for that crime from 1994–1997 before being acquitted at trial. He recalled that before he went to jail, the enterprise was involved in an ongoing dispute with a rival drug trafficking organisation based in 260 Park Hill, one building over from 240 Park Hill. After 1997, Bestman did not live in Staten Island because he feared retribution from Erron Lewis' brothers, but he did visit from time to time, saw the Christian brothers at 55 Bowen, knew that they had joined the Blood gangs by 1997, and believed they left the gangs in approximately 2000.

By early 2009, a vacancy had opened in the Senate with the death of Hannah Brent. Brent was a member of George's Congress for Democratic Change party. Brent had died from cancer. Her death drew tributes from across the country as many, including President Ellen Johnson Sirleaf, heralded Brent's remarkable accomplishment as one of a handful of women in the Senate. At her funeral, Sirleaf described the death as, "One of those events that break our spirit, shake our confidence and challenge our resolve. It is on such occasions," the President said, "that all Liberians must reach inner strength and hang on to faith and hope."[318]

Not too long after Brent's death, the struggle for her replacement intensified. George's party scrambled over a number of names to replace her. Weah's personal interest was Lenn Eugene Nagbe, a long-time friend with whom George had spent a lot of time. It was even rumoured that Lenn helped George with his studies in George's quest to get a university degree. But George's effort to push Lenn did not win the approval of the party, with many advocating for another woman to fill Brent's shoes. Enter Geraldine Doe-Sheriff alias "Lady Zico".

Geraldine was a popular female footballer for Invincible XI and many within the party felt that she would be the perfect fit to replace Brent.

By then, George had become a regular at the Monrovia Classic, an annual entertainment event of diaspora Liberians held in Atlanta, Georgia. At the event held in 2009, Weah arrived with James and the pair later travelled to Maryland where members of the party were set to meet at the University of Maryland to discuss the upcoming Senatorial by-elections in Liberia. It was decided there, that Geraldine would be the candidate, a decision that did not go down well with George.

The underlying factor was that George was broke and unable to travel and he did not want people to know he was having financial problems. Investments in his home in France and Florida, plus his radio station in Monrovia, had contributed to finances drying up. Very few at the meeting knew it, but finances were tough for George. Very few – except a handful of friends and associates around the two at the time – also knew that James was now bankrolling most of George's travel, hotel, car rental and spending money. So, James offered to finance George's trip to Monrovia to campaign for Geraldine. He even offered money to Geraldine for the campaign and bought her clothes. In those days, George's party was a major beneficiary of James' wealth. But what many did not know, was that, as Bestman resumed his drug business, he was also on the U.S. Federal Bureau of Investigation's (FBI's) radar.

On June 6, 2010, as the partisans were preparing to travel to Minneapolis, Minnesota, for the CDC-USA annual convention, George was scheduled to drive with some friends from Philadelphia to Maryland before flying to Minneapolis for the convention. While in the Maryland area, Weah and a friend were driving from another friend's house when they decided to pass James Bestman's house. Unfortunately for them, James was under surveillance by the FBI. And while George was at James' home, the FBI raided the property.

James, in handcuffs, immediately told the FBI that George was innocent and had nothing to do with whatever business he was involved in. "This man is innocent. I'm the one you want,"[319] he told the FBI officers. The agents then checked George's credentials and found out that he was a former UNICEF Ambassador and former World Footballer of the Year. All George's papers intact and nothing was found to link him to James Bestman's business. So, George was allowed to leave the grounds as James was taken into custody.

Then, according to a first-hand report, James gave some papers to Weah and told him to give them to Bestman's family. The next day, George flew to Minneapolis for the CDC convention. In the convention hall, George asked friends whether they had seen James Bestman. By then, the *Front-PageAfrica* newspaper got wind of what happened at James Bestman's house and broke the story on its online platform.

As George and his inner circle scrambled for answers, they found it difficult to explain George's presence in James' home at the time of James' arrest.

The day after James Bestman's arrest, James Butty of the Voice of America popular morning news magazine, *Daybreak Africa*, got George to speak about the incident at James Bestman's home.

George told the program that he was never handcuffed, while acknowledging that he was on the property when the FBI showed up. "I assure you, I will never get involved in any drugs and money laundering. I don't understand why any journalist would want to write stories and would not substantiate or corroborate his claims against me. As much as I believe in the freedom of press, I think, at the end of the day, when they are bringing the news, I think it should be news for the people to have peace."[320] George explained that he had known Bestman and had enjoyed a good relationship with him for more than 20 years, but that he never witnessed a drug raid or money laundering involving U.S. federal officials. "What happened there was, I was on my way to Minnesota to the (CDC U.S. members) convention, and I decided to pass to James (because) he should have been one of those who were trying to attend the convention. When I pulled into the driveway, Mr. James came down the stairs and I saw two officers that served him a warrant that he needed to come with them."[321] George said the officers then questioned him and asked him for his identification, and after checking his ID they thanked him. Then George asked one of the officers what had happened? According to George, the officer replied, "I don't know."[322] The officer told him that all he could say at the time was that there was a federal case, and he had a warrant for James.

George then said he and the officer laughed about it. "I told him that I must have come at the wrong time."[323]

It took nearly three years for the James Bestman case to go to trial. On April 6, 2012, the U.S. Attorney's Office found James Bestman guilty on two counts, including conspiring to possess 1,000 kilograms of marijuana or more, and money laundering. U.S. District Judge Catherine C. Blake sentenced James Bestman, age 38, of Laurel, Maryland, to 262 months in prison, followed by five years of supervised release, for distribution of marijuana and conspiracy to commit money laundering. Bestman was released in 2021 on grounds of good behaviour.

Testimony put forward at the two-week trial of Bestman indicated that he had 'conspired to distribute marijuana' from channels in the Southwest, then sent onwards to Ohio and the East Coast. At least 10,000 pounds of marijuana were distributed over the duration of the conspiracy evidence demonstrated. During 2004 and 2005 "according to witness testimony" Bestman was a supervisor in the organisation charged with the obtaining of drugs from a source based in Arizona. The FBI account continues, "Additional testimony showed that Bestman engaged in drug deals with other individuals and hired couriers to truck the drugs and money back and forth across the country. During this time, one of Bestman's couriers was stopped by police in the Midwest, and over $160,000 in cash was seized from a hidden compartment in the car. Witnesses also testified about Bestman's involvement in a drug deal in San Diego, California in 2010. Bestman and members of his organisation arranged to purchase 150 pounds of marijuana from an FBI and DEA source. When Bestman began directing where and how the drugs should be loaded and transported, police moved to arrest Bestman, who fled. Bestman was subsequently found hiding in the women's restroom of a nearby restaurant."[324] One last element of the evidence adduced that Bestman and an associate had participated in a scheme of money laundering relating to the purchase of a 2007 Mercedes in which "bank reporting requirements" were eluded and $20,000 stolen, which was intended as a down payment on the car from a co-conspirator. The report concludes, "United States Attorney Rod J. Rosenstein commended the IRS-Criminal Investigation and DEA for their work in the investigation and recognized the FBI, Baltimore Police Department, and San Diego, Police Department for their assistance. Mr. Rosenstein thanked Assistant United States Attorneys Mushtaq Gunja and Joshua Kaul, who prosecuted the case."[325] In the aftermath of the James Bestman saga, the lingering bad smell of the arrest became a haunting and nagging dilemma for Weah and his party. Nevertheless, Weah's popularity was still high.

In 2005, he placed first in the Presidential poll, but only managed 28.3% of the vote. He was defeated by Sirleaf in the November 8 runoff election, winning 40.6% of the vote compared to Johnson Sirleaf's 59.4%. However, Weah's party did win three seats in the Senate and 15 in the House of Representatives.

Weah had defied the odds with a strong showing in the 2005 elections. Yet he was still an untapped politician with a lot to learn. After more than a decade of civil war triggered by corruption, greed and bad governance, the James Bestman debacle was one of the many frailties that caused some sceptics to have second thoughts about Weah.

What had happened to his millions made during his football days? Where did his investments go? How did he manage his finances? Who was responsible and how did he suddenly find himself on the receiving end of handouts from a character like Bestman?

Weah had found himself in a rare company of former athletes whose money had run out after exiting the prime of their careers.

Research by Xpro, a charity for former players, claims that three out of every five Premier League players declare bankruptcy after retirement. According to *The Independent,* such figures are mirrored in American professional sports too. In 2009, a report found a whopping 78% of NFL players went bankrupt or suffered "financial stress" within two years of retirement. Sixty percent of NBA stars lost all their money within five years.

According to *Sports Illustrated,* most athletes lack the financial knowledge to manage the large sums of money they're earning. Former World heavyweight champion, Mike Tyson, and retired basketball great, Allen Iverson, are among many athletes who lived a lifestyle based on their peak earnings yet failed to think about the money they would need later in life.

Weah's link to Bestman raised a lot of concerns about his judgment, with many political observers unsure whether he possessed the discipline to oversee the economy of a nation emerging from war.

13

SACRIFICE

_____

I t didn't take George Weah too long to realise that the giant leap from footballer to President would not be an easy one.

Following a bitter loss to Ellen Johnson Sirleaf at the end of the 2005 Presidential elections, it was back to the drawing board.

The Carter Center, the National Democratic Institute (NDI) and most international observers had given the elections a thumbs up, despite claims from Weah and his supporters that the elections were rigged. The Carter Center is a not-for-profit, non-governmental organisation, that President Jimmy Carter and wife Rosalynn founded in 1982 to promote health and peace across the world.[326]

The Center's work in Liberia is supported by the Government of Ireland and USAID (U. S. Agency for International Development). In addition, the Carter Centre U.K. had, prior to the elections, implemented an electoral assistance program along with Electoral Reform International Services, supported by the European Commission.

The NDI is a non-profit organisation whose mission is to support and extend democracy across the world. Utilising a global network of experts who are volunteers, NDI's aim is to supply practical assistance to those political and civic leaders progressing democratic institutions, practices and values. The NDI's in Liberia provides assistance to civil society organisations concerned with election monitoring and voter education throughout the nation. Its programmes are supported by the National Endowment for Democracy and USAID.

A preliminary statement from the Carter Center released on November 10, 2005, provided a generally positive overall assessment of the process. Days later, on November 23, 2005, the National Elections Commission announced the official election results, declaring Johnson Sirleaf President-elect, having obtained 59.4% of the vote in the November 8 Presidential runoff.

The observers concluded, "While we are aware of several minor instances when polling officials did not follow procedures in completing record of count forms, as well as instances of several other irregularities, the Center and NDI have not seen evidence of systematic fraud or problems that would materially affect the election results."[327]

For Weah, the return to the drawing board would mean making the ultimate sacrifice, a sacrifice many of his followers dreaded. The grassroots Messiah was now forced into a position to do the unthinkable: play second fiddle to a more seasoned politician.

Weah needed a rapid transformation in his quest to rebound; he needed a bit of magic and perhaps some divine inspiration to fine tune his political credentials. It was clear to many that his flirtation with politics had exposed his weaknesses. Suddenly, he had slipped into political obscurity.

Around Weah, many of his closest advisors were convinced that he would need to take a backseat to the Presidency and run as a Vice-Presidential candidate to a more experienced candidate. This, they believed, would give him the necessary tutelage he needed to master the game of politics. It was an experiment worthy of a try, one that was floated and one to which Weah was open to giving close consideration, but at what price?

As head of a grassroots movement, Weah's supporters were adamant. They did not want anyone coming into their space. So, the experiment was bound to run into hiccups – and when the 2011 elections came around, the incumbent Johnson Sirleaf had ideas of her own, amongst which included muddying whatever pairing seemed threatening to her political survival.

Charles Brumskine of the opposition Liberty Party performed well in the 2005 elections, receiving nearly 14% of the vote, 6% less than the second-place candidate, Ellen Johnson Sirleaf. Although Brumskine was ruled ineligible to participate in the second round, he had performed well enough to establish himself as one of the leading politicians in Liberia. In the second round however, Brumskine angered Weah and his supporters when he snubbed the football icon and Sirleaf by choosing to sit on the fence.

Weah never forgot that, and neither did his supporters. The bad blood was evident six years later when discussions surrounding a potential pairing of Brumskine and Weah floated in the air. The sticking point for any discussion on the topic were the memories of the 2005 Presidential elections when Brumskine missed the opportunity to endorse Weah. Despite the hiccups, there were some people around the inner circle of both Weah and Brumskine who believed that a deal could be struck.

In October 2010, Lenn Eugene Nagbe and Abraham Darius Dillon travelled to Owings Mills, MD for a meeting with J. Fonati Koffa, a rising lawyer viewed by many as a star politician in the making. Nagbe Sloh, a political fireguard was also in attendance in what was expected to mark the beginning of an effort to broker a deal. Koffa recalls that a second meeting was held at Bodger Johnson's place in the Maryland area, during which Acarous Gray and Vah Isaac Tukpah were present.

Koffa recalls that the meeting was sponsored by James Bestman, the long-time friend of Weah. However, egos and the fight for positioning of the ticket would soon prove to be a deal breaker. "It boiled down to who would be first and who would be second," Koffa, who was one of the powerbrokers of the deal, recalls. "Neither party budged. I then lost participation in the process. Debar Allen, Brumskine, Nagbe Sloh and Israel Akinsanya took it from there. Israel and Eugene Nagbe became the chief negotiators. Brumskine travelled to Florida with Debar Allen and Nagbe Sloh. The meeting was cordial but not conclusive. They went to Ghana where there was an agreement of Brumskine first. Once the news hit the ground, Acarous Gray and Mulbah Morlu led a CDC revolt before the official announcement. Weah and his colleagues in Accra backed out. It is speculated that Weah had a change of heart while in Accra so sent a signal for the revolt. Brumskine and Weah never really clicked personally. That was a major problem."[328]

Despite the differences, speculation of the pairing sent shivers down the spine of the incumbent Sirleaf. Weah's 26% and Brumskine's 14% were great numbers which could spell trouble for Sirleaf's second term quest.

The discussions came on the eve of the CDC-USA convention in Pennsylvania, U.S.A, and after four weeks of intense negotiations which led to a reported mutual agreement between Weah and Brumskine. The agreement leaked to the *FrontPageAfrica* newspaper at the time was signed by Israel Akinsanya, Chairman of the Liberty Party, while Lenn Eugene Nagbe, Secretary General of CDC, signed for the CDC in the presence of Weah who, reportedly, had finally consented to a pairing which months ago appeared impossible.

Despite the fact that Brumskine did not endorse Weah in 2005, Weah appeared set to make the much-heralded marriage of political convenience work. The statement of mutual consent from the two parties, was preceded by a statement from Weah, dated October 14, 2010.

"Fellow Liberians, members of the Congress for Democratic Change (CDC), I have worked all my life for the success and viability of the Liberian nation. Both in my professional life and now in my political career, the welfare of the Liberian people have always been paramount to my own.

While I believe that a CDC government under my leadership is the best course to bring lasting and sustainable peace, security and prosperity to Liberia, I am not unmindful that even this great venture may be only achievable in small steps.

I remain convinced that the unity of the entire opposition is the best course to reversing the slide into elitism that I believe is leading to the reversal of any gains that has been made in our country.

We must defeat the current Unity Party government if we are to reverse the dangerous course upon which our country has been set; the course which leads to a mirror image of our ugly past and its domineering one-party political system. I believe that only a united opposition can achieve this national imperative.

Each of us who are leaders in the opposition community must be prepared to sacrifice personal ambitions to achieve a single slate of candidates – a more responsible, united and credible alternative for the 2011 elections. Enough time has been spent by each of us pursuing our personal ambitions and objectives while the Liberian people have endured the failed leadership of President Ellen Johnson Sirleaf. It is time to embark upon a new course for the opposition community and for the country.

Therefore, in order to unite the opposition, I am prepared to work with Cllr. Charles Brumskine to achieve a single slate of candidates for the 2011 elections and may consider all options for a united opposition ticket. I have today, authorized a representative CDC exploratory committee led by our dynamic Chairman Geraldine Doe-Sheriff to begin immediate consultation with the Liberty Party as to how best we can bring the entire opposition parties together for victory in 2011. Nevertheless, whatever path we choose must meet the full and unconditional approval of the CDC executive committee and all of those who have believed and supported my effort in these many years.

To preserve democracy, to prevent the present regime's subtle and overt attempts to create a one-party state and perpetuate itself into power, I call on all members of the CDC, Liberty Party and other opposition parties to join this effort and save our common patrimony, Liberia.

Fellow partisans, I cannot fulfil our mission alone. I want to empower you, to unite you, to share your desire for growth and positive change. We can make it happen together. MUYAN, MUYAN, CDC MUYAN!!!!.

Ambassador George Manneh Weah, Sr
Standard Bearer
Congress for Democratic Change, CDC[329]

The statement was soon greeted with angst, not just from the incumbent Sirleaf and her ruling Unity Party, but from elements within the opposition as well.

According to Akinsanya, in the days leading to a formal announcement and after further talks regarding the ticket in Accra, Ghana, key players both in the opposition and the government did not want the ticket. "The players and negotiators wanted to be the ones to put the ticket together, in order to have a say. But Sirleaf did not want that ticket as she knew it would be the end of her. So, the forces were against it from the day it was announced."[330]

Mr. Benoni Urey, a former aide to Charles Taylor, who was languishing in the United Nations Treasury and suffering under a travel ban due to his role in the Liberian civil war, was said to be one of the main figures opposing the deal. In fact, one of his peers overheard him exclaiming that he "would not sit and allow Akinsanya and Nagbe make the next President."[331] Another person who opposed the deal was Acarous Gray, an official of CDC. According to former cabinet minister and strong supporter of Ellen Sirleaf, Mr. Willard Russell, the Unity Party was concerned and reached out to Mr. Gray to lead the fight from within CDC to destroy the merger.

The marriage of political convenience appeared dead.

Brumskine rose to political prominence in the 1990s as an ally of Charles Taylor. When Taylor became President in 1997, Brumskine became President Pro Temp of the Senate. By 1999, however, they began feuding, and Brumskine fled the country after being threatened by Taylor's supporters. He returned to Liberia in 2003 with plans to run in the scheduled 2003 Presidential election. However, Taylor's resignation that year and the instalment of a two-year transitional government led to the elections being cancelled.

In 2005, Weah was highly critical of those in the educated elite who claimed that he was not fit to govern. "With all their education and experience, they have governed this nation for hundreds of years. They have never done anything for the nation."[332] However, after his lack of education hindered his political chances, Weah began pursuing a degree in Business Administration at DeVry University in Miami.

The deal's sticking point over who should head the ticket provided an anti-climax which was a familiar refrain for Liberia's political history. Nearly three decades earlier, in the October 1985 elections, President Samuel Kanyon Doe, was proclaimed the winner in an election he is widely believed to have lost to Jackson F. Doe of the Liberia Action Party. In that election, Jackson Doe secured 137,270 votes for 26.45%; Gabriel Kpolleh, a schoolteacher, secured 59,965 votes for 11.55%; while Edward Kesselly of the Unity Party secured 57,443 votes for 11.07%. The Liberian Constitution requires an absolute majority or 50% plus one to avoid a runoff but many political observers at the time believed that a united front against Doe may have made it tougher for the incumbent to steal the votes.

At the time, many political observers were of the view that if the four political parties put their forces together, they may have curbed Samuel Doe's margin of victory or left very little room for irregularities. Similarly, during the reign of President Charles Taylor, a similar scenario played out that saw Taylor win the Presidency by a landslide, with 75.3% of the vote, despite campaigning on the slogan: "He killed my ma, he killed my pa, but I will vote for him."[333] His closest competitor, Ellen Johnson Sirleaf, collected only 10% of the vote. Eleven other candidates failed to crack more than 5%.

Lost in the aura of Mr. Taylor's victory was the fact that the opposition took the power of the incumbent for granted.

At least thirteen political parties challenged Taylor in the '97 elections, prompting Sirleaf to stress years later in an interview with *FrontPageAfrica* the importance of opposition collaboration. "No political party as I see it, based on my political experience will win this election without a coalition. I don't think any political party can win on its own, given the number of parties. So, if you see people negotiating, dialoguing and all, it's because they all realise that some coalition has to be made for a particular party or parties to be competitive."[334]

Fast-forward to the 2011 Presidential elections, the incumbent Ellen Johnson Sirleaf highlighted the progress made in several areas during her first term while emphasising her expertise in nation-building and her administration's work in relieving the country's debt, paying civil servants on time, rebuilding the Armed Forces of Liberia, improving basic services and infrastructure, and restoring Liberia's international standing.

On the eve of the 2011 elections, the Brumskine-Weah ticket offered promise but as last-minute details of the deal became public, rumours and distractions drowned whatever promise the appetising ticket with enormous potential presented.

Under the deal, according to a copy of the agreement the *FrontPageAfrica* newspaper had in its possession, Brumskine would become standard bearer while Weah would be his Vice. The coalition would likely take a nomenclature like CDC, retaining a brand name that was the number one political brand in the country. The two parties would invite the other opposition party to a round table to conclude a power sharing arrangement that would include all of the major opposition leaders and their lieutenants controlling the state for six years after the elections. The deal included room at the table for the fledgling Democratic Alliance, of which Liberty was a member and Coalition for Democratic Change, a CDC bloc.

Partisans of Weah's CDC were in total disagreement. In fact, in a letter dated November 21, 2010, Mr. Mulbah K. Morlu, Jr., Chairman, Policy Committee & Secretary General, Elders' Council of the party, expressed his anger at the National Executive Committee of the party for going along with the merger plan.

He wrote:

Gentlemen.

It is our understanding that the National Executive Committee, to whom your membership belongs, has voted to instruct party leadership to expeditiously appoint an exploratory committee with delegated obligations to proceed with two-party 'Merger negotiations' arranged to consummate a cohesive institution-alization approach between the Liberty Party and the Congress for Democratic Change. It is also our understanding that your decision arises from a signed 'Resolution' affixed by thirteen or so members of the governing Executive Com-mittee of the Congress for Democratic Change, meeting under the cover of darkness for such purpose as set forth in that Resolution.

While we remain conscious of your constitutional authority as a major arbiter entrusted with a measure of power to litigate matters arising from internal party debates, your resolved determination to transact a combination between the two parties, being insensitive to recent past and current political realities floating the demographics, is a rallying call for the construct of a peaceful constitutional resistance to protect the arc of our revolutionary preamble against the threats your decisions advance.

As we ennoble the cause of this new challenge, which is an absolute consti-tutional obligation, we seek your kind forbearance to begin to see the unspecified consequential risk you subject 'The Movement' to by your 'Nightfall Resolution' signatures and the selfish decisions you have rendered:

(a) By signing a Resolution instructing the party to initiate steps to merge Liberty Party and the CDC, you have shown a flagrant disregard and callous contempt for the most relevant voices of the party, the masses who have been

enraged in their high numbers with unrelenting displeasures against the merger approach. This leadership mode being ultra-dictatorial, contravenes Article 4 Section 3 of the Constitution of the CDC, which unequivocally stamps that "The will of the people is the will of the CDC…and the business of the CDC is conducted in a free, open and transparent manner that makes the leadership accountable to the membership in accordance with the constitution."

(b) By your 'Nightfall Resolution' restricting merger conversations to two parties, you have jeopardized the once availing opportunity to coalesce the entire opposition bloc into a united force to defeat the oligarchy imperialist order of the failed Unity Party leadership. On the other hand, the collective decision of your assemblage meeting at nightfall at Party Headquarters has not only deteriorated and diminished the prospects of larger opposition collaboration but has similarly desecrated the wisdom of your signed communiqués; first in Accra with Cllr. Tubman, and later in Monrovia, at the Monrovia City Hall with three other parties, all of which were willing to emerge a single political party for the 2011 elections with our Standard Bearer, George M. Weah as leader. These blown chances deliberately orchestrated by a few on the Executive Committee, who have now passed it on to others, is counter-productive and selfish, suspiciously constituting the self-aggrandizing agenda of external forces hoping to exploit the CDC as a political donkey to power.

(c) Mockingly, the 'Nightfall Resolution' you signed on 19 November 2010 at around 7:30 P.M at our unlit and non-electrified Party Headquarters, where the Secretary General read the prepared document in the dark with the aid of Chairman Sheriff's mobile phone light, is an extreme travesty of the revolutionary mavericks that birthed the institution. That the two-party leaders initially signed a communiqué in Accra-Ghana to produce a 'single-slate of candidates' for 2011 elections, followed by a 'kangaroo Resolution' instructing a merger formality that brings the two parties and their standard Bearers together on one ticket, is to put the cart before the horse. This shaming contradiction betrays the surface intent of the conspirators, unravelling a deep-seated suspicion about a devilish agenda growing with speed in its fetus.

(d) Tragically, the 'Nightfall Resolution', if allowed to see daylight, is a cursed ink dried to paper that will alienate the CDC from the critical Islamic bloc and their affiliating sympathizers who are certain to vote-rebel against our

candidate based on the heightened religious one-sidedness of Cllr. Charles Brumskine.

Despite these obvious warnings of political disaster sufficiently sprawled on the walls of our consciences, it is by now unsurprisingly clear the suspected motivations that may have eclipsed the good judgments of some members of the National Executive Committee to circumvent good for evil. In a dauntless desire to navigate the crust of the artificial quagmire upsetting this great party, which provides a staircase of excruciating venture of investigative curiosity, it may interest a few of you to know that:

(a) Contrary to Part III Bye Laws, Chapter I, Codes of Conduct, Rule 5 of the Constitution of the CDC, which categorized it as "A serious offense for a party member to be acting on behalf of, or in collaboration with anti-CDC counter-progressive forces…" detrimental to the interest of the party, several party executives, without the least consideration for standards and codes, have been using the institution as a breeding ground to fertilize the advancement of Charles Brumskine and his Liberty Party;

(b) These party executives, who have been acting collaboratively with recognizable agents of the Liberty Party, have used and continue to use unconventional methods, and in several recorded cases unholy strategies to woo support for a Brumskine Presidency in disguise, said practices being disloyal and hypocritical, cannot stand up to the scrutiny of Part III Bye Laws, Chapter I, Codes of Conduct, Rule 6, no. 5 7 8.

(c) Evidence in avalanche proportionality continues to point to the widespread disbursement of bribe money and other forms of inducement traded by the Liberty Party to several senior party members in Monrovia to influence their support for the CDC/Liberty Party ticket. In some cases, Liberty Party's negotiators have been involved in street deals with some senior partisans, while other deals were struck from the patio of luxury hotels, with attractive sums passing under the table for 'Merger supports'.

That the Liberty Party allegedly utilizes bribery, dishonesty and croaked dealings to drive through a difficult barrier presumably to capture power is not only an act of political terror, but a serious constitutional outrage that must be investigated to its last source. Unlimited to this spectrum, the CDC's Byelaws and Constitution, specifically Part III Bye Laws, Chapter I, Codes of Conduct,

Rule 6, no.3, Article 2 AIMS AND OBJECTIVES, Section 4 forbids such heinous undertakings and require serious disciplinary actions against the culprits.

In similar context, the much-publicized Liberty Party/CDC merger as is being championed from the divisive bastion of unscrupulous political strategizing has become a curse that threatens the moral fabrics of our internal democracy. The CDC, Gentlemen, as you know it more, shot upward from the scaffold of sincere determination to introduce liberal structural reformative change to the body politics that has been hijacked by scoundrels for almost two centuries. This is a distinction that is supposed to separate us from the bulky political forces of indiscretion. It is therefore in this fact that we must reignite the spark to do our vast partisans justice by investigating the indictment of immoral political discourse chosen by a few at the character detriment of the collective.

And the fact that the National Executive Committee is at the epicentre of a bribery scandal that questions the moral integrity of the institution is one reason for the emergence of new critical voices (speaking out here) whose only interest is to dislocate the threats posed to our common patrimony by actors from both sides of the divide.

Therefore, given this very embarrassing background, our patriotic consciences impose upon us the duties to petition you to halt any further actions and advances on 'Merger talks', and we further request you to make a public statement of your intent to speedily launch an internal investigation into the Liberty Party bribery efforts and to return the 'Nightfall Resolution' to status quo ante as though it never took place.

While we may not have sufficient authority to coerce your actions on this matter within a three-day period, we would however like to inform you that your refusal or failure to dispose of the matter in the time sphere calculated supra will leave us with no other option to proceed without fail to the Supreme Court of the Republic of Liberia to pray a writ of prohibition against the 'Nightfall' Resolution, and we will further file a separate complaint before the Criminal Law court to dispense justice in the bribery scandal that has hit our noble institution.

In conclusion, we would like to reassure you of our continuous desire to remain peaceful, law-abiding and constructive in our current redemptive pursuits, though in a fearless manner, especially given our rights as enshrined in the Constitution (Article 6 Rights and Duties of Members, Section 1) to

"Actively participate and fully contribute to the discussions, formulations and implementation of policies, programs and action plans of the CDC..." and as well as offer constructive criticisms of any member, official, policy, program, activity or actions of the CDC..."[335]

With that deal all but dead, Weah and his supporters turned elsewhere for salvation with veteran ambassador Winston Tubman emerging as an unlikely pairing for the rising politician.

Weah's Congress for Democratic Change and Ambassador Tubman's National Democratic Party of Liberia (NDPL), the political brand of late President Samuel Doe, had signed a communiqué in which the pair agreed to work together to build a viable coalition. Tubman had previously been the political leader of the Liberian National Union (LINU). However, LINU gave Ambassador Tubman an ultimatum to resign from the party over political differences. Weah was still considered a political novice while Tubman came to the table with a wealth of experience. A renowned former diplomat and politician of American-Liberian descent, Tubman was also a former justice minister. He was born in the Maryland County town of Pleebo and the nephew of former President William V. S. Tubman, Liberia's longest serving President, who ruled Africa's oldest republic of 27 years. Winston obtained degrees from the London School of Economics, Cambridge University and Harvard University. In 1968 Tubman founded his own law firm serving as legal adviser to Liberia's Ministry of Planning and Economic Affairs during his uncle's administration as well as having long-standing United Nations experience. He worked in its Legal Office in 1973 and was Liberia's Permanent Representative to the UK (1979–1981) before taking a role in Liberia as Justice Minister under Samuel Doe (1982-1983). During the First Liberian Civil War, Tubman went (on behalf of Samuel Doe) to the United States to lobby its government to intervene. Latterly from 2002 to 2005 Tubman served as the Secretary General's representative and head of the United Nations' Political Office for Somalia.

Running on the NDPL ticket in the 2005 Presidential elections, Tubman was defeated in the first round, placing fourth with 9.2% of the vote.

Long before his diplomatic life, Tubman wanted to be a politician. "Diplomacy was the job they gave me. Before that I wanted to be a politician.

President Tubman, he was my model and he also identified me as the most likely to follow him."[336] But while Tubman was mesmerised by the idea of becoming a diplomat, fate had other plans.

On April 12, a coup was staged by an indigenous Liberian faction of the Armed Forces of Liberia under the command of Master Sergeant Samuel Doe, ending decades of American-Liberian rule.

"The coup happened and railroaded the whole thing," Tubman says. "If the coup hadn't happened, I would have continued on that road to becoming a diplomat, perhaps becoming foreign minister – like Cecil Dennis, more or less, Rudolph Grimes and other prominent Foreign Ministers like John Dennis, father of Gabriel Dennis, Edwin Barclay, CDB King – I would have followed those footsteps on the diplomatic line. But when the coup happened, I accelerated at perhaps looking at Liberia. So, I left the diplomatic arena and came home, looking for an opportunity to enter the political arena." [337]

Tubman describes Nathaniel McGill as the key to his linkup with Weah. "McGill had never met me although he had read about me – and I had the Tubman name."[338]

Early on, and as far back as the days leading to the 2005 Presidential elections, McGill saw Tubman as someone who could groom Weah and show him the ropes into politics. While many other politicians struggled to win Weah over and ride on his massive popularity en route to the Presidency, Tubman would have a much easier ride. By then, McGill was a strong ally to Tubman and felt that he needed to bring George Weah into the mix because Weah was very popular. "If he (McGill) could get George Weah into the mix, we would be off to a good start,"[339] Tubman recalls.

Tubman says he was in Kenya then, working for the United Nations. So, he invited McGill back to his office in Nairobi, the Kenyan capital. "We had a talk and he said, I should try to get some of my friends like the former United Nations Secretary General Kofi Anan, and international folks like the Americans and if they would talk with George Weah, George Weah would definitely accept it. That was his idea, he had formed this thing called LIBWIN (Liberians for Winston Tubman), and it had done well, it penetrated many counties and people were excited that we should try and get George Weah into our mix. Then I went to Minnesota, I met the guy who is now Finance Minister, Samuel Tweah. He was one of the main forces behind Weah. But I soon found out that they thought they already had a base and were looking for people to make the Weah project work."[340]

Tubman however recalls that Tweah was somewhat imposing. "He (Tweah) changed every document I put together around to make it look as if I was his mouthpiece and they felt convinced that this is what was going to happen. They were set and insisting on Weah settling for nothing less than the Presidency."[341]

So, in 2005, the discussions between Tubman and friends of Weah failed to materialise, although it would ultimately return to the table six years later. Tubman returned to the Samuel Doe arrangement and ran on the NDPL ticket in the 2005 elections. "I had history with the National Democratic Party of Liberia (NDPL), and I felt I should stay with them. So, I came back, and they invited me to be their candidate which I did accept and ran and the rest is history."[342]

In 2005, the Tubman name still carried some weight, but to this day, Tubman still believes that he does not think his strong performance in the 2005 elections was because he ran on Doe's party but rather on the Tubman name. He said that the campaign showed his family's name still resonated, especially in Tubman's hometown of Maryland County. "I got more from the Doe connection. The people of Maryland County, Tubman's hometown was enthusiastic about the Tubman success and in fact, we did much better in Maryland than NDPL did on its own. What happened there happened because of the history, who I was, the background – and people were tired with what Doe had done and they wanted some decency similarly to what we are having now under Weah. So, I pulled it off because I had those things going for me."[343]

Tubman says he could have done even better if his cousin, Shad Tubman had not joined the race thanks to Ellen Sirleaf's influence and run against him. "Ellen had done some studies that showed that I was the biggest threat she faced – and if I was, it was clearly because of the Tubman legacy. I had been through all of the countryside and was making great impact. Shad didn't go very far; it is sad that he fell for Sirleaf's political distraction. I came fourth and I think he came twelfth."[344]

Tubman believes that it was his strong performance that played a major role in convincing Weah to agree to be Vice President in the 2011 elections.

So, six years later, ahead of the 2011 elections, McGill had not given up on the idea of a Tubman-Weah partnership. Tubman recalls that McGill felt that if Weah was brought on board, they could go very far and so McGill did all he could to make it work and made a lot of efforts in that direction. "I met McGill in Florida, I met him in Ghana, and we had a lot of discussions. But I think it started before that. That campaign in 2005 when we first came together, we had a broadcast debate when the candidates were getting together, and people were saying that George Weah had no education for him to want to be President under the constitution. I said, no, I was involved in writing the constitution and the constitution doesn't have any such criteria that has to be met and therefore George is not barred from being President of Liberia."[345]

Tubman says his defence of Weah during the 2005 Presidential debate, left an impression on Weah. "He couldn't imagine that a Tubman would come to his defence in such a way and manner, in such a powerful show of support, one deftly defying political norms and conventions."[346]

Yes! George was impressed with Tubman, setting off what would later become a marriage of political convenience at the time. Weah never expected that a rival of his would use his platform to come to his defence like that, to say something supportive. "Certainly, it didn't benefit me; but it benefited him," Tubman remembers. "So, he had never met anybody who had that kind of objectivity – and he was stunned by that. And when it came to the time for deciding whether he would support me or not, I believe it was that unheralded moment in history which made the difference and proved to be the deciding factor in accepting to be my running mate. He felt that I was somebody who was able to make this kind of decision – and that I was selfless and influencing but he wasn't really ready to do that and what I was trying to do, I couldn't until I became President. Because until I became President, I knew he had to be the guy that brought the crowds and if he didn't it became a problem."[347]

This was evident on the campaign trail when, on most days, Tubman says, supporters struggled to get Weah "out of bed"[348] or away from his celebrity life to go on the campaign trail.

The experience of the 2011 Presidential elections showed a lot about Weah's character. Here was a former World Footballer of the Year venturing into a political arena but unwilling to put in the work. It is an age-old question which many find difficult to draw the line when it comes to celebrities and politics. If Weah was unable to speak to his potential constituents, how could he govern an entire country? How could he convince voters that he was ready for prime time?

Tubman recalls one instance when the campaign team was planning trips to one of the remote counties outside the capital, Monrovia. "We were supposed to leave at 8am, but Weah would just do as he's doing now as President, nothing would happen. He would just sit there until 12 midday – and finally when he was ready, we would go."[349]

Tubman says Weah really did not allow his team to use him in an effective way that could have made the difference. But Tubman is quick to acknowledge Weah's importance. "He brought the crowds; we had the experience with the National Democratic Party of Liberia where on our own we were able to muster fourth place. If he had been more disciplined and given us the support that we needed, we could have done better than we did and in fact, I think we did better than the results reported but we would have done even better."[350]

Despite what appeared to be a smooth pairing, aides around Weah were concerned that Tubman's ascendance would mean a diminishing role for Weah and his grassroots movement. Tubman recalls, "I remember when we were talking to him, some of his people were worried about me staying too long and stepping aside to let him become President. And I said to him we can come to an agreement and get someone like Reverend Isaac Winkler who would stand as a witness on the agreement, but George said, 'No! It's not necessary, when we come together, we would be like family and work together. There's no need to write this down. Once we work together, we would continue to work together. So, we do not have to come to any agreement.'"[351]

Tubman says Weah trusted him like a father figure. "Prior to seeing him, I was in East Africa, I wasn't aware of how important a star he was. But everywhere I went, when I said I'm from Liberia, people said: George Weah.

Football wasn't something I followed so I wasn't aware of what a great star I was dealing with. Everywhere I went, people were carried away by him."[352]

When the pair finally met face to face, Tubman said Weah felt comfortable. "I came home, and I saw him for the first time, he said to me, 'Chief, why didn't you tell me this, we could have gotten together sooner?' He really wanted that. I didn't know but McGill knew, and he said, 'What do we need to do to get George Weah on our team? If we can get him on our ticket, it would be beautiful.' And that's how it came about."[353]

Although Weah had decided on Tubman, after his fallout with Brumskine, he was unaware of the baggage that came with the choice. Tubman was coming to the table, on the heels of two very big legacies in Liberia – those of Tubman and the late Samuel Doe.

Aware of the pressure, Tubman told the *Daily Observer* in a 2005 interview that he was not running on a Tubman or Doe legacy but on his own.

"I'm running as a Tubman. My name is Winston Tubman. So, you can say a Tubman is running. But I'm not embarrassed or ashamed of the Tubman legacy because for one, the Tubman legacy mainly stands for was that [what] he did [with] the reunification policy, he tried to unite our people. And I want to build on that. But I'm building on it, not just because I'm a Tubman, but because I'm a Liberian and that's the way our country needs to go. Our country needs unification. If we have unification, we will have unity and peace in the country. And investors will come, development. President Tubman's time is remembered primarily because the stability contained then made it possible for many more things to be developed in the country. Bong Mines, Nimba and all the new investment that he bought enabled the country to have capitals that later Presidents were able to use. You know people say President Tubman didn't do this and he didn't do that, he stopped the road at his farm. It is very short-sighted to look at it that way because the things that he brought to the country, the investments that he made here made it possible for those who followed him to use those assets to borrow money and borrowing those funds they were able to build the buildings that they did. Had he not done that, they may not have been able to do so. When he came to power, there was nothing of the sort there, he had to use his ingenuity to bring those things about. So, if that's the kind of legacy you're talking about where he had the maritime program established, he had the open-door policy, he had the foreign scholarship program, that's the legacy I'll be proud to run on."[354]

On the Doe legacy, Tubman explained that he was running as the candidate of the National Democratic Party of Liberia because he wanted to unite the country. "I'm already in the National Democratic Party, many people say it is a Krahn party, well if that's true, now we have a chance to make it a national party. If you call me a Congo man, although my mother was Grebo and my father was Congo, I'm a Liberian, but now that I am in the NDPL we have a chance for people to come there in order to redress the imbalances that are there. The LIBWIN, my grassroots that follow me, for a long time, they wondered if this was the right thing to do, but a leader must lead otherwise there is no need having him as a leader. So, when I left and told them I was going to run within the framework of the National Democratic Party of Liberia (NDPL) they have all come around and say they are supporting me so I am confident that [the] move of running from a party like NDPL will bring more Liberians into it. And by bringing more Liberians into it we will make it truly national, and we would make it truly democratic. So that when that party wins the election, Liberia will be making a big step forward of unification and development for our country."[355]

Tubman had been in the party since 1989, joining the NDPL at a time when the war was escalating and when he said he wanted to try to get the international community involved in trying to stop the war. "You know a very funny thing happened. The day I decided to do that, I told Kenneth Best. We were at a funeral at the Trinity Cathedral, and I told him what I was doing and why. I don't think he was enchanted by it."[356] Best was the publisher of Liberia's largest newspaper at the time, the *Daily Observer*. Tubman says he felt that he needed to make an intervention that would try and change the situation although most Liberians disagreed. "They thought that the way to solve this problem was a different way, but I felt that the war could not be a solution to the problem and that we needed to try and find a negotiated settlement and the way to do that was I thought to involve international players, the United States in particular. And so, I knew that if I didn't have an identification with Samuel Doe, he wouldn't listen to me if I told him what he needed to do. So, when I joined the party just as I anticipated, he became ready to deal with me and allowed me to become involved in this problem. So that's why I joined the NDPL in 1989."[357]

Tubman says despite his strong bond with George, some stakeholders did not buy into the idea, owing to his family's history. After all, his uncle, William V. S. Tubman, had ruled Liberia for 27 years, still regarded as the longest serving President in the country's history, serving from his election in 1944 until his death in 1971. Regarded as the "father of modern Liberia", the Tubman Presidency was marked by attracting foreign investment to modernise the economy and infrastructure. Tubman also led a policy of national unification in order to reduce the social and political differences between American-Liberians and the indigenous Liberians.

Winston Tubman believes that part of the reason for the scepticism was that the Americans held the view that the Tubman era was still fresh in Liberia's history. "Our American friends didn't think we should have a Tubman becoming President so soon after President Tubman's 27-years in office and they probably felt that there was no way would they have escaped being blamed for it. People would have said, they (the Americans) had made me President and therefore, whatever road the country was on making George Weah, Congau domination and all would continue – and they would be blamed for it. So, they preferred Sirleaf to a Congau man – and there was no Congau person that was not a Tubman who could do what I was doing. If they hadn't had that view, I believe our victory could have happened, but they had that view, they felt that if they could prevent it from happening it would be something that would play continentwide because even today, I can tell you that certain African countries are not ready to elect a woman as President."[358]

The divide between the American-Liberians and the indigenous has been an unspoken concern for stakeholders with interest in Liberia. Ellen Johnson Sirleaf endured, and so did Tubman. Prior to the 2005 elections, Washington had reportedly favoured the country returning from war to be in the hands of an indigenous person. It was for this reason that Sirleaf, during her address to a joint session of the U.S. Congress on March 15, 2006, dedicated a good portion of her speech to shedding light on what she believed to be her indigenous lineage.

She told the joint session:

My family exemplifies the economic and social divide that has torn our nation. Unlike many privileged Liberians, I can claim no American lineage. Three of my grandparents were indigenous Liberians; the fourth was a German who married a rural market woman. That grandfather was forced to leave the country when Liberia, in loyalty to the United States, declared war on Germany in 1914.

Both of my grandmothers were farmers and village traders. They could not read or write any language, as more than three-quarters of our people still cannot today. But they worked hard. They loved their country. They loved their families. And they believed in education. They inspired me then, and their memory motivates me to serve my people, to sacrifice for the world and honestly serve humanity. I could not, I will not, I cannot betray their trust.

My parents were sent at a young age to Monrovia, where it was common for elite families to take in children from the countryside to perform domestic chores. They endured humiliation and indignities. But my mother was fortunate to be adopted by a kind woman, and both of my parents were able, through the system, to go to school, a rarity at that time for poor people. My father even became the first native Liberian in the Liberian National Legislature.[359]

In Tubman's view, the Americans pushed that line because it was necessary for the ultimate good. "They pushed it because they wanted to avoid making it appear that they had dominated the whole process and they had brought another Tubman who continued the kind of control that they had since the country became a republic and the 27 years Tubman ruled."[360]

Tubman himself was always aware of the controversy surrounding the indigenous lineage. "I remember working in a law firm in New York and one of the partners during a discussion about my Presidential aspirations when people were saying that a countryman should be the next President – and this man, a very foreign person said he thought it would be too big a jump, it would be like taking two steps, rather than one. Instead of jumping straight to an indigenous person, they should find someone who was from both sides, from both the American-Liberian line and the indigenous line, such as myself. By doing that it would be an easy transition. President

Tubman also felt that way. He knew that of all his family members, I was the one most likely to be groomed. I think that's the case. We cannot split the country into Country vs. Congau especially now that we are observing the bicentennial. McGill was the first to tell me about it."[361]

Regarding his own situation, Tubman says he too struggles with the perceptions about his identity. "I think it was the fact that although I was Congau or American-Liberian, my mother was a Grebo woman, and when you talk of Tubman's unification policy and all that, when it comes to integration – and although my American-Liberian friends never accepted that. When we were growing up in Maryland, everybody knew who I was – and the history was this, when you grew up in Harper, across the river, you would sow your royal oats, which my father did, which President Tubman did, his children did. When it became time to marry, these Harper boys could marry these country girls. My grandfather said to his son, Chris, 'If these indigenous women are good enough for you to lay with, and have these children, they are just as good enough for you to marry.' And my father married my mother. President Tubman didn't marry his Grebo woman, to the point where he wanted to settle down to the point where he went to the mansion with a wife from Sierra Leone and later went to Barclay, that kind of pull was always there."[362]

Tubman still considers himself indigenous owing to his mother's lineage. "In my case, I was really an indigenous person. I can't say if the boat came and said all the Congau people come aboard, where would I go? I knew where I belonged generally, and I felt that way – and I tried to behave that way because it was part of me, and I was proud of."[363]

In the aftermath of a bitter and contentious loss to Sirleaf at the end of the 2011 Presidential elections, Tubman began to sense some uneasiness in Weah's circle. Many of Weah's followers and party faithful who were against the merger and Weah's decision to go as a running mate to Tubman, suddenly wanted Tubman out.

The fact that sixteen other political parties chose to challenge Sirleaf's second quest made it an easy ride for Sirleaf who trounced her opponents in the first round of the Presidential election, with 43.9% of the vote, followed by Tubman with 32.7%. As no candidate received an absolute majority, Sirleaf and Tubman stood in a runoff election held on November 8, 2011.

Tubman alleged that the first round had been rigged in Sirleaf's favour and called on his supporters to boycott the runoff.

Tubman's pronouncement triggered a massive and violent protest during which one person was killed after shots were reportedly fired ahead of the runoff. After thousands of CDC backers assembled to persuade votes to stage a boycott of the runoff poll, rioting broke out. Police with the support of U.N. forces, blocked the way of CDC enthusiasts from marching through the city. Then shooting and stone-throwing broke out with some opposition parties firing at the police who responded with tear gas.

Opposition activists are said to have exchanged fire with the police, who also used tear gas. At the time, police spokesman George Badue said officers had not used live bullets. He said only tear gas was used by the police "to disperse the crowd so that people who were not part of the demonstration could move about freely".[364]

Tubman's running mate, Weah, condemned the shooting of "unarmed protesters" and called for the elections to be postponed. Tubman and the CDC claimed that vote-rigging was widespread but that was denied by Sirleaf and the electoral commission. Meanwhile, the political powers of the U.S., Europe and the African Union lined up against the CDC decision to boycott the runoff.

"It's a bad signal... political leaders must be prepared to win or lose,"[365] said former Ugandan Vice-President and head of the African Union observer mission, Speciosa Wadira Kazibwe.

An antsy Sirleaf slammed the protest saying, "I know that nobody in this country, no matter what the talk or rhetoric, nobody really wants us to go back to war."[366]

On November 15, 2011, the National Elections Commission declared Sirleaf the winner of the runoff with 90.7% of the vote. A few days later, Weah, in a poignant message to his partisans and supporters dated November 26, 2011, took offence at the protest and the Executive Committee's statement.

He wrote:

Pursuant to your signed statement of 26 November 2011, captioned 'Exec-utive Committee's position on the unauthorized street protests', in which you intentionally, criminally, unlawfully and purposefully misrepresented the official policy of the mighty Congress for Democratic Change as regards the ongoing intrinsic political scenario, we are obliged to institute restraining measures against your regretful rebelliousness.

Considering the gullibility of your assemblage yesterday when you congregated under the cover of darkness in Paynesville in the purported name of the 'Executive Committee of the CDC', contrary to Article 12 section 73 of the Bye Laws and Constitution of the Congress for Democratic, which requires 'The quorum for meetings of the NEC shall be absolute majority or of 50% + 1 of its total membership; you ignored an organic pillar of essential democratic decision-making, an unalterable doctrine of the CDC.

More so, having established beyond reasonable doubts that your series of secret meetings held over the period, which has culminated into a misleadingly unauthorized position of our noble institution, were politically motivated assemblies intended to hatch a conspiracy against the doctrine, manifesto and the grassroots philosophy of the mighty Congress for Democratic Change, your well-calculated act of betrayal is contemptuous and a direct flouting of Article 6. Rights and Duties of Members, Section 49 j of our constitution. It requires all party members to 'Refrain from publishing and/or distributing any media on the CDC without prior authorization which purports to be the view of any organized grouping, body, organ or structure within the CDC...'

In addition, inasmuch as some of you may be officials and members of the Executive Committee of the CDC, you spitefully overstretched your bound and subjected the noble character of this mass-based movement to intolerable disrepute against Article 6. Rights and Duties of Members, Section 49 h of the Constitution of the CDC, which calls on all 'To observe discipline, behave honestly, and execute dutifully and loyally all decisions of the majority and decisions of the leadership of the CDC.'

Similarly, your continuous surreptitious meetings and discussions with members of the Unity party; especially Hon. Edward Forh and Mrs. Geraldine Doe-Sheriff, which has led to deliberate leakages of official party conversations and decisions arising out of important hierarchical gatherings, constitute a breach of confidence and a punishable offense of the strongest magnitude, disapproved by the Bye laws and Constitution of the CDC as outlined in Article 5, under Membership, Section 41a quoted as follows:

'The following act shall constitute a breach of loyalty which every member owes to the CDC, whether committed by individuals or groups; misrepresentation or false suggestion of material facts and forgery...'

Henceforth, that you would resort to distortive utterances, divulging mis-information/propaganda and the widespread dissemination of unlawful statements wrongfully attributed to the Executive Committee, either exposes your shameful ignorance of the constitution of the CDC, or a deliberate conspiracy to engage in factional political activity against the interests of the millions of partisans of this revolutionary movement. No doubt, such a dichotic showcase perpetrates your 'Organized factional activity' as an advance of external or selfish interest, contrary to the collective objectives of our noble party. Permit me inform you notwithstanding, that the litany of excesses you stand guilty of are unpardonable constitutional breaches irreconcilable with the Constitution of the CDC, PART II BY-LAWS, CHAPTER 1. CODE OF CONDUCT, Rule 14, under Temporary Suspension, which authorizes the suspension/expulsion of a member considering the nature and seriousness of an alleged violation or offense...

Even more grievous is the unused unlimited access you have to the office of the Standard-Bearer and Vice Standard-Bearer, and other internally accessible mediums for the conveyance of grievances, which could have been positively utilized to address any reservations you may have contemplated before your unfortunate abuse of power.

Hence, your selection of the chosen course testifies to a calculated plot to mislead others in 'Participating in organized factional activity', contrary to PART II BY-LAWS, CHAPTER 1. CODE OF CONDUCT, Rule 7e of the BYE-LAWS and Constitution of the CDC, which forbids members 'Participation in organized factional activity that goes beyond the recognized norms of free debates and tolerance in the party, and which is tending to threaten its unity.' It is also necessary to inform you concurrently that by this flagrant disregard for the governing standards of the CDC, especially in your official capacities, you and your co-conspirators stand in breach of the constitution of the CDC for which disciplinary measure is necessary.

In furtherance, by this act of blatant disregard for the governing standards of the CDC, which you inspired and led, you have exposed the Congress for Democratic Change to unnecessary public ridicule thereby subjecting our *innumerable partisans to unjustifiable embarrassment and confusion, especially considering that the decision to hold public rallies and peaceful demonstrations is an inalienable constitutional right that will not be shied away from. ARTICLE 6. RIGHTS AND DUTIES OF MEMBERS, Sec. 2j of the constitution of the CDC repudiates your alleged actions, rendering you liable of a serious constitutional breach.*

In that direction, the democratic space and the dynamic political ideas we espouse cannot be sent off on a tangent by political casualness and compromise, most especially with the flagrant degree of callous political blasphemy you have committed against the CDC and its unmatched grassroots base.

In conclusion, it is important to note that as we remain focused on the continuity of our usual peaceful protests in larger dimensions in coming days, your poor leadership in the last weeks, a complete let down to the expectation of our partisans, supporters and sympathizers trouble us.

In this regard, unless measures are taken consistent with the rule of law to forbid recurrence, we may all fall short of the expectations of our people to provide exemplary leadership, as we prepare to inevitably take over the mantle of credible democratic authority shortly.

Therefore, it is the opinion of our leadership that you were in absolute disregard of the constitution of the party when you failed to consult the 1st partisan, who is Standard-bearer, and the highest ranking official of the party 'On all matters of vital importance' (relative to your issued statement) as provided for by ARTICLE 16. DUTIES, FUNCTIONS, AND RESPONSIBILITIES OF OFFICERS, Section 2, under Standard-bearer.

Hence, after initial findings, you (along with all county Chairmen that affixed signatures to a recent unauthorized document) are culpable of serious constitutional violations and are hereby relieved of your respective positions and subsequently expelled from the membership of the CDC.

Now that your membership has been removed from our official registry, you are kindly advised to turn over all party belongings entrusted to your care during the discharge of your official duties and responsibilities while you served in your various capacities.

Meanwhile, the National Secretary General of the party has been mandated to steer a National Secretariat that runs the affairs of the party until National Congress, slated for January 2012.

Thank you for your time of service as former leaders of the mighty Congress for Democratic Change.[367]

Weah had set the tone, sending a clear message to the international community that he was a man of peace, a former United Nations Goodwill Ambassador who was not about to see his peaceful persona compromised for the sake of power.

Despite Weah's position on the protest, his supporters insisted on Tubman's ousting from the party. The National Executive Committee of the revolutionary Youth League of the Congress for Democratic Change called for Tubman's expulsion from the party.

The league concluded that the statutory urgencies of the moment required the National Youth League to call on the Standard-Bearer of the CDC, Cllr. Winston A. Tubman to honourably resign his position as leader of the party in fulfilment of his one-term commitment. "The Youth League reminds Cllr. Tubman of his commitment in early 2011 to serve as a one-term Standard-Bearer, irrespective of the outcome of the general and Presidential elections, a process that has long come to a closure. The National Youth League believes there can be no better time than now for his wilful resignation to avoid the growing displeasure of thousands of the party's grassroots support-bases who are weary of any further continuity in his leadership."

The CDC, through its Secretary General Acarous Moses Gray, also followed up the youth's statement with a statement announcing Tubman's dismissal from the party.

The statement read:

Holding the conviction that we are called to lead the popular Party of our people for generations to come, against nepotism, corruption, ethnicity, lack of accountability, transparency, and ethics, through the struggles and sacrifices of the dominant constituencies of Liberia's democratic demography, the mighty

Congress for Democratic Change has with immediate effect relieved Cllr. Winston A. Tubman as Standard-Bearer of the party.

Cllr. Tubman's removal as Standard-Bearer of the institution is in fulfilment of a one-term agreement reached with the organization, which required a dutiful obligation to voluntarily relinquish office within a thirty-day period after the conduct of general and Presidential elections 2011. This timely decision by the party has become especially judicious, considering the post-ultimatum time luxury accorded him to prepare for a convenient exit.

As this mass-based grassroots movement continuously projects an ambience of discipline, trust and unblemished pledge to the national liberation struggle of the Liberian people, it remains drastically intolerant to the line, hook and sinker of selfish political engineering that has become entrenched in the domestic democratic psychology.

Hence, though the Congress for Democratic Change is not oblivious to widespread bureaucratic resistance to surmount the critical national challenge of distrust and self-centeredness, it however believes the task is achievable when public and private institutions hold accountable their emblem bearers.

In this regard, and in the spirit of preserving the illustrious democratic credentials of the CDC, the former Standard-Bearer, Cllr. Winston A. Tubman is further expelled from the institution; and his name is herewith obliterated from the membership database of the organization as he ceases to qualify for any party function, public or private. Cllr. Tubman's involvement in organized factional activity, and analogous counterproductive and outlawed undertakings, disallowed under Article 5, Membership, and Section 41 & 42 of the constitution of the CDC, authorizes the measure.

In its relentless pursuit of institutional superiority and conventional democratic brilliance, this great party of might and maverick, by its constitutional ascendancy onus, therefore, announces Ambassador George M. Weah as 1st Partisan and Political Leader until a feasible National Congress is held, which will elect a Standard-Bearer.

Ambassador Weah, in consultation with the National secretariat of the party (authorized by the constitutional powers of the former Standard-Bearer and Vice Standard-Bearer to steer the affairs of the organization until the holding of conventions), and the National Chairman shall proceed without fail to conduct the affairs of the Congress for Democratic Change.

In addendum, the leadership of the Congress for Democratic Change informs all its innumerable partisans of a launched restructuring exercise that has begun and is expected to climax with the holding of National Congress/Conventions at the end of a four-month working period. During this reasonable time stretch, the CDC anticipates a stronger restructuring measure of all offices, to include but not limited to the National Executive Committee, Regional Executive Committees, County Executive Committees, District Coordinating offices, Zonal overseers, collective national and regional auxiliaries, etc.

Conclusively, the leadership of the CDC applauds all of its members, supporters, sympathizers and well-wishers for the chivalrous and undeterred commitment displayed during the just ended general and Presidential elections. As Liberia leapfrogs into a stable democratic reality, CDCians will be remembered as eminent patriots and stakeholders of national peace, stability and indisputable political tolerance.[368]

Tubman explains that despite the angst from the partisans, it all boiled down to money, which was at the centre of the split. "After we lost, I had remained an attraction for funding. People like Snowe and others who were around Weah wanted to stop that because they didn't think that it would happen, that the money would keep coming in if I stayed there so they wanted me to resign, and I refused. I then decided to step aside from politics all together and went to South Africa."[369]

Tubman says during a conversation with President Sirleaf, shortly after she outsmarted the opposition to secure a second term, it was clear that something was amiss. "President Sirleaf said she didn't know what we felt but the sun had set; and I said, 'The sun cannot set if it hasn't risen.' George Weah, George Solo were there. They felt that this was a future that they could control but I had my own notions that I want to be in charge which is what I always wanted and if we had won that's what we would have done. We wouldn't have let them do what they are now doing. We couldn't do that until we had won."[370]

During one of the last conversations between the pair, Tubman remembers saying to Weah, "No matter what happens I'm grateful for you allowing me to run at the head of the ticket. It is something I will never forget."[371]

The relationship between the pair soured further in the aftermath of the 2011 elections and when Tubman declared his support for former Coca Cola executive Alexander Cummings in the days leading to the 2017 Presidential elections. It became increasingly clear that the pair would never see eye to eye again.

Weah felt snubbed. The man he had regarded and respected as a father figure had betrayed him.

According to Tubman, although Weah had expressed interests in reteaming with him to run again in 2017, he had his reservations, especially amid suggestions that the ticket be split this time around, with Tubman running second to Weah.

Tubman recalls, "I said to him, we didn't win in 2011 because of the factors that I had laid out. I said that Madam Sirleaf was not the incumbent now in 2017 and if we repeated the ticket, we could actually win. It is something I did not want to say publicly but I wanted to tell him to his face and when I finally met with him, I said to him that we should repeat the ticket that we had in 2011 we would win."[372]

Tubman reminded Weah of the factors which led to their failed bid in 2011. "I said that there were factors that prevented us from winning which were no longer in the way, that things had changed but he told me, 'The people say I must run on top of the ticket this time around.' He didn't tell me this directly, but he did say that to some of his aides who mediated during the time. He said that if I could agree to be his Vice President, that could be acceptable. But I couldn't do that because the logic was that I would groom him. We could work together and make an impression on the country and then at the right time, I would step aside and see to it that he became a solid successor." [373]

Tubman felt it was a ridiculous idea. "In my own mind, I sat down and said all that was just a baloney. Here I am now, going to be taught by the student who I was supposed to mentor into the Presidency. I wouldn't have accepted that. I never in fact said it to him directly, but he knew that was my position."[374]

The experience of the Tubman-Weah short-lived political marriage taught the veteran diplomat-turned politician one thing: he owed a lot to Weah for giving him a shot at coming within striking distance of the Presidency.

"We were close in the sense that he saw me as this elderly statesman who came to his defence when everyone said he shouldn't be allowed to run. I had said that he was entitled to run for the Presidency. He liked that; he was impressed by that. Other than that, we were never really close. The relationship we had was through McGill. I communicated through McGill to him and he to me, most times. So, we weren't close in the sense that we talked about football or women and stuff like that."[375]

Looking back, Tubman acknowledges that his last name inspired a mixture of acceptance and rejection. "There are lots of people, who even now think fondly of Tubman's legacy. I was talking to Richard Tolbert the other day and he was saying how the young people are not impressed by Tubman."[376] Tolbert was the son of Frank Tolbert, former President Pro Tempore of the Liberian Senate and elder brother of late President, William R. Tolbert, who was killed in the April 12, 1980, coup. Richard's father was one of thirteen former officials of the Tolbert government executed in the aftermath of the bloody coup d'état.

For Tubman, Richard's assertions may be true of the young people in today's Liberia, especially in the city areas but that's not true of the people in the interior parts of the country, and their parents, people for whom Tubman is still a legend. "They admire what he did. The Tubman name was never a negative thing outside the capital Monrovia. I remember when we were going around the country, canvassing views for the constitution, and all these progressives, Dr. Amos Sawyer, Wilson Tarpeh, H. Boimah Fahnbulleh and others, the people hadn't heard of them and weren't interested in what they had to say but when I was announced in each of these meetings, the Tubman name was like Mohammed Ali and that was always the case. I've never had a situation where people didn't like the Tubman name, it was quite the opposite."[377]

Despite his flaws, Tubman had scored a Pyrrhic victory over many of his political peers, who sought Weah's blessing and popularity in hopes of riding to the Presidency. However, like many before him who had crossed paths with the football icon, Tubman was fully aware that once Weah felt betrayed, ostracised or abandoned, the consequences would be just as excruciatingly painful as ever.

Weah had sacrificed his quest for power, partially acknowledging that his educational lapses validated chatters that he was a novice to the political arena. His father figure had let him down and, for what it was worth, he saw no reason to turn back the clock or leave a window of opportunity for Tubman to once again fall into his good graces.

14

RECONCILIATION

———

December 2012

Ellen Johnson Sirleaf knew how to keep her rivals and opponents close. When she won the Presidency in 2005, her first order of business was to bring a lot of her critics into her government.

So, in December 2012, just a year after her re-election, she announced that George Weah had consented to work with the government as its Peace Ambassador.

George was never against holding position, other than the Presidency, if he did not win. In fact, in 2005, in an interview with the *Daily Observer* newspaper, the then-candidate for the Presidency said his love for Liberia and its people would never keep him from serving. "If a government gives me a job to do for my country, I will be willing to serve because that is my binding duty as a Liberian. What Liberia and Liberians have done for me, I don't think I can run from my society because the national team sent me to Brazil for training and I became one of the world's greatest players."[378]

He went on to say that it was his duty to promote the community and help his country. "The question is a very good question because sometimes I ask myself: I have been working in the interest of Liberia for the past twenty years, you mean if the United Nations and UNICEF can use me to develop young people, my own country cannot offer me a job? You know sometimes you wonder why. But I will always serve my country, that's my duty."[379]

George Solo, who was the national chairman for Weah's Congress for Democratic Change (CDC), said that his acceptance to lead the national reconciliation process was a manifestation of Weah's commitment to peace in Liberia. "This is not a new agenda of Ambassador Weah. As you are aware, [he] was very instrumental in the disarmament of young people working as a UNICEF Ambassador. So, I think [Weah] has been a pillar of peace in this environment and he has been one of the custodians of the sustainability of the peace that we enjoy today. So, it's nothing new. It's just a continuation of the manifestation of his commitment to peace,"[380] he said.

George took on the post after Nobel laureate Leymah Gbowee stepped down in October that year as head of the national Truth and Reconciliation Commission after criticising Sirleaf for not doing enough to fight corruption. The appointment was welcomed by all and at the time seemed like a perfect opportunity for Weah. After all, he had been a UNICEF Goodwill Ambassador and is widely credited for spearheading the disarmament process during the country's bloody civil war. "I believe he will be the chief patron of the roadmap for national reconciliation, and I think Ambassador Weah is well-placed to handle the reconciliatory process because he is one of the aggrieved parties who has agreed to put his personal qualms on hold in the interest of Liberia. I think this is a symbol of patriotism that needs to be congratulated and emulated,"[381] Solo said.

The appointment however was not without concerns. There were members and supporters within Weah's party who felt that taking a job would mean selling out to the Sirleaf government, a point Solo points out was far from the truth. "I don't think the appointment changes the dimension of the opposition of the Congress for Democratic Change to the ills in our society. I don't think this changes the perspective and psychology of the Congress for Democratic Change of equal rights and accountability and proper governance. I think this further manifests that we are willing to stand up for all these positions and highlight all these necessary changes in our society, with the frame of mind that the bedrock for all of these different implementations and exhibition of our civil liberty need to be on the basis of peace."[382]

John Morlu, who served as Auditor General in Sirleaf's government from 2006 to 2011, said he warned Weah against accepting the position. In a critique of his appointment as Peace Ambassador, he wrote, "After the 2011 elections, I advised George Weah and George Solo to focus on business so that they would not have to live at the financial mercy of the Sirleaf's regime. It fell on deaf ears! Mr. Weah and Mr. Solo held multiple discussions with Robert Sirleaf and his team to trade the Senatorial seat in exchange for cash and access to some oil block, but it seems Mr. Solo just overplayed his hands, trying to out-fox his political leader. This is the unfortunate problem in the Congress for Democratic Change (CDC): political leaders trading places, while the interest of the rank-and-file are undermined. In all of this, where is the commitment to principle?"[383]

The appointment for some, was also a chance for Weah to address the concerns about his persona, his temperament and whether he could harmonize and reconcile the country amid questions about his severed relationship with former teammates on the national team, the Lone Stars.

For some like Dionysius Sebwe, the reconciliation issue is a key reason he and others were against Weah's Presidential quest. "That's why it was mind-boggling to me when the man said he wanted to be President. It's not that I hate the guy. You know up to now when he calls us to play football with him as President, I always say that I do not hate George, I just disagree with him politically because where this country was, President Sirleaf took it to a level, and we needed somebody with the requisite skills set to take it to another level, but George didn't have it."[384]

Dionysius is not alone. James Debbah feels the same. "That's why I always tell people. George is the President. He needs to institute the reconciliation. You can't unify the country if you can't unify where you came from. Look at those that were with that man for the last 20 years. Nobody with him anymore. It's sad, from the background George came from and he's not doing anything. George is a disappointment. I tell people and they say I shouldn't be that critical but 80% of those who played with him, he hardly sees them. George Weah has to change – and he's not willing to change. He thinks he knows it all. The man cannot learn."[385]

Weah's inability to unify has been a key reason many saw him as the wrong person to unify Liberia. Today, many of the former footballers with whom he shared dressing rooms and played with back in his day, think it is unforgivable that he cannot let go of the past.

Debbah also laments the situation with Frank Seaton. He was a member of the national team. He died on February 12, 2013. Debbah is angry that George did not attend Frank's funeral because he and Frank had a beef until his death. "The man never showed up for the funeral because he and Frank Seaton had some kind of squabble. So, what? How can you do that? The man was your teammate, you played together and were very close. We all were very close."[386]

Jonathan "Boye Charles" Sogbie, who is now a member of Senate following his election in 2019, says he feels justified for never supporting George's bid for the Presidency. "Today, George Weah is President. We see what is going on. So, my issue with this brother is real. I tell him what's happening, what's not happening. So, then, I'm saying don't go for the Presidency because you're not prepared. He contested 2005, he did not win, he contested 2011, he did not win, 2014, he decided to run for the Senate, I decided to support him because it is a pedestal, something he could learn from – if he wanted to go further it would be a good stepping-stone."[387]

George did go further, but Jonathan says he remains open to reconciling with George. "I'm not an enemy but I'm also not a fool. I remain open, I do not seek to compromise my principles. We will have to work together when we respect ourselves, we will have to reach each other on the level, like they say – on the level. I respect him as a President, I'm a lawmaker. We can work like that but when we meet as brother to brother, we will speak on that level. He has not reached out to me, he has not."[388]

In late 2020, Jonathan says he reached out to the President Pro Tempore of the Senate, Albert Chie, with respect to reconciliation. "I said I am open to meet with him. He's the President of our country, it would be good to speak to him, not only for myself but the Liberian people. That will be a good example of the reconciliation he preaches about and doesn't practice."[389]

When the Pro Temp approached Minister of State Nathaniel McGill, concerning reconciliation with President Weah, Jonathan says McGill told the Pro Temp to tell him to tone down his conversations in the senate. "They say because I'm harsh in speaking and I do not speak in favour of the government. I don't know what I'm supposed to say. I told the Pro Temp, I did not request a meeting, why should they be giving conditions? Those are not the conditions I want to accept just to meet the President. So, I'll just keep functioning the way I'm functioning. So, that's what it is."[390]

As *FrontPageAfrica* was to explain, in November 2014, George Weah stepped down as Peace Ambassador, explaining that he did so because he did not want to fall into conflict with the Code of Conduct as he was embarking on running for the Senate.[391] Prior to his resignation in November 2014, there was speculation that his office was not being supported by the government as there was a posture of non-co-operation between his office and the President's, especially after he declared his intention to contest the senatorial elections.

At the time, Sirleaf's son, Robert was also contesting the senatorial seat of Montserrado County.

George announced that he had received a check from the government to carry out a project under this office, but that he returned the check upon his resignation, although he did not disclose the amount on the check.

George was stepping down as Peace Ambassador, but he had a more ambitious undertaking. He had failed to win the Presidency in 2005, ran number two to Winston Tubman in 2011 but it seems he had come to the realisation that, with Johnson Sirleaf in the final leg of her second term, it was time to give his Presidential quest one more try, but first, he would embark on a quest for the Senate to gain valuable experience and silence his critics.

As an opposition figure, Weah often painted himself as a unifier. He paid his dues as a footballer, and as a UNICEF Goodwill Ambassador, undertaking initiatives with it to combat, through education, the growth of HIV/AIDS in Africa and promoting attempts through the vocational training of child soldiers, certain programmes to reintegrate them into the societies of war-troubled nations. As President, however, Weah is still haunted by familiar echoes of his past that many of his friends and peers say may never go away: his ability to hold on to a grudge. The irony of Weah's persona has made life difficult yet complicated for many who have crossed his path. This is why many found it a bit puzzling in the President's message for the Bicentennial celebration, that President Weah made a stunning declaration that the foundation of a new Liberia rested on national unity and reconciliation, which, according to him, is paramount in achieving socio-economic growth.

In essence, Weah was sounding off as Allafrica.com reported, "that the issue of unity and reconciliation must become the imperative agenda of all current and future national development policies"[392] and that projects and programs emanating from these "policies should focus on eliminating all forms of discrimination and exclusion in Liberia."[393]

To the contrary, critics of Weah often hammer away at the one-sidedness of his government, where he and his officials have stuck to their decision not to keep any member of the opposition in government.

In contrast to his predecessor – Johnson Sirleaf, who included several members of the opposition, including members of Weah's own party in her government – Weah, as President, failed to embark on a unifying venture to maintain the peace in the aftermath of a brutal civil war and a successful democratic transition. But here he was, celebrating the Bicentennial, preaching that reconciliation was the only option for the country's survival and continuity as it strived to recover from the devastation and division that characterised the civil conflict. "We must focus on promoting unity amongst all Liberians, wherever they may reside, and encourage all to make meaningful contributions to the nation-building tasks of our country," Weah said. "Redefining Liberia's identity and building a shared sense of nationalism should be at the centre of continued reconciliation in Liberia."[394]

For many of his critics however, the model President Weah was pitching for genuine national unity and reconciliation in Liberia was simply uninspiring. Yet, Weah, the President, was asking Liberians to embrace the tenets of National Unity and fight intolerance and impatience toward one another. "Let us fight hatred and malice," he declared. "These are all negative vices that detract from our higher purpose of oneness and national coherence. Because there is so much more that unites us than that which may tend to divide us, let us celebrate the complexities of our rich diversities, and live in peace, unity, and harmony as our brothers' and sisters' keepers."[395]

Emerging from war and in the midst of a post-war democratic transition, Liberia has always been in desperate need of its Nelson Mandela moment. The late South African President who was released by South Africa's government after 27 years imprisonment, and 4 years later elected the nation's first black President in 1994, made it his life's work to preach forgiveness and reconciliation. Mr. Mandela once noted, "Forgiveness liberates the soul, it removes fear. That's why it's such a powerful weapon."[396] When he assumed the mantle of authority in May 1994, he said, "The time for the healing of the wounds has come. The moment to bridge the chasms that divide us has come. The time to build is upon us."[397] Mandela chose forgiveness over hate, particularly of the remnants of an apartheid regime which had ridiculed and humiliated him during his days in prison.

The issue of reconciliation was a somewhat complicated one for Liberia's post-war resurgence. When Johnson Sirleaf was inaugurated in January 2012, not many Liberians viewed her as a unifier. She had acknowledged funding the civil war and supported Charles Taylor. So, her inauguration pledge calling for reconciliation was greeted with scepticism. Although clear in her speech that, "no task will be more urgent and more compelling; no cause will require my personal attention and engagement than national reconciliation."[398] Sirleaf struggled with the issue although she did embrace many with opposing views into her government.

In contrast, her successor, Weah, fitted the bill. In the eyes of most Liberians, he had not been involved in the civil war, although he too continues to struggle with personal demons of his own. However, he pledged that it would be, "my task, my duty, and my honor, to lead this nation from division to National Unity, and toward a future of hope and prosperity"[399] and "I have here taken an oath before you, and before the Almighty God, to uphold our constitution and to preside over this Government and this country to the best of my abilities,"[400] he said at his inauguration.

For the likes of James Debbah, Jonathan "Boye Charles" Sogbie, Dionysius Sebwe and many who still consider themselves victims of Weah's personal hatred against them, the jury is still out on a man often presenting the appearance of a unifier but far too often finding himself unable to put aside petty differences for the sake of peace.

15

WEALTH

———

June 2014

How much is George Weah worth?

Questions about George's wealth have been a major point of speculation since he hung up his football boots. In three major transfers of his professional football career, George accumulated a total of US$16,652,000. But when world football's governing body, FIFA, began looking into Qatari football officials in the wake of damaging claims about the legality of the bidding process for the 2022 World Cup, eyebrows were raised.

An investigation by the *Sunday Times* in 2014 alleged that Mohamed Bin Hamman, a former Vice-President of FIFA, paid US$5m (£3m) in total to football officials in return for support of Qatar's winning bid. Najeeb Chirakal, a former aide to Bin Hammam, was banned for life by FIFA as a result of the investigation. FIFA ethics committee judges ruled that Chirakal was involved in "several unethical payments made on behalf of a third party to various football officials between 2009 and 2011."[401]

The Denver Post summarised on January 20, 2017: "In the two-year period to 2011, Bin Hammam was Asian Football Confederation President and a FIFA powerbroker. His FIFA ambitions were fuelled by helping Qatar win the hosting rights for the 2022 World Cup. The ethics committee said charges proven against Chirakal included bribery and corruption, offering gifts, conflicts of interest and failing to cooperate with investigators. Chirakal worked in Qatar for Bin Hammam, who was banned for life by FIFA in 2012."[402] Chirakal was identified by Price Waterhouse Coopers (PwC), and outed via leaked emails in *The Sunday Times* as a central nexus for Asian and African officials soliciting cash payments from Bin Hammam. One of those communications published by *The Sunday Times* of London, included an email from Chirakal to George Weah, sent on February 16, 2010.

The email read:

Dear Mr. George
The payment has been transferred to your account and please find the
bank receipt.
Kind regards
Najeeb[403]

George had written Najeeb on February 7, 2010, for help:

Mr. Najeeb,
Greetings to you and all, I want to thank you for the respect given to me
through all these years. I write to remind you about the promise President made
to me in regard to my school fees last term. I am sending this account information
because it is the right one. As we spoke this morning, I need President help as
soon as possible I beg your indulgence. On the other hand, President also wants
my assistant to do some work for him in Liberia. So don't forget to let him know.
If he wants to send to him or to me, it will also be good. I am awaiting his early
response.
Thanks
Ambassador Weah[404]

In another of the published emails, Lenn Eugene Nagbe, then a close aide to George wrote, "George has repeatedly spoken of his support for our future plans in world football and we all look forward to your power. However, it will require a total of 50,000 to secure the election results."[405]

In October 2012, Chirakal was provisionally suspended by the FIFA ethics court for failing to cooperate with its investigation into his boss.

Former U.S. federal prosecutor Michael Garcia was leading FIFA's probe into the voting on the 2018 and 2022 host countries.

When the communication to Bin Hammam's aide was made public, George said he had a constitutional right to talk about anything outside football. "He has been a special friend." While declining to discuss why he might have sent Bin Hammam his bank details, Bloomberg News reported that George, in a telephone interview, acknowledged that he was questioned by a FIFA Panel regarding the scandal as many as five times by a team investigating allegations of corruption in bidding to host the World Cup. He told Bloomberg that the team led by Michael Garcia asked him about the 2010 e-mail published by *The Sunday Times*. In the email, George sent his Bank of America account number in Pembroke Pines, Florida, to the assistant of Bin Hammam, who was then on FIFA's executive committee.

George, who has homes in Florida and his native Liberia, told Bloomberg News that he first met Bin Hammam in Paris in 1998. Bin Hammam was a "father figure" to him, and any interaction with him had been personal and not related to Qatar's bid. Weah said by phone, adding, "I have a constitutional right to talk about anything outside football. He has been a special friend."[406]

Weah said the FIFA investigators taped an interview with him in New York and spoke to him "two, three, four, five" times in total.

The Italian sports newspaper, *La Gazetta dello Sport*, reported in June 2010 that the payment to George was to ensure that he would press for the re-election of Izetta Wesley as President of Liberia Football Association. Wesley had also accepted money from Bin Hammam, and the bribe to George ensured that the voice of Liberia was retained within FIFA.

The *Sunday Times* reported that one month after the communication between George and Bin Hammam's aide, the same amount was transferred to George's private bank account.

The FIFA saga not only raised questions about President George Weah's wealth, but it also raised concerns over what happened to the nearly US$20 million he earned as a professional footballer and through the advertising deal with Diodora. Those questions were further heightened, nearly eight months into Weah's Presidency when massive property structures began popping up across the city.

One of the properties to raise eyebrows was a 17-unit state-of-the-art multi-complex, which the President began constructing three months after he was sworn into office in January 2018. Amid huge public outcry, Weah seemed undeterred by claims of overnight wealth accumulation. Prior to the commencement of the construction, the area was used as a football pitch by members of the community.

President Weah also demolished his US$150,000 9th Street beach-side property for reconstruction while at the same time renovating the Jamaica Resort Beach property and building the RIA Highway complex.

Critics of the President soon began to question why he did not carry out such development of his personal properties prior to becoming President. Others wondered why such a project was so much a priority for the President when the country was experiencing a nosedive in the economy.

In the wake of all this, President Weah shot down criticisms about his refusal to declare his assets as required by the Code of Conduct.

The only assets made public to date, are those declared by Weah prior to becoming President. When he contested the Presidency in 2005, Weah declared US$3,290,000 in cash, personal and real properties in Liberia and the United States of America. He declared a total of US$335,000 as income realised within the borders of Liberia and abroad during the last twelve months. The amount represents US$250,000 from a real estate in the USA, US$60,000 from his supermarket also in the USA and US$25,000 from another real estate in Liberia. In total, he declared US$2,950,000 as the value for his real and personal properties both in Liberia and the United States. Weah valued his 9th Street residence at US$150,000; his real estate at the ELWA Community, Rehab Road in Paynesville at US$100,000; a US$1.5 million residence in Florida, U.S.A. and a US$1.2 million super-market in Miami, Florida. At the time of the declaration in 2005, he also declared a zero liability, an indication that the Presidential Aspirant owes no financial obligation or otherwise to anybody.

Nine years later, when he ran for the Senate, George declared that he owned a home in Florida, worth $1.4 million, plus a residence valued at $0.9 million, according to the 2014 disclosure form.[407]

Issues surrounding the President's wealth came to the fore amid his reluctance to declare his assets. Cllr. James Verdier, who was head of the Liberia Anti-Corruption Commission when Weah took over in January 2018, told the *FrontPageAfrica* newspaper in January 2019 that concerning the regulations regarding declaration of assets, officials were to declare these to the LACC within 30 days after their confirmation. Section 10.1 of the revised Code of Conduct referencing declaration of Assets and Performance Bonds states, "Every public official and employee of government involved in making decisions affecting contracting, tendering or procurement, and issuance of licences of various types shall sign performance or financial bonds and shall, in addition, declare his or her income, assets and liabilities prior to taking office and thereafter: (a) at the end of every three years; (b) on promotion or progression from one level to another; (c) upon transfer to another public office; and (d) upon retirement or resignation."[408]

Critics then began taking President Weah to task over promises made prior to becoming President and one he made on his inauguration day. President Weah said, "I further believe that the overwhelming mandate I received from the Liberian people is a mandate to end corruption in public service. I promise to deliver on this mandate. As officials of Government, it is time to put the interest of our people above our own selfish interests. It is time to be honest with our people. Though corruption is a habit amongst our people, we must end it. We must pay civil servants a living wage, so that corruption is not an excuse for taking what is not theirs. Those who do not refrain from enriching themselves at the expense of the people – the law will take its course. I say today that you will be prosecuted to the full extent of the law."[409]

In the President's defence, most of his officials, who themselves have not had their assets made public since the President's announcement, have struggled to explain their sudden, unexplained wealth.

Samuel Tweah, Finance and Economic Planning Minister told a state radio interview in 2019 that President Weah had the ability to acquire any property. "He was born to make history. He made history in football; he'll make history in politics; you're wasting your time. Some people are born, and you can't fight it. What 'God' has chosen; man can never fight. There is a reason why 'God' took him from Gibraltar to become the President today. So, whether you write fake news on *FrontPageAfrica*, you go on some kind of show and lie about a man who earned money – US$80 million and more – the man whose son is a millionaire, the man who made a lot of money, to say he ain't got money to build his own house because he's President, that's a black wicked evil lie."

The US$80 million figure has been thrown around for much of Weah's political life, but nothing has ever been put on paper, particularly in the two assets declarations in the public domain from his failed 2005 Presidential bid and his victorious 2014 Senatorial elections. According to the LACC, the President had since declared his assets, but it has no intentions of making it public – there is no legal requirement for this to be published.

A January 2021 investigative report by Radio France International reported that Weah's assets abroad are more clearly defined with publicly available documents in the US. These publicly available documents reveal a few details about Weah's properties in New York and Florida. For example, the report states that Weah and his wife Clar bought a house in the gated Pembroke Falls community, North of Miami, for $374,900 in 2004, according to records from Broward County, published by RFI. "The Weah family previously owned a house in the nearby town of Davie which sold in 2011 for $740,000. It had two mortgages secured against it. Another property in Plantation, in the same Miami area, was bought in 2002 and sold 11 years later."[410]

The report cited a commercial property near Fort Lauderdale identified in George Weah's asset declaration that has a title deed in the name of Clar Weah, and currently appears to be rented to a car garage specialising in customisation and alloy wheels. "The building, bought in 2002 for $460,000 with a mortgage, had a zoning agreement for it to be used as grocery store or delicatessen. However, Clar Weah was cited in 2004 with non-compliance of city ordinance for vacant or abandoned real estate."[411]

According to the report, "George's wife, Clar, in May 2005, took out a loan worth $100,000 from Associated Grocers of Florida for the business Flavors Supermarket & Jerk Center, of which George Weah was a director. The address listed for this company was their property, but the supermarket business was dissolved by state authorities in 2006 for not filing an annual report,"[412] the report noted. "The property was in 2009 leased to a company running a restaurant specialising in southern U.S. cuisine. But just a year later, Jamaican-born Clar Weah started eviction proceedings, saying the tenant had not paid rent. The tenant, 4J's Florida Holding Corporation, argued that Weah had not fixed a leaking roof."[413]

The court ruled in Clar Weah's favour and ordered the tenant evicted. "Clar Weah appears to manage the building, her name appears on property tax records, and was fined once in 2011 and later in 2018 for breaking Broward County local regulations. She also filed a notice to repair the roof in 2013."[414]

The RFI report also stated that George and Clar had interests in New York City and Clar rented commercial space in the Jamaica neighbourhood, signing a lease agreement in December 2011.

The contract ran until 2016, but she vacated the premises in 2012, breaking the conditions of the lease. According to the report, Clar's name also appeared on a mortgage foreclosure in 1998 of a residential property in the Queens borough of New York. "Then George Weah himself signed over his power of attorney in 2005 to Michael Duncan, Clar Weah's brother, before the same property was sold to Amelia Duncan-Fagon and Orvin Fagon. Perhaps again related to Clar's family, her maiden name was Duncan before she married Weah."[415]

A Staten Island property completes the list. This was sold in 2005, yet there was another in the Queens neighbourhood though the ownership was transferred from his football agent Alaji Sidibay back in 1993 when he was still playing for Paris Saint-Germain. The report noted that the property it was, "currently the subject of court proceedings for unpaid property tax bills of more than $10,000 as of September 2020. Several summonses have been served on the address." As with others in the Weah property portfolio there is a sense, if not of neglect then of an absence, of full attention being paid to all of their holdings.

Questions about Weah's finances were also raised when in 2016, Meapeh Gono, who accompanied him to the meeting in Minneapolis when he was pondering a run for the Presidency, filed a case against him in the State of Georgia for failure to pay child support, forcing him to make monthly payments. That case was a major distraction for George during his 2017 Presidential run.

In France, Weah is widely admired and holds French citizenship according to most accounts. A Radio France International report published on allafrica. com reminded its readers that the former footballer, with his former press agent Caroline Angelini, embarked on a business venture titled Weah Sports back in 2014. Each held half of the shares. It did not appear in Weah's asset declaration in 2014, likely due to timing. Using the slogan "Bring It On" the sporting clothing brand was based in Pacey-sur-Eure, Normandy and started with high hopes and wide publicity targeting European and African markets. However it failed, suffering a judicial liquidation process in 2015. Weah Sports was removed from the company register in 2019. President Weah has also come under fire over his foreign travels. For most of his foreign travels, the President uses a Dassault Falcon 900EX jet registered in France to Bonkoungou's company EBOMAF, a pan-African construction firm. The private jet came under scrutiny after the Falcon jet's owner, Bonkoungou, entered into an agreement with the Liberia government in 2019 for a $30 million investment into a milling plant to process wheat into flour. EBOMAF also signed a $420m financing deal with the government to fund road building. The deal also drew criticism from the International Monetary Fund over a lack of transparency in the finance agreement, encouraging the government to cancel a road construction deal. In January 2021, the Plenary of the Senate instructed the Ministries of Public Works, Justice and Finance to terminate or cancel the EBOMAF along with another controversial deal, ETON, which was projected to be worth around US$536 million.

The Senate took the decision after debating a report from its Judiciary Committee which advised earlier that if the deal remained as it was it could lead Liberia into future financial obligation. According to the Committee, legal procedures and best practices were not followed in acquiring the deal.

The ETON deal was a US$536 million financing agreement for the construction of 505.3km of roads including the corridor from Grand Bassa County in Buchanan through Cestos City in Rivercess County to Greenville City in Sinoe County onward to Barclayville City in Grand Kru County – a 316km road. The two deals were signed by President Weah amid controversy in June 2018, just six months into his Presidency.

The EBOMAF SA Loan would cover the paving of 323.7 km roads including the Somalia Drive via Kesselley Boulevard to Sinkor in Monrovia

(16km); and Tappita to Zwedru in Nimba and Grand Gedeh Counties; and from Toe Town in Grand Gedeh County to Ivory Coast Border, a 10.2km road. It included the 185km road from Zwedru in Grand Gedeh County, to Greenville in Sinoe County.

The ETON Financing loan covered 505.3km of roads including the corridor from Grand Bassa County in Buchanan through Cestos City in Rivercess County, to Greenville City in Sinoe County onward to Barclayville City in Grand Kru County; in total, a 316km road.

The road construction also included the corridor between Barclayville to Sasstown road (21km) in Grand Kru County, while the Barclayville to Pleebo road (75km) in Grand Kru and Maryland Counties would be constructed and paved.

The ETON Financing Road Agreement would also cover Western Liberia counties including the Tubmanburg to Bopolu (52km) road in Bomi and Garpolu Counties, and the Medina and Robertsport (41.3km) road in Bomi and Gbarpolu Counties.

The President was expecting to have both road construction projects completed in the first term of his administration.

Lingering questions surrounding Weah's wealth, including the unexplained, have surfaced for much of the duration of his first term. He had built a massive and luxurious 68-apartment multiplex, renovated his 9th Street home and his Jamaica Resort off the Robertsfield Highway, all in the first year of his Presidency. A lot of his ministers and officials in his government followed suit.

It is an issue key stakeholders in Liberia's future paid keen attention to and sought answers.

Issues of wealth involving Presidents, particularly in Africa, arise when most of those living at the bottom of the economic barrel struggle to find food on a daily basis, why many youngsters parade the streets in between traffic engaging in petty trade as breadwinners for their families and why after more than 176 years of independence, the issue of corruption persists.

This is why, during a visit to Liberia in February 2022 to commemorate the 200th anniversary of free black men, women, and children from the United States arriving on Providence Island, Dana Banks, a Special Assistant to U.S. President Joseph R. Biden lamented that like many democracies, Liberia still has work to do to seriously address and root out corruption.

Banks averred, "We bring this up as your friends who are eager to help. Corruption is an act of robbery. It robs Liberia's citizens of access to health care, to public safety, to education. It robs you of the healthy business environment we all know Liberia could have, which would lift countless Liberians out of poverty. It subverts economic opportunity, exacerbates inequality, and erodes integrity. It eats away at the democracy you have worked so hard to build."[416]

While commending Liberia for having a host of anti-corruption institutions, Banks was blunt in stating, "The truth is that the government fails to adequately fund them and exerts its influence upon them. Too many of Liberia's leaders have chosen their own personal short-term gain over the long-term benefit of their country."[417]

Banks declared that the expectation that the United States, and the rest of the international community, can take the lead in solving the longstanding problems of Liberia was a fallacy. Only Liberians can solve their own problems, saying: "So let me be clear. The United States is a proud and dedicated partner and friend of Liberia. But ultimately, only the Liberian Government and the Liberian people can tackle corruption, fight for accountability and transparency, and move this country forward."[418]

The stern words from the U.S. came amid what Banks pointed out as a "rash of dangerous coups across Africa."[419]

In May 2021, the Malian Army led by Vice President Assimi Goita captured President Bah N'daw, Prime Minister Moctar Ouane and Minister of Defence Souleymane Doucoure. Goita of the junta that led the coup d'état, announced that N'daw and Ouane were stripped of their powers and that new elections would be held in 2022. The takeover marked the country's third coup d'état in ten years, following the 2012 and 2020 military takeovers.

In neighbouring Guinea, on September 5, 2021, Col. Mamady Doumbouya declared himself interim President after deposing Alpha Conde, a leader who once put his faith in Doumbouya to help him keep his grip on power.

On January 23, 2022, a coup d'état led by Paul Henri Sandaogo Damiba was launched in Burkina Faso after gunfire erupted in front of the Presidential residence in the Burkinabé capital Ouagadougou. On January 24, 2022, on television, the army announced Roch Marc Christian Kaboré had been removed as President. Later they declared that not only the parliament but also the government and constitution were voided.

All of this was reminiscent of Liberia's own origins of civil disturbance, going back to the April 12, 1980 coup, and the reasons behind it. Ironically, the American-Liberian dominance of governance and wealth was a key reason Doe and his low-ranked officers staged the coup.

The outcome of bad governance, economic mismanagement and autocratic overreaching has largely been blamed for uprisings in Africa. Echoes of similarities and Weah's own naivety point to what many political observers see as detrimental to his own political survival.

16

JEWEL

———

Long before she was Jewel Howard Taylor, First Lady to former President Charles Ghankay Taylor, Jewel had only run into George Weah a handful of times. Little did she know that one day, their paths would cross in the way they did.

Jewel was a U.S. resident living in the state of New Jersey. She went to see a friend on Staten Island in New York. When she arrived at her friend's apartment, there was the friend's cousin, George Weah. George was visiting his relative when Jewel arrived and was just about to leave the apartment. Because George was traveling, he and Jewel exchanged pleasantries and he left.

The two would meet a few years later. But this time, Jewel was the First Lady of the Republic of Liberia. She had married Charles Taylor, the former warlord, whose National Patriotic Front of Liberia was responsible for launching the brutal civil war that led to the demise of the Samuel Doe government.

George and the Lone Stars were attending a state dinner for the national team, hosted by President Taylor. It was on the eve of the team's departure for the 2002 Africa Cup of Nations finals in Mali. There, Jewel was introduced to George by President Taylor. The two exchanged pleasantries and good wishes for a victory for Liberia with vague recollection of that first meeting in New Jersey. The pair would not meet again until January 2006 during the inauguration of President Ellen Johnson Sirleaf.

First Lady Jewel Howard Taylor was now Senator Jewel Howard Taylor. With her husband fleeing into exile and a new democratic government ushered in, Jewel had used Taylor's popularity in vote-rich Bong County, the third most populous county in Liberia, to clinch a seat in the Senate.

In July 2003, three years prior to Sirleaf's inauguration, rebels belonging to the Liberians United for Reconciliation and Democracy (LURD) had initiated a siege of Monrovia. Several bloody battles were fought as Taylor's forces halted rebel attempts to capture the city.

The pressure on Taylor increased as U.S. President George W. Bush stated twice that month that Taylor "must leave Liberia". On July 9, Olusegun Obasanjo, Nigerian President volunteered safe exile for Taylor with the requirement that he took no part in Liberian politics. Taylor's condition in response was to say he would leave office if Liberia received a contingent of U.S. peacekeeping troops. President George W. Bush however urged Taylor to resign as vital for any American involvement to be instigated.

At the same time, several African states, in particular the Economic Community of West African States (ECOWAS) under the leadership of Nigeria, sent troops under the banner of ECOMIL to Liberia. Bolstered by logistical support from a Californian company called PAE Government Services Inc., which was given a $10 million contract by the U.S. State Department, a 32-member U.S. military assessment team was deployed as a liaison with the ECOWAS troops, on August 6, 2003.

On August 10, 2003, a reluctant Taylor was to appear on national television declaring he would resign the next day. Power would transfer to Vice President Moses Blah. As his parting shot in the farewell address, he hit back at the Bush administration, bitterly declaring his departure would hurt Liberia. He resigned the next day with Blah serving as President until a transitional government was established.

Present at President Taylor's farewell were Ghana's President John Kufuor, South African President Thabo Mbeki, and Mozambican President Joaquim Chissano, all representing the African regional council. The U.S. brought in a Joint Task Force – Liberia's Amphibious Ready Group of three warships with 2,300 marines – into view of the coast. Taylor flew to Nigeria, where the Nigerian government provided houses for him and his entourage in Calabar.

So, there they were, George and Jewel at the inauguration of Sirleaf, perhaps without any inclination of what the future had in store for them.

George had lost the 2005 Presidential elections to Sirleaf. In a race that featured twenty-two candidates eyeing the Presidency, Sirleaf, a former World Bank employee and finance minister, finished second to Weah after the first round of voting. Sirleaf eventually won the second round 59%–41%, according to the final National Elections Commission tally.

Sirleaf, unhappy that George was trying to taint her victory, reminded the press that the former World Footballer of the Year had 72 hours to bring evidence of wrongdoing concerning her campaign under Liberia's election laws. Sirleaf declared that followers of Weah simply didn't, "want a woman to be President in Africa"[420] characterising the charges against the legitimacy of the vote as lies. This response was effective and December 22 saw Weah roll back on the protests.

Thus, in January, Sirleaf became the first democratically elected female Head of State in the history of the African Continent, and the first native female African head of state since Empress Zewditu, who ruled Ethiopia from 1916 to 1930.

Six years later, in a move seen as an acknowledgment by George that he lacked experience and had leadership lapses, he ran as Vice President to veteran Ambassador Winston Tubman. Sirleaf once more trounced the ticket and maintained her grip on power for another six years.

In the months leading to the 2017 Presidential elections, George and his team sensed that this was their time and that picking the right running mate would be crucial. The choices were few with Weah forced to choose between Jewel and Alexander Tyler, the former Speaker of the House of Representatives. Weah's choice was limited owing to the new-found alliance with two other political parties, Jewel's National Patriotic Party and Tyler's People's Democratic Party of Liberia. Both choices were entangled in controversy. The former speaker was dubbed "Corruption King Kong" by the media and was at the heart of an alleged corruption scandal that split the legislature in late 2016 and created a deadlock in the legislature. Tyler was among several current and former officials at the centre of a massive corruption scandal who were charged with 'economic crimes' along with London-based Sable Mining.

At the time, the London-based watchdog group, Global Witness, alleged in a damning report that Cllr. H. Varney Sherman, former head of the ruling Unity Party, orchestrated a vast political patronage network based on bribery on behalf of Sable Mining. Sable, co-founded by former England international cricketer Phil Edmonds, sought to gain a foothold in Liberia's lucrative iron ore industry between 2010 and 2012.[421]

Both Sherman, Tyler and many of those charged in the scandal denied the allegations. But Global Witness alleged that Sable's bribes were mostly paid out by Sherman, totalling $960,000 (860,000 euros).

The scandal came a year before Mr. Tyler stepped down from the then ruling Unity Party and formed his own party, the People's Democratic Party of Liberia (PDPL). The Global Witness report alleged that Tyler received a bribe worth $75,000 in a bid to get the Sable-friendly legislation through parliament with changes that included relaxing laws on the tender process.

Thus, for many Liberians, Tyler was persona non grata, a face many wanted out of the political arena due to the litany of allegations dogging his political life.

Jewel, on the other hand, had a less-tarnished political career, but as the former wife of President Charles Taylor, who was imprisoned in the UK for war crimes, she was still a force. However, she was still tainted by her close affiliation with a brutal era in the country's history as well as by allegations that her ex-husband was furtively helping her campaign.

Despite her flaws, Weah knew that Jewel was the lesser of two evils and that Jewel, owing to the Taylor name, would help him play well in the vote-rich Bong County, which was set to be a key battleground in the 2017 national elections. Joseph Boakai, the UP's candidate, also had strong support there.

Although Weah enjoyed immense popularity, his experience from the 2005 elections made it clear that he needed some kind of merger if he wanted to take his quest for the President to the next level. So, a merger was a no-brainer. Running on their own, both Tyler and Jewel stood no chance. Liberians had become fatigued with the ruling Unity Party, which had ruled for the past twelve years and were clamouring for change. Weah knew that with his popularity and a jolt from one or two other political parties, he stood a strong chance.

In the end, Weah settled for Jewel for one key reason. Besides hailing from the vote-rich Bong County, she had been married to Charles Taylor who used the county as his stronghold during the civil war.

Bong County, located in the north-central portion of Liberia, measures 8,772 square kilometers (3,387 sq/mi). As of the 2008 census, it had a population of 328,919, making it the third-most populous county in Liberia. With Weah widely expected to sweep the southeast, the party needed a strong force from a county like Bong to enhance its strength.

So, in 2016, the party of Charles Taylor – the National Patriotic Party – met in their National Convention and decided to join a newly formed coalition, called the Coalition for Democratic Change. The Coalition was made up of three political parties: The Congress for Democratic Change, the National Patriotic Party and the Liberia People's Democratic Party (PDPL)). The arrangements, which brought the three parties together, determined that the Congress for Democratic Change would produce the Presidential candidate and that the candidate would choose the Vice-Presidential candidate from one of the other two constituent parties.

Jewel says at that point both parties began to lobby so that their Standard Bearer would be the Vice. "After many negotiations between the three parties, the choice was then left to Ambassador Weah. He then began having conversations with both Hon. Alex J. Tyler and me. Our conversations took about six months of talking, about trust, roles, responsibilities, collaboration, coordination, commitment, and shared visions. The last series of conversation between the both of us even involved national and religious leaders, who spoke of the need for the both of us to work together for a better Liberia."[422]

Even at this point, Jewel says George reminded her that he had still not decided, but was still considering both herself and Alex, and that when he made up his mind, he would let them know. According to Jewel, this happened around October of 2016, when she met with George at his Rehab Road residence. In that meeting, George was clear with Jewel that he was looking for a partner to help him govern.

Jewel recalls, "George was convinced that my gender, education, and my many years of experience and strong advocacy would be needed in

helping him lead the nation. He was keen to note the pending lack of a
female at the helm of Government and the need to answer to the cry of the
Liberian women for a female at the top."[423]

George also expressed his joy that they would be a winning combination
and would work together to change the lives of their people for the better.
"George then asked me if I would be his running mate,"[424] recalls Jewel.

She agreed, but only with George's promise that they would work as a
team and that he would allow her to support the gender equality agenda
and continue her assignment as a gender rights advocate, trainer, and mentor,
both at home and abroad.

George provided a resounding approval for Jewel's plans. "He said, 'But
of course this is how we both will work for our people and build a better
Nation.'"[425] The pair shook hands and sealed that commitment with a hug.

At the time, Jewel says George asked that she keep the discussion to
herself. "He had given me his word, but it would become official at the
December 2016 Coalition Acceptance Rally, held at the CDC National
Headquarters in Congotown."[426]

Leaving George's home after being told that she was the Vice-Presidential
pick, Jewel says she got in her car and as she drove back home, she felt
humbled but with a lot of strong emotions running through her mind. How
did she get to this point? Was this possible or real? Was she ready for such
an assignment when they had not worked together closely before? Could
this union really work? Could she trust his word? What if they actually won,
and he changed? What could she do? What would she have to give up for
this journey? What kind of Vice President could she be in order to build
confidence and trust? As a strong female, how would she keep the relationship between herself and her boss?

When George finally made the announcement on January 21, 2017, at
the CDC Rally, the crowd went wild. In their view he had chosen the right
running-mate.

For Jewel, the moment was so overwhelming that both she and George
and many of the partisans had tears of joy in their eyes. "They could finally
see a combination team, which would light their path for a better life for
the majority. For him, I can only surmise that he knew that he had made

the right decision and he was now certain that the Presidency was closer than ever before."[427]

With the announcement official, Jewel was still in shock, yet humbled, imagining how a regular person like her could make it to that level. But deep down, Jewel was afraid and wondered if the ticket could even win. Her fears were genuine. After all she was the former wife of Charles Taylor who had spent years under a United Nations assets freeze and travel ban.

When she first ran for the Senate in the 2005 elections, Human Rights Watch named her among a few others as "a threat to the peace process in Liberia" or for being "engaged in activities aimed at undermining peace and stability in Liberia and the sub-region,"[428] because of lingering ties and close contact with Taylor.

With so much baggage, many political observers were unsure what to make of Weah's decision to embrace Jewel in a marriage of political convenience. For Weah, it was all about solidifying his base. He already had a strong hold on Montserrado County, now he needed a jolt to take him over the top. In 2005, he had played it safe, picking J. Rudolph Johnson as his running mate. Johnson was a former foreign minister, serving from 1987-1990. He was the standard bearer of the Independent Democratic Party of Liberia (IDPL) but also had baggage as serving as foreign minister under the reign of the dictator Samuel Doe. Although Johnson hailed from another vote-rich county, Lofa, he lacked the stature and political weight to propel a candidate like Weah to the Presidency because he was not seen as a strong presence in the county.

Sensing that he was knocking on the doors of the Presidency, Weah was not about to make any mistakes. It was not about picking a more experienced candidate this time but rather, picking someone who could help secure the votes. So, despite her flaws, her not-so-pristine image or the substantial baggage which she carried, Weah knew it was worth the sacrifice to pick Jewel. It was a gamble worth taking, even at the expense of alienating the international community which was not so keen on embracing the wife of the former President blamed for the deaths of scores of Liberians in a senseless and bloody civil war.

Jewel was fully aware of the baggage she carried. As many questions reverberated in Jewel's mind, seemingly with no ready answers, she was full of hope and was determined to make sure she and George put their very best feet forward. "All we needed to do was put together a credible team of experts and influencers from all walks of life who would work closely with the both of us and consult together with the team on every issue and ensure a consensus on the way forward thus securing us a victory."[429]

At this point, Jewel recalls that she lifted her eyes and voice to the hills from whence her help came. "I asked God, my life giver, to grant us mercy, grace, provision and wisdom for victory."[430]

Victory came in emphatic fashion. Despite cries of foul play from the other political parties, George, Jewel and the Coalition for Democratic Change emerged the winners of the 2017 Presidential elections.

George Weah (CDC) and former Vice President Joseph Boakai (Unity Party) competed in a runoff on December 26, 2017 after neither candidate acquired a majority in the first round of the Presidential vote, ahead of the other contenders. The second round was originally scheduled for November 7, 2017, but was postponed after the Liberty Party standard-bearer Cllr. Charles Walker Brumskine, in third place, challenged the result in the Supreme Court. Had Charles Walker Brumskine's challenge to the first round result not been rejected by the Supreme Court a re-run would have been set in motion for the first round. But as it was, the second round on December 26 was held with George Weah emerging victorious with 60% of the vote.

George and Jewel were inaugurated on January 22, 2018. In the days that followed, Jewel's worst fears began to become a reality. While there were a lot of rumours in the air about strains between the pair, things quickly began to surface in the public eye when on April 2, 2018, South African anti-apartheid campaigner and former First Lady Winnie Madikizela-Mandela died, aged 81. Winnie and Nelson, both jailed during the apartheid era, were a symbol of the country's anti-apartheid struggle for three decades. With the funeral set for April 18, 2018, President George Weah dispatched a delegation to the funeral.

Although Winnie and Nelson were divorced, Liberia played a major role in the struggle to end apartheid, but Jewel was not amongst them.

On April 19, 1962, Nelson Mandela paid a visit to Monrovia to garner support for the armed struggle. In an address to the Liberian Transitional

Assembly during a visit to Liberia on July 6, 1994, Archbishop Desmond Tutu spoke of Mandela's visit to Liberia and how Liberia made a generous donation to ANC's struggle against apartheid.

So, Winnie Mandela's funeral was an important one. Jewel, who had been promised a prominent role in George Weah's government, was told she would not make the trip to the funeral. Instead, President Weah was dispatching his wife, Clar Weah, along with Foreign Minister Gbezohngar Findley, even though the Vice President had expressed interest in making the trip.

Snubbing Jewel for the Winnie Mandela funeral triggered what would mark the beginning of many difficult moments for the Vice President. It soon became clear that President Weah and his aides began to see Jewel as a threat. Leaks from the Vice President's camp signalled distrust about her ambitions for the immediate future. In fact, months into the new regime, Jewel began quietly soliciting the help of some regional leaders in a bid to help soften the deep strains between her and President Weah.

Weah had said all the right things about Jewel during his quest for the Presidency. After all, he wanted the votes and he wanted Bong County but even he knew that Jewel had her own ambitions. So did those in his inner circle who reminded him daily about Jewel's interests in the Presidency someday. Those thoughts scared Weah and created a rift between him and his Vice President.

Things became so bad that Weah began taking issue with everything Jewel did, like the time she decided to make a trip outside Liberia without informing President Weah. In fact, many Liberians were baffled that the Vice President chose a private radio station to go public with her apology in the aftermath of the controversy, and not the state radio, the *Liberia Broadcasting System*, where she apologised for traveling without the knowledge of President Weah. In pleading for compassion and forgiveness, the Vice President pledged never to run amok against the President. For the Vice President, traveling without the President's knowledge contributed to an already fragile relationship between the pair while expressing that the situation had been "amicably resolved."

While calling for compassion and apologising for her error, the Vice President went to great length to justify why it was necessary for her to travel, citing the vacuum created with the departure of former President Ellen Johnson Sirleaf, and her personal quest to become the face of women on the African continent. "I would, therefore, have to make representations on the women's behalf."[431] Nevertheless, the Vice President pledged to be obedient and law-abiding, hoping that President Weah could forgive her for the misstep.

Suddenly, reality was sinking in for Jewel. At the height of the 2017 Presidential race, Jewel had boasted that unlike her predecessor, former Vice President Joseph Boakai, she would be a more robust Vice President, a small jab thrown at Boakai, who had declared during a debate ahead of the 2017 Presidential elections that during his time as Vice President under former President Sirleaf, he was an 'old race car' parked in the garage because he was never given any responsibility for anything substantial.

Jewel now realised what she was dealing with and what she had gotten herself into. Weah was a man full of insecurities. It was no secret that he had a vindictive persona and disliked anyone trying to downplay him or take him for a ride.

Now, Jewel was about to eat her own words. Like Boakai, she too was not an old car parked in the garage. In picking Jewel to be his Vice President, Weah had boasted that she would be given the wings to fly, that she would never be an old car parked in the garage. Jewel remembered that. She recalls, "The truth is that the statement was made by the then Ambassador George Weah on the campaign trail. I was subsequently asked about it and reiterated that I would not be a parked race car in a garage. I had no regrets then and have none now. Thankfully, I have been actively involved in many state activities, including women's empowerment initiatives. So, I am definitely not a race car parked in a garage. In fact, I am not parked at all. Though I may not be running up to my highest speed, but I am on the road and intend to continue to be so, by the special grace of God."[432]

Despite her sense of denial, Jewel felt betrayed and somehow haunted by those words. "Those who know me will say in a heartbeat, 'She is not a quitter.' As long as I have life and breath and opportunities to continue to be a change agent, I will remain so."[433]

In September 2017, Jewel had spoken of her expectations for the role she was ascending to. "The President and the Vice President are elected on one ticket, so they are like one. They should be discussing the vision, the plans and progress of their country, that's the first place of the influence of the Vice President."434

Jewel went on to say that, "The office of the Vice President plays a key role in the governing process of the country, asserting that the Vice President signs every document that leaves the National Legislature before the President's perusal. The Vice President is a member of the cabinet."435

Ironically, that became one of the first hurdles for the Vice President in the first few days of the new government. This position led to even more strains between President Weah and his Vice President. In fact, some aides to the President attempted to stop the Vice President from presiding over the Senate in a bid to limit her leverage. At one point, the Vice President was summoned by the President Pro-Tempore Albert Chie who attempted to suggest that the Vice President should not preside over the Senate.

It is uncertain how much knowledge Weah had about this unravelling between his Vice President and his surrogates. Did he sanction these overtures by people close to him against Jewel?

One thing was certain, Jewel had the constitution on her side. This was key when a few senators cited Article 51 of the Constitution in defence of Jewel. The law states, "The Vice-President shall be President of the Senate and preside over its deliberations without the right to vote, except in the case of a tie vote. He shall attend meetings of the cabinet and other governmental meetings and shall perform such functions as the President shall delegate or deem appropriate; provided that no powers specifically vested in the President by the provisions of this Constitution shall be delegated to the Vice-President."436

Surprisingly, the push against the Vice President presiding over the Senate was reportedly backed by Senator Varney Sherman (UP, Grand Cape Mount) and the Pro-Temp, Albert Chie.

At the end of the day, those fighting Jewel realised that constitutionally, the Vice President had the mandate.

Jewel also came under fire from members of her own party within the three-party coalition, who took her to task. They felt marginalised and excluded from jobs and accused Vice President of not prioritising jobs for partisans.

Jewel would acknowledge later that she was indeed going through a lot of challenges. "It has been a very challenging period for me. And the truth is that life comes with many experiences, both happy and sad. During my political career, I have had many challenges and many victories also; and so, I surmised that this new journey would be similar but that whatever came my way would only be stepping-stones for greater works. Looking back, I can say, without fear or favour that on the one hand, I have no regrets that amongst the many who participated in those elections, I was chosen and voted into office as the first female Vice President of my beloved Nation, Liberia, to serve and be a positive agent of change."[437]

Jewel says her election as Vice President broke another part of the glass ceiling for greater gender equality, even though it was clear that she was being marginalised. Weah had become President and really didn't care what Jewel thought. The votes had long been counted, the purpose of choosing her had been accomplished, he was President of the Republic of Liberia.

Despite making her best attempt to put on a straight face, Jewel says her one regret is that she had not been given the full opportunity to serve alongside the President as it should have been, and as intended by the framers of the Constitution. "Thus, being denied the space and fortitude to bring to the table as his able advisor, my many years of public and private sector experiences, my educational expertise and my sphere of influence as an able and capable partner for the benefit of our government's vision for the people."[438]

Amid the challenges, Jewel recalls that she was determined to do what good she could in her sphere of influence.

For Jewel, being left out of the governance process at the Presidency/Executive Branch in Liberia, has been troubling. "The role ascribed to the functions of the Vice President have been ignored and set aside. Thus, denying me of having the full range of opportunities to be an advisor and helpmate to our President in particular and help make my nation better in general."[439]

Despite being in a coalition with George Weah's CDC, Jewel says many were feeling betrayed. "The National Patriotic Party is a de facto member of the Coalition, without much input in the Governance process. The majority members of the NPP feel betrayed and left out of the process they brought to life, with no hint of any benefits which accrue to them. The agreement between the parties expires in October 2022 but all options remain on the table as to the way forward. The NEC of the Party along with party stalwarts will make the final decision as to the way forward taking into consideration the collaborative spirit in the Coalition and the prevailing socio-economic conditions of the Liberian people. It would thus be unfair [of] me to place my opinion, especially as a single individual, as the central point for discussions on the future for the decision to be taken affects the lives of many others."[440]

Jewel's lingering battles have always centred on distrust from close associates of President Weah. "It seems as if I have become an 'expendable asset'. And I have to draw my answer from the perspective of the campaign – and I knew that I was a key figure in all of us. Whether it was deciding how many T-shirts you bought, or the fact that the Liberty Party had bought a hundred vehicles and we didn't have any and people were agitated, 'we need you now, we need vehicles, we need motorbikes.' And I don't remember any issue being discussed that my opinion wasn't sought. So, I think during the campaign, there was a level of respect that I received from everyone, especially the young partisans. But we get into governance and there's a lot going on. The camaraderie that we enjoyed during the campaign seemed to have dissipated. And people begin to get involved with their own work at different levels. And so, we meet but there was now more rivalry."[441]

Nevertheless, Jewel says, she believes that the inner wrangling and power struggles around the Presidency were cause for the lingering uneasiness between herself and the President, a situation which made others believe that her position as an elected Vice President could be treated with disdain and disrespect.

That disrespect came in many forms for Jewel, including denying her office the funds it needed to operate.

As the former wife of a former President lingering in a London prison for war crimes committed in Sierra Leone, Jewel is reminded every other day about the stigma her name carries. "Yes, the Taylor name still carries some stigma, but it is my responsibility, in spite of the challenges, to continue to leave positive lasting legacies, which I hope will diminish whatever stigma this name carries. All of us have names. We each have names, connections, history, legacies, whether positive or negative, from both sides of our family – what is from your mother's side or from your father's side? And you will find out that in African societies, if you show up and they say what is your name? And you said my name is Jewel Howard Taylor, then other things come up. Or is this a Taylor that did this or did that – and is it the Taylor who did this or did that? So, those names carry a lot."[442]

As a candidate running for President, Weah had said all the right things about Jewel even coming to her defence whenever rumours about her last name appeared to hurt his chances of winning. He told journalists covering one of the campaign stops in October 2017, "She's my colleague in the Senate. She's a hardworking woman. Now, she's a former wife of Charles Taylor. She is a Liberian, capable, qualified, and Liberian people love her. I also believe in gender equality, so I think having a woman as my Vice President is a good thing."[443]

It was a Jekyll and Hyde transformation of sorts, from Weah the candidate to Weah the President. As President, Weah transformed into something else when it came to his relationship with Jewel, so much so that in December 2018, the Liberia National Rural Women (LNRW) with membership throughout the fifteen counties made an intervention and called on President Weah and the Vice President to settle their "in-house political differences and move on with the country's development agenda."[444]

Ms. Kebbeh Mongar, LNRW National President, said reports in the media concerning a rift between the President and his Vice President was not a good sign for a developing country like Liberia. "I just want to tell our President and the Vice President that if there is a problem between them, it will be important to sit on a roundtable to find common ground, instead of them being in the media. We want peace among our officials, because if we (women) hear that confusion exists among our leaders, it brings fear to us."[445]

Amid the noise of division between the President and his Vice President, it took three years into the administration for the two to be seen publicly together, an acknowledgement of a rift that seemed detrimental to the ruling party's quest to maintain power in the 2023 Presidential elections.

In June 2021, while on a 'thank you' tour of Bong County, the pair appeared united. Weah in particular played down the beef between himself and his Vice President. "In 2017," he said, "Jewel Howard-Taylor and I came here in Salayea District to ask for your vote, and you voted us. Three years into our first term, we have come back to tell you thank you for your votes. The team you elected is a very good one and I hope we will continue to work for the Liberian people beyond the first six-year mandate you people gave us. I have a Vice President whom I rely on so much in this government for key decisions."[446]

A key reason for the strains between Weah and his Vice President had been concerns that Jewel was more educated, more intelligent and could easily take charge of a room with her eloquence, a contrast to Weah who was a total opposite. It was something President Weah acknowledged when he told the crowd in Salayea District, "People say Vice President Jewel Howard-Taylor is smarter than me, but I say to myself, I am smart because I selected a very smart Vice President in Jewel Howard-Taylor. I am enjoying working with my Vice President, and I hope we can continue this working relationship beyond our six-year mandate." [447]

The show of unity in Salayea came amid rumours of the President planning to split with his Vice President and look for a new running mate for the 2023 elections.

Several close aides to Weah, including Monrovia City Mayor Jefferson Koijee, brushed off the speculation and described Howard-Taylor as a "political asset" to the ruling party.[448]

Asset is a necessity in politics. For Weah, Jewel has always been his reluctant but necessary asset: his key to the Presidency. The marriage of political convenience was a means to a political end and one from all indications that Weah has proven time and time again, he was willing to live and die by – even it meant defying the norms of political convention and international rebuke.

17

INAUGURATION

———

January 2018

Long before Ellen Johnson Sirleaf's final days as President, she was often bombarded with questions about her life after the Presidency. "I always told people that when my Presidency is over, I wanted to feel normal again."[449] Her definition of 'normal' was driving herself in a black Toyota Land Cruiser to the ceremony marking the transfer of power to Weah on January 22, 2018.

Until that day, Liberia had not had a peaceful, successful democratic transfer of power from one government to the next in decades. The last time it happened was in 1944 after the 1943 elections, which brought Liberia's longest serving head of state, William V.S. Tubman, to power. The election was held in May 1943 along with a constitutional referendum. Tubman ran unopposed. He was preceded by President Edwin James Barclay, a politician, poet and musician who was President from 1930 until 1944. Barclay's support for Tubman in the 1943 Presidential election was borne out of the miscalculation that Tubman would be a one-term President – a deal that would feature the re-emergence of Barclay, which ostensibly never happened.

The transition was important for a country which had been dominated by a one-party rule for decades. The True Whig Party controlled the political governance with Barclay's reign propelling Liberia as a strong ally of the United States during World War II.

Barclay's paternal grandparents had emigrated with their children in 1865 to Liberia from Barbados. Not so many immigrants to Liberia were from the Caribbean yet the foundation of the English language heritage and mixed race ancestry would have ensured the Barclays had an affinity with the American-Liberian elite. Edwin's father, Ernest Barclay and his uncle, Arthur Barclay, became important politicians in Liberia.

Barclay become President of Liberia in 1930 after a secretary of state role from 1920–1930 under President Charles D.B. King and Vice President Allen Yancy who were both forced to resign owing to the Fernando Po crisis, which culminated in exporting Liberian slave labour to a Spanish island on the west coast of Africa.

Barclay was selected to complete King's term as President. He was elected in his own right for the first time in 1931.

In December 1942, Liberia had to elect a successor to President Barclay. Six candidates ran for the Presidency to succeed Barclay in December 1942, with the frontrunners Foreign Minister Clarence L. Simpson and Tubman. It was Tubman, age 48, who via election who claimed the Presidency on May 4, 1943, being inaugurated on January 3, 1944. The policies of the Economic Open Door and National Unification defined his Presidency historically, within a period of high foreign investment and strong economic growth. Tubman endeavoured to balance the interests of American-Liberians and indigenous populations as the 1950s saw unprecedented growth for Liberia, the second highest in the world. Tubman died in 1971 at a clinic in London after a prostate operation by which time Liberia boasted the largest rubber industry in the world and a sizeable merchant shipping fleet. Under his Presidency, Liberia had attracted both substantial foreign investment (said to be already US$1 billion by that point) and was exporting iron ore with some success. William R. Tolbert, Vice President from 1952–1971 succeeded but Tubman's authoritarian form of rule had begun to attract opposition and there were calls for prosperity to be more widely shared. At last, in 1980, the long reign of the True Whig Party was shattered when the People's Redemption Council led by Master Sergeant Kanyon Doe, staged a violent coup. The ensuing civil wars and violence spanning over 14 years, destroyed the economic prosperity of Liberia's golden age.

With Sirleaf bracing herself to step aside after serving two terms in office, Liberia was poised in 2018 to witness, for the first time since 1944, a democratic transfer of power from one civilian government to another. Sirleaf's electoral victory was historic when she became the first female President in any African country in 2005. She served two six-year terms – the maximum – and pledged to step down once the new leader was elected; a promise she kept.

Now, Weah intractably assumed command of political authority against insurmountable odds.

His critics and opponents had made fun of his lack of formal education, a handicap which was a key reason why he lost the elections in 2005 to the Harvard-trained and more experienced Ellen Johnson Sirleaf. It also played a major role in Weah's decision to play second fiddle, six years later, as running mate to Ambassador Winston Tubman in the 2011 general and Presidential elections.

Weah outsmarted many of his political opponents, forming what was seen as an unpopular alliance with Charles Taylor's National Patriotic Party (NPP), and Alex Tyler's People's Democratic Party of Liberia (PDPL). Nathaniel Barnes' Liberia Destiny Party later joined the alliance.

Many political observers at the time said if Weah and the CDC had not abandoned the Ganta Resolution, he would not have been able to form a coalition with NPP and the LPDP and could have very well been entangled in a similar predicament that was plaguing members of the Collaborating Parties that includes LP, ANC, ALP and UP.

At the time, Mr. Weah came under a lot of scrutiny for embracing the political arm of former President Charles Taylor. In hindsight, however, the move paid off and proved Weah to be a political genius as the former World Footballer of the Year now fully became entrenched in politics.

Weah's decision to pick the former First Lady appeared to be a major decider. He had defied the critics who said it was a bad idea, but he knew the votes from Bong County would come in handy and they did. Jewel had delivered.

The truth of the matter is that Weah and the CDC's decision to form an alliance with the NPP and the LPDP was not only greeted with mixed reviews but also thwarted the efforts resulting from what became known as the Ganta Resolution.

Many of the key figures behind-the-scenes of those discussions at the time said Weah felt some degree of disrespect amid dissenting egos incapable of striking a deal or coming up with a clear-cut conclusion, settling in the end, for a vaguely worded statement agreeing not to attack or castigate each other.

Things were so heated during the discussions that the Ganta Resolution was forced to caution signatories to the pact, concluding, "Opposition political parties that are signatories to this declaration hereby make a seldom pledge not to castigate or denigrate each other in any manner and form. In the event of disagreement among or between political parties the matter shall be referred to the joint technical committee for resolution."[450]

What made the Weah arrangement with the LPDP and the NPP work, was simple.

Weah had insisted on – and gained – agreement from the other two parties that he must head the ticket under the new formation, now branded the Coalition for Democratic Change. The NPP and LPDP obliged on grounds that Weah had the numbers.

With that out of the way, it was a foregone conclusion that former First Lady, and influential Senator from vote-rich Bong County, Jewel Howard Taylor, would serve as running mate to Weah, edging out LDP leader Barnes and embattled former Speaker Alex Tyler.

The new bloc had, thus, satisfied Weah and the CDC's long-held view that its political leader must head any ticket. Mr. Nathaniel McGill, Chair of the CDC at the time had been adamant that the CDC would not go second to another party.

Ironically, Weah threw pointed jabs at the other politicians who he believed had been unable to form an alliance, going so far as to slam Senator Johnson who, he said, abandoned the opposition in the second round of the 2011 Presidential race. "We all say the same thing but in different tones. We have been in this for more than 10 years, speaking of the ills in society and the reason why it continues is because we refused to come together [due to] our self-ego and personal aggrandisement. If we have the interest of the Liberian people, why are we all running? I believe in teamwork, and I think with a better team, one idea and one vision, we can liberate our people."[451]

Now, it was time to get down to business. Inauguration day was here.

The President-elect, George Weah was on the verge of inheriting one of the countries hit hard by the deadly Ebola virus pandemic. The country was still recovering from the shocks of the health crisis that took thousands of lives and devastated the economy when the COVID-19 pandemic started.

Despite its abundant natural wealth and favourable geographic location, Liberia still ranks among the world's poorest countries. In 2016, for example, just two years before Weah would ascend to the Presidency, more than 2.2 million Liberians were unable to meet their basic food needs, according to the World Bank. "Of which almost 1.5 million (68%) resided in rural areas, 1.6 million were below the food-poverty line, and 670,000 lived in extreme poverty. Regional and urban-rural disparities in poverty rates widened in the wake of the Ebola crisis and the collapse of global commodity prices."[452]

Despite the country being rich in natural resources, which include iron ore, diamonds, gold, fertile soil, fishery, and forestry, the economic potential of these assets remains largely untapped.

Moments before delivering his inaugural address, Weah appeared humbled and thankful for the trust and hope Liberians had placed in him as he delivered his inaugural address.

Ironically, his inauguration took place at the very stadium in which he had scored so many goals as a footballer for both his team, Invincible XI, and the national team, the Lone Star.

Weah said, "I have spent many years of my life in stadiums, but today is a feeling like no other. I am overwhelmed with the crowd and the energy here today, and I guarantee you, when we finish, there will not be a winning or a losing side. Today, we all wear the jersey of Liberia, and the victory belongs to the people, to peace, and to democracy."[453]

Weah's message, interrupted by cheers and applause, spoke to the hearts and minds of tens of thousands of Liberians, glued to their televisions and radio sets in communities across the country. "It is to you; we are responsible to deliver the change you deserve. Indeed, we must deliver the change that our people need, in order to transform their lives for the better. I promise to do everything in my power to be the agent of positive change. But I cannot do it alone. First, I call upon the revered institution that host us today and from which the Vice President and I come– the Legislative – our co-equal branch of government, to work with me to create and pass essential laws that are needed to complete the foundation of this nation."[454]

Weah spoke with passion as he pledged to unite the country and deal with some of the fundamental issues such as freedom of speech, and how national resources and responsibilities are going to shift from the nation's capital to the counties. "The people expect better cooperation and more action from their government. We can do better, together. Today, we Liberians have reached an important milestone in the never-ending journey for freedom, justice, and democracy; a search that has remained central to our history as a nation. Many of those who founded this country left the pain and shame of slavery to establish a society where all would be free and equal. But that vision of freedom, equality, and democracy is far from being fully realised."[455]

Paying homage to his predecessor, Ellen Johnson Sirleaf, President Weah hailed the departing President for laying the foundation upon which his government could stand and grow.

For Weah, the inaugural ceremony signalled more than a peaceful transition from one democratic administration to another. "It is also a transition from one generation of Liberian leadership to a new generation. It is indeed a confirmation that democracy exists in Liberia, and that, it is here to stay! We have arrived at this transition neither by violence, nor by force of arms. Not a single life was lost in the process. Blood should never be the price tag for democracy. Rather, this transition was achieved by the free and democratic will of the Liberian people, guaranteed by the rule of law. This inaugural gathering also celebrates an important precedent: that we Liberians can, and will, rely on established institutions and the rule of law to resolve our political disagreements. This demonstrates the maturity of our institutions and that we as a people have learned valuable lessons from our brutal history."[456]

Realising the grave divide which has defined Liberia for more than a hundred years, Weah pledged that during his tenure as President, the loudest battle-cry would be for unity. "We should all strive to put aside our differences and join hands in the task of nation building. We must learn how to celebrate our diversity without drawing lines of divisions in our new Liberia. We belong to Liberia first before we belong to our inherited tribes or chosen counties. We must not allow political loyalties to prevent us from collaborating in the national interest. We must respect each other and act as neighbours, regardless of religious, social and economic differences."[457]

For a man often criticised for not being a great speaker, Weah's delivery although not perfect spoke to his base. Even he was quick to acknowledge his lapses when he declared, "My greatest contribution to this country as President may not lie in the eloquence of my speeches, but will definitely lie in the quality of the decisions that I will make over the next six years to advance the lives of poor Liberians."[458]

Weah was ascending to power at a time when many Liberians had become fed up with the departing Sirleaf's government failure to tackle corruption. To that end, Weah asserted that the most effective way to directly impact the poor, and to narrow the gap between rich and poor, was to ensure that public resources did not end up in the pockets of Government officials. "I further believe that the overwhelming mandate I received from the Liberian people is a mandate to end corruption in public service. I promise to deliver on this mandate. As officials of Government, it is time to put the interest of our people above our own selfish interests. It is time to be honest with our people. Though corruption is a habit amongst our people, we must end it. We must pay civil servants a living wage, so that corruption is not an excuse for taking what is not theirs. Those who do not refrain from enriching themselves at the expense of the people – the law will take its course. I say today that you will be prosecuted to the full extent of the law."[459]

Like his predecessor, President Weah offered hope to the country's private sector, declaring Liberia as open for business. "We want to be known as a business-friendly government. We will do all that is within our power to provide an environment that will be conducive for the conduct of honest and transparent business. We will remove unnecessary regulatory constraints that tend to impede the establishment and operation of business in a profitable and predictable manner. As we open our doors to all foreign direct investments, we will not permit Liberian-owned businesses to be marginalised. We cannot remain spectators in our own economy. My government will prioritise the interests of Liberian-owned businesses and offer programs to help them become more competitive and offer services that international investors seek as partners."[460]

The fanfare of the elections was over and like most of his peers in the sub-region, President George Weah was about to put his promise of unity, change and transformation to the test. Like President Muhammadu Buhari in neighbouring Nigeria, Weah ascended into the Presidency with the weight of history on his side. He was the first opposition figure to win an election in post-war Liberia. On a continent where beating an incumbent government is a daunting challenge, Weah achieved a feat no one had imagined.

In Nigeria, Buhari was the first opposition figure to win a Presidential election since independence in 1960 and like Weah he had pledged change. "I belong to everybody, and I belong to nobody,"[461] Buhari told cheering crowds at his inauguration in the capital, Abuja, as he vowed to tackle "head on" the issues of corruption and the insurgency from militant Islamist group Boko Haram.

For Weah, the rugged campaigning of the elections was over. It was time to get to work. In Africa, honeymoon periods are short-lived. The expectations are just so high when so many are yearning for so much. Like his predecessor, Ellen Johnson Sirleaf, the weight of an entire nation now rested on the shoulders of the President.

18

JUNE 7

———

H enry Costa was up by 4 a.m. on the morning of June 7, 2019, to say his prayers. It was a Friday and the perfect time for the much-anticipated protest against the George Weah-led government. Although the government was only in its second year, the reality was beginning to sink in that the honeymoon period was nearing its end.

In the view of many, the protest was a necessity. The administration had begun straying away too early with a number of scandals and controversies; press freedom, corruption, bad governance, gross disregard for human rights and a sense that Weah's Coalition for Democratic Change, which had run a campaign on the backs of the grassroots, was slowly losing its footing, and falling into familiar failures which governments before had to endure.

Henry was the leader of the Council of Patriots and hosted a popular morning show which was often critical of the government. But even he knew the repercussions of what was about to go down. "I prayed for the protest to be peaceful, to be successful in attendance and for nothing to happen to the people. Then, I went to the radio station and did the show that morning and afterwards, some of the people came to my station, and they escorted me, and we walked to the protest ground."[462]

As the crowd assembled, Henry was aware of the striking historical references regarding protests and Liberia. "There was a sense of trepidation,

I was afraid that something might happen, and I did not want it to stain my future. People kept telling me if anything happen, it will be like Baccus Matthews, that thing haunted them for the rest of their lives. So, that was always hovering over my head, in the back of my mind. So, when it all passed off peacefully without anyone getting hurt, I was so happy."[463]

The fact that the day came and went without any violence was a huge relief for Henry and the organisers of the protest.

In September 2018, just nine months into the Weah administration, the nation was rocked by reports that sixteen billion Liberian dollars (US$100 million) had gone missing from the Central Bank of Liberia. This would become a big story as explained later in this chapter.

Contrasting dramatically with the jubilation of supporters on Weah's 2017's election victory, scores of demonstrators carrying signs called Weah a "traitor" and his government corrupt. They gathered before the President's office to state their case.

The last time Liberians assembled in such numbers was on April 14, 1979, when the then Minister of Agriculture, Florence Chenoweth, proposed an increase in the subsidised price of rice from $22 per 100-pound bag to $26. Chenoweth asserted at the time that the increase would "serve as an added inducement for rice farmers to stay on the land and produce rice as both a subsistence crop and a cash crop, instead of abandoning their farms for jobs in the cities or on the rubber plantations".[464] Critics lambasted the proposal as self-aggrandisement, pointing out that Chenoweth and the family of President William R. Tolbert operated large rice farms and would therefore realise a tidy profit from the proposed price increase.

The Progressive Alliance of Liberia called for a peaceful demonstration in Monrovia to protest the proposed price increase. On April 14, 1979, about 2,000 activists began what was planned as a peaceful march on the Executive Mansion. The protest march swelled dramatically when the protesters were joined en route by more than 10,000 "back street boys," causing the march to quickly degenerate into a disorderly mob of riot and destruction.

Widespread looting of retail stores and rice warehouses ensued with damage to private property estimated to have exceeded $40 million. The government called in troops to reinforce police units in the capital who were overwhelmed by the sheer numbers of the rioters. In 12 hours of violence in the city's streets, at least 40 civilians were killed, and more than 500 were injured. Hundreds more were arrested.

Such were the times, and such were the fears of the current realities facing the June 7 organisers. Not only was the pressure on Henry and the organisers, but pressure was also mounting on President Weah and his government. Although the riots of 1979 and the protest of 2019 were 40 years apart, the Weah administration was quite aware of the implications. After the riots of 1979, President Tolbert's credibility was severely damaged. The following year, in January 1980, Tolbert permitted the Progressive Alliance of Liberia to become officially registered as the Progressive People's Party. Three months later, Tolbert was assassinated, and his government overthrown on April 12, 1980, in a military coup led by Master Sergeant Samuel Kanyon Doe, almost a year to the day after the 1979 rice riots.

However, the June 7 demonstration was more than just a protest. Organisers hoped that by rallying thousands in the streets, the Weah administration would take notice and address some of the pressing concerns in the country.

Among the victims of the early days of Weah's reign was Patrick Honnah, a popular talk show host who had his radio station licence revoked shortly after the Weah administration was inaugurated into office. A year before the protest, the Weah government announced the suspension of the licence on June 18, 2018. Just at this point the government said the decision related to the need to review standards and governance was because of technical and other anomalies. Such discrepancies included frequencies allocated twice to television and radio operations and such issues. As the review process commenced on June 20, 2018 – according to a government communication – relevant organisations involved were requested to submit themselves for participation in the reviewing process. While several other stations were licenced, Patrick and his station Punch FM never received the go-ahead to operate.

"I think it is unfortunate that President Weah, who had been a peace ambassador and a UNICEF Ambassador, would allow his government's name to be tainted on issues regarding the trampling for rights and speech,"[465] Patrick said at the time his licence was revoked.

Even Jonathan Paylayleh, a local correspondent for the BBC, had a stake in the protest. On March 22, 2018, his experience with President Weah came exactly two months into Weah's Presidency.

"It was quite unfortunate, to say the least," Paylayleh recalls. "I was speechless, finding it difficult to understand why he chose to attack and bully me so publicly."[466]

Weah had preached tolerance and unity but it was clear from the very beginning of his Presidency that he did not fancy facing the press and one of his first victims was Paylayleh.

Like his predecessors, Barclay, Tubman, Tolbert, Doe, Taylor and even Sirleaf, Weah soon found himself entangled in some of the very lapses that led those before him astray. In the months after his inauguration, echoes of bad governance and corruption began to fill the air. The June 7 protest chronicled a litany of issues dogging Liberians and many began to wonder who was really running Liberia.

It all started during a news conference in March 2018 when Paylayleh was accused by the President of undermining him during the height of the civil war when the President was advocating for peace and disarmament.

The accusations resurrected familiar refrains from the President's critics that he held grudges for long spells against anyone who crossed his path. Paylayleh had asked the President a question about the establishment of a war crimes court in Liberia during the visit of U.N. deputy Secretary-General Amina Mohammed.

The President had just returned from a visit to France and threw a jab directly aimed at the BBC correspondent, as he called for the evaluation of what he called "fake news" being disseminated in the international community.

The President, without naming names, insinuated that some journalists were sending hate messages that could destroy the nation. He emphasised the need to filter and counteract fake news which, he said at the time, was counterproductive to the development of the nation.

Days later, Minister of Information, Cultural Affairs and Tourism (MICAT), Lenn Eugene Nagbe, accused the BBC correspondent of being a member of the propaganda machinery of the National Patriotic Front of Liberia (NPFL) of former President Charles Taylor.

As the Paylayleh saga generated international attention, President Weah back-pedalled on his talk, telling journalists a month later that he had nothing personal against Paylayleh. The President went on to say that his response to the BBC correspondent was inversely proportional to his critical question posed to him during the media stakeout in the presence of the visiting UN Under-Secretary.

Weah had assumed command of the state with a lot of expectations both among his generation of young, desperate and disadvantaged supporters and international players who saw his coming to power as a new beginning. Unlike several other politicians, Weah was and still is presumed to have stayed clear of the brutal Liberian civil war, and so upon taking office, international advocacy groups, including Human Rights Watch, were keen to see how the former football star was going to handle the issue of unresolved impunity associated with the running of the affairs of Liberia over the years.

Paylayleh was aware that Human Rights Watch expressed the hope that President Weah was going to prioritise the setting up of a court to look into Liberia's immediate ugly past. And so, when the United Nations Deputy Secretary General, Amina Mohammed, held talks with President Weah that day – and the two were taking questions from reporters at a press stakeout – Jonathan simply wanted to know from the guest, if the United Nations was going to assist Liberia in setting up a war crimes court like it did for Sierra Leone.

"President Weah's portion of that question was simple. I tried to seek his response further to calls by groups like Human Rights Watch to prioritise the setting up of the court. It was while responding to this question that Mr. Weah became furious and branded me as one person who was against him when, he claimed, he was working for human rights and peace during the years of conflict."[467]

Paylayleh's persistent attempt at seeking clarity from the President triggered fears for his life, partly due to Weah's supporters who could either misunderstand and misinterpret such an assertion and get him into trouble.

Sam Mannah, who was the President's Press Secretary, and Representative Acarous Moses Gray, were some of the associates of Weah who elevated the attacks on Jonathan and created a situation that presented the BBC correspondent as someone who was truly against the young government and its leadership. "They accused me of all sorts of things including being a supporter of ex-President Charles Taylor. Their sustained attacks on me put my life at risk."[468]

Paylayleh never really recovered after that. He says the fear still exists. "People, including some of those working in the Weah government, advised me to stay away from Liberia because of the level of dislike that the President had developed for me."[469] Out of fear, Paylayleh left the country for a breather and to reassess his life and his work under such extreme pressure.

Paylayleh was back home after three weeks. "I returned home because I have always decided to live here at home. I didn't leave when there were calls for me to do so when I covered the war in Liberia and rebel fighters were openly declaring they would kill me if and when they entered Monrovia. So, I didn't feel the Weah attack should run me out of Liberia. This is why you still see me in Liberia."[470]

The truth is, since the situation with President Weah and because of the possibility that anything he reported or said could be misunderstood and misinterpreted, Jonathan has been very careful in reporting on issues in Liberia and in his government, fearing this could cause more problems for him. "We promoted Mr. Weah a lot when he was an international soccer star. We followed him, we were all excited that a Liberian was raising the flag of our country as the country descended into a civil war. I was one of the first persons, if not the first, to report about his intention for the Presidency when he had indicated that to me. He was open to me at the time, allowing me into his home whenever I sought an interview."[471]

When Weah's Congress for Democratic Change felt cheated in the first post-war elections of 2005, Jonathan was one of the few journalists taking interest in reporting their concerns. "I was not liked by people in the new government of Ellen Johnson Sirleaf because of that. There are so many things I did for Mr. Weah both as an international footballer and as a political leader before he became President."[472]

For Paylayleh, the payback came in the form of the alarming situation in which he now found himself. "I didn't expect that he was going to hate me so much. His office does not invite me to any Presidential events. Some security personnel and loyalists around him have proven they don't want to see me at his events. But I always wished Mr. Weah the best and am hoping to look for an opportunity in the future – maybe after he has left the Presidency – to really ask him to name the wrongs for which he has chosen to target me in this unwarranted hate campaign. The intent will be to know my wrongs, talk about them and move on."[473]

For many journalists like Paylayleh, President Weah had become an exact replica of the iron-fisted rulers of the past, who wreaked havoc on free speech and the free press.

The contradiction was evident. While cracking down on critical media, the Weah government was publicly repealing harsh media laws that saw journalists suffer excessive jail sentences and fines. Besides the attack on Paylayleh, the radio station *Roots FM* by Henry Costa (June 7 protest organiser), also endured attacks and was shut down. While listeners to the popular show saw the closure of *Roots FM* as another example of the government's lack of tolerance for opposition voices, the government said it shut the station down because *Roots FM* was broadcasting on frequencies that it didn't have a licence for. It also accused the station of inciting violence. "FM 102.7 was engaged in broadcasting specifically hate messages at peaceful Liberian citizens and other forms of extortion and blackmail,"[474] Solicitor General Sayma Syrenius Cephus told journalists.

Complicating matters for Weah, in 2018, the Press Union of Liberia (PUL) issued a stern warning, saying it was alarmed by the hostile anti-press sentiment. The PUL sent an open letter to the United Nations warning of the "pace at which official intolerance for independent journalism and dissent is escalating in Liberia."[475]

Ironically, President Weah had repeatedly talked of his support for free speech and free press. When he was sworn in as President in January 2018, Weah affirmed his commitment to freedom of expression, saying: "We could not have arrived at this day without our voices been heard loudly, and all our views, no matter how critical, being freely expressed in an atmosphere void of intimidation and arrest."[476]

For Patrick and Jonathan, June 7 presented a chance to form part of a historical journey aimed at alerting the Weah administration about what was unfolding before their very eyes. The protesters had a laundry list of demands and needed answers: the dwindling economy, in which many were lingering at the bottom of the economic ladder and of course, the sixteen billion in newly printed bank notes destined for the Central Bank of Liberia...

The banknotes were ordered before the Weah administration took office in 2018 although the administration faced criticisms that it handled the delivery of the money poorly. The House of Representatives, during the Presidency of former President Sirleaf had passed a resolution for the order of 5 billion Liberian dollars, from the company Crane AB, to remove and replace old banknotes on the market. The Central Bank requested additional 10 billion Liberian dollars, but the request was denied by the Senate. The bank went ahead anyway and engaged the company to print the additional banknotes. "CBL (Central Bank of Liberia) management subsequently explained to Kroll that due to the urgency for new banknotes, the CBL did not follow its own internal tendering policies for the procurement of Crane AB,"[477] the Kroll report – commissioned by USAID from Kroll Associates to investigate the case – concluded.

Under President Weah's predecessor, the Liberian economy suffered under the 2014-2016 Ebola flare-up responsible for thousands of fatalities, dwindling foreign aid and weak prices for exports notably rubber and iron ore. In March 2019, the International Monetary Fund revised down Liberia's economic growth forecast for the year. This fell by 4.3% nearly to zero from 4.7%; whereas in December inflation soared to a high of 28.5%; hugely impacting prices of routine foodstuffs and other items. For those lingering in abject poverty, Weah had been in their shoes. He grew up in the slums of the city, adopted football and became a world class striker. His election was expected to usher in a new era, but things didn't seem that way. Dogged by the same criticisms of corruption which haunted the Sirleaf administration, Weah's back was against the wall as protesters zeroed in and made their voices heard.

The protest organisers, the Council of Patriots, circulated a petition making accusations concerning government violation of press freedoms, failure to support education and health projects and the misallocation of public funds. President Weah was himself vehemently accused of constructing "scores of luxury homes" after failing to declare his assets or make them public.

The protest paid off.

Having received a request to the "international" community from Liberia's government and certain civil society groups, the U.S. Embassy (via USAID) commenced to commission an independent investigation from Kroll Associates Inc, a company known for their "expertise in forensic investigations."[478] Their brief as the statement published on the report's release said was, "to research matters stemming from allegations in the press that a container of new Liberian Dollar (LRD) banknotes had "gone missing" upon arrival in Liberia."[479] In February 2019, the report prepared by Kroll Associates Inc. was released.

To the surprise of many Liberians, the Kroll analysis, while confirming that new banknotes totalling LRD 15.506 billion were received into the CBL's reserve vaults, found no information to support allegations that a container of banknotes went missing. The report, however, did raise concerns regarding the overall accuracy and completeness of the CBL's internal records. The Report identified systemic and procedural weaknesses at the CBL and identified shortcomings in Liberia's fiscal and monetary management processes that were longstanding.

The report baffled a lot of Liberians, who, still to this day, do not believe that no money went missing. What made many even more angry were redacted portions of the report which Kroll and the USAID refused to make public. The USAID did however issue a word of caution that the report be read in its entirety and encourage pragmatic responses from the Government of Liberia and its people.

What followed after the Kroll's finding was chaos, confusion and a state of uncertainty regarding the redacted portion of the report, a wave of arrests and some mysterious deaths in the aftermath of the report's release.

A month after the report's release, Charles Sirleaf, the son of former President Ellen Johnson Sirleaf, was arrested in relation to the illegal printing of more than $104m (£78m) worth of local banknotes. Charles was deputy governor of the Central Bank at the time of the incident in March 2018. Milton Weeks, the bank's governor, was also picked up in connection with the money saga, although the USAID-sponsored report had said no money went missing. Kroll explained that, despite repeated requests, the bank did not provide any explanation as to who had approved the injection of new banknotes into the Liberian economy without first removing the equivalent quantity from circulation.

Separately, the Weah administration released its own report, days after the Kroll's report and it too said it found no evidence of the existence of containers full of banknotes. It said that an investigation needed to be carried out into a separate US$25 million that was withdrawn from Liberia's Federal Reserve account in New York in July that year by Mr. Weah's economic management team.

The mop-up exercise saga dealt another blow to the Weah administration.

The Liberian Auditor-General's Report of Factual Findings of the application of $US25 million concluded that at least 15 entities received US$491,697 but denied that they participated in the exercise.[480] Another 27 entities received nearly US$703,000 but were not registered with Liberia's Business Registry. Additionally, the report noted that 52 entities received nearly US$1.1 million but refused to respond to calls and text messages from auditors to confirm receipt of the money. 8 entities recorded in the CBL records as receiving over US$163,000 were not in operation when the auditors visited them.

The report noted, "The money issued from the vault daily and disbursed to beneficiaries from the bank's United States Dollars operational vault was not posted to the bank's accounting system in real time. For example, money taken from the vault between the periods July 17–31, 2018 was not posted to the vault until August 1, 2018, in lump sum. The lump sum amounts posted were without supporting schedules…"[481]

The General Auditing Commission (GAC) in its factual findings further said it "…was informed by the CBL that there is no amount classified as mopped up cash currently sitting in a separate vault as was the case during the period of the mop-up exercise. The Assistant Director for Banking Operations confirmed on April 24, 2019, that the total amount mopped up was subsequently re-infused into the economy to service CBL customers' demands during and after the Christmas Season…"[482]

Amid the controversy surrounding the release of the two reports, things were about to heat up. In March 2019, Matthew J. Innis, Deputy Director for Micro-Finance in the Regulation and Supervision Department at the

Central Bank of Liberia (CBL), was found dead along the 72nd Boulevard on the outskirts of the Liberian capital, Monrovia. Matthew had left his home on the morning of Saturday, March 2, 2019, telling his daughter and other family members that he was going to work, which was not a regular Saturday routine for him. When the family didn't hear from him for nearly the whole day, they tried to reach him via his mobile phone but by 4 p.m., couldn't get hold of him and never heard from him again until they discovered that he was involved in an alleged hit-and-run accident at 2 a.m. Sunday in his neighbourhood around the 72nd Junction on the Somalia Drive.

"By 2 a.m., we only heard a group of young men banging on our gate saying that Matthew had been hit by a car and his body is on the road," an eyewitness told the *FrontPageAfrica* newspaper. "Before we got to the road, his body has been removed. We were told that the police had taken him to Stryker Funeral Home and the police was driving his car."[483]

In the days after Matthew's death, the family insisted that they suspected foul play; that he did not die of a "hit-and-run" accident. The Bethel Cathedral of Hope Church was in shock to learn that Matthew had died in such a violent manner, and wanted answers. "We call on all members of Bethel in Liberia, those around the world and all members of the Body of Christ to remain calm as we demand answers to our many questions," the church said in a statement on March 4, 2019. "We ask for a swift and speedy investigation by the Government of Liberia to enable us understand fully the situation surrounding Brother Innis' mysterious demise."[484]

Under the leadership of Bishop Dr. M Wolo Belleh, Diocesan Bishop, and with the approval of His Eminence Bishop Dr. Darlingston G. Johnson, Presiding Bishop of the Bethel World Outreach Ministries International, the church sought many answers to questions they felt they just could not figure out:

Who informed the police of the accident, and at what time?

1. *Who were the police officer(s) who were first responders to the accident scene?*

2. *How did the police get to the accident scene and why was Brother Matthew's car used to take him to the ELWA hospital, instead of an ambulance or some other emergency vehicle?*

3. *Is there a hand-over report or accident report at the local Depot in the 72nd area where the Police came from that catalogued the incident?*

4. *Why did the police not wait for member(s) of the family before removing Brother Innis' body from the hospital to the funeral home?*

5. *Are there any fracture(s) on the body?*

6. *Was Brother Innis alive when the police got on the "accident" scene?*

7. *Has the Liberia National Police (LNP) made any arrest of the driver that allegedly "hit" him or did anyone identify the vehicle that "hit" him? We were informed that the phone used by Brother Innis was returned to the family by the Liberia National Police and was positioned at factory mode —meaning, calls made and received by Brother Innis might have been deleted.*[485]

While the church was deliberating on what its next course of action would be, another death shocked the nation. Kollie Ballah was a driver of one of the trucks which drove some of the LD16 billion from the Freeport of Monrovia to the Central Bank. Like the Matthew saga, Kollie's family was unsure what to make of alleged report that he was killed instantly when his truck ran out of control while en route to Zorzor, Lofa County on Monday, February 11, 2019.

Relatives told newspapers that Kollie used to drive the truck that carries Central Bank money to the different destinations. He reportedly knew a lot and was ready to tell the truth before his death.

Like Matthew's case, this one remained cold.

One year after the deaths, it appears the court system itself was struggling to deal with the aftermath of the missing billions and the US$25 million mop-up money. In May 2020, former Deputy Governor of the Central Bank of Liberia, Charles Sirleaf, was relieved of all charges against him. His boss, former Executive Governor Milton Weeks was also set free, as were several other executives of the bank arrested in the aftermath of the saga that had the Weah-led government on edge for the most part of its first two years in office.

June 7 had come and gone, but the issues triggered much scrutiny on the many lapses in the Weah government. President Weah had been put on notice and already had his work, cut out for the challenges ahead.

19

PAYBACK

———

The 2017 Presidential elections that brought George Weah to power had come and gone. But for the football icon, there were still a few scores to settle.

In Africa, many rulers and leaders use power to their own advantage, most times to their own detriment. If a perceived enemy falls on the wrong side of the government of the day, they could be scorned for life; or at least for the duration of the time a sitting government stays in power – and President Weah was sure to pay back anyone who had crossed his path in the past.

The elections were marred by allegations of fraud and irregularities with four of the other political parties which contested raising qualms. The former ruling Unity Party and the Liberty Party all raised challenges.

While acknowledging that the first round of voting was, to some extent, characterised by fraud, irregularities, and disregard of the New Elections Law, the Supreme Court of Liberia said it had not been established that such malpractices were on a scale that warranted a rerun of the entire elections as requested by the Appellants (Liberty Party and Unity Party), which made the allegations.

Associate Justice Philip A. Z. Banks III, who read the ruling on behalf of the Bench, said, "that notwithstanding our findings that indeed there were some irregularities, fraud, and violations of the New Electoral Law, as well as Rules and Regulations of the NEC, we hold that there is no evidence to show that those violations were in such magnitude that they rose to such level to warrant setting aside the results of the Presidential and Representative Election held on October 10, 2017 and ordering a rerun."[486]

The ruling stemmed from the Bill of Exception filed by the opposition Liberty Party in conjunction with the governing ruling Unity Party after the NEC Board of Commissioners upheld the ruling of the NEC hearing officer that the two parties failed to prove allegations of fraud outlined in their complaint.

The Liberty Party, led by Cllr. Charles Walker Brumskine, who came third in the October 10, 2017, elections with less than 10% of the votes, took the lead in protesting the election results, claiming that it was marred by fraud and lacked the minimum requirement to be regarded as free, fair and transparent.

According to the Supreme Court, "Fraud may be established by not only directly but by inclusive circumstances which by their weight may constitute proof; from the facts and circumstances of the instant case, the 1st and 2nd appellant established by proof that fraudulent acts were perpetrated at a few polling centers during the Presidential and Representatives Elections conducted on 10 October 2017."[487]

However, in the mind of the Court, both the ruling Unity Party and opposition, which joined forces to prove that NEC orchestrated fraudulent acts during the October 10 elections, failed to show that the evidence of fraud pervaded the entire spectrum of the elections throughout, or in a considerably wide part, or in most parts, of the country. "We have not seen from the records that the appellants demonstrated that there was a conspiracy by the NEC as an institution, or that the NEC sanctioned the conduct of those persons who were alleged to have committed elections violations or irregularities. We do not believe that the evidence reached that threshold,"[488] Justice Banks asserted.

Weah, was on his own, having been on the verge of winning the Presidency which had eluded him for more than a decade. This time around, it was not Weah who was protesting election results, but those standing in the way of him and the Presidency, those claiming that the announced results were fixed to his advantage, partly because he had the support of the outgoing

President, Ellen Johnson Sirleaf who, at the time, was at odds with her Vice President, Joseph Boakai.

According to Justice Banks, as important as the evidence was, the fraud and irregularities complained of and shown by the testimonies and witnesses were limited to the generality of the elections rather than indications of widespread intentional gross conspiracy conduct by NEC as an institution.

Associate Justice Banks noted that despite proving that fraud occurred at a few polling places, this did not constitute reason enough for the Supreme Court to speculate that such irregularities, fraud, and disregard of electoral laws occurred in all parts of the country. On this note, the Supreme Court said it could not sanction a rerun as the evidence provided did not merit the annulment of the October 10th elections. According to Justice Banks, the Bench also took into consideration the consequences such a decision may have on the country. The Liberty Party's appeal for a rerun of the October 10th elections was thereby denied.

However, as precondition for the runoff election, the Supreme Court mandated and ordered the NEC to fully comply with the standards of publications of the Final Register Roll (FRR) as in keeping with law. The NEC had also been ordered to conduct a full clean-up of the FRR to have it comply with the provision of the law. It was also mandated that the FRR be available in published hard copies to all Election Magistrates and polling places across the country in accordance with law prior to the conduct of the runoff election. Contentiously, the NEC was also mandated not to allow anyone whose name was not in the FRR to vote during the runoff. It was noted that the FRR was the only electoral document which spoke to the eligibility of voters. "Poll watchers who did not register at their places of assignment and those whose names are not in the FRR should not be allowed to vote." The Chairman and members of the Board of Commissioners of the NEC and other staff of NEC were then prohibited by the Supreme Court from public utterances and pronouncements relating to any matter that may emanate from the runoff.

In the end, the former ruling Unity Party (UP), through its standard bearer Vice President Joseph Boakai, accepted the Supreme Court's final ruling on the runoff of the 2017 Presidential and Legislative Election and urged the National Elections Commission (NEC) to make public the Voters

Roll and address other irregularities to ensure a transparent runoff election. Former VP Boakai told a news conference that the Supreme Court was the highest court in the land and the final arbiter of the dispute, which had come down with its decision. He said, "We would therefore like to state without equivocation that the Unity Party accepts the ruling of the High Court. This decision, and the road we took with collaborating parties, are unprecedented and should give all of us hope that the future of our democracy and country is bright. Liberians can now celebrate the triumph of the rule of law! Liberians can now celebrate their resolve to pursue non-violent means of solving problems."[489]

On the contrary, Cllr. Charles Walker Brumskine of the opposition Liberty Party (LP), said he and his partisans were disappointed by the Supreme Court's ruling, which among other things, had violated "our equal protection right, as provided in Article 11(c) of the Constitution. The Court ordered the correction of some of the things that we complained of, that made the electoral process unconstitutional and unlawful that contributed to massive fraud, and pervasive irregularities, as conditions for holding the runoff, but failed to similarly ensure equal protection for the other eighteen political parties." He concluded, "Finally Liberians can disagree and not kill each other and destroy our country. I have always said, our legal action and pursuit of justice was not just about me, or just about the Liberty Party." He said the Supreme Court can rule against an aggrieved political party, and its judgment is accepted, notwithstanding "our disagreement, as to both the Court's determination of the facts and their conclusion of the law. Our people are truly witnessing the transition from negative to positive peace."[490]

Despite the objections to the High Court ruling, the Standard Bearer of the opposition Alternative National Congress (ANC), Alexander B. Cummings, said after all considerations, prayers, and consultations, the ANC had decided not to endorse any of the political parties for the runoff. "We are asking all partisans to vote [with] their conscience, and what they believe in their hearts to be right for the country given the two choices. This was not an easy decision, but one we believe serves the best interest of our party and the country."[491]

Also Benoni Urey, All-Liberian Party (ALP) political leader suggested that President Ellen Johnson Sirleaf had tampered with and influenced the results of the October 2017 poll. At Unity Party Headquarters on Thursday, December 7th just after the Supreme Court's ruling, Mr. Urey put the blame entirely on Sirleaf's shoulders.

"You know all the problems in Liberia is Ellen Johnson Sirleaf. She had promised more than one party that she would take them to second round."[492]

The silver lining of the court ruling was a dissenting voice. Associate Justice Kabineh Ja'neh disagreed with the rest of his peers on the bench, opining that some acts committed by the National Elections Commission (NEC) in the October 10, 2017 Presidential and legislative elections were "fraudulent and calculated to cheat."[493]

Weah held that in the back of his mind. He knew that Ja'neh was not in his corner when it mattered most. He also knew there would be hell to pay once he assumed the Presidency. Whatever Weah was about the embark on, whatever agenda he had on the table, it was clear at that point that Ja'neh would be a stumbling block. Ja'neh's professional roles included Liberian Minister of Justice and Attorney General (2003–2006) Republic of Liberia and Chairman of the Mano River Union Security Council. In 2004, Justice Ja'neh was awarded a certificate in Harmonisation of the International Penal Code in Beijing, China.

In 2006, he was nominated and subsequently appointed Associate Justice to the Honourable Supreme Court Bench of the Republic of Liberia. Prior to his legal sojourn, Ja'neh ruffled feathers during the civil war as a senior member of LURD (Liberians United for Reconciliation and Democracy). The Movement for Democracy in Liberia (MODEL), with LURD, both fought against the former President Charles Taylor who, a year before, had escaped to exile in Nigeria. These two organisations agreed a peace settlement with the Taylor government's remnants a week later.

Justice Ja'neh, the only one on the five-member Supreme Court bench to oppose the High Court ruling which dismissed massive fraud allegations and called for annulment of the results to conduct rerun elections on grounds that evidence was insufficient, stated, "I am further deeply troubled and perturbed over the majority decision of the bench. This direction leaves this nation with more questions than answers."[494]

Justice Ja'neh said he believed that there was enough evidence to show that the October 10 polls were conducted in violation of Liberian law and standards for credible election, thus the need to set aside the results. He pointed to what he considered to be contradictions in the majority opinion when they acknowledged that some fraud did occur and that NEC had a dirty voters roll.

According to the Associate Justice, the majority Justices seem to "ignore what the other side of the dirt is,"[495] wondering how the dirt impacted the valid votes cast in the recent Presidential and legislative elections. "It's deeply disconcerting to say the least" to talk about how the level of the violations would not have altered the results of the polls, suggesting it could be "pretence". The dissenting Supreme Court Justice went on to say that "fraud by law is proven when it vesicates everywhere."[496] Justice Ja'neh then took his colleagues on the bench to task for what he considered as downplaying a very crucial plaintiff witness testimony of U.S.-trained Liberian IT/data expert, Jeff Gblebo. He said Gblebo's testimony pointed extensively to some evidence of fraud in the October 10 polls, recounting how examination of the NEC's voters roll data given to political parties on a flash drive "demonstrated evidence to prove fraud."

Justice Ja'neh further argued that the data expert's analysis discovered two separate voter rolls and missing polling places amounting to some 35,000 registered voters. Gblebo's analysis, he said, discovered 58 pages of voters' registration numbering 200 voters where the same ID number had been assigned to multiple names. "I find it unfortunate how I've found it difficult to harmonise my legal opinion with that of my colleagues. But this (his opinion) should be filed and put on record for posterity to judge,"[497] Justice Ja'neh concluded his dissenting opinion.

Justice Ja'neh may have been the lone voice of reason on the High Court but his action to dissent was about to cost him.

Shortly after his inauguration, one of President Weah's first orders of business was to get back at Justice Ja'neh. The President and his aides had come to the conclusion that Ja'neh would be a problem if he stayed on the bench. Thus, the government began putting into play a motion for impeachment.

It all started in 2018 when two members of the House of Representatives and executive members of the Coalition for Democratic Change, Representatives Acarous Moses Gray and Thomas P. Fallah, filed an Amended

Petition before the Speaker of the House of Representatives, seeking to initiate impeachment proceedings against Justice Ja'neh. Ironically, House Speaker Bhofal Chambers also happened to be an executive member of the CDC. At the Supreme Court's October hearing it was noted that, "The petition submitted by the two lawmakers called on the Plenary of the House of Representatives to impeach his Honor Kabineh Mohammed Ja'neh for alleged misconduct, abuse of public office, wanton abuse of judicial discretion, fraud, misuse of power and corruption."[498]

The crux of the case against Justice Ja'neh was triggered by allegations regarding his role in a controversial US$27 million road fund and a land dispute involving the embattled Justice and a private citizen, Madam Annie Yancy Constance.

It was alleged by lawyers representing the House of Representatives that Justice Ja'neh issued a prohibition to stop businessmen Musa Bility of Srimex and Abdallah Sheriff of Conex returning, to Government coffers, the required surcharge levied on fuel and gasoline that was to be used for the road fund.

The total money amounted to US$27 million for the 2017/2018 budget year, an amount owed by the petroleum importers. Petroleum importers had agreed with the Liberian government the public would be charged 25 cents extra for every purchase to top up the road maintenance fund which they would pass on. The estimate of the money to be raised this way for 2017/2018 came in at US$31 million.

The money was an extra charge which reportedly had nothing to do with the profit or operational funds of the importers. Their duties were to simply remit the extra 25 cents on a gallon of fuel or gasoline to the Government to be used for road maintenance under the road fund. The petroleum importers included Srimex (Musa Bility), Connex (Abdallah Sheriff), Aminata & Sons (Siaka Touré), and Kailondo Petroleum (George Kailondo). Of the US$31 million owed to the road fund by the importers listed above, Srimex and Conex owed over US$11 million.

As *The New Dawn* reported, lawyers for the House of Representatives claimed "that after the two companies refused to turn over the collected revenue to the Government and, knowing that 'their business partner' Justice Ja'neh was the Chamber Justice at that time, Justice Ja'neh asked the companies to file a writ to the Supreme Court praying for a stay order against government request for a turnover of the revenue collected purposely for the road fund. According to the House of Representatives, the alleged action by Justice Ja'neh amounted to "abuse of power and gross breach of duty."[499] The lawyers further noted that Justice Ja'neh's action in issuing the writ of prohibition which stopped the Government from collecting the US$27 million of the road fund money deprived the state of much needed revenue. The House of Representatives alleged that Justice Ja'neh received kickbacks from his two friends who were his business partners and that he was getting more money from the deal since the importers had been unable to repay the Government despite stipulations for repayment that had been made.

On being quizzed about the road fund case, Justice Ja'neh fell silent but subsequently explained the whole Supreme Court Bench had determined the cancellation. The decision had not been down to him alone. Debate in the lower house of the national legislature was tense with lawmakers divided on the plan for impeachment. According to *The New Dawn,* Rep. Edwin Melvin Snowe of Bomi County, "accused Rep. Acarous Gray of attempting to intimidate the Judiciary Branch of Government with cheap impeachment proceedings."[500] Rep. Snowe, who appeared to be very annoyed by the action of his colleague, intimated that such a bill had no basis but only intended to scare Associate Justices from performing their statutory duties. The Bomi lawmaker went on to warn Rep. Gray to stop that form of intimidation or it would create a bad image of the Liberian Legislature. Rep. Snowe then expressed disappointment in Rep. Gray for bringing himself low, saying Justice Ja'neh had violated no law as claimed by Rep. Gray.

Rep. Snowe insisted that Rep. Gray's action was for the sole purpose of scaring members of the Judiciary and was senseless. Joining Snowe in voicing criticisms, Rep. Samuel Kogar from Nimba County who hailed from the same area as Justice Ja'neh, termed the impeachment action as "nonsense". According to Rep. Kogar, the impeachment plot had no weight to be placed on a draft agenda of the House. But despite the objections, Rep. Gray, the mastermind of the impeachment plot against Justice Ja'neh, pressed on, insisting that Justice Ja'neh violated laws of the land. He argued that the only penalty for allegedly violating the laws was to remove Justice Ja'neh from the bench to prevent him from contaminating other justices on the High Court. Rep. Gray added that there was nothing that would stop him and his colleagues from launching the impeachment proceedings against Justice Ja'neh – and he was right.

As *The New Dawn* noted, the Liberian Constitution (Article 71) mandates good behaviour when holding office for "the Chief Justice and Associates Justices of the Supreme Court and the judges of subordinate courts of record." However these officers it noted may be removed by impeachment or conviction if there is proven to be "misconduct, gross breach of duty, inability to perform the functions of their office, or conviction in a court of law for treason, bribery or other infamous crimes."[501] Ironically, Rep. Gray never really provided a clear reason as to why he wanted the Associate Justice impeached but it was clear within the corridors of power that the move had very little to do with any violation, but more to do with Ja'neh's dissenting opinion during the 2017 political season.

At the conclusion of the "trial", regulated by no rules of procedure as mandatorily required in impeachment proceedings under Chapter V, Article 43 of the Liberian Constitution (1986, as amended), the Liberian Senate tried and voted Ja'neh "guilty" of "collusion between the Respondent Associate Justice (Ja'neh), SRIMEX Corporation and CONNEX Corporation to deprive the Liberian Government of the surcharges collected from the public, which was and still is intended to be used as matching funds to the Millennium Challenge Compact's funding for construction of new roads and rehabilitation of old roads and that such deprivation would have resulted in millions of United States dollars going to these two (2) companies for their benefit and the benefit of Respondent Associate Justice; which if proved would clearly constitute 'official misconduct' and 'gross breach of duty.'"

For Ja'neh, the sole reason for which he was impeached was because of his 2017 dissenting opinion from that of his colleagues, who ruled that the reports of fraud during that year's elections were not egregious enough to require a re-count.

Ja'neh later explained that, prior to the impeachment proceeding, Senator Prince Y. Johnson visited him and asked him to accept a certain amount of money (not disclosed) and leave the Supreme Court's bench without an impeachment, but he declined on grounds that he could have never accounted for said amount, more so that he did not work for said money. "My own Senator from Nimba County, Prince Johnson, came to me and told me that the George Weah led administration was not interested in working with me and as such I should accept a payoff and leave without impeachment. I only asked him, 'What could I have said tomorrow to my children, friends and the general public about such money?' I obviously refused."[502]

According to the former Associate Justice, Senator Johnson was not happy with the decision to refuse the offer. "He was not happy, but I had to stand my ground for the cause I believe in," he said, adding, "in the first place, what did I do wrong to leave the Supreme Court, or is it President Weah's farm or Speaker Bhofal Chambers' plantation that they should choose at any time to decide who serves at the Court? That, I could not reckon with; so, I refused to give in."[503]

Ja'neh noted that the case about the government's arbitrary imposition of taxes on petroleum products was not overseen by him alone, but also the Chief Justice, Francis Korkpor and the rest of the Associate Justices. "They, too, should have been impeached, if that is what they believed, that I deserved impeachment from the Bench. We all agreed on the ruling that the government was wrong by imposing the taxes without Legislative approval and the government accepted the ruling and promised to meet with the petroleum importers and settle the matter out of court. All of my colleagues, including the Chief Justice, signed that decision. Why, then, I alone should be punished?"[504]

Ja'neh argued that the entire impeachment proceeding was bogus and completely against Article 73 of the 1986 revised Constitution of Liberia. This says, "All persons shall be entitled to freedom of thought, conscience and religion and no person shall be hindered in the enjoyment thereof except as may be required by law to protect public safety, order, health, or morals or the fundamental rights and freedoms of others."[505]

Ja'neh emphasised that no judge was to be punished, according to law (unmentioned) for a decision or opinion rendered in court while still actively involved in the adjudication of a case. He expressed his disappointment in Chief Justice Francis Korkpor for knowingly presiding over what he knew was wrong but ignored. "To me, the chief priest of the justice system is unfit to continue serving in that role. He has given in to the ruling establishment and [is] dictated to most of the time. What the Legislature or the Executive branches of government want done, that is what happens with Korkpor in charge of the Judiciary,"[506] he alleged.

Ja'neh expressed frustration that under the Weah administration, orders from Supreme Court were no longer respected by both the Executive and the Legislature because there was simply no one like him (Ja'neh) on the Supreme Court's Bench who consciously rejected manipulations, influence and intimidation. He said, "When I was there, one thing I realised was that the Executive had so much control and what kept playing on the justice system was the total control of its (Judiciary) budget. I worked things out with my colleagues and today the Judiciary has financial autonomy. No more President deciding when and how to pay the Justices."[507]

However, he pointed out that, in spite of the financial autonomy, the Judiciary's budget was still tampered with every fiscal year. "The budget was US$20 million but, when Weah came to the Presidency, they brought it down to US$17 million. In fact, it is on the book, but it hardly comes in full in the fiscal years under Weah. That is killing the justice system. This is why we are going nowhere except backward."[508]

Cllr. Arthur Johnson, the lead lawyer for Ja'neh, was furious, asserting that the Liberian Constitution was being violated in the impeachment proceedings. He claimed that the entire impeachment trial was in violation of Article 43 of the Liberian Constitution.

He told legislative reporters following the High Court ruling, that the alleged violation of the constitution and the rule of law was the main antecedence for the bloody civil war, warning that if Liberians were not careful, similar conflict could arise in the future. "The antecedence of the conflict in Liberia; the 15-year conflict, one of the major factors was when people were disinterested, when people were frustrated, when people felt there was no remedy at the level of the court. That brought the conflict in this country. And we are repeating history, and this is a very bad precedence. And in order for the nation to know, what we are doing is in the interest of the rule of law and not only Justice Ja'neh."[509]

For Cllr. Johnson, the lack of access to justice was a functional element responsible for the 15-year conflict and Liberia should dare not to repeat such an ugly history.

The lawyer averred that, "The lack of access to justice was the functional element responsible for our 15-year conflict. And the crisis of identity when it continues to exist in a country, there is a tendency for us to repeat our history. We were here for 15 years; we saw the conflict. We never left this country. Many persons are not aware, many persons that hold positions of trust, some of them cannot tell you what the causes for the conflict in Liberia are, but when you read the Truth and Reconciliation Commission report, there is a recommendation that identifies the antecedence of the Liberian conflict, and that is recommended. One of it is that people abused the rule of law."[510]

At the close of March 2019, the George Weah Government 'removed' Associate Justice Ja'neh from the Supreme Court of Liberia.

Despite being ousted from the bench, Ja'neh did not waiver but instead took his fight to the Economic Community of West African States (ECOWAS) Court. In 1975, the court was founded with the goal of socio-economic integration of the Member States of the Community with the Community Court of Justice following in the early 1990s when the ECOWAS treaty was revised. The Court was then to operate as the judicial arm of ECOWAS. As the Court itself describes matters, it is made up of "five independent Judges who are persons of high moral character, appointed by the Authority of Heads of State of Government from nationals of Member States for a four-year non-renewable term upon the recommendation of the Community Judicial Council."[511] The court agreed that Ja'neh's rights were violated, that the Weah administration had turned a blind eye to justice and wrongly removed Justice Ja'neh from the High Court bench. In November 2020, it ruled that Ja'neh's removal was illegal. The Court also ordered that the impeached former Justice be reinstated. For Ja'neh, this was a last resort, a chance to have a credible international body look at the case against him and things in perspective. The government had argued that the ECOWAS Court of Justice was "incompetent to review, interpret, and apply the national constitution and domestic laws of Member States" in the Ja'neh case. Solicitor General, Cllr. Sayma Syrenius Cephus, for the government claimed that the court had no jurisdiction to consider or determine on the suit filed by Cllr. Ja'neh which maintained that his impeachment by the Supreme Court Bench had violated his "human rights, particularly the right to a fair hearing and impartial trial."[512] In his argument, Cllr. Cephus asked the Court to "declare that the application is inadmissible" since the impeachment of the "Applicant was done through a political process that also followed the due process of law as laid down in Section 43 of the 1986 Constitution of Liberia."[513]

However, the Court denied the Liberian government's argument and said that the matter was "admissible and within the jurisdiction"[514] of the court. The judgment of 73 pages with Justice Edward Amaoko Asante presiding, concluded that the court could hear human rights cases. Moreover that the court had established violation of Ja'neh's entitlement to a fair hearing and right to work.[515] Contrary to Cllr. Cephus's argument, the Court's ruling, pursuant to the 2005 ECOWAS Supplemental Protocol, which was codified, stated that the Court had jurisdiction "to hear human rights cases and expands the admissibility rules to include disputes between individuals and their own member states."[516]

For Ja'neh, the ruling was a validation. "The facts in the matter illustrate that I, as Justice presiding in Chambers, issued 'a stay order'. This order basically halted the collection of surcharges on petroleum product, thereby suspending any collection of surcharges on petroleum product pending a determination of the controversy. For this judicial action taken by me, the Honourable Liberian Senate concluded and found me guilty of collusion. Interestingly, Mr. Justice Philip A. Z. Banks, III, who preceded me as Chambers Justice, had in fact issued stay order in a similar matter involving Srimex. The stay order issued by me was actually in favour of Conex and Aminata, not Srimex. Both stay orders were to remain in place pending hearing and adjudication of the matter by the Honourable Supreme Court of Liberia."[517]

Ja'neh explains that in the principal argument in the petitions filed by the petroleum dealers was one basic contention. "The petitions contended that that the Legislature had not passed any law imposing surcharge/tax on petroleum product. That the Legislature is the sole authority empowered under the Liberian Constitution to impose tax. That the Legislature not having not passed any law to that effect, any collection of surcharges was without the pale of the law."[518]

The impeached High Court Justice states that it was interesting to note that, following the issuance of the two stay orders, the Weah Government approached the Supreme Court seeking its approval for an out-of-court settlement of the case. "All the Justices, including Chief Justice, Korkpor, Sr., signed and approved the request of the Liberian government. This led to withdrawal of the case from the Supreme Court of Liberia."[519]

In the face of the formal withdrawal of the case, sanctioned by the Supreme Court of Liberia, Ja'neh says, it beats any reasonable imagination that the same case could be relied upon by the Weah Government as a basis to impeach and remove a Justice of the Supreme Court accusing him of 'collusion' with petroleum dealers for the purpose of depriving the Liberian Government of legitimate revenues.

Ja'neh insists that that the real reason for his impeachment and subsequent removal from the Supreme Court was never, and could never have been, about the issuance of stay orders placed on collection of surcharges but rather a payback by Weah to avenge his dissenting opinion in the 2017 elections impasse. For Ja'neh, there is preponderance of evidence demonstrating that finding him guilty of 'collusion' with petroleum dealers was simply a cloak and a pretext. "I was impeached and removed predicated on the wrath of Weah Government against me for delivering a 'Dissent Opinion' in the October General and Presidential Elections of 2017 attacking the results of those elections. In my 'Dissenting Opinion', I articulated that there was preponderance of the evidence demonstrating that the 2017 elections were marred by irregularities and fraud such as to warrant a re-run of the elections. I also declared in that dissent that, to the extent that the Supreme Court majority Opinion did conclude that the elections were indeed marred by irregularities and fraud, the Opinion of the Majority to uphold the results of the same elections in the face of acknowledged irregularities and fraud, and not ordering a re-run of the elections, was without the pale of the law."[520]

For Ja'neh, by any reasonable measure, it would seem that the Weah Government considered his dissent as an attack on its legitimacy. "It did not take kindly to my dissent. Shortly after he was sworn in office, Mr. Weah determined that Justice Ja'neh had to be plucked out of the Supreme Court Bench, whatever the costs,"[521] Ja'neh says the 'Dissenting Opinion' he delivered was indeed the real and ultimate reason propelling his impeachment and removal from the Supreme Court. As a matter of fact, he says, the Weah

Government seemed to have conceded this vital point in its answer filed in response to his complaint, lodged before the ECOWAS Community Court of Justice. In that answer, according to Ja'neh, the Weah Government argued "that the removal of the Applicant (Mr. Justice Ja'neh) was by 'the political process of impeachment supported by the relevant provisions of the Liberian Law, the most important of which was the rights, privileges and benefits of DUE PROCESS OF LAW…'. The Weah Government further argued in that answer that there was no basis, either in law or in fact, to support my complaint because '…his [Complainant's] entire, trial, conviction and removal from office were all supported by, and consistent with relevant provisions of Liberian Laws, the most important of which was that he was accorded all the rights, privileges and benefits of DUE PROCESS OF LAW…'"[522]

Interestingly, Ja'neh had argued in his complaint lodged before the Regional Court of ECOWAS that his 'impeachment', trial and removal from office were carried out without any prescribed rules of procedure to regulate the impeachment and trial proceedings. Ja'neh had also contended that the entire trial proceedings – impeachment, trial, conviction and removal from office – violated Article 7 of the African Charter on Human and People's Rights (ACHPR).

Not only did the Court award Mr. Justice Ja'neh US$200,000 for 'moral damages', but further ordered the Weah Government to reinstate Mr. Justice Ja'neh 'forthwith'. With very little regard for the Rule of Law, the Weah Government has, for the past 15 months, outrightly refused, neglected and failed to comply with the decision of the ECOWAS Regional Court.

Looking back, Justice Ja'neh says, with available evidence, his removal from the Supreme Court by the Weah Government, was for singular reason of my dissent in the 2017 election.

Ja'neh insists that, "to remove a Judge because of judicial decision constitutes a direct violation of the Liberian Constitution. This development raises a number of fundamental legal questions: whether decisions/actions taken by a 'Judicial Officer' through questionable process may be exposed to attack on grounds of propriety and legitimacy? Within this context, could one present a case to compel recall of all the decisions the 'Justice' ascending to the Bench through a flawed and illegal process participated in? These in my mind would be pivotal lingering questions that should demand appropriate answers by the Honourable Supreme Court of Liberia."[523]

Noted human rights lawyer, Aloysious Toe agreed.

For Toe, both Acarous Moses Gray and Thomas Fallah of the ruling CDC, had the blessings of the President to launch the impeachment proceedings against Ja'neh. Toe believes the pair, "brought falsified and trumped-up charges against Ja'neh in a devious display of a high-risk suicidal political gamble." In Toe's eyes, Ja'neh was "not guilty of the charges levied against him, he did not interpret the law in the code of conduct debate to 'satisfy his personal ego and vested interest' as falsely claimed by Gray and Fallah."[524] Moreover, Justice Ja'neh's judicial conduct and opinions were immune from sanctions and were protected under Article 73 of the Liberian Constitution. In Toe's eyes, the "outrageous claims and contentions by Acarous Moses Gray and Thomas Fallah were simply and factually incorrect; legally unsound; sentimentally overblown and overstated" and included "intentionally misstated facts and pertinent information." He believes the pair "mischievously withheld factual information favourable to Justice Ja'neh, presumably to frame Ja'neh in what was a likely political witch-hunt." Toe believed that both Acarous Moses Gray and Thomas Fallah had "one and only one mindset, regardless of the truth and regardless of the future consequences of such thoughtless thinking. They believed that 'if you want to kill a dog, it must be guilty at all costs', even if the facts prove otherwise."[525] For Toe, no matter whose interest is affected by its opinion, an independent and impartial judiciary is the pillar of the Liberian democracy and the foundation of peace and a guarantee of security. He says, "when the judiciary is arm-twisted, coerced and threatened with war drums of impeachment because of a decision which elected officials disagree with, as was done in the 1980s era of Samuel Doe, the tragic consequence is a pretext and justification for a 1990 war of Charles Taylor, a repeat that none of us ever want. To threaten judges who issue an unfavourable decision…falls outside the bounds of appropriate and constitutional conduct by lawmakers, and disagreement over a ruling does not constitute grounds for impeachment."[526]

According to Toe, "Acarous Gray and Thomas Fallah simply did not understand the facts and the law involved in the case against Ja'neh. Yet they cared little or less to know the facts and the law. Gray and Fallah do not have the law and the facts on their side; but they have the power, albeit devoid of reason. But as you know, naked power, devoid of reason, is reckless and abusive; and power allied with ignorance of the law and facts, is the worst enemy of justice."[527]

But Toe was not alone in the condemnation of Justice Ja'neh's removal.

Cllr. Tiawon Gongloe, President of the Liberia National Bar Association, said at the time that the removal of Associate Justices in Liberia had always been controversial as they had been controlled by the politics of the day and not the controlling law of the day. Gongloe recalls how, in 1915, Associate Justice Thomas McCants Stewart was removed for political reasons. Stewart, an American lawyer, born to a prominent attorney in New York, studied law in Minnesota and became the first African American lawyer in the state of Oregon. His lack of financial success in Oregon led him to eventually move to San Francisco where failing vision led him to commit suicide. Stewart was Associate Justice of the Supreme Court of Liberia from 1911 to 1914.

For Gongloe, given that the removal of Justice Ja'neh was "devoid of any legal reason, it can be concluded that his removal was for political reasons."[528] He asserts that the justice's removal set a bad precedence which was not good for Liberia. According to Cllr. Gongloe, while both the House of Representatives and the Senate have the rights to respectively impeach and remove a justice, such a process must be in keeping with the law. In the United States, for example, Gongloe says, "only one justice of the 112 justices that have been appointed since 1790 has been impeached, but none has been removed from the bench. In 1804, Associate Justice Samuel Chase was impeached by the House of Representatives, but the Senate in 1805 acquitted him. Hence, he was not removed."[529] The case against Ja'neh was just the beginning and President Weah and those within his inner circle still had a few more tricks up their sleeves. The ruling CDC had been a thorn in the flesh of former President Ellen Johnson Sirleaf. They criticised her every move and barely let any misstep go without putting the former President in check. No longer in the opposition, but rather, now running the affairs of state, the tide had changed, and the shoe was now on the other foot.

Prior to becoming President in 1933, Franklin Delano Roosevelt was a vocal critic of President Woodrow Wilson. In the *Kansas City Star* newspaper in May of 1918, Roosevelt's predecessor as President and relative as fifth cousin Theodore wrote, "to announce that there must be no criticism of the President, or that we are to stand by the President, right or wrong, is not only unpatriotic and servile, but is morally treasonable to the American public."[530]

In Liberia, the irony for President Weah was that criticisms of his government were unacceptable and so were dissenting voices. That is the very reason why he did not want Ja'neh on the High Court bench.

It was the same reason perhaps that he and his inner circle went the distance to prevent Brownie Jeffery Samukai Jr., who served as Minister of Defence during the Ellen Johnson Sirleaf administration, from taking his seat as Senator from Lofa County.

For much of the latter stages of the Sirleaf era, Samukai found himself drawn in a lengthy battle with widows of former Soldiers of the Armed Forces of Liberia. The saga involved an account established in 2009 as a compulsory contributory savings fund, which deducted salaries from all ranks of the AFL to serve as a supplementary pension benefit to provide assistance to wounded soldiers and to families of deceased soldiers. The payment, made out of the AFL Pension Account at the Ecobank-Liberia, was reportedly authorised by former President Johnson Sirleaf, and all of the disbursements made out of the pension scheme received written authorisation from the former President.

Another payment from the AFL's pension scheme was based on written communication and authorisation by the Ministry of Justice. President Sirleaf reportedly instructed the then Minister of Defence Samukai to pay US$50,000 from the AFL pension funds as gratuity to Hajji Fantima Wali, widow of the late Nigerian General Suraj Abdurrahman.

Operation "Restore Hope" and Operation "White Shield" were some of the projects on which the Ministry of National Defence withdrew money from the AFL Welfare Fund, for which authorisation was made by former President Sirleaf for payment. The first was a project aimed at securing the border between Liberia and the Ivory Coast, and resulted in the discovery of arms and ammunitions in an area called the Garleo Forest. Operation White Shield was a project where soldiers of the Armed Forces of Liberia set up check points to restrict the movement of people from Ebola-affected areas as a safety measure against further spread of the disease. On January 17, 2018, President Weah, then President-elect, held a meeting at his Rehab Community, Paynesville, with former Minister of Defence Samukai along with senior members of the AFL hierarchy, where the outstanding issue of a refund of the AFL Welfare Fund was discussed, and President Weah confirmed and reiterated in that meeting that he and ex-President Johnson Sirleaf had met and discussed the situation and agreed that, during the passage of the 2018 budget, all monies spent from the AFL Welfare Fund would have been refunded.

For much of the early days of the Weah Presidency, it appeared that Samukai was in the clear and far removed from the noise of the AFL widows' payments saga. For a while, it appeared that very little was being said about the controversial fund. However, murmurs about the saga began to unfold when Samukai announced his intent to contest the Senatorial seat for the vote-rich Lofa County in the December 2020 midterm elections.

After the Sirleaf Presidency, Samukai spent a great deal of his time entrenched in the fourth most populated county in Liberia which boasts 276,863 people. Located in the northernmost portion of Liberia, the county is bordered by Bong County to the south and Gbarpolu County to the west. The north-western parts of Lofa borders next-door Sierra Leone and the north-eastern parts border Guinea. Mount Wuteve, the highest mountain in Liberia, lies in the north-central part of the county.

Samukai was a proud son of the county and confident that he had put in the work to be elected. After the votes were counted, Samukai, running on the ticket of the opposition Collaborating Political Parties (CPP), who was winning out with the most votes. On December 8, 2020, eleven candidates competed for the Special Senatorial Elections Cllr. Joseph Jallah was second with 13,968 votes, behind Samukai with 20,431.

Days after the results were announced, the Board of Commissioners (BOC) of the National Elections Commission (NEC) reaffirmed and confirmed its earlier ruling declaring Collaborating Political Parties Candidate Samukai as winner of the December 8, 2020 Special Senatorial Elections in Lofa County.

He had been declared the winner, but the work was only just beginning. In the corridors of the Weah government, Samukai, like Ja'neh, was a threat the government could do without. And so, just as they did with Ja'neh, key aides to the President began to put a plan in motion to ensure that the former Defence Minister never set foot in the Senate, even though he had won the seat.

For Weah and his government, the plan was simple. Samukai had already been embroiled in the saga of the AFL widows' money. Now, all that was needed was for state prosecutors to make a case that the public would buy.

Samukai first had to deal with a case filed by the opposition Movement for Progressive Change (MPC). In a filing to the Supreme Court, the party sought to put a halt to Samukai's certification by the National Elections Commission (NEC). On Tuesday, March 2, 2021, John D. Barlone, Chairman-emeritus of the party, told a news conference that the decision taken by the party's executives was, related to Samukai's connections to misapplication of AFL funds when Defence Minister. Barlone said the senator-elect had been "indicted and convicted as an economic criminal through the final ruling of the Supreme Court", and that such a person lacked the, "moral integrity to uphold public office."[531] He went on to outline several claims that prompted the decision of the party's Executive Committee to write to the Supreme Court, mentioning, "criminal facilitation, economic sabotage and misapplication of public funds as crimes that Samukai was found guilty of."[532] He said, "You may have recalled that Mr. Brownie Samukai once pleaded guilty through the wisdom of the most powerful Supreme Court on all charges levied against him, and he was also mandated by the same court to restitute the sum of US$1.4 million within a grace period of six months or one year's time, if not he might likely be sent to jail for at least two years."[533]

In January 2022, the Full Bench of the Supreme Court handed-down its final ruling in the case involving Samukai and one of his deputies and the comptroller, for the crimes of "Money Laundering and Economic Sabotage". In its ruling on January 27, the Supreme Court ordered the Sherriff to "arrest, incarcerate, and place in a common jail" the former Defence Minister.

On Tuesday, March 24, 2020, the Criminal Court 'C' had found the former Defence Minister Samukai and his deputies guilty of corruption, but defence lawyers took exception to the ruling and announced that they would file an Appeal to the Supreme Court.

Mr. Samukai had been facing trial for misappropriating some US$1.3 million. His leadership of the Armed Forces of Liberia had received huge amounts for the AFL's Compulsory Contributing Fund which the Government of Liberia had sent to the Ecobank Liberia Ltd. It included US$460,000 in addition to US$687,656.35, making a total sum of US$1,147,656.35.

The Lower Court, presided over by Judge Yamie Gbeisay, said there had not been sufficient evidence to convict the former Defence officials of the crimes of Money Laundering and Economic Sabotage.

The Supreme Court ruled on February 8, 2021 and upheld the lower court's guilty verdict and sentencing, also said that it was law extant in the Liberian jurisdiction that "All public officials and employees shall obey all lawful instructions issued to them by their supervisors and shall decline to obey orders he or she knows or ought to know to be wrong or unlawful." [FN] Also that the High Court said "Public Officials and Employees of Government shall be held personally responsible and liable for his or her own acts of commission or omissions, done either mistakenly or deliberately ..."[534] Consequently, the High Court said officials and employees of government who were adjudged to have one unlawful order shall be held personally responsible and liable for their acts of commission or omission as in the instant case.

The case against Samukai was filled with potholes. For example, why did the government and the Elections Commission allow Samukai to take part in the elections, knowing full well he had all these charges hanging over him? Why did the Weah administration drag the case on for so long? Perhaps the government did not see victory on the cards for Samukai.

Interestingly, in March 2020, Deputy Finance Minister for Fiscal Affairs, Samora P.Z. Wolokollie, confirmed in court that the Weah-led administration had paid US$460,000 into the Armed Forces of Liberia's (AFL) Pension Account as reimbursement funds toward the US$1.3 million used from the AFL Pension Account.

Several media outlets reported that Minister of National Defence Daniel D. Ziankahn also acknowledged the payment of the amount alluded to by

Deputy Finance Minister Wolokollie into the AFL pension account by the Weah administration through the Ministry of Finance.

The two ministers, Ziankahn and Wolokollie, made the assertions on March 13, 2020, at Criminal Court 'C' when they took the witness stand. They were testifying in the economic sabotage case involving former Defence Minister Brownie Samukai and his two former deputies. The court requested the pair's attendance to ask if the Weah-led administration had paid into the AFL Pension Account as partial reimbursement towards US$1.3 million. This President Weah had undertaken to ensure. In court Minister Wolokollie explained that the amount had been paid into the AFL's account with input from the National Security Council of Liberia. "At the receipt of the request coming from the Ministry of National Defence, the Ministry of Finance proceeded in line with its budget execution process and with the advice from the National Security Council of the Government of Liberia, to make payment to the Ministry of National Defence in the amount of US$460, 000."[535]

On January 27, 2022, Samukai and his associates were convicted and ordered to be imprisoned for embezzlement.

Weah had a difficult dilemma hanging over his head. Although the High Court had found Samukai guilty, actually putting him in handcuffs and sending him to jail came with a political risk. Weah and his inner circle folks feared political backlash in the vote-rich county if Samukai was humiliated, embarrassed and thrown in jail. Away from the public glare, both President Weah and others in the government were in serious discussions with Senator-elect Samukai to find a way out of the political time-bomb waiting to explode. Shortly after the High Court ruling, President Weah placed a call to Samukai and expressed concern about his safety. The President assured Samukai that he would try to solve the problem and that he would not go to jail. The President even asked Samukai whether he was out of the country. It was widely believed that Samukai politely told the President Weah that he had not left the country but would inform the President if it came to that.

Was President Weah being sincere with Samukai or simply playing the role of the innocent good cop, trying to assure the former Defence Minister that he had no hand in what was unfolding? In the aura of the moment, there was a generally held view within the decision makers of the government that very high-level politicians and people of the opposition had intended to get Samukai to launch his bid to become either Vice President or Presidential candidate upon taking his seat. Around the Presidency, President Weah had told aides that he saw Samukai as a threat and vowed that the former Defence Minister would never take his seat as Senator, no matter what.

Standing his ground made things even more difficult for Samukai although the former minister appeared to leave the door open for working with the Weah administration's agenda in the Senate. Deep down, Samukai was hoping for clemency, hoping that President Weah would go a step further in expressing support for his wellbeing. But Samukai also knew that hope was a dangerous undertaking, especially for Weah, renowned for holding things in and not one to let go. With full Presidential clemency, Samukai could take his seat and help where there were regional and international challenges.

President Weah had nearly conceded but came under enormous pressure from his Minister of State for Presidential Affairs, Nathaniel McGill; Finance and Economic Planning Minister, Samuel Tweah; supported by Mayor Jefferson Koijee and the Justice Minister Frank Musah Dean, who were all against the idea of a Presidential pardon. Weah's inner circle was more open to the idea of a Presidential pardon on the condition that Samukai relinquish his fight to take his seat.

Besides the political undertones, there was also the fear that Samukai was in contact with former and present military personnel within ECOWAS to organise some support against President Weah. Both President Weah and Samukai dismissed this report with Samukai reportedly indicating to President Weah that he was not meeting any military or security personnel anywhere whatsoever.

However, Samukai's whereabouts were still a mystery. Although he had been in touch with the President, no one really knew where he was. There were some suggestions that the former minster had informed the President that he was leaving the country for personal and safety reasons.

On February 22, 2022, President Weah granted an executive clemency to Samukai, suspending his two-year jail sentence handed down against him which had been upheld by the Supreme Court. Announcing the pardon on behalf of President Weah, Minister McGill said the President's decision was fully in accordance with the Liberian Constitution's Article 59 that grants the President such clemency powers. "The President of Liberia, pursuant to Article 59 of the 1986 Constitution which vests in him the power and authority to grant reprieves, suspend fines, sentences and pardon anyone convicted and sentenced for a crime has, with immediate effect, ordered the suspension of the two-year prison sentence imposed on Mr. Brownie J. Samukai, following his conviction by the Honourable Supreme Court of Liberia."[536] A day later in response to criticism, McGill confirmed that the clemency extended was not a full pardon but rather "a suspension of his jail sentence to allow him find means to refund the money for which he was sentenced."[537]

In the meantime, the President directed the Minister of Finance and Development Planning (MFDP) to make full payment of the outstanding balance of the AFL money, while Mr. Samukai went through the Stipulation Payment Agreement.

In spite of the pardon and suspended sentence, there seemed to be three parallel backdoor discussions in order to find a way to grant Samukai and his colleagues a constitutional reprieve and allow the government to exploit Samukai's popularity in Lofa county. Allowing Samukai to relinquish his quest for the seat he successfully contested was right up President Weah's alley. It was, after all, the climax of a fulfilment for the President. It is the same reason he sat in his office and watched his long-time rival and cousin, James Debbah, wait for him in the rotunda of the Executive Mansion, as Weah watched from his CCTV cameras. There is something about humiliating others that seemed to tickle Weah. It is the same reason he has not spoken to John Brownell since he won the Presidency. Brownell, like Debbah "Boy Charles", and many of those he played football with on the national team, the Lone Star, are no longer on speaking terms.

In Brownell's case, he isn't even sure how it all started. "We were both so cool. All I can say is that the man created his own problem. We never really had any differences that I can remember. I do know that he falsely accused me of dating his baby mother, MacDella Cooper, the fashion model."[538]

The irony of Brownell's confusion is funny. Brownell, who was a striker for local football club, Mighty Barrolle, during the 1980s, recalls that Weah once humiliated him by dating his girlfriend and making fun of the incident after taking the girl to Ghana. Years later, Weah would then accuse Brownell of dating MacDella.

For Brownell, the accusations could never have been so far from the truth.

"Yes, MacDella did invite me to a program, we took photos but there was nothing to it. I never got anything personal with him and I could never have dated MacDella knowing fully well she had a child with George. Even though he did the same to me, I could never stoop to that level. But he told a lot of people that I went behind his back and stole his girl."[539]

Little did Brownell know how deep the feud he knew nothing about extended.

Shortly after Weah won the Presidency in 2018, Brownell and a handful of friends from Weah's football days went to see the new President. Led by Sinoe County, District No. 2 Representative, J. Nagbe Sloh, Brownell had hoped to share some advice on leadership with his friend. To Brownell's dismay, aides to the President only allowed Rep. Sloh in to see him. After waiting hours outside the President's home at Rehab Road, Rep. Sloh came out to say that the President would not be seeing anyone in the group, particularly Brownell. Rep. Sloh told Brownell how the President had seen him on the CCTV camera and had the worst things to say about him. "I was surprised to know that he told the lawmaker, I always made fun of him and how I was always fonder of James Debbah. This is a man, I spent money behind in 2005 for us to go to Liberia for the elections. I always encouraged him to use his celebrity status for dialogue and unite the country. To my utmost surprise, when he came into power, I became an enemy. George Weah has taken the Presidency as a vindictive tool for people he has had problems with and surrounded himself with a bunch of thieves."[540]

Brownell, like many others who have crossed Weah's path, have one thing in common. They have become his lifelong enemies for simply not being on the same page with him.

Remember James Nyepan Verdier Jr.? He would know. James was amongst a few Liberians who had assembled in Pembroke Pines, Florida, back in 2004 and involved in a series of discussions at varying levels about the new Liberia and its political and impending electoral processes. James had encouraged Weah to go back to school and although his advice fell on deaf ears, he knew it could come back to haunt the football legend. Weah did not listen to James then but would later retreat to his advice when he lost the 2005 elections as a standard bearer and the 2011 elections as Vice standard-bearer to Winston Tubman in his party's quest for power.

For James, the fact that Weah was later admitted to two universities to study for a bachelor and graduate degrees, suggests that, had Weah listened to his advice in the first place, things perhaps would have been different. "I intend to submit a bill for professional fees relating to the piece of advice I provided in 2004, which he pursued with success."[541]

It took a long time – more than a decade to be exact – but Weah finally won the Presidency. By then James Verdier was head of the Liberia Anti-Corruption Commission.

James was appointed by former President Ellen Johnson Sirleaf as head of the LACC on February 24, 2014, replacing Cllr. Frances Johnson Morrison who had previously headed the National Elections Commission and had been Minister of Justice under the Sirleaf administration.

Weah never forgot his 2004 run-in with James Verdier. And just like Ja'neh, Samukai, and others, it was payback time. Two years into his term, President Weah began to tighten the screws around Verdier and the LACC. In a letter dated February 26, 2019, addressed to another Commissioner at the LACC, the Minister of State for Presidential Affairs and Chair of the Cabinet Nathaniel F. McGill wrote, "In consideration of the current situation at the Liberian Anti-Corruption Commission (LACC), the President has instructed that you serve as Officer-In-Charge of the Liberia Anti-Corruption Commission (LACC), and mandates you to take charge of the tasks and functional responsibilities of the Office, thereof, until further notice. The new Officer-in-Charge is LACC Commissioner Charles J. Gibson, a former Government Auditor with a background in business."[542]

The decision to side-line the LACC head directly related to an earlier request from Minister McGill at the direction of President George M. Weah to have the LACC Executive Director provide a list of all individuals who had declared their personal assets in keeping with the law. The President had come under heavy criticism after he gave a rather weak response to a BBC interviewer's questions as to why his officials had not complied with his directive last December to declare their assets. At the time, the President responded that all he could do was ask his officials to comply since it was the law, rather than exercise his executive authority for full compliance.

An angry Verdier felt disrespected. In a detailed response to Minister McGill's letter dated February 22, 2019, he enumerated a seven-count explanation to Minister McGill's request for information which included details on a prior communication to the Office of the President about those officials who had and had not declared their assets in the three branches of Government and the responsibility of the head of each branch of Government to ensure compliance with the country's Asset Declaration Law.

Verdier reminded Minister McGill that he was still in charge of the LACC and that the commission was composed of five commissioners nominated by the President and confirmed by the Liberian Senate. One of the commissioners served as Chairperson and one as Vice Chairperson. The Chairperson and Vice Chairperson of the Commission should be appointed by the President for a term of five years each and should be eligible for appointment for one additional term of five years. To ensure continuity, and subject to confirmation by the Liberian Senate, the President should appoint three additional Commissioners for terms on a staggered term basis.

Verdier went on to reiterate to Minister McGill that his position as LACC Executive Chairperson was tenured. He was appointed to the LACC following successful stint as National Officer for Justice and Security at the United Nations Development Program (UNDP) in Liberia. He was a career lawyer specialising in criminal, domestic relations, civil, corporate and constitutional law with emphasis on the poor. He was appointed on February 24, 2014, by former President Ellen Johnson Sirleaf to replace Madam Frances Johnson Morris Allison who moved into private legal practice in Liberia.

The Weah Administration had signalled its preparedness to cut tenured positions to allow the President a free hand to stack strategic public positions with loyalists in order to solidify his administration's hold on power and to carry out his policies. And James Verdier would be one of the first casualties.

The Weah administration did not stop there. In fact, the government, through the Minister of Information, Lenn Eugene Nagbe, defended President Weah's commitment to fighting corruption amid accusations that his administration was attempting to hamper the country's anti-corruption body.

Verdier did not hold back and criticised the Weah government for not delivering its funding and their threats to remove him. He told Radio France International in an interview that the anti-corruption agency's experience under Weah was dire. Absence of funding had caused problems, leading to fears that the government was planning to install a political appointee at the expense of the anti-corruption body's tenured chairperson. "We don't have funding, we have struggled to actually have this administration put itself behind the fight against corruption and make some bold statements regarding transparency, accountability and ensuring that we can fight corruption."[543] Minister Nagbe countered (also on RFI), "If you look at Liberia's current national budget this year (2018) there has been more allocation in our budget for transparency institutions including the corruption commission."[544]

It was clear that President Weah did not want James Verdier in his government. After all, he had defied the odds, taken his chances, and put Verdier and many others who did not believe he could, to shame. It was for this reason that Weah was a bit sensitive when it came to anything negative being said about him or his government. This was also evident when he announced his government's plan to introduce two controversial loans, ETON and EBOMAF. The President just couldn't understand why a majority of Liberians were not buying into the deals which looked promising on paper. But these deals had all the markings of a shady transaction, unlikely to yield any dividend for Liberia or for the Weah administration.

Nevertheless, Weah appeared antsy whenever anyone raised a question about the loans, going so far as to slam his detractors, saying, "My people, don't listen to those criticising me for lobbying for loans. Those doing so are enemies of the country. The loans I am taking will be able to complete the roads in three years. When I am asking partners for loans, any of them who tell me that they want to complete the roads in six years, I can say no because I know in the next six years, if I don't do anything for you, I will not be re-elected."[545]

Many political observers had taken a keen interest in noticing that some close to Weah, particularly those enjoying his confidence, were those willing to toe the line, willing to accept anything he said, without offering a dissenting opinion.

Some think that, in the last five years of his Presidency, President Weah has shown all the symptoms of a rising dictator. Besides launching a spiteful campaign of slander and vilification against the independent press, he has had statues built in his image, named public structures in his name such as the 14th Military Hospital (recalling the jersey he wore during the prime of his football days), and had markets named in honour of his wife, Clar. Instead of using the press and critics to motivate, Weah the President has labelled critical voices against his regime as "enemies of the state."

As a footballer, Weah became accustomed to scoring goals on the world's biggest stage and hearing his name shouted in chorus. As a leader of Africa's oldest republic, the football icon soon fell prey to hero worshipping by sycophantic followers singing only the songs he wanted to hear. Like the emperor without clothes, Weah had suddenly found himself obliged to accept the norms that came with the Presidential territory.

Weah's inaugural speech reflected humility from a man acknowledging his education lapses, when he declared, "My greatest contribution to this country as President may not lie in the eloquence of my speeches but will definitely lie in the quality of the decisions that I will make over the next six years to advance the lives of poor Liberians."[546] As President, however, Weah was suddenly showered with awards and with aides wasting no time in referring to him as Dr. Dr. George Weah, representing the number of doctorate degrees he had received since becoming President.

The humility was gone. Suddenly, the perception of being educated meant so much more than the raw, untapped portrayal Weah had embraced prior to becoming President. The truth is, President Weah had soon fallen prey to the errors of his predecessors. The trappings of power had gotten the best of him. The likes of Samuel Doe, Charles Taylor, William V. S. Tubman and even Ellen Johnson Sirleaf had been overwhelmed by sycophancy, self-seeking flatterers praising the powerful just to gain their approval.

As President, Weah has been unrepentant in accepting the realities of the job, aptly summed up by America's 33rd President Harry Truman who once said, "The President is always abused. If he isn't, he isn't doing anything." Truman's logic was simple, "I want people around me who will tell me the truth, who will tell me the truth as they see it, you cannot operate and manage effectively if you have people around you who put you on a pedestal and tell you everything you do is right because that in practice can't be possible." For Truman, the message was, "When you get to be President, there are all those things, the honours, the twenty-one-gun salutes, all those things. You have to remember it isn't for you. It's for the Presidency."[547]

Weah, like many before him, had lost touch with the reality and had fallen prey to the trappings of power. He had allowed his inner circle, led by his influential Minister of State, McGill, to ambush his Presidency. Suddenly, the voices of the unheralded masses who embraced his political naivety became eclipsed by the few who had his confidence, the few who had his ears and the few who were willing to ignore the wrongs and would poorly advise the President, even to his own detriment and Presidential legacy.

20

OPPONG VS. SALINSA

George "Oppong" Weah and James "Salinsa" Debbah are household names in Liberia. Before going professional, Oppong played for the Invincible XI while Salinsa played for the Mighty Barrolle.

The duo's most dominant display for Liberia came in August 1988 when they each scored to lead Liberia to an emphatic 2–0 victory against a powerful Ghana Black Stars team in the qualifying round for the 1990 World Cup. The victory ensured Liberia could advance to the group stage where they were placed in Group B with Egypt, Malawi and Kenya. Newspaper headlines the next morning were filled with praise for the Duo: "Oppong Open It; Salinsa Close It,"[548] led the *Sports Chronicle* newspaper while the *Daily Observer* ran a banner headline, "VICTORY: Lone Star Smashes Black Stars 2–0, Qualifies for World Cup Round Two."[549]

Egypt would eventually top the group with eight points with Liberia in second place with six points.

Growing up in Monrovia, George was always compared to the Ghanaian great, Charles Oppong. George grew up on the Capitol Bypass in Monrovia, Montserrado County, with his parents William Tarpeh Weah and Anna Quayeweh Weah (both deceased). His ancestry derives from the Bassu and Kru ethnic populations with his mother from Grand Bassa County, his father from Grand Kru County.

Born in a Christian home, George converted to Islam in 1989. However, in a bid to keep alive his grandmother's religious tutelage, he reconverted to Christianity following her death in 1994.

His father worked as a mechanic with LIBTRACO on Johansen Drive while his mother was a marketer. Dr. George Manneh Weah was reared by his late grandmother, Emma Forkay Klonjlaleh Brown, a devout Christian. He is one of dozens of children brought up by his grandmother.

James hailed from Grand Bassa County, located in the central-most portion of Liberia. Since he was 10 years old, James has been called several variations of Salinsa. James simply impressed people with his dribbling skills. They would say he packed up his opponents like sardines in a can. Over time, he would be called Salin or Sardines but once he made it big, it was Salinsa.

A year later James transferred to Olympique Lyonnais. In 1995, he moved south and a little east in Ligue 1 to OGC Nice, where he played until 1997. That same year, James had yet another transfer to the Belgian side Anderlecht. He moved back to Ligue 1 for one season with Paris Saint-Germain in 1998. On leaving PSG, James travelled to Turkcell Super League side Ankaragücü for the 1998 and 1999 seasons and later to the Greek side, Iraklis. In 2001, James would move to Al Jazira Club in Abu Dhabi, United Arab Emirates, and onwards to Muharraq Club in Bahrain, in 2003. In 2008, four years after leaving Muharraq Club, he experienced the Indonesia Super League with PKT Bontang for a solitary season.

Like George, James had a somewhat colourful football career, although not as successful. In the twilight of his career, he hit a low point when, during a July 2004 FIFA World Cup qualifying match against Togo in Monrovia, as captain, he refused to be substituted in the 53rd minute, instead waiting until the 68th minute to leave the pitch. The match resulted in a 0–0 draw, causing the team to leave the stadium under the protection of an armoured personnel carrier. In September 2018, James made a final appearance for the national team, at the age of 48, making him, at the time, the third oldest international player on record.

James found it difficult to accept that he was at the tail end of his career. The man dubbed in Liberia, the nation's "most celebrated player" was long past his prime and it was evident from his dismal performance against Togo that he had very little to offer. Every time he touched the ball, he was booed by disenchanted fans who became even more antsy over James' refusal to leave the pitch or be substituted. After thunderous boos from the fans who once applauded his plays, James finally left the game, paving the way for an up-and-coming striker, Isaac Tondo, to take his place.

In just over 90 minutes of a crucial football game, Liberia's most celebrated player had become its most unpopular.

Lone Star Coach Kadala Kromah was angry after the match, claiming that James' refusal to leave the pitch upset his game plan. "It was bad for us; the entire team was affected psychologically. If he had come out when we called him, we would have had ample time to reconsolidate."[550]

James would later acknowledge that he had allowed his emotion to get the best of him. The reality was, James had passed his prime, he had become a shell of what he was for many years wearing the red, white and blue. James knew the sun had set on his career but sought reprieve from a nation unhappy with what had just gone down. "As a professional I should not have done that but again if you judge me from this game, it's not fair. They should look back at what I have done for Liberia and my voluntary return, they should be grateful and treat me with respect. I have no regret; the fact is that the mistakes came from the technical staff who did not formulate the system that we played. It simply did not work."[551]

The sun had indeed set, and the Togo game would mark James' last. It also marked the end of an era. James and George had formed a deadly strike force for Liberia. Whenever they faced off in a rival IE vs. Barrolle duel, it was fireworks. Their partnership on the national team was one of the most-deadly duos in African football.

The relationship between the pair dates as far back as their days in elementary school. "If you look at it, he's my next of kin," James says. "His mother, Ma Anna Weah is related to my mother, Ma Wachie Debbah because they were first cousins."[552] Both George and James attended grade school at the Garretson W. Gibson Junior High School (named after Liberia's fourteenth President) in the 7th grade before George switched schools and went to the Ellen Mills Scarborough. "George was always migrating between schools. From Scarborough he went to Muslim Congress."[553]

James would move on to graduate from the Wells Hairston High School after completing Junior High at GW Gibson. George remained at the Muslim Congress School until James and others recruited him for Wells Hairston. George stayed at Wells until the 10th grade. "I graduated and left him at Wells," James recalls. "He didn't graduate. He left Wells in the 10th grade – that's the last time I saw that man in school."[554]

The pair split up when late President Samuel Kanyon Doe arranged for several young players on the national team to travel to Brazil for training. "We were still in school when this trip came up for Brazil," James recalls. "I couldn't go because I was graduating. So, I stayed, and George went, and they stayed up to seven months in Brazil. By the time the team returned, James says George got an opportunity to go to Cameroon where he secured a semi-pro contract with Tonnerre de Yaoundé."[555]

Debbah would soon follow George's footsteps via semi-pro contract in Cameroon with Union Duala before venturing into Europe.

Despite the history between the pair, the relationship has been soured over the years. While James is still unsure how or why the beef started, it may have been triggered by James' unwillingness to embrace George's quest for the Presidency. In the run up to the 2005 Presidential elections, James criticised George's decision to seek the Liberian Presidency. "I will be doing a lot of injustice if I vote for him,"[556] James told a news conference in Monrovia.

James said at the time that his disqualification of George was not based on the fact that a lot of people said he was not educated. "My reason is that he does not have the necessary governmental experience. He will be brought to public ridicule, as he is a political novice who would not understand the intricacies of politics. All the things he has worked for over the years could be taken away from him, if he does not perform [as President]."[557]

Weah shot down James' comments, also telling the BBC, "I regret that my cousin does not seem to understand why I am getting into politics at this time. James knows I have the leadership ability, which was evident when I played and captained the Lone Star. If he says I'm a novice to the Presidency, he should know that no one goes to the Presidency with the requisite experience, except that person has served before."[558]

The relationship between the pair has been going downhill ever since – or maybe it began even long before.

George lost his quest for the Presidency in 2005 but eventually won in 2017. Despite attempts by James to reach out to his cousin, George has not returned the favour. James says all of those who played with Weah tried to embrace him. "He ascended to the Presidency," says James, "but everybody can't be for you. I've never been a member of his party. It's not that I hate George, but I've never been a member of the Weah's political party, the CDC, because I'm from the opposition bloc – and I told him clear."[559]

James feels that George had a serious problem. After George's 2017 victory, some mutual friends suggested to James that he should reach out to George. It seemed George was open to the idea and so, on September 12, 2018, James invited George to play in an international friendly match to retire his number 14 jersey. Ironically, prior to that game, James was the oldest player ever to play in a FIFA-sanctioned match for Liberia, in that controversial AFCON game against Togo. Now, George, at 51, was about to outdo him. George wore his famous number 14 and James, his famous number 10. George also took the record away from Greek captain Yorghos Koudas, who was 48 when he played his last game in 1995. James, who regularly played alongside George during the Lone Star's golden era at the turn of the century, would now find himself third on that list.

Each player was part of the Liberian side contesting the 1996 and 2002 Africa Cup of Nations, the only tournaments where the Lone Stars were to make the final stages. Their closest to a World Cup appearance also featured Debbah and Weah when they narrowly missed out on qualification by a single point.

So, for James, the retirement game was a step in the right direction.

"Since that man became President," he says, "I've only seen him two times in person. He called me the first time during his retirement jersey game. Zeogar Wilson, the Minister of Sports called me and said, 'My man, the President was just talking about you and said you are the only person he wants to play with for his retirement.' I said OK, I will come."[560]

However, James had his reservations. "I really never wanted to go but Musa Bility, a mutual friend who was a former head of the Liberia Football

Association, called and said, 'Just go, so people cannot say you're the problem.'"561

To James' surprise, George gave him the cold shoulder. "I go to play the game; we're supposed to meet at the stadium, but we first met at the Golden Gate Hotel. Everybody stood up when it was announced that the President was arriving. We stood up, the President who I played with all those years and my own cousin approached me. As I showed up my hand to greet him, he passed by me and shunned me in front of everybody. I said to myself, what? This guy left my hand hanging. Everybody noticed it."562

Samuel Tweah, the Minister of Finance, Nathaniel McGill, Minister of State for Presidential Affairs, and the late Munah Pelham Youngblood noticed the cold shoulder. According to James, Munah was very understanding and reasonable. "Munah came to me and said, 'Jimmy what did I just see? What's going on?'"563

James told Munah, "I don't know. Maybe it was an oversight. I will go back to the man. We went into the dressing room – about to wear our clothes, I reached out to him again. As soon as I approached him, he got up again and left. So, I said, 'What the fuck?' I went to Zeogar and said, 'But why did you all bring me here to embarrass me?' I decided to leave but some of the players pleaded with me to stay. I played the game. After the game, the man was gone. He did not even sit to talk to anybody. I said OK, I'll let it slide."564

James would get a second opportunity, and maybe a third. "The second one George did to me was the LFA awards night. I was scheduled to give the most valuable trophy and highest goal scorer award. When I got there, the program was changed on me. So, when my part came – in fact before my part came – Edwin Snowe, a Senator in the upper house of the national legislature went up to me and told me that I would be receiving the Most Valuable Player award."565

James said he was OK with it. He remembers that when the program finally commenced, Weah took to the stage, grabbed the microphone and went into a public display of support for him, while the cameras were rolling, saying all the right things and making sure that there was no sign of a beef between he and James.

James recalls George saying, "I can't give the presentation without the recognition of somebody here who has made immense contribution to Liberian football in the presence of our most valuable player and highest goal scorer of all time, James Salinsa Debbah, my brother, my cousin."[566] George even went to James and gave him a big hug. "He came to me, hugged me and said, 'My man, just call me, I got your back.'"[567]

Days later, James sent messages and even tried to call George, but to no avail. "I called him for days and he never answered my call. I texted him several times, he never replied. I let it slide."[568]

The third time James recalls was sometime in 2019. "The last one after which I threw in the towel and said I would never deal with this guy again. It was in March, Bill Twehway, Managing Director of the National Port Authority (NPA), called me and said, 'Jimmy, my man, the President was just talking about you – man. He has something for you – and he wants to see you.'"[569] The NPA is one of the biggest and most lucrative state-owned enterprises in Liberia and Bill was at the helm. He had previously served in the national legislature as a Representative from Montserrado County, District #3, representing the former ruling Unity Party. He was elected in 2012 but lost his seat six years later in the 2017 Presidential elections. A long-time friend of Weah, Bill had become a key member of the President's inner circle. In fact, he had become so close to Weah, that he was often called, "Gbeh-kugbeh Junior", one of Weah's middle names. In essence, Bill was Weah's political son.

James remembers Bill asking him to be at his office at 11 o'clock.

Bill said to James, "You brought your car, right?"[570] Bill then signalled James to follow him.

As James recalls, "I drove behind Bill and when we got behind the mansion, we parked the car. He said let's go upstairs."[571]

But as both men moved past the security check, Bill turned to James and said: "Wait down here. Let me go and check upstairs to the President's office."[572] James clearly understood that this was a matter of protocol. And so he sat in the veranda of the Executive Mansion, waiting, and waiting, and waiting before venting out his steam.

"I sat down in the veranda waiting for more than five hours. I was sitting down in the place five hours and fucking embarrassed."[573]

Trokon Roberts, the head of the Executive Protective Service, was on his way out when he noticed James was sitting there. Trokon asked James what he was doing in the veranda? Trokon said that, because of his past history with the President, James should not even be downstairs but rather that he should be upstairs. Trokon asked James who was facilitating his visit. When James told him it was Bill Tweahway, head of the NPA, Trokon said, "Well, if its Bill, it will be alright."[574]

James waited for another hour. In total, James sat in the veranda for six hours, 27 minutes, fuming with anger. Bill Twehway finally came out and said, "Jimmy, let's go home, everything's alright."[575]

James, angry and confused, felt embarrassed. He turned to Bill and said, "I thought we came to see the President?"[576] Bill told James not to worry, but to get in his car and follow him.

James recalls that he drove behind Bill as he was instructed. "We went to one spot on sixteen street in Sinkor to an apartment building where he joined some small girls, just dancing. He remembers Bill saying, "Dammit, I like my job to the Port – man, the job got leverage, I'm enjoying myself."

"What the fuck!" James said to himself. "This man brought me here to talk about himself?"[577] Then, James turned to Bill and asked him what was going on?

Bill said something to the effect that he was traveling the next day to Rivercess County but assured James that when he returned, everything would be alright. In other words, he would try once more to fix whatever issues there were between James and his cousin, George Weah.

What made James even more angry came a few days later when a mutual friend called him to say that he had run into the President who was attending a function at the U.S. Embassy. James said George told the friend, "Oh, Jimmy was at the office yesterday."[578]

James was puzzled. "I said, 'So that man saw me on that CCTV and just decided to humiliate me. What is that?' From there I drew the line and said, 'Fuck it!' If George cannot pick up phone to call me, I'm not going there. George owes me an apology. I can never go to him, why would I? I rather eat grass than to go to George Weah. I've played my part."[579]

For James, George had always been that way. "A lot of people don't see because he's a superstar. It should always be about George. If it's not him it's no one else. Look at the other time when the Liberia Football Association tallied the highest goal scorer of all time. When it emerged that I was the highest goal scorer, the man said they should do the tally again."[580]

In all of George's accolades, James says he and other members of the football fraternity had been there to celebrate with him. "We hailed him as the King but still the man wants everything for himself."[581]

James, like most of the members of George's football fraternity, has issues with George, even accusing him of stepping on their achievements and successes. "He played no role in me going professional. That's why I'm always surprised when people say the man took me to France. Took me to France, where? He didn't take me to France. I went on a trial that was arranged by Laye Sidibe, not him, that man never even wanted me to go to France. He was never involved. Even Jonathan "Boye Charles" Sogbie helped more people than him, he took more than three players to France – and I can say it to his face. That man didn't want anyone to succeed. Look at Alexander Cheneken Freeman. Cheneken had a contract in Malaysia, he played with Stephen Keshi for a team called Perlis FA. When Keshi moved to Racing Club Strasbourg, he apparently had a good relationship with the coach and so he recommended Cheneken to the team. But they needed a reference. So, Keshi said, 'You can call George Weah.' When they called George, he said, 'He did nothing. Cheneken wasn't fit to play in Europe, he's not the kind of style you want.'" [582]

"Who are you to determine that?"[583] James lamented.

George's beef with James continued even after he won the Presidency. George's predecessor, Ellen Johnson Sirleaf had appointed James as a member of the board of the Liberia Maritime Authority. One of George's first actions as President was to remove James from the LMA board. He did the same for Jonathan "Boye Charles" Sogbie who had been appointed by Sirleaf on the board of the National Oil Company of Liberia.

In addition, James had been appointed as head coach of the Liberian national team by Sirleaf. During his time as manager of the team, the Lone Stars did fairly well but faltered due to the lack of support. James says the decision to fire him was highly political. Mustapha Raji, the head of the Liberia Football Association had called him and said, "You know I want you to stay with the team but the government in power is saying you're not part of the ruling party, you're not a member of the Coalition for Democratic Change."

After all James says, George had moved him from the Maritime board. "So, I said no problem."[584]

For George, James will always be his cousin. In a 2004 Interview with the *Daily Observer* newspaper, George, then a candidate for President, said he had no idea what the noise was all about between him and James. "My cousin James and I have a very healthy relationship. We may have some little talk about coming to practice on time and the like, but that's normal. But to say we have friction is just not true and could never happen, because I respect James Salinsa Debbah a whole lot. He's my icon, I came after him. I played the game to the best of my ability, but Debbah and I personally lived together. He's my cousin and there's no way we can play together twenty years on the national team and today we resign from the team then we would have problem? No! Debbah is one of our serious campaign commanders. He was at the AME Zion and had debates at the college. He was beside me; we talk about issues. So, I don't know where the information is coming from. We need the right information because we are moving toward reconciliation and you, the media, are the source of communication. So, when you hear these news stories, do just what you're doing now. You come and inquire and then you will have your answer, but there's no way Debbah and myself have any friction or problems."[585]

In Debbah's view, the way he was treated – being made to sit for hours in the rotunda of the President's office – was not just disrespectful but downright humiliating and demeaning. He was James Salinsa Debbah, Liberia's most celebrated footballer. Outside of Weah, Debbah was the next best thing. Here he was, sitting and waiting, putting up a straight face as bystanders and passersby who noticed him walked by, forcing himself to explain why? Why was he waiting to see the President? His cousin, his teammate? Why was he made to wait?

Even as Debbah struggled for answers, Weah's own denial that he had no issues with his buddy further validated the fears many had about him, that he hung on to grudges. But what was it that pushed him over the edge? What made Debbah feel hated by the President? Was Weah still holding to what Debbah had said about him years ago? That he was not quite experienced enough to be President? Or that Debbah threw his support behind Weah's rival, Charles Walker Brumskine of the opposition Liberty Party?

James Debbah had joined a long list of former friends, loved ones and peers who fell out of favour with Weah, who doubted Weah's leadership credentials, somewhere or sometime in his past. For now, it fell in the category of the unexplained – or even the Twilight Zone - but for the history books, it is something the football icon-turned President will likely be unable to shake off, regarding his state of mind, his preference for hate over love and his desire to payback and not reconcile.

Mahatma Gandhi once wisely said, "An eye for an eye only ends up making the whole world blind."[586] For everyday people, grudges can be painful. For leaders of people and nations, the failure to forgive can be a recipe for anger, bitterness and animosity. For George Weah, it remains an inexplicable part of his character.

21

GOODRIDGE FALLOUT

———

Until the attempt to burn down George's home on 9th Street Sinkor, George and Reginald Goodridge had become, not the best of pals, but really good friends – and potential business partners.

George and Reginald go way back. In fact, not many people know that in 1993, it was Reginald who came up with the branding of a big parade for George, whom he dubbed "Black Diamond". "I have always been in the promotional business,"[587] Goodridge says.

In 1993, he had started a company he named Diligent Associates through the late Fred Deshield. The plan was to sell diamonds to a company in South Korea. George met up with Goodridge shortly after the company was formed and the pair struck a friendship.

Goodridge recalls, "We met in Saye Town and he liked me immediately. He said, 'Papay, come to Paris because this thing you're talking is a good thing.'"[588]

It was a year before George won the FIFA World Best and Africa's Best Football Award. Murmurs were already in the air that Weah was on course to clinch the World Best crown. "For me, from a marketing perspective, I thought that we could transform it into a Michael Jordan through sports,"[589] Goodridge recalls. But a major stumbling block in the way of the partnership progressing was the presence of Sylvester Williams, alias Careca. Careca was

George's cousin and errand man, handling most of his daily runs. "Careca had George like a noose,"[590] Goodridge says. But George was so impressed with his business plan, he invited him to Paris.

"I went to Paris twice and I did a whole package. It caught the eye of a South Korean businessman who got interested and was prepared to pump a lot of money into it. We could have made about US$300 million in the first year alone,"[591] Goodridge thought at the time.

Goodridge spent a lot of time in Paris with George and his wife, Clar. "So, I spent some time with them in Paris. I know Clar like the back of my hand and we went everywhere together. In that very same Mercedes convertible, they claim I took from his 9th Street home, we drove from Paris to Brussels."[592]

Goodridge even suggested to George that they arrange a massive parade for him in Monrovia. "I put together a program to bring him home and we had this massive homecoming with the designation Black Diamond. I created that – at the time the Interim Government of National Unity (IGNU) was in charge, and we had this open convertible which drove him through the city. We had this massive program at the SKD stadium. So, he was impressed."[593]

The IGNU was formed in Gambia under the auspices of ECOWAS in October 1990 and Dr. Amos Sawyer became President and by 1992, numerous militias and political factions had arisen during the Liberian civil war that were included in the transitional government that emerged.

The parade left a lasting impression on George and would pave the way for a budding friendship. "He told me, Papay, I don't know you for long and you can pull this kinda crowd for me? So, come back to Paris, let's do this deal."[594]

In Paris, the businessman flew in from Seoul. "We were in this five-star hotel and everything," says Goodridge. "We had dinner in the evening before. At the time, this guy Aaron George, was Ambassador in Paris – a Masonic brother, we're cousins. And so, the embassy was opened to us."[595]

At this time, there were rumours in Paris that George would be leaving Paris Saint-Germain for AC Milan in Italy. As news spread of George's imminent departure for Milan, Goodridge says he was taken aback at the reaction from PSG supporters. "I always had a front-row seat in PSG stadium," says Goodridge, "and the word got out through the media, through a leak and it got out that day they were playing; they had this massive screen and they started to boo at him, Le nègre, calling him Nigger."[596]

Goodridge recalls, "George's face came on a massive screen in the stadium, 'a big closeup', with tears rolling down his eyes and he could not play. After three minutes, the coach took him out. It had not been made official, but the rumour started. I felt bad, I felt terrible for this guy."[597]

Later that evening, Goodridge met George and tried to console him. "I said, 'My man don't worry. Tomorrow, you will be signing a big deal in Italy, and you will be making much more money from the promotions deal than the chicken change they paying you here.'"

George said, "OK!"[598]

The following morning, George and Goodridge were due to meet with the South Korean businessman. "We were supposed to have met at 9:30 – 10:00 that morning at the hotel. So, I woke up early and went to the hotel to meet the businessman. We went over every detail of the business package – and 10:30 no George, 11:30 no George. The guy had to catch a flight at 3pm."[599]

At about 12:30, Goodridge called Clar, George's wife. "Where's George?"

"I don't know," said Clar. "He left early this morning."

At 1:30, the businessman said, "Well, I got to go. Whenever George is ready, let's do this thing."[600] The businessman flew back to Seoul, leaving Goodridge embarrassed and in a state of confusion.

Finally, at about 2:15 in the afternoon, George finally appeared, bristling with smile, telling Goodridge, "Don't mind that fucked up man,"[601] referring to the Korean businessman.

Goodridge later learned that George had flown to Italy early that morning where he had put ink to paper on a US$8 million contract with AC Milan. Goodridge said he was disappointed that George, who had the world at his feet, only signed for US$8 million. "I was so dejected."[602]

So, for all the stuff George had done, the marketing, the parade and work on the business plan with the South Korean, Goodridge says he was owed about US$52,000. "George paid 5,000 Francs which is about US$6,200 and I returned to Liberia."[603]

George said, "Don't worry Papay; money is not a problem."[604]

While in Paris, Goodridge noticed that George was having serious financial issues as well as delinquent tax problems. "So, before I returned to Liberia, he was having financial issues. George was in the seventy percent bracket in France because of his income. He had not paid for several years, which was one of the reasons why he had to leave France and go to Italy, to AC Milan."[605]

George told Goodridge to relay a message to President Charles Taylor. "Please tell the President it's not easy here."[606]

At the time, Goodridge says he wasn't really with the Taylor government. "I was shuttling back and forth doing my magazine. And so, George said 'When you get back to Monrovia, just tell the President, anything he can do to help me I will appreciate it.'"[607]

Lewis Brown, who was National Security Advisor to President Taylor at the time, says Goodridge's views about the Weah/Taylor relationship cannot be easily discounted. For Brown, Goodridge's claims to have been the go-between Weah and President Taylor cannot be dismissed. He says, "In any case, I had no idea of Weah's tax issues in France, nor was I aware of President Taylor's discussion to help resolve it. One important feature of the Taylor Presidency was his ability to compartmentalise. Only those directly handling certain matters were privy to details of it."[608]

However, Goodridge recalls that Weah had actually sought his intervention on Weah's house on 9th Street which was burned by rebels. "That very house on 9th Street, Weah had issues with the owners of the land, and he asked me to tell President Taylor to please intervene."[609]

Goodridge returned home and relayed the message to President Taylor. "President Taylor asked, 'How's you and your friend?' I explained to him and delivered the message from George."[610]

So, when an opportunity came for President Taylor to visit France for a meeting with President Jacques Chirac, it offered a perfect opportunity for Weah to address some of the tax issues which had been dogging him. According to Goodridge, George had sought help from President Taylor regarding his tax bills. "When President Taylor met Jacques Chirac, they were able to resolve George's tax problem. The late opposition leader Charles

Brumskine, who was President Pro Tempore of the Senate at the time, was in that meeting."[611]

Looking back, Goodridge is not so sure how his relationship with George turned sour. They had studied business prospects and shared a lot of fond moments. But things were simply never the same after their last experience in Paris. Over the past few years, Goodridge appears to be feeling the pinch of the fallout.

On Sept. 6, 2011, Weah and Goodridge met for the first time when George visited the Masonic Lodge in the Mamba Point enclave, not far from where Goodridge took charge of the black Mercedes convertible. A friend pointed to George, telling Goodridge, "That's your man there."[612] At some point during the evening at the Lodge, George reached over to Goodridge who went on to give him some pointers about politics.

Weeks later, Goodridge pondered, "It seems to me that after all of this stuff, I would have thought that this matter would have been behind us. I keep hearing from people that he still talks about it privately, he's still har-bouring this grudge and all of that kind of stuff. I wish this brother would have found a way to put an end to this thing, but it has not happened."[613]

In the years that followed, Goodridge became entrenched into politics. After all, he came from the cloth of the True Whig Party, the oldest political party in Liberia and one of the oldest on the continent of Africa. Founded in 1869, the TWP dominated Liberian politics from 1878 until 1980 when the Samuel Doe-led coup d'état ended the reign of William R. Tolbert. Although opposition was never outlawed during the TWP reign, in those years Liberia was governed as a one-party state. The party's complicated history made it difficult for entry into a modern era of politics. Not many Liberians were running to jump on a party with a history of ruling Liberia for more than 100 years, and under whose reign lay the blame of Liberia's chequered past. Thus, Goodridge spent much of the past decade trying to rebrand the party with the help of a few smaller parties under The Rainbow Alliance which was comprised of seven registered political parties and cer-tificated by the National Election Commission on August 31, 2020.

The seven political parties are Movement for Economic Empowerment, Redemption Democratic Change, True Whig Party, Union of Liberia

Democrats, Victory for Change Party, Vision for Liberia Transformation and Democratic Justice Party.

With his feet firmly rooted in politics, Goodridge, now the head of the opposition Rainbow Alliance, was puzzled that Weah continues to hang on to the past. "He must know that in the formation of the Rainbow Alliance, a lot of people have been wooing us, Alexander Cummings of the Alternative National Congress and Joseph Boakai of the former ruling Unity Party."[614]

Goodridge's political alliances were bound to collide with Weah at some point. It was just a matter of time before he and Weah crossed paths again.

In mid 2021, the Rainbow Alliance collaborated with the CPP in defeating the referendum. This was followed by a meeting between Goodridge and Cummings. The ANC leader had called Goodridge and said he wanted to come to his office at the E.J. Roye building which was also used as the headquarters of the Rainbow Alliance.

Ironically, after that meeting, Goodridge received a letter from the Monrovia City Corporation and the next day, the City Corporation sent officers to occupy the building. Goodridge began to sense that President Weah was working behind the scenes, using the court system to get back at him due to their previous disagreements.

Goodridge and the TWP had been embroiled in a nagging court battle over the EJ Roye Building, which served as the national headquarters of the TWP during its reign. After years of feuding about the rightful ownership of the E.J. Roye Building between the government and TWP denizens and loyalists, Monrovia's Civil Law Court 'A' suddenly came down with a ruling in favour of the Government of Liberia.

Goodridge recalls that sometime in March 2021, he received a strange call from the clerk of the Supreme Court regarding a property he owned on the Tubman Boulevard. "This matter has been in court for 20 years – back and forth but it would have been difficult for these guys to win outright. The clerk told me by telephone that the Chief Justice will be ruling on your case."[615]

Goodridge was shocked at the ruling, especially since he and the Chief Justice Francis Korkpor had been friends for a long. time "We've drunk beer together and visited each other. That man read that ruling against me and looked up in the air and knocked his gavel. I was so dejected. That property is worth half a million dollars, now it's all gone. A life's work gone in vain."[616]

Goodridge and the TWP had argued that the building was allegedly confiscated from the party by the junta in 1980; and not from a third party, referring to the government. They had asked the court to declare their rights as concerned partisans "because the government was illegally occupying the party's headquarters under the pretext of enforcing the military junta decree."[617]

"Our ownership rights over the E.J. Roye Building is a public knowledge and has never been in dispute, until two years ago when the government purportedly enforced a PRC decree #11 of April 12, 1980," Goodridge says the lawsuit alleged, adding that they, "illegally entered upon our property, physically took down the party's flag and started evicting our partisans and businesses that we placed on the property."[618] The TWP argued that the government made the move on the understanding that the military junta in 1980 had expropriated the building. Goodridge further alleged that even if the government had ended up de facto owning the building, the decision was made without any proof of a title deed.

The court record quoted the concerned TWP partisans: "Government has shown no evidence that the property was confiscated, and that it belongs to her by proof of a title deed."[619]

The TWP also claimed that there was no evidence to the extent of an eminent domain or condemnation proceedings: "instead they are using their various connections and powers to forcibly seize our property. They have not shown any inconvertible document to prove that the building is con-fiscated and is now owned by the government."[620]

In counterargument, government lawyers said although Goodridge and his colleagues had challenged the government's rights to the property, "It is not precluded by law from developing property in the absence of a restraining order or a writ of injunction from a court of competent jurisdiction."[621]

The TWP also alleged that the 2014 temporary restraining order had lapsed; and by operation of law, for them to obtain another restraining order they should have first filed a new petition for preliminary injunction, "setting forth the grounds for their request to be dismissed, because it should have been accompanied by the appropriate bond, which they failed to do." The TWP continued in its argument, "There being no new application or petition for preliminary injunction and no bond filed, the restraining order issued does not have any legal basis and must be denied as a matter of law."[622]

The day after the ruling, Goodridge received a call from Nancy Blah. Blah, the widow of former President Moses Blah, was a good friend of both Goodridge and the Chief Justice. Her late husband succeeded former President Charles after he agreed to move into exile following mounting pressure from the international community, especially the United States of America, to salvage the peace process and prevent Liberia from plunging into another round of civil war.

Goodridge had been supporting one of Nancy's daughters with a scholarship at the United Methodist University. Nancy told Goodridge, "Brother, when we heard about the thing, we went to our friend the Chief Justice, our Nimba man too. And we asked him, he said his hands [are] tied because the President's hands were behind this thing."[623]

For Goodridge, the 25 or 26 year grudge between him and Weah was making life really difficult and the defeat in the court illustrated how far Weah was willing to go to get even.

Goodridge, like most of those who crossed paths with Weah, knows that the football icon never forgets. James "Salinsa" Debbah experienced it, Jonathan "Boye Charles" Sogbie and many others who played football with Weah on the national team were quite aware too.

For Goodridge, not even his standing with the opposition Rainbow Alliance was good enough for Weah to see reason to let go.

It is one of those things Goodridge believes may just never go away. "I'm standing and I'm stronger than ever," he says. "It was a big loss for me at this age, but I'm standing and waiting and biding my time. So, all this thing about house getting burn and what not. I didn't even know his house had gotten burned. To this day, I have no idea why he accused me of burning his house and stealing his vehicle. I knew nothing about Charles Taylor's National Patriotic Front of Liberia. I was never part of the formation or whatsoever. I never took up arms or never led men in arms."[624]

22

EXPERIMENT

———

Winston Tubman had his doubts. Although he had headed a ticket with Weah as his Vice in the 2011 Presidential elections, he foresaw some of the pitfalls likely to dog the Weah Presidency. "I think we are in a tricky spot right now – and the Weah experiment isn't working, and we need a real leader."[625]

Since Weah's ascendance to the Presidency, Tubman had been watching from a distance with a lot of 'what ifs' and 'what could have been', had he and Weah gone all the way in that controversial 2011 election. "Right now, if I was in the government, I'm not sure what we would talk about other than how the country was being run which I don't think he has much interest in. We were close in that he saw me as a father figure who was honest and prepared to support him – and didn't believe in any country, Congau dom-ination – and he liked that, and he often said that we were friends."[626]

The term "Congau people" has been used in Sierra Leone and subse-quently Liberia to denote free-born or enslaved African Americans. These peoples ended up in the Congo basin area and found their way to Liberia after being released by the British navy who had taken over slaving vessels and released them. Some Afro-Caribbeans (mainly Barbadians) were also to join them.

Tubman says he's really not surprised at Weah's governance style. "He had no idea of what it took to be President. He said to me once, 'Just let me do my thing.' 'You can continue running the show' he said that. And that is what is happening now. People like McGill and Samuel Tweah are running things and he has no idea what is going on and cannot really influence anything."[627]

Tubman had earlier spoken of Weah's lacklustre interest in campaigning. If he wasn't willing to do the work, how could he lead?

In the first few years of the Weah Presidency, the answers were laid bare amid lingering questions. Who was really in charge of the government? Who was running the affairs of the state? All this amid rumours that President Weah worked mostly from his Jamaica Resort and abandoned the seat of the Presidency, performing most of his duties from the confines of his home at his private Jamaica Resort.

A major issue Weah had since becoming President is what many consider to be the outsourcing of the Presidency to his two key lieutenants – Minister of State Nathaniel McGill and Minister of Finance, Samuel Tweah.

How would Tubman have handled things if he and Weah had won in 2011? "I think we would have done our best," Tubman says. "We would have prevented ourselves from being bulldozed by those in his circle because we would quickly find ways to bolster security including using foreign help; but I think the country was ready to move forward – and to bring the old order back that would have meant another 30 years of dominance by them – and it would have meant a domination of the Congau or American-Liberian element and people would have been insufferable."[628]

Taking over from Johnson Sirleaf, President Weah was in the midst of inheriting an economy badly hit by downturns in world prices of iron and rubber, hitting Liberia's exports and economy hard. Longstanding poverty – where some 80% of the population lived on less than $1.25 a day – had been worsened by the Ebola crisis of 2014–2016.

Amid the uncertainty and apprehension of the Weah Presidency lay a bundle of hope and optimism marking the country's first electoral transfer of power since 1944.

By May 2019, rumours already began to fill the air that many in President Weah's circle had begun to lead him astray. There were echoes that the new administration already became embroiled in a series of corruption scandals including the missing billions and most importantly, reports that the government was dipping into donor funds for donor projects. Was the President naïve about his surroundings? Did he understand the nature of the job? How much was he involved in the day-to-day running of the country?

On street corners and in small shops, many sought answers to these questions to which, perhaps, only Weah or those in his inner circle were privy.

In the midst of these staggering reports were concerns from the International Monetary Fund (IMF) that the economy had contracted by 1.4% in 2019, down from 1.2% growth in 2018. Inflation was on the rise which, at this point, was undermining household purchasing power.

In only its first year, President Weah's government was already beginning to struggle to deliver on ambitious 'Pro-Poor' campaign pledges. Weah and his team had adopted a Pro-Poor policy aiming to directly target poor people, or what many consider to be a plan to reducing poverty. However, from the outset, the term was being misinterpreted by Weah and those within his inner circle to mean eating and drinking in what was considered to be poor and dilapidated areas or restaurants frequented by those below average income and borderline poor.

Many were confused as to how the policy would be shaped to improve the assets and capabilities of poor people. How would the policy be designed with emphasis on the needs of those languishing at the bottom of the economic ladder?

After year one, and delivering his second Annual Message to the nation in January 2019, the President announced several Pro-Poor bills he was forwarding to the national legislature for ratification. As *FrontPageAfrica* reported, these acts included, "an Act to Ratify and Authorize the Payment by the Government of Liberia of Tuition Fees for all Undergraduate Students in all Public Universities and Colleges, the National Youth Act, the Liberia Technical Vocational Education and Training Commission Act and the Revised Liberian Bank for Development and Investment Act."[629] The President also sought to push an Act to Ratify the Investment Incentive Agreement between Liberia and Fouta Corporation Act, ratifying the agreement for the Establishment of the Export-Import Bank (AFREXIMBANK) and an act to Amend the Revenue Code of Liberia to reform Excise Tax Law (2018).[630]

Additionally, the President sought a proposed amendment to extend the time required to renew resident permits. "In Liberia we have businesses and other people who have lived here for 30 to 50 years but have to renew resident permit every year," he disclosed. "This will have to change."[631] For President Weah, those who resided in the country for five years or more, without a criminal record, would be eligible under the proposed amendment. "The amendment proposed will also allow permit holders to no longer be required to obtain permits to re-enter the country,"[632] he announced. "We will also look into revising the requirement for annual renewal of work permits for a longer period."[633] He told the nation that these legislations would help smooth and enhance efforts toward accomplishing the Pro-Poor Agenda for Prosperity and Development (PAPD) outlined in October 29, 2018, that was to return power to the people, stimulate employment, boost the economy, ensure peace and lead to better governance and transparency.

"The overall objective of the Pro-Poor Agenda for Prosperity and Development and its ultimate goal is to lift our people from poverty to prosperity,"[634] the President announced.

Placing an emphasis on agriculture, President Weah acknowledged that the sector was a major impetus for economic revitalisation. He went on to bemoan the minute returns realised from the enormous investments put into agriculture, stressing, "This will have to change. Our international partners will agree with me that endless national and foreign resources have been and continue to be poured into agriculture yet returns on these investments are almost negligible. We will craft new practical and realistic agriculture policies, incentivise the sector by providing access to credit, reducing tariffs on agriculture implements, and provide small machines, modern seeds and fertilisers."[635]

President Weah suddenly found himself staring at substantial obstacles to broad-based, sustainable development. Additionally, coming on the heels of the global darling, Ellen Johnson Sirleaf, the government still faced corruption and flaws in infrastructure (notably electricity provision) which coupled with a business environment lacking in competition that was impeding growth in the country. All the big export businesses from palm oil to diamonds, and rubber to gold and iron ore were crucial for tax revenues and foreign currency exchange but those industries were providing few high-paying jobs to local Liberians, and much of the population relied on subsistence agriculture. Nearly one-third of Liberians faced moderate to severe chronic food insecurity despite the country's fertile land, extensive coastline, and abundant rainfall.

Additionally, after just one year, the administration found itself battling issues of human rights which had improved considerably since the early 2000s. However, corruption, episodic security force abuses against civilians, and discrimination against women and marginalised communities persisted.

The administration was also coming under fire for what many believed to be a clamp-down on the free press. Reporters like Paylayleh and Honnah faced harassment and occasional violence from government officials, including legislators, and some journalists reportedly self-censored to evade persecution.

President Weah also faced criticism over his government's failure to address the issue of accountability for wartime abuses which remains a highly sensitive issue, with several key figures from the civil war era having strong influences in elected and appointed offices.

All this was besetting the nation when several perpetrators of wartime abuses were facing trial in the U.S. court system, most on "immigration-related fraud or perjury charges related to nondisclosure of involvement in such abuses in applications for U.S. asylum, residency, or citizenship.[636] Among them was Alieu Kosiah, a former commander of the United Liberation Movement of Liberia for Democracy (ULIMO) faction, a rebel group that participated in the First Liberian Civil War (1989–1996) which fought against the National Patriotic Front of Liberia, led by Charles Taylor. After the war, Kosiah moved to Switzerland, where he obtained permanent residence. On November 10, 2014, Swiss authorities arrested him in connection with accusations that he was involved in mass killings in parts of Liberia's Lofa County from 1993 to 1995. Criminal complaints were filed against him by several Liberian victims, represented by Alain Werner, Director of Civitas Maxima.

The Swiss organisation which facilitates the documentation of international crimes, and pursues the redress of such crimes on behalf of victims who do not have access to justice, has been a breath of fresh air for victims of the civil war.

Mothers, fathers, sisters, brothers and children of war victims have been starving for justice and craving that those who committed atrocities would be made to pay. In the aftermath of a serious war crimes court to address casualties of war, Civitas rose to the occasion, collaborating with and building the capacity of local grass-roots partners to document crimes in the state where those crimes were committed. The organisation also generated awareness and informed debate around victims' cases, with a view to empowering local communities to pursue their own quests for justice.

This was crucial in bringing case against the likes of Kosiah, who was accused of ordering civilian massacres, rapes, and other atrocities in northern Liberia during the nation's First Civil War. Kosiah was charged on several counts, including having ordered, committed, or participated in the murder of civilians and soldiers hors de combat, having desecrated the corpse of a civilian, having raped a civilian, having ordered the cruel treatment of civilians, having recruited and used a child soldier, having ordered several pillages, and having ordered and/or participated in the forced transport of goods and ammunition by civilians.

The Swiss Federal Criminal Court postponed the trial several times due to the spread of COVID-19. Finally, the Court decided to proceed with the preliminary questions and the hearing of the defendant from December 3 to December 11, 2020. The rest of the trial – the hearing of the plaintiffs and the witnesses, and the final pleadings – took place from February 15 to March 5, 2021.

According to Civitas, on June 18, 2021, Kosiah was sentenced to 20 years in prison, from which his over 6 years of pre-trial detention was deducted and was ordered to pay over 50,000 CHF to the seven plaintiffs who testified against him. Although the former warlord has appealed the case, those who believed he committed atrocities have been relieved that they have been able to see him face trial for alleged crimes that includes, ordering the killing of 13 civilians and 2 unarmed soldiers, murdering four civilians, raping a civilian, ordering the cruel treatment of 7 civilians, infringing upon the dignity of a deceased civilian, repeatedly ordering the cruel, humiliating, and degrading treatment of several civilians, repeatedly inflicting cruel, inhuman, and degrading treatment on several civilians, repeated orders to loot, and using a child soldier in armed hostilities. The crimes for which

Kosiah is acquitted included recruiting a child soldier; attempted murder of a civilian; complicity in a civilian murder; and giving orders to loot in one instance.

What made the Kosiah case interesting was the fact that it marked the first time a Liberian national was tried for war crimes in relation to the Liberian Civil Wars, and the first time the Federal Criminal Court held a war crimes trial.

Another intriguing case that grasped the attention of the world was the case of Agnes Reeves Taylor, a former wife of the former dictator Charles Taylor, who was arrested by the Metropolitan Police Service in London in June 2017 and later charged with torture for her alleged involvement with atrocities committed by Charles Taylor's rebel group, the National Patriotic Front of Liberia (NPFL), during the First Liberian Civil War. Reeves Taylor was charged with seven counts of torture and one count of conspiracy to commit torture in relation to her involvement with the NPFL during the First Liberian Civil War. She was the second person formerly associated with the NPFL that has been charged with crimes committed during Liberia's civil wars. On December 6, 2019, the Central Criminal Court decided to dismiss the charges against Agnes Reeves Taylor.

Shortly after the UK court ruling, Agnes returned to Liberia, claiming that the Central British Court had dismissed the charges against her. In May 2022, Agnes filed a suit before the Civil Law Court in Monrovia for damages for malicious prosecution/wrong, accusing the institutions, as well as Hassan Bility and Werner of allegedly conniving and inflicting untold suffering and pains against her.

Bility, the director of the Global Justice and Research Project (GJRP), a non-governmental organisation dedicated to the documentation of war time atrocities in Liberia and to assisting victims in their pursuit of justice, has been working with Civitas to bring cases against perpetrators of the war.

Agnes asked the civil law court to hold both Bility, Werner and their institutions to pay over US$1 million for their alleged false accounts which led the criminal justice system in the United Kingdom to prosecute her for alleged torture charges, though the U.K. court systems later dismissed the charges against her.

FrontPageAfrica would later report, citing U.K. court records that Agnes was not released based on her innocence of the allegations brought against her by Mr. Bility's GJRP and Civitas Maxima.

The newspaper reported on May 13, 2022 that on December 6, 2019, the Central Criminal Court (The Old Bailey) in London decided to dismiss the charges against Agnes after the UK Supreme Court confirmed, in a historic judgment on November 13, 2019, that members of non-State armed groups may be prosecuted for crimes of torture under section 134(1) of the UK Criminal Justice Act 1988, thus legally paving the way for the case against Agnes Reeves Taylor to proceed to trial. "However, after rendering its judgment, the U.K. Supreme Court sent the case back to the Central Criminal Court to consider further evidence from the prosecution's expert and apply the legal standard confirmed by the Supreme Court to the facts of the case."[637]

Many activists and political observers say, Agnes returned to Monrovia in a bid to avoid the next phase of trial mounting against her.

The case against Kunti K., a former ULIMO commander, arrested in 2018 on suspicion of crimes against humanity and torture allegedly committed during the First Liberian Civil War (1989–1996) was a less complicated legal affair. Kunti was arrested as he was trying to flee.

Civitas documented that in the spring of 2019, the French and Liberian authorities collaborated on a fact-finding mission relating to proceedings in Lofa County, north-western Liberia. This marked the first time since the end of the Second Civil War in 2003 that Liberian authorities had proceeded, along with foreign authorities, to undertake crime scene reconstructions relating to war-time crimes. These reconstructions took place in the presence of the French prosecuting authorities, investigating judge, defence lawyers, and the civil parties.

In September 2019, Kunti K. was released from pre-trial detention due to a procedural error. Kunti K. was subject to conditions of release, including being prohibited from leaving France. In January 2020, he was arrested again as he was trying to flee France.

Also on the Civitas radar was Michel Desaedeleer, a U.S. and Belgian citizen, who was arrested in September 2015 in Malaga, Spain, following

the issuance of a European arrest warrant against him. He was then transferred to Belgium where he was charged for war crimes and crimes against
humanity, being accused of having participated with Charles Taylor and the
rebels of the RUF in Sierra Leone in the trade of so-called "blood diamonds".
The arrest came after several citizens of Sierra Leone, victims of enslavement
during the civil war, filed in Brussels in January 2011 a criminal complaint
against Mr. Desaedeleer who then resided in the United States. They were
represented by the Belgian lawyer Luc Walleyn. This was the very first time
that someone was "arrested and indicted for participation in the blood
diamonds trade."[638] Desaedeleer passed away in Belgian custody on 28
September 2016, a few months before his trial was scheduled to commence.

The case brought against Mohammed Jabbateh, aka Jungle Jabbah in
April 2016, trumpeted another milestone for Civitas. Jabbateh was arrested
in Pennsylvania, U.S.A.

Civitas documented that on the 2nd of October 2017, the U.S. Government's immigration fraud case against the Liberian citizen, Pennsylvania
resident, and alleged war criminal, began in Philadelphia. "Jabbateh was
charged with two counts of fraud in immigration documents and two counts
of perjury for having lied to authorities about his war time activities. He
was a ULIMO commander, then later ULIMO-K post-faction split, during
the First Liberian Civil War and responsible for commanding atrocious
wartime crimes including murder, conscription of child soldiers, and can-
nibalism. A jury convicted him on October 18, 2017. On April 19, 2018,
he was sentenced to 30 years in prison, the maximum possible sentence for
his charges. This sentence is also one of the longest sentences for immigration
fraud in U.S. history. Civitas Maxima and the Global Justice and Research
Project had collaborated with the U.S. authorities on the investigation
since 2014."[639]

According to Civitas, the Jabbateh trial was the first ever trial against a
ULIMO commander and the first time that victims testified in a criminal
trial about crimes committed during the First Liberian Civil War. On September 8, 2020, the United States Court of Appeals for the Third Circuit
in Philadelphia rejected Mohammed Jabbateh's appeal, upholding his conviction and 30-year prison sentence. The Appeal Court's decision describes
Jabbateh's actions as being carried out "with bone-chilling cruelty" stating

that, "The horrors recounted at trial, retold only in part here, are indescribably tragic" and "None, including the jury that weighed impartially the mountain of evidence marshalled against Jabbateh, would view his conduct as anything less than monstrous."

In May 2014, Juconti Thomas Woewiyu was arrested at the Newark Liberty International Airport in New Jersey, U.S.A, upon his return from a trip to Liberia. Woewiyu was charged with 2 counts of fraudulently attempting to obtain citizenship, 4 counts of fraud in immigration documents, 3 counts of false statements in relation to naturalization, and 7 counts of perjury.

Woewiyu founded the NPFL with Charles Taylor and served as Spokesman and Defence Minister until political dissonance led him to create and lead the NPFL-CRC during Liberia's First Civil War (1989–1996). June 11, 2018, marked the start of Woewiyu's immigration fraud trial. Over 35 witnesses testified to his direct and indirect involvement with war crimes during the civil war. After 13 days in court, the jury found Woewiyu guilty on 11 of 16 counts on July 3, 2018. His maximum possible sentence is 75 years in prison. Woewiyu died on April 12, 2020, of COVID-19, in Philadelphia, U.S. He was still awaiting his sentencing. His trial marked the first time ever that somebody who held a ministerial position during the First Liberian Civil War faced justice and the first time that the atrocities of the NPFL – the most violent rebel faction active from 1989–1996 – were documented in a courtroom.

One case that generated a lot of attention was the case against Martina Johnson, a former front-line commander of the National Patriotic Front of Liberia (NPFL). She was arrested in 2014 on suspicion of war crimes and crimes against humanity allegedly committed during the First Liberian Civil War. She was arrested in Belgium, a country where she resided since 2003. This was the very first time an alleged Liberian perpetrator was criminally charged for crimes under international law committed in Liberia during the First Civil War. Liberian victims implicated Johnson as having participated directly in mutilation and mass killings in late 1992 during the "Operation Octopus", an infamous military offensive by Charles Taylor's NPFL on the capital Monrovia. She was placed on conditional release shortly after her arrest.

The case against Gibril Massaquoi was unique for a number of reasons. For the first time in the history of war crimes cases involving Civitas, judges from Finland where Massaquoi was arrested, travelled to Liberia to interview witnesses. The judges toured the northern parts of Liberia, where the alleged atrocities were committed as part of a first-of-a-kind trial of a warlord accused of committing atrocities during the country's civil war.

The trip to Liberia was important as it offered the judges an opportunity to gather witness testimonies and hear evidence on Liberian soil – the first time war-crime proceedings have taken place in the country.

According to Civitas, the judges' presence in Liberia set a "monumental precedent in the ongoing struggle for accountability for the world's worst atrocities and crimes".

Massaquoi was a member of the Revolutionary United Front (RUF) inner circle during the Sierra Leonean Civil War, was a Lieutenant-Colonel and spokesman of the rebel group as well as an assistant to the group's founder, Foday Sankoh. In 2005, he testified in open session before the Special Court for Sierra Leone (SCSL) in the case against members of Sierra Leone's former Armed Forces Revolutionary Council (AFRC), a rebel group that allied itself with the RUF rebels in the late 1990s. On March 10, 2020, Massaquoi was arrested in Tampere, Finland, by the Finnish police who suspect that he had committed war crimes and crimes against humanity in Liberia between 1999 and 2003. The crimes he allegedly committed include homicide, sexual violence, and the recruitment and use of child soldiers.

After days of trial, the Pirkanmaa District Court in Tampere, Finland, on April 29th, 2022, issued its judgement, and announced the dismissal of all charges, and found that there was reasonable doubt that the defendant committed the offences that he was charged with.

The Massaquoi verdict was a blow to Civitas. In a statement hours after the verdict, Civitas declared: "The world watches with horror as atrocities are committed in Ukraine and as international and national entities are grappling with the challenges of bringing to accountability those responsible for grievous crimes. The Gibril Massaquoi trial reminds us that national jurisdictions play a critical role in ensuring that war crimes and crimes against humanity are prosecuted, regardless of the nationality of the victims, and the time since these were allegedly committed."[640]

For Civitas, the Massaquoi trial was a complex case of intertwined conflicts with a former insider witness of an international court. "The Massaquoi trial will surely become an important reference on the concrete challenges of universal jurisdiction. And the Finnish experience will be an important case study for other countries who are committed to the principle," Civitas concluded in a post-trial statement, published by *FrontPageAfrica*.

In the pursuit of justice for perpetrators of Liberia's civil war, the issue of holding those accountable and responsible has always been a nagging issue. It certainly was at the start of Ellen Johnson Sirleaf's government when she was forced to turn over former President Charles Taylor for war crimes committed in next-door Sierra Leone. And for her successor, President Weah, the issue proved to be equally thorny. All of the trials involving alleged perpetrators against victims of the civil war were taking place outside the jurisdiction of Liberia, but Liberia was failing to tackle the issue head on.

Weah had already flip-flopped on the issue and was uncertain about his administration's policy regarding war crimes. Pressure was mounting from all over and human rights organisations were clamping down on the government's throat.

Elise Keppler, Associate Director, International Justice Program of the watchdog group, Human Rights Watch (HRW) took issue with President Weah on the eve of his address to the U.N. General Assembly in September 2020. She reminded the President of his speech a year earlier when he gave hope to victims of brutal crimes committed during the country's civil wars and spoke about pursuing a war crimes court for Liberia. President Weah had said that he was engaging the national legislature, the judicial system and international partners on the court's creation. However, HRW was unhappy with the snail's pace at which it was moving. In a letter sent on the eve of the President's address to the U.N. in September 2020, the watchdog group recalls, "Liberians suffered tremendously during the wars, which spanned more than 14 years starting in 1989, and left tens of thousands of dead. Warring parties gunned down civilians in their homes, marketplaces, and places of worship. Women and girls were subjected to horrific sexual violence including gang rape, sexual slavery, and torture. Villages were destroyed. Children were abducted and forced into armed service."[641] HRW said while the Weah government had begun to allow foreign investigators into Liberia to investigate war crimes for overseas prosecutions, not one alleged perpetrator had faced a court of law in Liberia.

The problem stemmed from the fact that he was reluctant to address the issue because a lot of those who were involved in the war were amongst Weah's key advisors and played prominent role in his inner circle.

And the international community was taking notice. On October 6, 2022, U.S. Ambassador At Large for Global Criminal Justice (GCJ), Dr. Beth Van Schaack, during a visit to Liberia, held meetings with major stakeholders concerning Liberia's transitional justice mechanisms, especially the implementation of the Truth and Reconciliation Commission's recommendations.

Dr. Schaack, who advises the Secretary of State and other Department leadership on issues related to the prevention of and response to atrocity crimes, including war crimes, crimes against humanity, and genocide, lamented to journalists at a news conference on October 6: "There has been no accountability here on the criminal side, or the civil side for those who have been most responsible for those abuses… I will be having some meetings with members of the government and I plan to ask: what the status of the draft statute is and why it is not being put forward; what are the blockages and how can the blockages be solved?"[642]

Dr. Schaack described the TRC report and its recommendations, as an "excellent" exercise in gathering the views of many survivors across the country. "I have studied your system and read your Truth and Reconciliation Commission report which was an excellent exercise in gathering the views of many survivors across the country as to what happened during the two consequential civil wars."[643]

Amongst President Weah and his aides, there is often the perception that the administration despite its flaws, was being picked on by the U.S. and other international bodies regarding the issue of war crimes. After all, his predecessor, Madam Ellen Johnson Sirleaf, besides turning over Charles Taylor to the international community, shortly after taking over, had not really done much to bring those responsible for the war to book.

This was evident on September 30, 2019 when President Weah expressed his confusion, while addressing the United Nations' 174th General Assembly. The President said while he understands the rising chorus of voices from many quarters, calling for the establishment of an Economic and War Crimes Court, his administration was "at a loss to understand why the clamor for the establishment of the Court is now being made, almost a full decade after it was first called for, and during which time no such pressure was brought to bear on the government that grew out of the Accra Peace Accord."[644]

Dithering on the issue of war crimes has been a norm for Weah, during the past five year. Limping into the crucial elections in 2023, the issue is unlikely to go away and many, including war crimes activists and advocates like Human Rights Watch appear perplexed that justice remains elusive for victims amid growing concerns that victims of the civil war are drawing even further away from seeing justice in their lifetime.

Among them was Emmanuel Shaw, a former Minister of Finance, who served from 1989 to 1990. He was a close confidante of former President and convicted war criminal, Charles Taylor. Also in the President's inner circle was Charles Bright. Bright was one of the prominent figures of the Civil War, who had served as Finance Minister in the Taylor government and was appointed by Weah as an economic advisor. Bright was General John T. Richardson's principal deputy, remembered for taking over the Housing Bank in Monrovia in military uniform when in Taylor's National Patriotic Front of Liberia.

The presence of these two officials in Weah's inner circle resurrected echoes of the baggage which had dogged Weah's bid for the Presidency, especially after he tipped the former First Lady, Jewel Howard Taylor, as his running mate.

Reports of the Taylor-era figures in Weah's inner circle triggered Liberian, regional, and international organisations to write to President Weah on September 10, 2020, "asking Weah to use his speech at that month's General Assembly to request U.N. assistance in setting up a war crimes court, reviving plans for justice, and rekindling the hopes of victims and their families."[645]

Complicating matters, Bhofal Chambers, speaker of the lower house of the national legislature, declined to introduce a resolution in the court in October 2019, "despite strong backing among lawmakers. Human rights activists who have championed accountability have faced increasing threats, as have witnesses to civil wars-era crimes."[646]

Ironically, on December 9, 2021, coinciding with International Anti-Corruption Day, the United States government declared its solidarity with all those committed to confronting and ending widespread corruption by slapping sanctions on Senator Prince Y. Johnson, one of the most brutal figures of the Liberian civil war.

Johnson, a former warlord and member of the Liberian Senate, is the former Chairman of the Senate Committee on National Security, Defence, Intelligence, and Veteran Affairs. In 1990, he was responsible for the callous murder of former Liberian President Samuel Doe. Johnson is named in Liberia's Truth and Reconciliation Report as having committed some of the worst atrocities during the country's First Civil War. According to the U.S., Johnson, as a Senator, had been involved in pay-for-play funding with government ministries and organisations for personal enrichment. As part of the scheme, upon receiving funding from the Government of Liberia (GOL), the involved government ministries and organisations laundered a portion of the funding for return to the involved participants. The pay-for-play funding scheme involved millions of U.S. dollars. Johnson had also offered the sale of votes in multiple Liberian elections in exchange for money.

Pursuant to E.O. 13818, Johnson was designated as 'being a foreign person who is a current or former government official, or a person acting for or on behalf of such an official, who is responsible for or complicit in, or has directly or indirectly engaged in, corruption, including the misappropriation of state assets, the expropriation of private assets for personal gain, corruption related to government contracts or the extraction of natural resources, or bribery.'

This included those within the Government of Liberia who stood up against corruption, committed Liberian citizens and organisations seeking to challenge the impunity of corrupt officials, and international organisations supporting anti-corruption efforts. The U.S.A. trumpeted the Johnson sanction as one small part of its anti-corruption effort.

The sanction slapped on Johnson marked the official start of the Summit for Democracy, which highlighted corruption as one of the three areas most critical for democracies to address.

In his June 2021 action establishing the fight against corruption as a core national security interest, President Joseph R. Biden said, that

"Corruption corrodes public trust; hobbles effective governance; distorts markets and equitable access to services; undercuts development efforts; contributes to national fragility, extremism, and migration; and provides authoritarian leaders a means to undermine democracies worldwide. When leaders steal from their nations' citizens or oligarchs flout the rule of law, economic growth slows, inequality widens, and trust in government plummets."[647]

In response to the sanctions, the U.S. Mission in Liberia said that it had long reported on the pervasiveness of corruption within the Government of Liberia, including in the annual Human Rights Report. "Organisations such as Transparency International also score Liberia very poorly in terms of corruption. But more than that, Liberian Government officials and citizens themselves regularly report on corrupt government activities that reach across all sectors of governance and society. No government is free from corruption, but no government can improve its democracy without simultaneously attacking corruption, and that effort must start at the very top, both in word and in deed."[648]

The U.S. issued a word of caution to all three branches of the government of Liberia, to acknowledge that public officials should not receive financial benefit from their positions other than their salary and should take all necessary measures to stand up to the corruption that continues to erode the trust between the government and its people. America's interest in Liberia dates to a historical past with Liberia, often the beneficiary of massive U.S. aid. Since the end of Liberia's second conflict in 2003, the United States has provided more than $2.4 billion in State Department- and USAID-administered assistance to support Liberia's post-war stabilisation and development. This does not include nearly $600 million in emergency assistance for Liberia's Ebola response, aid channeled through other U.S. agencies, or U.S. funding for a long-running U.N. peacekeeping mission that completed its mandate in 2018. Current U.S. assistance, which totaled $96.5 million in fiscal year 2019, centres on supporting agriculture-led development and strengthening the health system, public service delivery, civil society capacity, and justice and security sectors. An ongoing $256.7 million Millennium Challenge Corporation (MCC) Compact seeks to enhance Liberia's power sector and roads infrastructure.

The war crimes issue aside, international stakeholders began to raise concerns about governance of Liberia under Weah. In an op-ed on January 28, 2019, Elizabeth Donnelly, a former Deputy Director, Africa Programme at Chatham House, described President Weah as a conflicted leader. "George Weah's election as President of Liberia in January 2018 was widely hailed as a popular victory over ineffective or corrupt politics and was the first peaceful handover of power since the end of the Liberian civil war. Seen as a victory of the people over a political system viewed as ineffective (at best) or corrupt (at worst), Weah's election brought with it the high expectations of not just his support base but the country as a whole. However, despite early signs that he would take on bureaucratic excess and corruption, rebuild infrastructure and drive economic development, Weah's first year in office was haunted by the old guard of Liberian politics, hampered by limited resources and dogged by controversies over missing money. Continuity seems to be winning out over change."[649]

Weah had faced dogged questions about his ineptitude and inexperience to lead Liberia. But now he was facing even more severe questions about his choices and his selection of people to help him lead.

The likes of Cllr. Winston Tubman and Cllr. Varney Sherman had earlier expressed the view that Weah would be a ceremonial President, surrounded by the right and experienced people. Weah had his own agenda, his own plans about how he wanted to lead, and it was nothing like what others envisioned for him.

Raising questions about the administration's expressed willingness to clean up graft, waste and corruption, Donnelly recalls how, within hours of taking over the Presidency, Weah had issued an ultimatum to outgoing government ministers and civil servants: return all government equipment, including cars, or face arrest. Weah himself took a pay cut. Such moves were applauded by the media and the public at large and raised hopes of a change in political culture. But his early actions and populist rhetoric were in tension with the realpolitik demands of managing an entrenched political class and a political system designed to defend their privilege. Weah was surrounded by people linked to past corruption and mismanagement, or with ties, direct or indirect, to key figures in Liberia's civil war.

The report also raised questions about Weah's ties to the former warlord, Prince Johnson, who reasserted and redefined his influence and power by blocking appointments and insisting on more people from his home county of Nimba being appointed. Donnelly wrote, "Weah's Vice President, Jewel Taylor, has links to war criminal and former President Charles Taylor. Such alliances and appointments may be the price of getting anything done, but they also highlight unresolved issues around justice and war crimes, and risk complications in Weah's relations both with his support base and Liberia's foreign partners."[650]

President Weah also came under fire for presiding over an environment of intimidation and stifling of the freedom of the press, including examples of personal attacks on journalists and the closure of the newspaper *Front-PageAfrica* and the arrest of its staff.[651]

The President did not stop there. He also fired Konah Karmo, head of the secretariat of the Liberia Extractive Industries Transparency Initiative, a key voice for transparency in the country, and appointed a loyalist in his place. Domestic and international criticisms were growing by the day.

Donnelly summed up President Weah as a 'conflicted leader', saying he was, "A man of the people, who identifies with the poorest of his compatriots, but also someone who is accustomed to the trappings of the elite and who has seemed to welcome back a political old-guard mired in past corruption and mismanagement scandals. The real George Weah remains elusive."[652]

Criticism of the Weah government resulted in great loss for Liberia, especially regarding the Millennium Challenge Corporation, an independent U.S. Government foreign aid agency based on the principle that aid is most effective when it reinforces good governance...

In late 2021, for the first time since 2009, Liberia fell sharply on the annual assessment of the Millennium Challenge Corporation, a collection of 20 independent, third-party indicators that measure a country's policy performance. Every year, each MCC candidate country receives a scorecard assessing performance in three policy categories: Ruling Justly, Investing in People, and Encouraging Economic Freedom. Liberia first qualified in 2015 during the reign of Weah's predecessor, Johnson Sirleaf, when the compact grant was signed in a bid to support the energy sector, providing access to reliable and affordable electricity and build the foundation for the periodic maintenance of primary roads in the country. In 2016, Liberia received a grant of US$257 million from the United States through the MCC to enhance its electricity and road projects. A total of 85% of compact funds have since been committed in contracts, while 73% of total compact budget has been disbursed. The total compact comes to about $256.7 million. When *FrontPageAfrica* reported on Liberia's Millennium Challenge Corporation (MCC) "scorecard", the five-year compact was already past its halfway stage and intending to impact an estimated half a million Liberians before it concluded in 2021.[653] In June 2021, Jonathan Nash, the Chief Operating officer of MCC visited Liberia and held several meetings with top government officials. During that visit, Nash stressed the need for the government to successfully implement its part of the current compact and at the same time focus on maintaining its grades on the scorecard. He also emphasised that if Liberia must regain another compact, it must first perform on the upcoming scorecard. In Monrovia in June 2018, he said, "To obtain a second compact, the board looks at the extent at which a country was able to deliver and have a high-quality implementation of the first compact. The board generally looks for improved performance on the scorecard over time as well. I'm here to engage with President Weah and his administration to review the progress that has been made to date and to take a look ahead at the challenges and opportunities that lie ahead for the completion of the particular compact."[654]

Since the MCC Chief Operating Officer warned Liberia about the possibility of losing another compact, the government under President George Weah had appeared to be lackadaisical about the ramifications of its policy action. Consequently, these missteps might certainly disrupt the much-publicised Pro-Poor Agenda which would heavily rely on international funding from donor countries.

The Weah administration, under mounting criticisms over bad governance, was losing its grip and the U.S. was losing patience. On Thursday, August 26, 2021, U.S. Ambassador Michael McCarthy toured the Liberia Electricity Corporation's (LEC) Bushrod Island facilities in order to better understand how U.S. assistance in the power sector has been used, and what the challenges are to the sector. Interestingly, the U.S. Embassy and Liberian Government had just celebrated, on January 21, 2021, a bittersweet moment with the end of the MCC Compact, a U.S.-funded, $257 million, 5-year effort, which was primarily focused on rehabilitation of the Mt. Coffee Hydropower Plant, the largest source of power in the country and Liberia's most valuable fixed asset. During his visit, the Ambassador learned that commercial losses including theft and unpaid bills accounted for over 50% of the electricity produced by LEC, seriously threatening the financial viability of the organisation.

And just like that, the program aimed at addressing limited access to reliable and affordable electricity in the country and poor-quality road infrastructure, was being erased even as Liberians struggled for stable electricity. The compact had funded the rehabilitation of Liberia's largest power source, the Mt. Coffee Hydropower Plant, supported the creation of an independent energy sector regulator, developed a training program for technicians in the electricity sector, supported improved delivery of electricity services by the LEC, and established a data-driven road maintenance system.

Ambassador McCarthy later hosted a press conference at the U.S. Embassy in Monrovia following the visit and came up with a dismal conclusion. "I was both impressed and discouraged by what I saw and heard."[655] He continued to say that the LEC's international management team had greatly improved LEC's operational readiness and facilities. However, widespread power theft and unpaid power bills placed LEC in a financial crisis from which it could not recover without immediate intervention and support from the Liberian Government. The Ambassador highlighted four main messages in a call-to-action for the Liberian people.

First, he emphasised that electricity generation, transmission, and distribution is very expensive. "Utilities around the world invest large sums in infrastructure, operations, and maintenance in order to 'keep the lights on', and they receive very low return on investment. Liberia's power sector is no different, except that it is losing money every day. Nowhere in the world is electricity free. I pay an electric bill at my home in the United States. As Minister Tweah said last week, Liberia is no different: if you want electricity, you must pay for it. Nobody has ever promised free electricity to the people of Liberia."[656]

Second, Ambassador McCarthy pointed out that more than half of all electricity LEC generates is not paid for. He put it in clear terms, saying,

"Each connection that isn't generating revenue is a step toward the collapse of the electric grid ... About two-thirds of the electricity being generated by LEC does not result in revenue [due mostly to power theft]. Without that revenue, how can LEC fix the technical issues? How can they quickly respond to power interruptions? How can they continue to connect more of Liberia to the power grid?"[657] He acknowledged that electricity is expensive in Liberia, but that it would be difficult for that to change because "for each person that illegally connects to a power line, they are making everyone else underwrite the cost of power and making it harder to reduce the cost for those who do pay. They are also making all connections less reliable, which will lead to even more maintenance costs down the road. The only way to reduce the cost of electricity is for every LEC customer to be properly connected and to pay their electricity bills."[658]

Third, the Ambassador asked all Liberians to do their part to ensure that LEC could continue to provide electricity. "Here and now," he said, "I call on every user of electricity in Liberia to pay their bills in order for the power sector to survive here."[659] He pointed out that there was not a single culprit, but that instead, power was being stolen by individuals as well as some large users who were clearly using their political connections to keep from paying, and that the Government of Liberia had much to do to fix the problem. "It's not enough to say that the power theft situation is complicated, or that it's hard to fix. In order to protect our investments, and your future, and to set Liberia on the path to opportunity, we need to see action – payment of electricity bills, prosecutions, convictions – and we need to see substantial sentences and fines for power theft. This needs to be a systemic focus – nothing will improve without a strong response across the judicial system, supported at the highest levels of the Liberian Government. In his speech commemorating the delivery of electricity to Peace Island, President Weah called for this as well."[660]

Finally, Ambassador McCarthy asked both the Liberian Government and the Liberian people to take power theft more seriously. "Having invested so heavily in the power sector here, it's not too much for the U.S. Government to ask that the Liberian Government do more to protect our investments and its own power sector. We have been told by multiple sources that there is a well-organised electricity theft cartel that benefits well-connected

businesses and even government officials. We know that some LEC investigators trying to fix this problem have been harassed by some representing
themselves as security officials. This is absolutely unacceptable. As major
investors in Liberia's power sector, we call on government officials to do
everything possible to stop this corruption and prosecute the perpetrators,
no matter how important they may be."[661]

Ahead of the 2023 elections, President Weah had a lot going for him,
despite the lapses in governance and the failure of his administration to
address burning and lingering issues affecting the poor and those languishing
at the bottom of the economic ladder.

First, the opposition was in tatters, disorganised and unsure of itself.
Speculation was rife that President Weah and his team had planted spies in
the opposition to disrupt the chemistry and ruin what was seen as the only
viable alternative. The Collaborating Political Parties were comprised of the
former ruling Unity Party of Johnson Sirleaf's Vice President Joseph Boakai,
controversial businessman and former Charles Taylor aide, Benoni Urey's
All Liberian Party, the Alternative National Congress of former Coca Cola
Executive Alexander Cummings and Charles Brumskine's Liberty Party.
Brumskine himself had succumbed to cancer shortly after his third failed
attempt at winning the Presidency. His party, now in tatters with a vacuum
to fill due to his death, scrambled for leadership with those looking to fill
Brumskine's shoes while struggling to hold the party together.

Despite his reservations about President Weah, Winston Tubman was
often not so sure that the current field of contenders, some of whom ran in
the 2017 elections would cut it. "I don't think Cummings fits the bill. He
did well in Coca Cola, but he doesn't have the charisma – and he doesn't
have any anchor."[662]

Cummings lack of a base was also a problem, as Tubman suggested. "He
went to Maryland County and said that was his home, but he was never
accepted there and he has never made any real effort to make that place his
home. So, he would be seen as just another American-Liberian. The best
chance he has is to run with the former Vice President Joseph Boakai as a
running mate. I don't see Liberians embracing an unknown Congau man,
not even for a Tubman. I mean they did for me. So, I think it's difficult, if

we don't get that to happen, him becoming Vice President to Boakai, but if it doesn't happen that way, I don't see how it works."[663]

Toward the end of Weah's first term in office, it was evident that the administration had fallen short of not just its own expectations but those of many Liberians whose hopes appeared to be dashed. In a January 2021 report, Naymote Partners for Democratic Development concluded that the President had fulfilled only seven of his 92 promises, of which five had been completed during his first year in office. These include revising the national school curriculum, passing a long-awaited land rights law and capping the salaries of senior government officials at $7,800.

While touting some progress on the President's 38 pledges, Naymote lamented that on the economic front, these included steps to reduce tariffs on basic commodities, upgrades to key infrastructure such as roads and the introduction of loans for small businesses. However, Weah's government had failed to begin work on 32 promises, the report said. There were "no tangible actions on promises around accountability and anti-corruption,"[664] the group said, explaining that those pledges included setting new rules to prevent public sector graft and pursuing legal action against companies involved in bid-rigging and other corrupt practices.

The economy worsened with inflation hitting 30% and civil servants reporting months-long delays to salary payments.

The Weah experiment was in full gear midway into his six years in office. But what was evident from the start was the scale of the challenges that many had envisioned and which many felt would make or break the football icon. The expectations, the headaches, the heartbreaks and the disappointment, were mostly the result of President Weah's own doing and those of his inner circle.

Weah's dilemmas could very well be owed to his background as a footballer. After all, he was a celebrity. Celebrities often shy away from the press and rarely desire anything negative to be said about them in the public domain.

Unfortunately, Weah quickly appeared to be mastering the game of sycophancy and the patronage system of his predecessors. He had become accustomed to hearing only the good things that his inner circle was telling him. He was like the emperor without any clothes, and little different to former President Tubman, who perfected the patronage system of doling out gifts and cash to voters and supporters. Weah was doing everything he could to complete his transition from footballer to President.

23

FAMILY AFFAIR

———

Clar Marie Duncan migrated with her family from Jamaica to New York in 1978. Only thirteen years-old at the time, Clar remembers living in Brooklyn, New York. She spoke to Rabin Nickens on Cultural Caribbean TV shortly after her husband was inaugurated as President. "I did all my schooling in New York and everything about me – I was moulded in New York. So, I have to give thanks to New York for that. Even though I was born in Jamaica."[665]

Clar says she always had an eye for business. "Growing up in New York City, we're surrounded by so many businesses and my brother and I, he's the President General of the Universal Negro Improvement Association (UNIA). We always wanted to own our own businesses and we started our first business in Brooklyn in Nordstrand Avenue. Unfortunately, it didn't work out. Later on, we moved to downtown Brooklyn. It was very difficult because we had so many businesses in the area."[666]

Clar would later move to Florida where she and her brother tried their hands at a number of unsuccessful business projects. "We tried something there also but with the hurricane and everything we just decided to give it up – and later on when we moved to New York, I said to my brother, let's try one more time – and the one more time that we did it, right now we're owners of two restaurants by the name of Jamaica Breeze, we're co-owners, we own a warehouse that does restaurant supplies. In all, we have three businesses that we are managing currently."[667]

A businesswoman and trained medical practitioner, Clar first met George when she worked as a bank-teller in New York. "It's funny how I met George. At the time, I was much younger. I was working in Chase Manhattan Bank, and he had a manager who managed him in Europe, who I did most of his banking for him at that time and he told me he had some players who he wanted me to come and do business with, and George was one of them."[668] That manager was Laye Sidibe, Weah's first football manager.

It was on one of Weah's visits to the Chase Bank in 1991, that Clar recalls him asking her for her phone number. "Because of the time difference, he was working in France at the time, and he asked me for my home number and asked if he could communicate with me because of the time difference – and that's how we became friends."[669] Clar was no fool. She knew what giving her number to Weah meant. "I knew what he wanted. No one asks me in my place of business for my personal number. I knew what he wanted, and I give it to him, that was September of 1991."[670]

The following year, when Weah came to New York for the summer, the pair spent some time together and in the months that followed, as the relationship blossomed, Clar took Weah to Jamaica to see her homeland.

"I travelled back and forth to France, and I guess he figured that I was someone that he liked," Clar recalls. "It was very difficult because at the time I was very calm and shy, so, I mean I embraced it and we went to Jamaica and after that I travelled back to Europe, and he asked me to marry him – in the space of I think a year or so."[671]

Weah's venture into politics was unexpected. "I was surprised because living with a superstar, as anyone knows, is not easy and I kind of wanted that part of our life to end in the sense that we could have more of a stable life together because George being a soccer player, he travels a lot, and I was always at home with the kids."[672]

Clar was really looking forward to life after football and spending quality time with her family, but Weah had other plans. "I really wanted to just hang out with my husband and the kids but after he told me that the people of Liberia were requesting for him to lead them, I was surprised but I also didn't want to be selfish because I understood and knew what the people of Liberia were going through at the time and they needed someone that they loved and someone that they trusted, someone they believed in that had their interests especially the poor people of Liberia."[673] Reluctantly, she embraced Weah's quest for the Liberian Presidency and never looked back. But embracing her husband's sudden turn from footballer to President came with a lot of ups and downs amid public reports of Weah's infidelity and a number of kids outside his marriage. One of the more high-profile extramarital affairs involved MacDella Cooper, a former fashion model, who met Weah at the tail end of his football career just as he was transitioning into politics.

In 2014, MacDella shocked many when she announced that Weah had fathered a child with her. Cooper has children by Dick Parsons, of Citigroup fame, and the late advertising exec Thomas Tafuto. MacDella did not hide the fact that Weah was the father of her child and openly boasted to the *New York Post*'s Richard Johnson, "He's going to be the next President of Liberia. You have a future First Lady here."[674]

MacDella was alongside Weah and cheered him on when he was inducted into the Mexican Football Hall of Fame in November 2013. The pair also showed up at a 2013 gathering in Monte Carlo with Prince Albert and his Princess Charlene.

At the time, MacDella appeared hopeful that she and Weah would go all the way amid reports of a somewhat rocky relationship with Clar at the time. "He is someone who has a big heart. We are going to change Liberia,"[675] she told the *Post*.

Weah did go on to win the Presidency, but it was with Clar, not MacDella, by his side.

Issues of infidelity aren't rare for African leaders. George's dilemma never seemed to bother Clar, at least not publicly. Yet, reading about one's husband's infidelity in the New York tabloids became an embarrassment. Rumours about the pair having relationship problems often heightened whenever there was a MacDella Cooper sighting with Weah or a report that he had fathered another child outside his marriage.

For Clar, the Presidency changed her life drastically. "I'm embracing it. I'm not the same person I was before. I have the same personality, I'm very calm. With my husband being the superstar, I'm always in the background.

I do a lot of work for him and the children, but I always try to not let that control who I am but now being a First Lady, I have to be out there. There are so many people out there who are now dependent on me, not only my husband but they depend on the First Lady."[676]

Besides his child with MacDella, Weah had three children with Clar, another by Meapeh Gono, a former Assistant Minister of Labour and one off-the-record source suggested in an interview there were a further six other children bringing the number of children to 11, some by women in Ivory Coast, Nigeria and Ghana. In 2017, Meapeh described Weah as a "deadbeat father" but received a backlash after backtracking from her aforementioned statements about Weah and endorsing him for the 2017 Presidential race.

The child support case dogged Weah in the months leading up to the 2017 Presidential elections but did very little to derail his Presidential hopes. Meapeh went public after a court in the U.S. state of Georgia issued a warrant charging Weah with child abandonment. The *FrontPageAfrica* newspaper published the warrant which alleged that Weah had failed to pay for child support.

Despite the saga, Weah's spokesperson, Sam Mannah, said the warrant "was a calculated propaganda trying to diminish our political momentum."[677] Mannah later backtracked to say that the warrant was withdrawn after lawyers for Weah spoke to court officials. It was filed in relation to an allegation of failure to pay child support in the U.S. state of Georgia. Reuters reported that the crime (if proven) was "punishable by up to 12 months in prison" and that on April 18, 2016 the Newton County Court had gone so far as to issue a warrant for Weah's arrest for child abandonment.[678] Meapeh Gono, the 10-year-old girl's mother filed the petition. Georgia takes such matters very seriously with the law automatically considering it a felony should the non-custodial parent (in this case, Weah) not be in the state.

According to the court document, defendant Weah requested that his child's mother repay his attorney's fees, adding that this request was denied. "It is hereby ordered, defendant's request for an award of litigation expenses and attorney's fees is denied," the court ruled. "The defendant's (Weah) request for an award of litigation expenses and attorney fees having come before this court during the motion for Attorney Fees hearing on October 31st, 2016, along with the court considering applicable law and pleadings".[679]

The court further concluded that neither party would be responsible for paying litigation expenses and attorney fees.

Prior to the warrant being filed, Weah hired a lawyer to take in a check of US$160, claiming that he only made US$1090 as Senator in Liberia and that he has two other minor kids born in 2000 and 2012 and can only afford to pay US$160. *FrontPageAfrica* newspaper reported that the check never reached the mother. Senator Weah's lawyers had hoped to convince the judge that he did in fact submit the check.

According to the communication published by *FrontPageAfrica*, the State of Georgia had requested the state of New York through the City Court of New York Law Department Family Division to investigate the finances of Weah further and effect support and also have him repay arrears for any income-based social services the child may have received.[680]

At the time, Weah was listed as a resident of Rose Dale, New York.

Weah's extramarital issues, although never really addressed by Clar or him publicly, brought some embarrassment to the Presidency and raised questions about his stance on women and gender issues.

Before the marriage, it was widely speculated that the pair's marriage was on the rocks. In fact, most insiders believe that had Weah not won the Presidency, Clar would have pushed for divorce. So, what changed? The luxurious life that came with the Presidency appealed to Clar. Being First Lady changed her perspective on things and perhaps it was worth the risk to hang on.

This is as close as Clar would get to the celebrity culture that drew her to Weah when he was in the prime of his football career. The multi-car motorcades, access to everywhere she wanted to go, having security and servants catering for her every wish – these were the sparks that relit Clar and Weah's relationship and probably saved their marriage. But the issues of infidelity would drag on and bring extra difficulties for Weah who had to endure endless baiting from a few of his exes.

For example, during the 2020 Senatorial Midterm elections, MacDella Cooper entered the world of politics and became one of Weah's opponents. Cooper had run for Liberian President in 2017 achieving a modest 0.7% share. Later she ran again for office in the Montserrado County Senatorial elections, on July 2, 2020, again unsuccessfully.

Now, she had created the Movement for One Liberia as a way to improve opportunities for women in legislature, a platform she says created a pathway for more female representation in the legislature.

In the midterm elections that followed, MacDella was not a candidate but made sure to stick it to her former lover. Although she had supported Weah in the second round of the 2017 Presidential elections, the relationship had grown sour. Of all Weah's girlfriends, MacDella and Meapeh were the only ones who had gone public. MacDella had made headlines in the *New York Post* about her desire to become First Lady and Meapeh took Weah to court for child support in the U.S.

After endorsing Weah, it was widely speculated that MacDella would have been rewarded with a ministerial post at the Ministry of Gender. But Clar was having none of that. Of all Weah's sidechicks, MacDella was the smartest, most elegant and because of her model background had somewhat of a stature that was comparable to Clar's.

Clar had given Weah a simple message: don't bring her anywhere near this Presidency. Weah obliged.

For MacDella, the snub was a slap in her face but even though she had shared a child with Weah, it was time to take the gloves off. By the time the December 2, 2020, midterm elections came around, MacDella was in battle mode. When Weah's ruling Coalition for Democratic Change announced the list of candidates, it was missing women and MacDella saw an opening to stick it to Weah.

Weah had ordained himself as the 'feminist-in-chief' of Liberia because of his government's expressed priority of women's rights issues and their economic empowerment. At the International SHEROES Forum held in Monrovia on October 17, 2018, Weah conferred the title upon himself, reaffirming unwavering commitment to the pursuit of the feministic ideals that guarantee the rights and wellbeing of women.

In reality, activists took the government to task, declaring that the decision of the party ran contrary to any claims by the President and his government that they were working to empower Liberian women.

Some 15 senate seats were up for grabs during the 2020 midterm elections, but there was one big problem: there was only one woman, Senator Nyonblee Karnga Lawrence, among 29 male senators at the Senate.

MacDella took on Weah's party's decision, describing the omission of any women on the ballot as an affront to the women of Liberia. "The fact that we have a President who is the feminist in chief, he should always be cautious about women's participation, the roles that women can play to help us lift our country,"[681] MacDella told Radio France International in an interview. She went on to call on President Weah to make good his promise of being the feminist-in-chief of the country. Cooper also criticised the appointment of only three females by the President out of 19 major ministries, including Jeanine M. Cooper, head of the Ministry of Agriculture, Wilhelmina Jallah, Minister of Health and Social Welfare, and Williametta Piso Saydee-Tarr, Minister of Gender, Children and Social Protection.

In his defence, Weah countered that he had also appointed a woman to be the first female deputy Chief of Staff of Armed Forces of Liberia, and that the Deputy Inspector General of the National Police was also a woman. The President also boasted of appointing many women to ministerial positions and to boards of state-owned enterprises.

Nevertheless, MacDella said Weah was not doing enough. Under the Weah administration, MacDella opined, Liberia had become the, "worst place for women and girls due to the increase in sexual and gender-based violence and their exclusion from the decision-making processes."[682]

During the lockdown due to the deadly COVID-19 pandemic, there were approximately 700 reported rape cases. But MacDella did not stop there. She went on to accuse the Weah government of reversing the gains made to champion women's representation during the Ellen Johnson Sirleaf administration.

In 2018, Weah stated that the National Elections Commission guidelines to have 30% of women in government should be raised to 50% women's inclusion, but later had to backtrack on his comment.

President Weah's infidelity issues had caught up with him and this was tainting his stance on women and gender issues. When the July 2019 Independence Day celebration came around, Leymah Gbowee, the orator of Liberia's 172 celebrations, expressed dismay at the dearth of women appointed to cabinet positions in the Weah government. In her speech, the Nobel laureate called on the President to remember that Liberia was not a political party but a nation for all Liberians. "In order for us to move forward together, we must recognise that men as well as women, the blind, the physically challenged, and youth groups are equal parts of the society."[683]

The President had also been mute on a number of high-profile issues involving attacks against the female gender by members of his own government. In February 2022, Isaac Doe, a married Deputy Minister of Sports in Weah's government walked in on his girlfriend with another man at the popular D'Calabash spot. He followed her as she left with the friend, dragged her out of the car he had bought her and beat her up. Videos of the incident went viral on social media, but Weah's government kept silent.

Similarly, Augusta Tarwin, a female Commander of the Crime Services Division of the Liberia National Police, was threatened with dismissal by her boss, Deputy Inspector General for Operations in the Liberia National Police, if she failed to drop physical assault charges against Executive Protection Service (EPS) Director Trokon Roberts. Officer Tarwin had filed a written complaint to the police inspector general Patrick Sudue indicating that, on February 16, 2022, the EPS boss, Roberts, along with six well-armed men allegedly dragged her out of her Zone-5 police depot along the Roberts International Airport Highway and brutalised her for carrying out her assignment. Officer Tarwin had reported impounding a black Chevrolet jeep transporting contaminated rice. The officer's complaint was greeted with threats that she would be dropped from the force.

For many gender activists, Weah's extramarital activities made it difficult for him to really enforce himself as feminist-in chief and actually tied his hands to do much, giving his officials a free ride to do what they please.

Despite the extramarital drama, Clar still relished her First Lady role and never seemed bothered by the side distractions, although some were simply unavoidable.

One of Weah's known mistresses was Tangie Banto. Long before the Presidency, when things were going bad between Weah and Clar, Tangie, like MacDella, filled in the gap and played a prominent role in Weah's life. Tangie had met Weah back in 2004 in Minneapolis, Minnesota, during one of the CDC-USA meetings. The two exchanged numbers and didn't reconnect again until 2011 when they started dating and actually lived together for a while. For much of the first few years of the Weah Presidency, Tangie, a no-nonsense, fiery woman, never shied away from controversy and made her voice heard on her Facebook page, especially when she felt she was getting the short end of the stick from another one of Weah's sidechicks.

In a Facebook video that she posted that went viral, Tangie went in full attack mode on another woman, rumoured to have had an affair with Weah, Saifuah Mai Gray, who was appointed by Weah shortly after winning the Presidency to head the National Oil Company of Liberia (NOCAL). In the video, Tangie accused Saifuah of spreading lies about her to the President that she (Tangie) was sleeping with Eugene Nagbe, the Minister of Information, Culture Affairs and Tourism who was, at the time, the Chief Spokesman for the Weah government. Using every imaginable curse word she could think of, Tangie vented her frustration on Saifuah, going all out to send a clear message that she was having none of it. Clar was no fool. But Tangie's video had gone viral. Amid the chatters about what had been said about the President, the First Lady continued to carry on with her role. After all, her office had a hefty US$1 million in the national budget. Now, Clar wanted a motive, something to keep her busy and away from the distraction, and so, she turned to charity and goodwill.

Throughout her life, Clar had a passion for charitable work. Now, in her role as First Lady, she had a reason to back a number of causes. "I'm a woman and I think I can see things a bit differently," Clar says. "What women are going through in Liberia, I kinda feel for them. So, they're now embracing me, they're now relying on me, and I have to come out of that shell. I was cool, calm, but now I have to embrace my role that God has given me and I have to come out of that shell and be there for the people of Liberia and so my life has changed drastically within Liberia and also outside Liberia because once you're a dignitary, people see you differently, there are a lot of expectations and I have to step up to it and so my life has drastically changed."[684]

Since becoming First Lady, Clar has been impressed by the overwhelming support from her adopted nation. "The reception from Liberians has been very well. In the beginning I was afraid because of my personality. I've always said to my family, I didn't know in the beginning how I will perform as a First Lady because I felt I wasn't good with public speaking, I felt that to get up in front of people was very difficult for me but now that I've done it and the people of Liberia, the people I'm surrounded by were helping me

to acclimate very well in the Liberian society and they're helping me tremendously, we have great people there and I love them dearly."[685]

Long before assuming her role as First Lady, Clar had an ambition of
her own. Growing up in New York City, she adored Oprah Winfrey. "To
be honest, I don't know if I will ever get to meet this person but I've always
been inspired by Oprah Winfrey because I felt that – my brother said to
me one time that I want to do – and I didn't know I was going to be a First
Lady, but I always said, I want to do what Oprah's doing, I want to help
people."[686]

Clar's brother Michael would often tell her that her dream had was
fulfilled. "My brother looked at me one day and he said, you know Clar,
you're doing exactly what Oprah's doing but on a smaller scale. You're like
the poorer Oprah, I remember him saying that and it meant a lot to me
because I didn't have what Oprah had but she has inspired me so much, she
has gone through so much in her life and to see what she has done for herself
and for people of the United States also, and to see how people revered her,
I just wanted to be like her. I know it was within me and I didn't know I
was going to be blessed and be given a platform like this to a nation where
people are relying on me and where I have to do exactly what Oprah is
doing – or has done."[687]

As First Lady, Clar has already seen the challenges at first hand. "We
have so many challenges in Liberia, I just cannot be the First Lady who
focuses on one issue, like other First Ladies. Liberia has many challenges,
we have the kids in the orphanages who are living in deplorable conditions,
we have the elderly who are not being taken care of, we have the young
women in the streets who are hooked on drugs, and we have to implement
ways of getting them off the streets, we have so many issues in Liberia."[688]

Clar says that part of her role as First Lady is to see beyond the norms
of reality. "People are begging because they don't have jobs, the education
system is poor there, so my goal is to restore that, their dignity, my goal is
to give these people hope. This is where my foundation falls in, to restore
the dignity of the beautiful people of Liberia."[689]

However, Clar's vision was always greeted with controversy. In October
2018, eyebrows were raised when the fiscal year 2018/2019 budget allocated
a total of US$1 million for the Office of the First Lady under the Ministry

of State for Presidential Affairs/Humanitarian Outreach. The controversy was further heightened when Clar, during the launch of her Clar Hope Foundation, declared that she needed more as she sought international help to raise money for Liberia. The First Lady explained she had been unable to engage with Liberian affairs during the Civil War since her husband's international football career was all-consuming and child care was her priority.

Now, as First Lady, she could.

Clar said at the time, "A lot of you people are not familiar with me, but I have been in Liberia a very long time. Yes, the war – I married George Weah. There was a time we were going to the neighbouring countries, we were in Ivory Coast, we were in Ghana in the refugee camps, many of you don't know that I had kids to take care of in the U.S. George told me he was going to be struggling – I was taking care of the kids and I wasn't able to come and do some of the works that I always wanted to do. When George got elected to be President, I realised that my life has to be here. I don't think that Liberia needs an absentee First Lady because I know that you guys have not had a First Lady in a long time."[690]

Clar's quest for more money was seen as a clear contradiction to Section 9.6 of Liberia's Code of Conduct regarding the use of public office for private interest is clear: "No Public Official or Employee of Government should use an official position to pursue private interests that may result in conflict of interest."[691] Crafters of the code of conduct put those laws into place with the idea of preventing public officials and employees of government from giving preferential treatment to individuals, corporations or institutions, while performing official duties.

Launching her foundation that year, the First Lady presented it as a non-political initiative aimed at creating an equitable society in Liberia where women and children are healthy, are provided education and fully empowered to lead a prosperous life. When the foundation was launched, the First Lady listed the construction of a maternity hospital, schools and the Hope Community for the less fortunate as well as advocating against gender-based violence and implementing agricultural programs among the goals for the organisation.

But then came the bombshell. While addressing a gathering about the foundation, the First Lady revealed that while the government was allocating some money for her office in the national budget, that money was simply not enough and that she would need an additional US$10 million to complete her ongoing projects and maintain them after completion.

The First Lady explained, "I just want to say something about funding. The government funds me and all of you need to know this – the government funds me, yes! But the projects I want to do for the Liberian people – US$500,000 – can't do it. A million dollars can't do it. I'm usually a reserved person, I have a heart for people, I go places and I beg for help on behalf of the Liberian people. I don't do it for myself, I do it for you because I want to better your lives. I give thanks to the Liberian people for whatever they give me but a lot I have to do; I have to go to the international community. To do what I want to do, the government cannot give me 10 million. I need 10 million to do the project but after we have to continue for the community to grow. I don't want to stop in Monrovia. As soon as the President and government begin to build the roads, I want to build another one in that area. We will continue to beg on your behalf, for our children, they are our future – so I just need your support."[692]

Shortly after the launch of the foundation, records from the Division of Corporations in the U.S. State of Florida obtained by *FrontPageAfrica* showed that the Weahs did register a foundation named "The Weah Children Foundation Inc." However, the document filing number N0400000005623 showed that the foundation was never active since its formation on March 30, 2004. The account is still listed as inactive. Administrators of the account posted that the account was dissolved on September 14, 2007.

Clar came under fire first at the time of the foundation's launch in Liberia. Critics questioned the Weahs' decision to start a foundation now when they could have done so when Weah was in his prime or after his retirement from football.

For Clar, the US$10 million would go toward her ambitious Clar City of Hope project, which began construction in 2018 in Marshall territory off the outskirts of the country's capital, Monrovia. When completed, the project would include an administration building, a social club, school, library, nursery, restaurant, dormitory, vocational centre and a sport centre square.

Further complicating matters for the First Lady, *FrontPageAfrica* reported that the project bordered a conflict of interests because the land was purchased in the name of the First Lady and not the government or her office, meaning funds raised on behalf of Liberia as stressed by the First Lady would go toward her personal project and not Liberia. Questions were also raised about the ownership of the project when the Weahs leave office in the future and whether the government of Liberia would retain ownership.

Despite concerns regarding breach of the Code of Conduct and conflict of interest, the First Lady insisted that she was determined to see the project through. "I'm doing this from the bottom of my heart and the only thing I can ask – I'm not here for the fame. I'm not here for the money. Like I said last night, how much money do we really need to survive? What would it take for all of us to care for one child, how many cars do we need to drive? This is the food for the thought. But we have to be our brothers' keepers. I'm your First Lady and the only way I can survive is with your help. Try to work with me to build City of Hope, try to work with me to help the elderly."[693]

The First Lady added, "I love kids and I had my own experience growing up where my father died when I was very young, and as I grew up, I became confident in myself. Sometimes, it just takes one person, you don't need that many people, you just need one good person to effect change."[694]

She explained that on coming to Liberia she began by visiting orphanages and started repairing a few of them. This is when she says, it became important to her that she couldn't go back and say everything is satisfactory when kids were not eating and sleeping well. "So, I took that on. So, moving through Nimba, moving through Bassa and other places, I started moving away from the kids and started looking at the elderly and I wanted to see how they were living and the conditions there were so bad and of course as a mother, as a wife and First Lady of Liberia, I could not ignore that."[695]

The First Lady said she saw a lot of elderly that were not eating well. "I went to the Superintendent of Bassa and said is there something you can do for me, could you give me a piece of land to build an elderly home. Once the home is done, if there are any nurses available, I can place them there to work and care for the elderly. My facility has a place for young girls."[696]

Despite the First Lady's expression of good intent, many international stakeholders raised concerns, particularly with the President and his wife establishing a foundation while in office.

The foundation controversy was just one of a nagging number of issues dogging Clar and her family's interest in Liberia.

Clar's brother, Michael Duncan, was in a long line of succession to Marcus Garvey as head of the UNIA.

Visiting Liberia in 1923, a delegation from the Universal Negro Improvement Association and African Communities League (UNIA-ACL) sought approval for their settlement schemes. The idea was to obtain permission from Liberian President Charles D. B. King to buy land for agriculture and homes for the UNIA members wanting to live in Africa and to survey the conditions they might find later on arrival if approved.

Nearly 100 years later, Michael was leading a movement to revisit the arrangement in hopes of rekindling a promise, which President King later reneged on to Garvey. Now, with immense access to power through his sister as First Lady, Michael could pull some strings, not just for the UNIA but for his personal business as well. Like Clar, Michael also came under scrutiny amid allegations that the Armed Forces of Liberia were using troops and resources donated by the government of China to mine gold on behalf of Duncan and the First Lady. The AFL told the *FrontPageAfrica* newspaper in a stern denial that its troops were not working on mines but were building roads.

In his capacity as head of the UNIA, Mr. Duncan, who has led the organisation since August 2016, was responsible for the entire working and carrying out of all commands.

In a Facebook livestream in September 2018, firebrand radio commentator, Henry Costa, displayed photographs he alleged showed the use of trucks donated by the Chinese government to the AFL being used to mine gold in Grand Kru County. Mr. Costa alleged that the mining operation was taking place in Grand Kru in a village called Ma Mary Village, Parluken City, Forpoh District.

Michael, who had launched an unsuccessful 2013 bid for the 31st Council District seat in New York, and was a regular visitor to Liberia since his sister and her husband ascended to the seat of power, quickly dismissed the report. He told *FrontPageAfrica*, 'Since I was 17 years old, after reading Marcus Garvey's book, it was my vision to live in Liberia. I first visited in 2015, and prior to that, I travelled to South Africa in 1996. It has always been my dream to not just visit but to live and become a citizen and spend to rest of my life in Liberia. We have to work to bring back the Garvey mission. We are not interested in mining; we are interested in agriculture. My idea is to help develop Liberia anyway I can; to develop our people and use the Garvey vision to self-empower Liberians to work with the people as Mr. Garvey prescribed."[697]

Mr. Duncan explained that he learned about Marcus Garvey in high school and had been a "Garveyite" ever since. "At that point I learned about Garvey's interest to form a city or start a program in Liberia as it relates to the black man," Mr. Duncan said. "What we did in 2015, we started the UNIA local division, James Stewart."[698] The division was named after James R Stewart who was from the U.S. state of Ohio, but Stewart moved the Association's headquarters to Monrovia where it remained until his death in 1964. It was again moved to Youngstown, Ohio. But by then, the organisation was a shadow of its former self, and became disoriented.

Asked whether he had made any effort to reach out to the Senate or the national legislature, Mr. Duncan said, "This is not to deal with the government. We are working through the people. It is our idea to build it from the ground up. I am the 11th President General of the UNIA. We are taught to respect the local laws and we intend to respect the laws of the government and abide by those laws. Everything we do, we will make sure it is legal. We want to reach the common men and women and help them realise their fullest potential. Now, I have a farm that I am working on right now. We do not have an office per se, but we intend to have an office space soon. We have a structure on the farm where we can take care of the community."[699]

Michael further explained that the emphasis is on the elders and the indigenous people. "That's who we are here for. My objective here is to reach the common men and women and from there, we will grow. We are not only doing this in Liberia but in other countries as well. We are in Ghana, Sierra Leone, working in Guinea, Zambia, South Africa and in Zimbabwe. Our objective is to organise humanitarian programs to build communities in countries wherever we are. It entails creating local missions and influencing people to control their economies. Liberia has a very fertile soil for agriculture. There was a lot of farming here before, but the war took a toll. Currently, we have hired 27 people and as we grow, we will hire a lot more people. We are doing this jointly with the chiefs, the community elders to help make their communities better, that's the main objectives."

Asked what kind of farming he is involved in, Michael said he has managed to sow "15,000 heads of cabbages, 4,300 of kilos of watermelon, 15,000 plants of cucumbers and 7,000 heads of soursop."[700]

Michael told the newspaper that 20% of the soursop was processed for export while the rest would be used for the communities. "I have a local business in the U.S. and the produce from the farm will be used to supply that business. We have a distribution business in U.S., and we can supply them from right here. The rest of the produce, including corns, is for the local market. We already started distributing and we will soon start harvesting the cabbage. So, our concentration is on agriculture because it can help the local people and connect the local villages. We are working and training them to farm. What we have done so far is to train the locals with seeds so they can farm on their own."[701]

All this, he said, was aimed at "steering the local people back into agriculture again."[702]

The controversy has also been stirred up by some noise over the farm property and whether it was purchased from the villagers or obtained through concession rights. Under Liberian law, only Liberian citizens or qualified foreigners can own land. Foreign companies investing in agriculture in Liberia may sign a long-term lease, renewable for the life of their investment.

In September 2018, President George Weah, who took office in January of the same year, signed a land reform law giving local communities greater rights over "customary land" and let foreigners and charities own property. First drafted in 2014, the Land Right Act has nonetheless been criticised by some who say it weakens the rights of Liberians who live in rural areas, notably women. Previously, the government could grant private companies long-term leases on non-titled lands that cover most of the West African country settled by former slaves from the United States and Caribbean.

Under the new law, local communities could now claim ownership of customary land based on oral testimonies of community members, maps, signed agreements between neighbouring communities and other documents. The law allowed foreigners, missionaries, educational and charitable organisations to own land as long as it was to be used for the purpose given at the time of purchase. Previously, the Liberian Constitution provided that only "people of colour" can become Liberians and only Liberians can own property. During his inaugural address in January 2018, President Weah described such archaic clauses in the land law as "unnecessary, racist and inappropriate" for the "21st century"[703] and pledged to push for all races to apply for Liberian citizenship and for foreigners to be allowed to own property.

The UNIA-ACL is a black nationalist fraternal organisation founded by Garvey, a Jamaican immigrant to the United States. The Pan-African organization enjoyed its greatest strength in the 1920s and was influential prior to Garvey's deportation to Jamaica in 1927. After that, its prestige and influence declined, but it had a strong influence on African-American history and development. The UNIA was said to be "unquestionably, the most influential anti-colonial organisation in Jamaica prior to 1938."[704] The organisation was founded to work for the advancement of people of African ancestry around the world. In the 1920s, it worked to arrange for emigration for African Americans who wanted to go to African countries of which the most important by far was Liberia.

Four years after the UNIA-ACL's mission to Liberia, then Chief Justice of Liberia, J.J. Dossen, wrote to UNIA conveying the government's support. He wrote, "The President directs me to say in reply to your letter of June 8 setting forth the objects and purposes of the Universal Negro Improvement Association, that the Government of Liberia, appreciating as they do the aims of your organisation as outlined by you, have no hesitancy in assuring you that they will afford the Association every facility legally possible in effectuating in Liberia its industrial, agricultural and business projects."[705]

However, two months later, President King unexpectedly ordered all Liberian ports to refuse entry to any member of the 'Garvey Movement'. In the days that followed, Liberia entered into an agreement with the Firestone Rubber Company for a 99-year lease of one million acres (4,000 km²) of arable land. The deal allowed Firestone to extract and process rubber for the world market.

King had originally intended for Liberia to lease the land to UNIA at an unprecedented dollar an acre ($247/km²). The commercial agreement with Firestone dealt a severe blow to the UNIA's African repatriation program and inspired speculation that the actions were linked.

In his book, *The Open-Door Policy of Liberia. An Economic History of Modern Liberia* Dr. Van Der Kraij asserts that, initially, President King welcomed the Garvey Movement, notably the mass-emigration of blacks to Africa. But later, King refused cooperation with the Marcus Garvey Movement after being put under pressure at the behest of the French and British Governments.

Things took radical turn when, in 1924, emissaries of the Universal Negro Improvement Association, who arrived in Monrovia on July 30, were deported the following day. It was the plan of this Association to establish a great Negro Empire, with Marcus Garvey as President General and which, with Liberia as a centre, was to extend over the entire continent to which negroes were to be brought from all parts of the world. The Presidential act aimed at deporting these persons was approved by the legislature. King had reportedly been warned by neighbouring powers that they would "not tolerate the presence in Liberia of an organisation working for the overthrow of European supremacy in Africa."[706]

This still makes it possible that the French and British governments exerted pressure through the U.S. government.

At the time, the UNIA had launched the Black Star Shipping Lines among other business ventures and began to look to Liberia as the only independent state in Africa as the site of a Pan-African empire that would work for the upliftment, redemption and empowerment of people of African descent all over the world in the long-term, and the decolonisation of Africa in the short-term.

Garvey had previously launched the Liberian Construction Loan program to raise US$2 million for the UNIA settlement in Liberia, and a sizable loan to the government aimed at bolstering UNIA's work. Some historians say Garvey and the UNIA fell victim to U.S. interests in Liberia and this may have contributed to Liberia breaking its promise to Garvey. At the time, the UNIA loan was seen as an alternative to a US$5 million loan offered to Liberia by the U.S. Although Garvey and his supporters managed to raise almost $150,000 worth of bonds to finance the scheme, it did not materialise as the U.S. intensified its hold on Liberia, dashing the UNIA's hopes.

Years later, President William Tubman imposed severe restrictions on the immigration of Black Muslims, and other American and Caribbean Nationalists.

As Garvey's vision nears 100 years, interest is being resurrected. In February 2019, members of the UNIA-ACL, led by Duncan, paid another visit to Liberia from January 27 to February 2. They issued a statement in which they said they were on a mission to complete that which its founder and first President General, Garvey, had sought to accomplish in 1920. The statement said Liberia was the place chosen by Garvey to launch this mission in 1920, and although he did not achieve the desired success, all was not lost. "Today, nearly 100 years later, present members of the organisation see this mission as timely and very relevant at this time to help realise the hopes and aspirations of people of African descent."[707]

During that meeting, the delegation met with President Weah and his Jamaica-born wife, Clar. The delegation would conclude in a statement that it had held extended discussions with the Minister of Agriculture to look at establishing cooperation between the UNIA-ACL and Liberia. Meetings aimed at strengthening relationships between the UNIA-ACL and the various indigenous groups in the country were also held during the visit.

At the time, Michael expressed confidence and pride that the UNIA-ACL was determined and fully committed to realise Garvey's hopes and dreams of a better place in the world for people of African descent, and he was urging these people to start coming together in any way they could and to work towards achieving their goals for the future.

Garvey's group was also behind the founding of the Citizens Nonpartisan League, in defence and support of Didhwo Twe and Thomas J.R. Faulkner. Twe, was a representative in the Liberian legislature and a presidential candidate in the 1951 general elections. He was an advocate of Liberian native rights and the first Liberian of full tribal background to seek the Liberian presidency on an official, transparent basis. A U.S. Library of Congress document shows that Twe had a good friendship with Mark Twain and that Twe assisted Mark Twain with his short book, *King Leopold's Soliloquy.* Thomas Jefferson Richlieu Faulkner emigrated to Liberia in 1881, is credited for exposing the ignominy and horrors of Fernando Po to the world in 1929. A professional engineer who installed and operated an ice factory, ice cream plant and telephone system, Faulkner was famous for running the popular TJR Faulkner Ice Cream and Confectionery, and attempted to bring electricity to Monrovia. He became Monrovia's mayor and ran twice unsuccessfully as a Presidential candidate.

The group was also instrumental in exposing the Fernando Po forced labour crisis which raised the entrenched power structure of King-Yancy, American-Grebo, Monrovia-Cape Palmas at the time. The Citizens Nonpartisan League, led by Justice Frederick Johnson and Gabriel Johnson, held huge rallies in the streets of Monrovia and forced the legislature to compel King and Yancy to resign.

In his quest to make Liberia his home, Mr. Duncan had always hoped that his venture in President Weah's hometown would appease villagers although many were unsure to what end it justified the means considering the timing and family ties so close to the powers. "I just want to say that I'm an African born in Jamaica, who grew up in the U.S. – and now in Liberia. I expect to make Liberia my personal home. Since I read Garvey's book, I fell in love with Liberia. The villages and people have accepted me. So, I would like to make this my personal home where I intend to spend my last days. I want to make a difference and say I help everyday people. I think I've been able to do that with the hiring and employment of people in the communities. Within the next year, we will be hiring two to three hundred people."[708]

With Weah's Jamaican clan enjoying a comfortable seat at the high table with unfettered access to power, the million-dollar question many wanted to know was, 'Why now?' Why had Liberia suddenly become a haven for investment for Clar's family and why the sudden interest? What was it about Liberia that appealed to Clar and her family that had them all of a sudden so engaged? Was it the power that Weah now possessed? It was an open secret that Weah and Clar hardly slept under the same roof for months leading into the Presidency. Now, she and her family were deeply involved in everything. Was it the money, the fame, the new-found opportunities?

Something must have been a driving force for Clar to turn a blind eye to Weah's infidelities. Not many women could stomach open rebuke about their partners on social media by other women, especially a sitting First Lady.

Extramarital affairs involving leaders are nothing new. In February 2010, South African President Jacob Zuma admitted that he had cheated on his wife with another woman, acknowledging to the press that he had a love-child. The issue did very little to rattle Zuma. In fact, there were no political implications for Zuma or for his ruling party, the African National Congress (ANC). What the Zuma incident showed was something more. It spoke to the character of the country's politics and its electorate. Zuma may have been saved politically, but his extramarital issues undermined his government's efforts to fight the spread of HIV. At the time, South Africa had the highest number of citizens infected with the disease: 5.4 million. But even with that, Zuma's behaviour did very little to match the 1998–99 impeachment effort that U.S. President Bill Clinton faced over his affair with Monica Lewinsky, or similar ones that led to the resignation of Britain's Defence Minister, John Profumo, in 1963.

For Weah, extramarital woes proved to be a complication. Just as Zuma's love child undermined his government's fight against the deadly HIV, Weah struggled to sell himself as a true feminist-in-chief owing to his alleged ill-treatment of the women he was involved with, including issues of child abandonment and his failure to pay child support to his children born out of wedlock.

Oftentimes, it appears President Weah chose an inadvisable path when it came to his responsibilities toward his kids born out of wedlock, particularly Hilareal George (aka Georgie), the child he had with MacDella. He reportedly ignored invitations from MacDella's counsel and close friends. A mutual friend between Weah and MacDella expressed the need for Weah to take on his role as Georgie's father and pay up back child support payments.

The burden of having so many to cater for can be daunting, even for a President, so, burdensome that on more than one occasion, Weah used his church pulpit to take aim at Liberians who texted him for money. The President told worshippers at his church in October 2020 that out of every 1,000 messages he receives, 999 were insults. He declared that he would not offer help or assistance to people who continuously showed him disrespect through text messages. "You are arrogant and you're asking me for something small; I will not do it. You can't be asking for help and disrespecting the President."[709]

Even as he struggled and was bombarded with issues of child support payments, President Weah was often tormented by pleadings from everyday Liberians and friends asking for handouts. "Some of you telling me to pay your rent; you get your ma and pa and you asking me to pay your rent; why you can't go live with your ma. The money you want to pay your rent [with]; you can use it with your mother to do business."[710]

For MacDella, Meapeh and others, the competition for Weah's ears and attention regarding child support payment could be a nagging headache.

When she was not busy holding his government accountable for governance lapses, MacDella tried to focus President Weah's attention on raising his son, Georgie. The issue had prompted many to question Weah's character as a parent and his unwillingness to engage in a rational problem-solving exercise to address MacDella's concerns about raising Georgie. Weah's failure to heed the appeals to his conscience regarding his role as a father and refusing to take pride in his son's upbringing, raised mounting questions about the consequences that could arise for him and perhaps bring embarrassment to his Presidency and to him personally. The treatment toward Georgie was yet again a missed opportunity for Weah to stand on the high moral ground at a cost that, for someone of his stature and wealth, would seem minimal. For Weah, the cost of forsaking that opportunity was virtually incalculable.

More importantly, Weah's failure to adequately tackle abuses involving officials in his government raised eyebrows about his quest to cement himself as a leader dedicated to tackling gender issues and abuses head on.

Writing in *The Huffington Post*, Dr Tomas Chamorro-Premuzic, an international authority in psychological profiling, talent management, and people analytics, offers an interesting theory on why leaders engage in extramarital affairs. "Leaders are generally overconfident. In fact, most people are, but this is especially true for powerful people, not least because of their past accomplishments. Overconfident people have an inappropriate sense of security, and this increases the probability of engaging in counterproductive and risky behaviours. For example, one of the reasons why most people decide not to pursue extramarital affairs is that they are afraid of being caught. The main reason why some people do pursue them is that they feel confident of not getting caught. This sense of invincibility makes infidelity extremely prominent among powerful people. Exceptional achievers who claim that extraordinary confidence is the secret of their success are more often its victims."[711]

For Weah, reports of multiple extramarital affairs were not only crippling his reign over the affairs of state but also drew him into a number of high-profile entanglements which brought the Presidency into disrepute.

One such saga involved Angela List, the wife of mining mogul, Paul List, who had been romantically linked to Weah years before the 2017 elections. List was a regular guest of the President in the aftermath of his historic victory. In fact, the general consensus amongst key aides in proximity of the Liberian Presidency was that List had unlimited access to most of the major concessionaires. As a Finance and Administrative Director of BCM International Group based in Accra, Ghana, List was linked to a number of mining operations in Liberia shortly after Weah won the Presidency. She was also one of the brains behind the Weah government's decision to hire a power barge that would sell electricity to the Liberia Electricity Corporation for distribution to Liberian consumers.

One of the high-profile controversies relates to an incident in February 2019 when BCM's country manager, Dionysius Sebwe, was ordered arrested on the orders of Minister of State for Presidential Affairs, Nathaniel McGill. Dionysius was one of the former footballers on the national team who did not get along with Weah during his playing days. Sebwe told the *Front-PageAfrica* newspaper in 2019 that he had travelled to Buchanan to pay some BCM International workers when he was informed of an order for him to be arrested. Sebwe explained that he believed at the time that his arrest was orchestrated by the ruling CDC due to his political differences with President Weah. Sebwe explained to the newspaper that prior to his trip to Buchanan, Minister McGill confronted him via mobile phone on the removal of the company equipment. "He called and said, 'My man, the President is concerned about the people's equipment, when are you getting them out of here?'"[712]

According to Dionysius, List, had travelled to Liberia during the inauguration and apparently explained the difficulties she was going through while getting the equipment out and settling their financial obligations to employees of the company. Sebwe explained that the company's manager, Joseph Edmund had recently visited Liberia arranging hire of a heavy duty crane from Bollore to raise equipment of BCM's including excavators and bulldozers amongst others, onto the low-bed trailers. But Edmund reportedly denied ever filing charges against him.

At the time of the incident, *FrontPageAfrica* reported that the Weah administration was in negotiations with a Turkish company, Karpowership, a private electricity exporter, owner, operator and builder of the first floating power plant fleet in the world. Under the plan, Liberia would enter into a ten-year contract in which it would purchase power from Karpowership even though it already had an absorptive capacity of only 24% of current installed capacity at Bushrod Island and Mt. Coffee. However, the issue was a lightning rod for trouble for the Weah government. Within the international community, many stakeholders who spoke to *FrontPageAfrica* on condition of anonymity feared that the signing of the agreement could lead to serious repercussions with the Millennium Challenge Corporation (MCC), the Norwegian government, the European Union, the World Bank and the German Development Bank.

In fact, at the time, most of the ministers in the government were against the agreement because it was being pushed by McGill, Minister of State for Presidential Affairs. There were even suggestions that McGill already received the backing of the President to sign off on the deal which, some key international stakeholders said, would tie down assets and restrict revenue for Liberia.

Ironically, prior to the ushering of the Weah government, the company had not done any mining or related operation.

List used her influence and ties to President Weah to stretch her interests in a number of projects in Liberia, including Putu Iron Ore, Wologisi, Tawana Resources Cape Mount Project and the Hummingbird concession which was vetoed by the President in July 2018. The President vetoed the ratified Concession Mineral Development Agreement between the government of Liberia and Hummingbird Liberia Inc., returning the bill to the

Senate with several recommendations. While the President's action was in line with Article 35 of the Liberian Constitution, *FrontPageAfrica* reported that the move was triggered by interests from List.

Interestingly, Article 35 states, "Each bill or resolution which shall have passed both Houses of the Legislature shall, before it becomes law, be laid before the President for his approval. If he grants approval, it shall become law. If the President does not approve such bill or resolution, he shall return it, with his objections, to the House in which it originated. In so doing, the President may disapprove of the entire bill or resolution or any item or items thereof. This veto may be overridden by the re-passage of such bill, resolution or item thereof by a veto of two-thirds of the members in each House, in which case it shall become law. If the President does not return the bill or resolution within twenty days after the same shall have been laid before him it shall become law in like manner as if he had signed it, unless the Legislature by adjournment prevents its return."[713]

In vetoing the concession, the President cited conflict in dates, authority to negotiate land expansion, negotiation of office space and support to community development by proposed concessionaire, telling lawmakers, "The document warrants review to ensure that provisions in the agreement are responsive to current and future situations."[714]

President Weah further claimed that the document had a date error which could not be corrected by his office. "In the agreement instead of the year 2018, the bill bears 2017, which period this government cannot account for." He continued, "There are several omissions of dates which my Office is not authorised to correct and without such corrections, I cannot affix my signature to the bill. I refer you to pages 7, 102 and 107. We also observed that pages 14 and 15 are unsigned."[715]

The President also told the lawmakers that in the ratified agreement, expansion of land area was vested in the Land and Energy Minister to expand the land area for exploration. He disagreed with the lawmaker's vesting authority of negotiating land expansion in an agent. According to the President, doing so was a "window of the unlawful act and pursuit of personal gain."[716] He told them that it would be wise that expansion of land is authorised by an appropriate authority.

Besides the Hummingbird concession, List and her company also reportedly showed interest in projects currently licensed to the Australian firm, Tawana Resources, which was involved in mining operations in the Mofe Creek project.

The company had transferred Mofe Creek assets and others in Western Australia to a wholly owned public company, SpinCo, before undertaking a capital reduction and distribution by way of in-specie distribution of 85% of all SpinCo shares to Tawana Resources' shareholders. The Mofe Creek project is located within one of Liberia's historic premier iron ore mining districts and is 10 km from the abandoned Bomi Hills mine, 80 km from the historic Bong Mine, 45 km from the Mano River mine and 20 km from the Bea Mountain resource.

Additionally, List and her company were also heavily tracking the Russian Iron Ore Company, Putu Mining Operations, which had been dormant for some time since it shut down its activities in Liberia. The Putu mine is a large iron mine located in south-east Liberia in Grand Gedeh County and represents one of the largest iron ore reserves in Liberia and in the world with an estimated reserve of 2.37 billion tonnes of ore grading 34.1% iron metal. In March 2017, Liberian authorities confirmed that Putu was exiting Liberia because it could not handle the mining process singlehandedly. "From all practical purposes, Putu is basically out of Liberia but technically the MDA is still valid though Putu walked away from the agreement,"[717] former Lands, Mines and Energy Minister, Patrick Sendolo, said in March 2017 during an appearance before a Senate committee.

Keeping track of Weah's extramarital affairs was not only a problem for Clar but for Liberia as well as issues of conflict of interests arose in the wake of Angela List's influence. Clar's debacle illustrated a lot about Weah's character as a leader. But the questions about her motive for hanging on to a man with a strong taste for women outside her marriage, raised a lot of eyebrows.

John Maxwell, a noted Pastor, Author and Speaker once wrote, "Power really is a test of character. In the hands of a person of integrity, it is of tremendous benefit; in the hands of a tyrant, it causes terrible destruction."[718]

In Clar's eyes, despite his philandering ways, George Weah was the best thing that ever happened to her. Since the day he spotted her in the bank and asked her to marry into the fame and fortune she has been able to fulfill dreams she never knew she had, and fulfill a belief she never thought was in her. The glory moments of his professional football days were becoming a distant memory and long gone, but both she, her family and Weah ran into a new lease of life with the dawn of the Liberian Presidency.

Anecdotes of promiscuity have dogged George Weah most of his adult life and once President, rumours began to swirl that all of the women appointed by him to key government ministries and/or agencies were either former or current girlfriends of his. The first person in his inner circle to confirm those rumours was the Chairman of the Congress for Democratic Change, Mulbah Morlu; when a secretly recorded audio of him, intoxicated and ridiculing the President, was leaked. The recording reverberated through Liberian society and caused what many believe to be an irreconcilable rift between the long-time friends and ultimately diminished Morlu in his role as CDC Chairman.

The Mulbah Morlu audio set off a trend for leaking the President's sexual exploits online, but it was the Tangie Banto's "leaked" voice message to the young female President of Liberia's national oil company that made it to YouTube. Tangie Banto, once considered the President's favourite girlfriend, has been with Weah throughout his financial highs and lows and according to sources, the thorn in his marriage to Clar. In her now infamous voicemail, Tangie berated Saifuah Gray over Gray's supposed failed attempt to head Liberia's maritime programme by lying to the President about another candidate for the same job, Eugene Nagbe. According to Banto's rant, Gray told the President that Tangie and Eugene Nagbe, who is married, were having an illicit affair. Tangie went on to tell Gray that Weah had discussed with her his sexual exploits with Gray and that they were essentially sister wives.

In her anger, Banto disregarded the dignity associated with, and necessary to, the Office of the President, and leaked her audio message online, while following it up with weeks of insults targeted at Gray. But even as both women went head-to-head with each other, Weah appeared unbothered. The social media firestorm would be short-lived with supporters and detractors of the President going at each other's throats on opposite sides of the aisle. The spat, played out on social media offered, a "fly on the wall" view of a regular occurrence that Liberians had become accustomed to but which was unlikely to rock the Weah Presidency.

24

POLITICAL WILL

———

For more than a century Liberia has been plagued by bad governance, corruption, greed, nepotism and a lack of leaders with the political will to do the right thing for those below the poverty line.

Liberians have always been sceptical about their leaders. Sometimes, they let things slide and at others they took matters into their own hands to the detriment of a nation which has often found itself at the dark end of uncertainty. As far back as October 1871, Edward James Roye, who led the country from 1870 to 1871, was deposed in a murky political coup d'état.

Even now the manner of Roye's deposition from office is disputed and the date which he died, with some favouring February 11, others February 12. For several months after he was placed in jail after his removal and the nature of his death is likewise mysterious and contested, with one version favouring drowning in an attempt to board a British ship stationed in Monrovia's harbour. The reasons for his ousting included the President's unpopular loans arranged with Britain and concerns that he would abort the forthcoming Presidential election.

A little over a hundred years later, another President suffered a similar fate when a bunch of low-ranked officers led by Master Sergeant Samuel Doe ended decades of American-Liberian rule with the toppling of William R. Tolbert in a bloody coup d'état. When Doe toppled Tolbert on April 12, 1980, he made sure to point out how the minority American-Liberian elites had ill-treated the ethnic majority. Doe took to the airwaves earlier that morning to announce himself as the new head of state. "I am Master Sergeant Samuel K. Doe. I have killed President Tolbert and we have taken control of the government. All soldiers report to the Barclay Training Centre. Do not take orders from your officers. All military officers stay in your homes. If you go out, you will be shot. Members of the Tolbert Administration turn yourselves in to the Post Stockade. People of Liberia, stay off the streets. We have won. In the cause of the people, the struggle continues."[719]

The 'we' signified the triumphant exclamation point for an ethnic majority which had for long felt disenfranchised, abused, abandoned and neglected.

Days after the coup, thirteen members of Tolbert's government were placed against poles on the controversial South Beach and executed by firing squad.

When President Ronald Reagan hosted Doe for a state visit in August 1982, two years after the coup, Doe remained defiant about the executions, telling *The Washington Post* in an interview, "It's the law of the country that people be executed for their crimes – both political and economic. They were guilty of crimes. I didn't decide the punishment."[720]

Perhaps Doe was right. As the *Post*'s Carla Hall wrote during Doe's visit to Washington, "Tolbert's government had been called oppressive. The ruling class that Doe and his army threw out had long guarded their wealth and power in Liberia, believing those with property should rule. They were the 'settlers', the minority ruling American-Liberian class, the descendants of the freed American slaves who founded Liberia in 1822. The indigenous population, known derisively as 'the country people' are generally poor and make up the majority of the country's 2 million people. 'If you were from a poor family, you would never go to the university,' Doe says of the old regime. 'You would never become a foreign minister.' Doe, the master sergeant, was born to 'country people.'"[721]

This was somewhat evident a year earlier when, on April 14, 1979, the Progressive Alliance of Liberia (PAL) staged a demonstration intended as peaceful to protest against the price increases. Two thousand souls walked towards the Executive Mansion but a further 10,000 "back street boys" joined and control was lost. Looting on a wide scale of rice warehouses and retail premises followed; the damage estimated at over $40 million. When the government's troops were called in neither they nor the police units could easily calm the large mob. Forty civilians lost their lives and 500 were injured in roughly 12 hours of violence.[722] In 2008, former General Coordinator of the People's Redemption Council, D. Karn Carlor, testified before the national Truth and Reconciliation Commission that approximately 300 PAL supporters died amidst the security crackdown. Hundreds more were arrested.

The rice riots of '79 and the coup of '80 redefined Liberia's standing on the global stage.

Prior to the coup, Liberia experienced rapid economic progress during the 1950's. According to the International Monetary Fund, the indications were at the time that, "real domestic product increased by approximately two and a half times during the period 1950–62, while exports increased from $28 million in 1950 to $67 million in 1962 and government revenues from $3.8 million to almost ten times that amount over the same period. In the early 1950's, the development of iron ore mining facilities at Bomi Hills and the phenomenal rise in rubber prices triggered by the Korean war boom were the major factors contributing to an upward spurt in the domestic product. The rate of economic advance slowed down as rubber prices fell in the post-Korean war period, but it picked up momentum again in the mid-1950's as the result of a gradual improvement in both production and prices of rubber."[723]

George Weah grew up in the slums and was one of those at the bottom of the pile. When he took over in January 2018, he understood, at least on paper, the challenges and responsibilities he was assuming. A mass of people was looking up to him when he said, "I further believe that the overwhelming mandate I received from the Liberian people is a mandate to end corruption in public service. I promise to deliver on this mandate."[724]

Many of those who identified with his upbringing and stellar rise from the slums of Gibraltar to a world-famous footballer had been holding their breath. It had been a long time since those below the poverty line heard from one of their own. "It is my belief that the most effective way to directly impact the poor, and to narrow the gap between rich and poor, is to ensure that public resources do not end up in the pockets of Government officials,"[725] Weah said upon taking the mantle of authority from Ellen Johnson Sirleaf.

When Weah and Tubman went their separate ways, Nathaniel McGill was forced to make a choice; to part ways with Tubman with whom he had enjoyed a somewhat cordial relationship, or to go with Weah, a popular football icon on the cusp of a political gamble.

For McGill, the choice was a no brainer. Tubman had long since passed his prime as a seasoned politician. His best days were far behind and in Weah, McGill saw the potential of what a political goldmine could be.

In the last face to face meeting between Tubman and Weah, it was clear that Weah wanted to part with the old guard with whom he had reluctantly flirted. He was tired of playing second fiddle and so, when he gave McGill the ultimatum to decide between him and Tubman, McGill decided to walk away with Weah, leaving Tubman in the cold.

The gamble paid off for McGill who became the party chairman of Weah's political party, the CDC, en route to formalising what would later become a rather formidable bond with Weah. It was one that would come to define the Weah Presidency and perceptions of who really was in control of the Weah government.

Immediately following Weah's inauguration in January 2018, McGill was handed the position of Minister of State.

The Ministry, created by an Act of the National Legislature in 1971, had often been viewed as a meaningless government entity, simply responsible for coordinating activities and operations of the Office of the President of the Republic of Liberia; and providing support to the President in carrying out the executive functions of the state through close consultation with the cabinet, key agencies and other institutions, including the private sector and civil society. Prior to the ushering of the Weah administration, the ministry was headed by Dr. Edward McClain who performed the role under former President Ellen Johnson Sirleaf.

McGill soon used his close proximity to President Weah to make the role of Minister of State more than just a ceremonial one. In only a matter of months, word on the street was that McGill was slowly establishing himself as the Prime Minister figure in the Weah administration.

Nothing got done without McGill's knowledge.

Truth be told, many came to the conclusion that President Weah had outsourced the government to McGill, giving the President time to engage in his favourite pastimes; playing football, basketball and making music. Weah's love for his favourite pastimes is often greeted with mixed reviews from Liberians far and wide. For example, when he released a song to be used by the United Nations to spread awareness about the new Coronavirus, the United Nations, with whom he worked as an ambassador, came calling, using the song to encourage people to take precautions. Upon the release of the song, Weah hoped to appeal to music lovers across the West African nation of some 4.5 million people to ensure COVID-19 would not spread further. But this was not Weah's first shot at music. During the 2014 Ebola crisis, when he was a senator, he collaborated with Ghanaian artist, Sidney, to release an awareness song. The song, "Ebola; Africa Must Stand and Fight Together", was used as part of the second phase of UNESCO's #DontGo-Viral campaign, aimed at informing and sensitising communities across Africa about the dangers of the disease.

In June 2021, the President also raised eyebrows when he released a reggae-themed birthday song to commemorate the birth anniversary of Bob Marley's widow, Rita.

Gloria Shalom, who watched the trending YouTube video found it interesting that the President was able to take time from his busy schedule to engage in a variety of extra activities. " Only in Liberia you can find a President as talented as George Weah. President, Pastor, Iman, Musician, and Footballer."[726]

Randgt, another YouTube viewer, was more blunt. "I don't know if I should cry, or laugh. It's heart breaking to see a 'leader' misplace his priorities and who fails to consider the optics of this childish behaviour. The only things I can think of that will motivate him to do this are marijuana and alcohol use. And those 'yes boss' that are his friends."[727]

The President though was never without his supporters. Isaac Dikenah showered praise. "Thank God for President Weah. This is wonderful!! His Excellency President Dr George Manneh Weah is multi-talented. BRAVO!!! The enemies of progress will always complain about everything. Let them continue to worry. Liberia is rising from the ashes of despair under the farsighted leadership of President Weah, and the CDC led Government."[728]

Mark Reeves agreed. "Great song President Weah. Keep doing what you love. I don't see anything wrong with a President singing or doing what he loves. But I know only foolish people have problem with it."[729]

While critics of Weah are often baffled over his insensitivities to the plight of those languishing at the bottom of the economic ladder, Weah often appears unmoved. So unmoved that he also found time to throw pointed jabs at his critics in another reggae-themed hit single, "Mr. Liar Man". The song appears to be an ode to those critical of the government and the President did not hold back in venting his frustration and anger.

Despite its motive, "Mr. Liar Man" marked the fourth song released by President Weah and the lyric was aimed directly at the President's critics: "In my own country, they're trying to track me down for what I don't know... But Mr. Liar Man, you know I did not do the things you say I do."[730]

Senator Abraham Darius Dillon, a senator from Montserrado County opined that he thought the President was referring to an official who worked for the state radio who was recently sacked after posting a criticism on Facebook of Mr. Weah's leadership of the country.

The song itself could have very well been about any of the President's many critics, including the media. What mattered to Weah most was that he felt at ease in those moments. Whether it's in the music studio he built in his 68-apartment complex or playing sports or games with many of his constituents, Weah was in his comfort zone.

The football icon-turned President often found a way to use his side attraction to throw pointed jabs at his critics, even from the pulpit where he preached most Sundays as pastor at his Forky Klon Church, located a stone-throw away from his massive 68-apartment complex building.

For example, during a New Year's Eve service at the church on January 1, 2021, President Weah used his pulpit to chastise some members of his government for being selfish and uninspiring and for making the living conditions difficult for ordinary citizens across the country. The President lamented that a lot of public servants, particularly Ministers, Senators, and Representatives including Directors and others, did not share with those in need in their respective communities and areas. He declared that it was rather unfortunate for those who were worthy to look down on those who were striving to earn their daily meal by not sharing with them.

As a result of public officials' failure to associate with community dwellers, the President went on to say that much of the burning and criticism goes to the Presidency simply because they are not getting what they want to survive.

The irony for many raising qualms about the President's method of leadership was that he could just as easily dismiss officials who he felt were not performing. Instead, the President turned to his comfort zone, where he often felt relaxed and composed to speak from his heart and say what he actually wanted to say.

It is by using such methods that many of the President's critics, including some members of the clergy, feel conflicted by the President's leadership trappings. This has led to concerns about his motives.

Solomon Joah, a Pastor of the Refuge Baptist Church in Monrovia, has been one of President Weah's staunchest critics. He believes that the President should not be allowed anywhere near a pulpit. Pastor Joah, who refers to himself as a 'Biblical Fundamentalist', threw pointed jabs at the President while appearing on the state radio, the Liberia Broadcasting System, in May 2019. "President Weah will disgrace the Church of God because he is not skilled in the things of the Bible,"[731] Pastor Joah stressed. He indicated that President Weah was not pastoring a good church and therefore no one should go there. Pastor Joah vowed to criticise any pastor who preached the wrong gospel just as President Weah was doing.

The clergyman's critique came just days after President Weah told a New Year's Eve service in January 2019, "Life is a business; what you do with your life will make you profitable or unprofitable. God gives to everyone talent according to their own managerial ability. God doesn't give you things that you can't take care of."[732]

Many of the President's critics believe the time spent in his comfort zone offered an opportunity for his Minister of State, McGill to exploit. Some believe the President not only outsourced the government to McGill but had sanctioned McGill to run things while he spent most of his time in his Jamaica Resort off the Robertsfield Highway, where he entertained guests and performed some government functions.

As the President took his eyes off the ball, McGill was busy asserting himself through surrogates at the helm of every major government ministry and agency.

In fact, in September 2018, the *FrontPageAfrica* newspaper published extracts from letters from the office of the Minister demanding appointments for members of the ruling Coalition for Democratic Change. As *FrontPageAfrica* noted, "Letters from both McGill and party chair Mulbah Morlu became the new fashion since the government took office in January", that year rendering the office of the Civil Service Agency almost close to being "useless."[733]

The CSA was established in 1973 to streamline the civil service and operate as a central government personnel agency. Regulated to be independent from all other Ministries and Agencies of Government, the CSA is tasked with managing the Civil Service especially its human resources in all respects. It also advises the Liberian Government in respect of appointments, terms and conditions and all personnel matters so that the Government can provide services efficiently for Liberia's citizens. Despite its laws and the government's own guidelines the CSA has not had a large say in recruitment and recommendations for key government hires. As *FrontPageAfrica* noted "This led to a lot of flawed appointments, causing serious embarrassment to the administration of President Weah where appointments had been dominated by partisans and loyalists of the ruling party."[734] Besides his influence over appointments in government, McGill successfully transformed the role into that of Acting President whenever the President travelled. Under normal protocol, whenever the President travels, the Minister of State for Presidential Affairs acts as Chair of the Cabinet in close consultation with the Vice President. For McGill, the President's absence often offered a chance to cement himself into the Acting President role, parading the city with multiple motorcade convoys and describing himself as acting President at every opportunity.

Mr. McGill's influence on the President was clear from the very start but while many were taken aback by his audacity within the role, some found it quite strange that the President allowed the minister to seize on his Presidency and do unconventional things to the President's own detriment. In the months that followed, many critics of the President began to see McGill as posing a serious danger to the Presidency. Did Weah endorse what McGill was doing? Was he content governing with the perception that McGill was running the affairs of state? Many within the President's circle seem to think that the President deliberately played the good cop/bad cop routine and allowed McGill to have his way.

A veteran human rights lawyer who was a key critic of the government went as far as calling for McGill to be sanctioned by the United States government for his alleged involvement in 'pay-for-play' politics. The accusations came amid concerns that McGill was using his proximity to the President and confidence reposed in him to influence the outcome of key by- and midterm elections.

In December 2020, the minister came under fire amid accusations that he was heavily involved in the harassment and flogging of Independent Gbarpolu County senatorial candidate Madam Botoe Kanneh, and the detention of members of her campaign team because of allegations of espionage in the midterm elections that year.

In a call to several local radio stations, the minister categorically denied ever getting involved in the controversies surrounding the conduct of the recent special midterm senatorial election and national referendum in Gbarpolu County, terming the allegation as baseless and only intended to bring his hard-earned reputation to public ridicule.

Even the opposition Collaboration of Political Parties (CPP) accused the minister of using his power and influence in government to instigate violence and disturbances to frustrate the electoral victory of Madam Botoe Kanneh.

Amidst he accusations, the midterm elections of 2020 dealt a painful loss to Weah and the ruling party and sent a clear message that the allegations of McGill's interference did little to influence the results.

A key reason for the ruling party's misfortune proved to be a controversial decision by Minister McGill to form an auxiliary grouping outside the party's existing structure which eventually denied President Weah the opportunity to score points over the opposition and solidify its chances for the 2023 elections. The McGill influence was also a factor in key by-election races in Bong, Nimba and Grand Gedeh counties where the ruling party lost dismally. In essence, McGill wrestled control of the party from the

Chairman Mulbah Morlu and sought to run the campaign from his office at the Ministry of State in a bid to cement himself as the command centre of the Weah administration.

For example, in the Grand Gedeh race, candidate Jeremiah Sokan surfaced through McGill and Senator Zoe Pennoh's connection, while Madison Gwion, a member of the ruling CDC, was heavily antagonised by Senator Pennoh who found himself entangled in a rivalry between the two Senators Pennoh and Albert Marshall Dennis.

Pennoh dictated the pace on everything taking place in Zwedru, the capital of Grand Gedeh, the hometown of late President Samuel Kanyon Doe. Ironically, Madison Gwion was the favourite of the party, but Pennoh-McGill decided otherwise because they didn't want Marshall Dennis to come out stronger in a Madison victory because of Gwion's very close ties to Marshall.

McGill had summoned Gwion to a meeting once and asked him to back off the race because they had chosen Jeremiah Garwo Sokan to run on the party's ticket.

The *FrontPageAfrica* newspaper reported that the ruling CDC Caucus in Grand Gedeh was heavily divided with Pennoh, Rep. Grant on one side and Marshall Dennis and others on another.

In Bong County, many feared that McGill was overzealous about making himself into a political alternative and prove to Weah that he could rally votes in key areas across the country and in the process cement himself as a possible replacement of Jewel Howard Taylor, who President Weah was rumoured to be contemplating dropping as his running mate ahead of the 2023 elections. In McGill's view, cash and scholarship interventions in vote-rich Margibi, Bong and Nimba counties would lead to important victories for the ruling party and get the attention of President Weah.

Nevertheless, in Bong, McGill came under fire from rival candidates accusing him of favouring one side over the other. Supporters of the National Patriotic Party (NPP) accused the minister of supporting two candidates in the race. The charges against the minister came days after he was seen campaigning along with Vice-President Jewel Howard Taylor in Gbarnga for the ruling party's candidate, Melvin Savage. Savage was endorsed at a political rally in Gbarnga by McGill, who reportedly contributed cash to his campaign.

But partisans of Howard Taylor's NPP accused McGill of also playing double standard by supporting an opposition candidate despite his public appearance with Savage. Terrance Benson, a partisan of the NPP, also accused McGill of financing the campaign of the People's Unification Party candidate James Kolleh in a bid to prove that the Vice-President had lost hold of the county.

Vice-President Howard Taylor had also been engulfed in a feud with President George Weah on a number of key political decisions in Bong County, ranging from her honour as the county's highest traditional icon to her refusal to endorse the candidate of the party in the 2020 senatorial elections in the county. Though Howard Taylor did not publicly endorse any candidate at the time, political pundits believed her actions may have hurt the party following the election of the opposition candidate Prince Moye. Additionally, partisans of the NPP feared that the reported feud between President Weah and Howard Taylor was still fresh and visible, accusing Minister McGill of being on a mission in Bong to deface the Vice-President. "We still think the internal fight within the ruling coalition is still visible and it could spill over to the November 16 by-election in Bong County,"[735] Deborah Flomo, partisan of the NPP, told the *FrontPageAfrica* newspaper.

Minister McGill and others tried to control the party from the outside instead of working with the party chair and hierarchy. "When that wasn't possible, they began driving their own alternative plans; work outside the party and make it seem you're simply zealous to foster the President's re-election strategy,"[736] said Mulbah Morlu.

For example, Rep. Melvin Cole, an antagonist of Vice-President Taylor, was McGill's chief executioner in the county. He was the sole authority there on McGill's behalf and also a fierce critic of the Vice-President with whom he was always at loggerheads. Cole was at the forefront of the scholarship efforts carried out by McGill without the involvement of the ruling party. All this was set against the backdrop that the ruling party had a leadership in the county led by Sayblee Weay, chair of the Bong County Chapter. As a result, the party was caught in the middle of the McGill/Jewel fight, with neither of them supporting the party's activities in Bong. McGill ran a private program to give himself a name brand while the Vice-President ran a pro-National Patriotic Party program. Consequently, party insiders were concerned that using resources in a by-election outside the party or creating the impression that 'money wins' continued to be a mistake that could come back to haunt the ruling party in 2023 as it did in the midterm and the by-elections of 2020.

In Bong, Savage was the choice for the party's county leadership, but his campaign was hijacked by two power interests, each determined to show that Savage's victory would be theirs alone.

The 2020 midterm elections in Nimba were always going to be difficult for a party which supported Sam Brown and which was projected to win the race in Nimba because of Prince Johnson. Brown was a member of the ruling party and had always supported it. However, Senator Johnson insisted that the party support for him would cut off his support for the party's 2023 ambition. The race in Nimba was eventually won by Jeremiah Koung.

The party faced a similar dilemma in Bomi with Snowe who had committed to supporting the ruling party in the 2023 elections, which the source says, was crucial to its decision to remain neutral.

Despite the ruling party's glitches, political pundits were unsure what to make of the results. Was the 2020 midterm a sign of things to come in 2023? The opposition itself had many reasons for concern.

George Wisner, a prominent member of the former ruling Unity Party, remembered thinking that the midterm election results suggested that the opposition alliance had to return to the drawing board and rethink its strategy when heading into the 2023 elections. "We reiterate that there is a need for the CPP to unite. Sorry, but those who argue otherwise, disrespect us, and even brand us for working to unite CPP, either need to see the psychiatrist or need to learn some basic lessons in political psychology."[737]

Like the ruling CDC, the opposition alliance had broken away from the unity formula that drove them to victory in midterm elections and the by-elections earlier that took Senator Abraham Darius Dillon to the Senate. Infighting and backstabbing over petty differences and ego-tripping amongst the leaders of the various parties making up the CPP coalition offered Weah and his party a lifeline.

Even as the opposition struggled to hold, McGill's influence on President Weah offered hope that the President's chances of re-election in the 2023 elections was still an achievable challenge. With the economy in turmoil and international stakeholders keeping close tabs on the unfolding developments surrounding bad governance, corruption and money laundering, President Weah faced a nagging dilemma as he headed into the reelection bid for 2023.

Attention once again shifted to the McGill influence.

In 2021, while recognising that the Weah government had made efforts to strengthen its Anti Money Laundering (AML) regime, the U.S. State Department said that significant challenges remained. For example, the State Department pointed out that the Central Bank of Liberia (CBL) did not robustly enforce AML requirements. Inter-agency coordination had improved, but key stakeholders had not produced actionable financial intelligence, conducted systematic financial investigations, or secured financial crimes convictions. Additionally, they noted that financial institutions had limited capacity to detect money laundering, and their financial controls remained weak. "Liberia's Financial Intelligence Unit (FIU) is under-funded and has experienced recurring budget cuts. The FIU also lacks the equipment and institutional and technical capacity to adequately collect, analyse, and disseminate financial intelligence. Liberia remains a cash-based economy with weak border controls and endemic corruption, leaving the country vulnerable to illicit activities."[738]

The State Department recommended that the government enhance the Central Bank's oversight authority and consistently provide adequate resources to the FIU and urged Liberia to continue to work with international partners to ensure its AML laws, regulations, and policies met international standards.

By late 2021, it was clear that those concerns from the State Department would trigger an opening for money launderers to exploit with the indictment of Korlane Investment Liberia Limited Liability Company. In late 2021, the company had been listed by the Financial Intelligence Unit as a shell company operating in Liberia. In December 2021, Korlane was indicted for money laundering, theft of property, wired fraud and criminal conspiracy. Those indicted were Korlane Investment Liberia Limited Liability Company through its President, and corporate agents, Evgeny Nikisuik, Patrick Hermann Wahi Diega and others to be identified. The indictment read, "That Co-Defendant Korlane Investment Limited Liability Company has perpetrated fraud by instituting scant and dubious deals by using Visa and Mastercards and processing miscoded gambling and or illegal gambling transactions in which accumulated hundreds of thousands of United States Dollars transferred to Guarantee Trust Bank (Liberia) Limited through dubious transactions."[739]

The indictment was complicated due to allegations of involvement of the Solicitor General Syrenius Cephus and the judge of the Monrovia City Court Judge Jomah Jallah. Both officials, according to call logs obtained by *FrontPageAfrica*, placed and received phone calls from Patrick Hermann Wahi Diega, a major suspect in the scandal. The calls were placed between December 2021 and January 5, 2022. *FrontPageAfrica* established that there were 115 incoming and outgoing calls between him and co-defendant Patrick Hermann Wahi Diega between December 2021 and January 5, 2022.

Korlane Investments Liberia LLC., was designated as a high-risk money laundering shell company set up for what appeared to be the sole purpose of laundering the proceeds of crimes generated through fraud, a predicated offence for money laundering. According to the indictment, the company filed Articles of Incorporation on October 12, 2021 for the provision of a variety of services from digital revenue collection to consultancy and project management. Between October 2021 and December 12, 2021, a little more than US$500,000 found its way from card accounts in Ecuador and Slovakia into Korlane's local account. The indictment stated, "In order to effectuate this dubious transactional activities, between the period of September 1, 2021 to December 17, 2021 or thereabout, the Co-Defendants used the business records of Korlane Investment Limited Liberia Liability Company and opened a current account with GT Bank Liberia Limited on account number 0123686/002/0001/000 through which it milked hundreds of thousands of United States Dollars by using miscoded gambling and or illegal gambling transaction, by manipulating Visa and Mastercard transactions wiring the huge sum of money."[740]

According to the indictment, co-defendants Evgeny Nikisuit, Patrick Hermann Wahi Diega and others to be identified had established Korlane as a vehicle and shell to undertake these questionable transfers by laundering six figure sums of U.S. dollars in Korlane's GT bank account and that of others in Liberia. As *FrontPageAfrica* pointed out, the timing was awkward:

"The indictment and the call logs involving the Solicitor General and a judge came to light just weeks after the administration of U.S. President Joe Biden unveiled steps to combat corruption globally, including assistance to foreign governments to increase financial transparency and new regulations on U.S. real-estate purchases to prevent money laundering."[741] The U.S. Government's Strategy on Countering Corruption just issued had five pillars, one of which was curbing illicit finance. The ambition was to target criminals and their networks with the ambition of furthering greater cooperation between federal agencies, including the State Department, Treasury, Commerce and U.S. Agency for International Development and law enforcement.

With so much riding on President Weah's legacy, his inability to make drastic changes to his government became a nagging concern, resurrecting echoes of similar issues that his predecessor, Ellen Johnson Sirleaf struggled with in her twelve years in office, warding off concerns that she lacked the political will to fight corruption, improve governance and make the necessary adjustments to keep her government from sinking.

In President Weah's predicament, most of the anticipated changes appeared to be in the hands of McGill. Of particular concern was the lengthy void at the Ministry of Public Works. Minister Mabutu Nyenpah suffered a stroke on September 3rd, 2020 and died a month later while undergoing care in Accra, Ghana. The job remained vacant for months. The President had settled on promoting his trusted aide, Trokon Kpui, who was Minister of State Without Portfolio. However, Minister McGill had his own plans. To the dismay of many in the President's circle, the minister delayed naming the President's preferred choice in Kpui but instead, pushed for the Acting Public Works Minister Ruth Coker-Collins to take on the job.

President Weah's failure to tackle the issues of corruption and bad governance and to control the grave influence of figures like McGill in his inner circle, points to what many leaders across the continent have struggled with, when poorly performing anti-corruption programs lead to bad governance.

But Weah was supposed to be different. His lack of political will to effectively govern suggests that he may have never really figured out the workings of the Presidency and no one could really blame him. The expectations were low, not for the nation, Liberia, but for Weah himself. He hardly participated in any debates and was never really expected to solve all of Liberia's problems overnight.

He never visited any town hall gathering to tell the people his plans and vision. He owed no one any apologies. In fact, he made it clear that no one should judge him on his eloquence, but on his performance. So, all they saw was a symbol of grassroots, the boy from Gibraltar who became a man and conquered the world of football. Weah was one of them, he had seen their struggles and experienced some himself. But was he really the right man for the job? Could he improve on the gains made by former President Sirleaf and continue Liberia's democratic transition and successful transfer of power?

It is easy to draw conclusions; but Weah is not just any ordinary man. He had defied the odds, defied expectations and fulfilled his dreams of becoming President of Africa's oldest republic. What he needed now was a clear-cut formula and the courage to lead with passion and conviction. What everyone saw was a President delegating his Presidency to his powerful Minister of State. The sad reality for many political observers is that Weah was elected by the people. But now, McGill was performing most of the functions of government, making all the calls, and most of the tough choices. As baffling as it is to many, Weah didn't seem bothered by the perceptions that he had outsourced his power and the votes of nearly five million voters to an appointed official, Nathaniel McGill.

25

ENDGAME

———

F rom the moment George Weah picked up a football, he never looked
back. Along the way of what was undoubtedly a wonderful football
career, were many glitches and hiccups, as well as a few doubting
Thomases.

Old man Kamara, the man who discovered Weah, spotted it. So, did
Coach Sithole, the outcast South African coach from next-door Guinea,
and later, the famed coach, Arsène Wenger, under whose tutelage Weah
would blossom into arguably one of the most gifted footballers of his
generation.

With so much promise, Weah saw a window of opportunity and did
not just seize it but exploited it to his own benefit. Whether it was an injury
to English football legend Mark Hateley during his spell at AS Monaco in
France that paved the way for him, or doubters who said he simply wasn't
strong enough when he moved to the tough Italian Serie A in 1995, Weah
defied the odds. He simply had a footwork that was unmatched and a knack
for scoring goals that was beyond his years.

Perhaps one day a forward like Liverpool FC's Egyptian striker, Mo
Salah will upset the odds to become the second African footballer to win

the coveted World Footballer of the Year, won by Weah in 1995. Until then, George Weah's football legacy remains intact.

When he finally decided to enter politics, long after the game had taken a toll on him, Weah was once again staring down a queue of doubters who had every reason in the world to justify why he would never succeed in politics, much less become President of Africa's oldest republic.

Among them was former U.S. President Bill Clinton who, in a July 2008 conversation interview with Jane Wales, Vice President of the Aspen Institute, had some unfavourable things to say about the football legend who had lost a controversial Presidential election to the Clintons' favourite, Ellen Johnson Sirleaf. "Ellen Johnson Sirleaf was opposed in the election after a distinguished career at the World Bank, after having been a political prisoner, she was opposed in the election by the country's only bona fide sort of cultural figure, a soccer star who was a movie star, handsome and everybody loves to watch him kick the ball and he was backed by all the wrong people and like we say at home, she beat him like a market dog in the election and the voters guided and knew exactly what was going on and they did not bark."[742]

At the time, many of Weah's supporters were taken aback. Clinton had gone gutter, a parlance for dirty politics by Liberian standards.

In particular, Professor Tarpeh believed that the comment from the former U.S. President was rather unfortunate. "It is unfortunate that President Clinton would use that kind of language. To describe someone who rose to the top of the world in football in that manner is very unfortunate. We can say that Ambassador Weah will continue to lead the masses. If someone can beat you 28–19, referring to Weah's margin of victory in the first round of the 2005 Presidential elections, as a market dog beaten, it is unfortunate."[743]

Weah was at a disadvantage, playing on an unfamiliar turf and against insurmountable odds. The education issue became somewhat of an embarrassment for Weah who initially claimed to have a BA degree in Sports Management from Parkwood University in London, later discovered to be from an unaccredited diploma mill which awards certificates without requiring study. Weah has since attained an undergraduate degree and a Master's in Business Administration from DeVry University in Miami.

Weah flipped the tables in 2011, deciding under pressure to run as a Vice-Presidential candidate to Ambassador Winston Tubman. In what many say was a prelude to his 2017 quest, Weah contested and overwhelmingly won the 2014 senatorial elections by defeating Robert Sirleaf, the son of President Sirleaf. Weah won a landslide victory, receiving 99,226 votes, which represented 78.0% of the total votes from the 141 polling centres. Sirleaf, his closest rival, received 13,692 votes which is nearly 11% in an election marred only by a low turnout.

The senatorial elections victory was seen by many as a litmus test for Weah's 2017 prospects. A good showing in the halls of the national legislature could make or break his political career; a bad showing could bolster the perceptions of Clinton and others that Weah was still challenged by the lapses eluding his Presidential quest. But many of Weah's supporters agreed at the time that his election to the Senate was a great and remarkable improvement on his political credentials from 2005.

For Professor Tarpeh, it all came down to whether Liberians were better off now than they were in 2005. "To categorise a man who has made it from the strength of his boots in such a manner is unfortunate but what is important now are results. Where are we now? Are we better off now? Granted, Senator Weah may not have gone to an Ivy League school, but it is about results and his passion for his people."[744]

No fan of Weah, former President Clinton had urged voters to take a different direction by choosing Sirleaf over Weah. "I was there a year or so ago, because we do aid work there and we are trying to build their health systems and Ellen asked me to meet with college students and in Monrovia, the capital, at night. Even then only about 20 or maximum 25% of the buildings had any electricity at night. I know these young people I met have a hard time washing their clothes and ironing them and things that we take for granted at home. These kids were dressed, they were incredibly dressed, well informed. Even though, [they] did not have newspapers, one guy writes the headline on a chalkboard with some chalk."[745]

At the time, many of Sirleaf's critics and Weah's supporters lamented that much of the country was still in darkness – and still is today – suggesting that the winner of the 2005 elections had performed below the expectations of her supporters like President Clinton.

Weah was not without his own supporters. Academy Award winner Denzel Washington, presenting Weah with the 2004 ESPY's award said, "George Weah is one of the greatest soccer players of our time, from a nation where chaos has been the rule and where children are born killers."[746] But was he a good politician? A good President?

Heading into the 2023 Presidential elections, the jury is still out. Even Weah's harshest critics and supporters agree on one thing: that his biggest obstacle to the Presidency was translating his football success into the political arena and an unheralded trait holds the key. No one has seen this first-hand more than George Solo. Solo, a former chair of the CDC, was a vocal presence and key henchman for Weah and the CDC. Solo and Weah parted ways over ideological differences on the revolution. "He wanted a kingdom, and I wanted an institution,"[747] Solo says, recalling the circumstances that led to the fallout, shortly before Weah embarked on his 2014 quest for the Senate.

Today, the pair are no longer on speaking terms and Solo has turned out to be one of Weah's harshest critics. Despite the differences, Solo attributes Weah's success to his ability to adapt. "One of the major skillsets that George Weah has that everyone overlooks is his adaptability. I've seen George Weah beating drums with people from Grand Kru County, beating that drum like he crafted it. I've seen him play football like I've seen him amongst diplomats and all capacity."[748]

For Solo, Weah's ability to adapt gives him an edge over his current opponents in the political arena, despite the fact that he has handicaps in areas in which they seem to thrive.

"So, if all of our time as members of the CDC, and all of our revolution, the adaptability was to change the life of the Liberian people, then fast-forward to today, look at all of the people around George Weah, look what's been done, it means, he has adapted to his new surrounding – and his new surrounding includes not taking Liberians seriously. His new surrounding includes making music. His new surrounding includes no direct agenda to change the lives of the people. But again, we are all product of our environment. That's his gift. Take corruption for example, if you put me in the vicinity of corrupt people, I will condone their actions, you put me in the vicinity of accountability, I will be accountable but if you put me in a free for all with no position, with really no direct critique and no conversation with the ruling party, this is what we have now with Weah."

Solo laments that Weah has not been held accountable by the opposition in a way that will put the government under pressure to perform. "We put clothes on and went toe-to-toe, standing up against President Sirleaf and now that the CDC is in power, things are no different, perhaps even worse."[749]

Right now, Solo says, Liberia is being run as a monarchy. "But even the monarch does not have enough professional support to propel an agenda. Then you have a dysfunctional opposition that further dampens the hope of the Liberian people by saying maybe we will just live with the devil we know than the angel we don't know; because these people are themselves confused. Then, thirdly, we have to look at capacity, across the board as a nation. Whoever is the President, what is the capacity that is there to support them? What policies, processes and laws do we have? We have the Liberia Anti-Corruption Commission (LACC) that picks and choose who to go after. We still have people like Prince Y. Johnson who was a warlord but is still active in government."[750]

He says that until Liberia can clear out all of these lingering issues, including the possibility of sanctions to scrutinise and fix our country, there will always be lingering issues. Solo says Weah has failed, and the failure is a reflection of the Congress for Democratic Change. "From the day we decided to move away from the plan to redeem the Liberian people to a monarchy approach, the good, the bad and the ugly and to make statue of the leader, CDC lost its way, and the Liberian people are feeling the pinch of it. The revolution that we started is not the revolution that is being man-ifested. The road that we started on is not the trajectory that the CDC is on. CDC has failed the people, but George Weah did not fail the Liberian people, CDC failed the Liberian people on the basis of refusing to build and maintain an institution. They wanted a king, and they got a king."[751]

26

GIBRALTAR

———

Riddled with potholes, zinc shacks and makeshift football fields, the Gibraltar area of Claratown represents the poorest of the poor in the Liberian capital Monrovia. It is here that poverty meets hard times, where only one in ten youngsters is likely to become anything resembling a success.

Ironically, Gibraltar occupies a central point of Monrovia, near the historic Bushrod Island, named after Bushrod Washington, the first President of the American Colonization Society (ACS) and a nephew of President George Washington. The ACS operated under that name from 1837 – having been founded in 1816– and promulgated the cause of emigration to Africa of free and enslaved African Americans.

It is surrounded by the Atlantic Ocean, the Saint Paul River, the Mesurado River and Stockton Creek, a tidal channel that connects the two rivers. The surrounding area of Gibraltar also contains the Freeport of Monrovia, the major national port of Liberia, and a variety of businesses. It also contains numerous residential areas and government buildings.

Old Lady Margaret Nah, considered a godmother to many in Gibraltar, says the area's founding fathers named Gibraltar, Gee-Bla-Tah, meaning in the Kru tribe, 'Come and knock your chest'. "When you come here, like a real man or woman, knock your chest to do something good,"[752] she says.

Gibraltar's proximity to the capital and industrial base makes it an important commercial area for the country. It is here that youngsters stuffed socks with litter, plastic and papers to form a substitute football, where the breadwinners were kids who should be in school but who found themselves spending most of their time on the streets selling basic necessities just to help their families put food on the table or pay their way through school. Most barely got a chance to see the inside of a school.

It is here that George Manneh Weah earned his stripes for the game of life.

Football was Weah's ticket out of the hard-knock, poverty-stricken community that offered very little but dreams and aimless expectations. "A combination of luck and hard work enabled me to make my improbable journey from the dusty football fields of Claratown to glamourous stadiums in Europe,"[753] Weah would write in a *New York Times* Op-Ed, shortly after ascending to the highest position in Liberia, the Presidency.

J. Odalfus Wesseh (Odalfo) grew up to the Weah euphoria. Now the Youth Advisor of Gibraltar, Odalfus is just glad that someone from the ghetto made it out, conquered the football world and became the President of Liberia. "If George Weah can do it, why can't I?"[754]

In this ghetto, the people that Weah left behind wouldn't have it any other way. Win or lose, pass or fail, President or not, George Weah has given them hope. "Weah has paved our road and re-roofed our homes since he got elected. People who are saying George Weah is not doing well, they do not have eyes to see. Since he took over, and he met a broken economy, he has been trying to fix it over time."[755]

In 2018, shortly after his inauguration, Weah announced plans to transform Gibraltar, commencing with the re-roofing of all the homes in order to spare inhabitants of impending embarrassment in the wake of the fast-approaching rainy season. When Weah assumed office, most of the homes in the community were in a state of dilapidation as a result of being built over the past three or four decades.

During a visit to the Gibraltar Community in April 2018, President Weah told the community that he would embark on the re-roofing of all the homes in the area. The Liberian leader told residents of the community that he had special love in his heart for them and the community. This was intensified by the fact that he had been working with them long before his election as President of Liberia. "The arrangement will allow community dwellers to leave their respective homes and move to either a home of friend or family member for about five months to allow construction works take place before returning home," the President said, adding: "The project may go slow but will not take more than five months to have every house in the community fully re-roofed for residents to return."[756]

The project however was not without controversy. In December 2018, the *FrontPageAfrica* newspaper obtained and published documents and vouchers showing that the Ministry of Finance and Development Planning had approved more than US$1 million for the re-roofing of 205 houses in Gibraltar, Bushrod Island in fulfillment of a Presidential promise.[757] An investigation by the newspaper into how the project was carried out discovered that two vouchers were raised amounting to US$1,075,000 though the project was estimated at US$800,000 from the outset. The contract was awarded to a Lebanese dealer in building materials, BMC, headquartered on the Capitol By-Pass, and to Sam Sidani, another Lebanese who is believed to be the owner of Hotel Buchanan in Grand Bassa County. The contract award to the Lebanese raised eyebrows at the time at the sincerity of President Weah's January 22, 2018, inaugural speech in which he said, "As we open our doors to all foreign direct investments, we will not permit Liberian-owned businesses to be marginalised. We cannot remain spectators in our own economy. My government will prioritise the interests of Liberian-owned businesses and offer programs to help them become more competitive and offer services that international investors seek as partners."[758]

For Weah, the Gibraltar neighbourhood adjoining Claratown on Bushrod Island is a historic community. Here, the President was raised and here, his first steps were taken on the glittering journey that became his football career and subsequent celebrity. Weah himself has indicated he retains no remorse or embarrassment at having grown up in a poor community noting all its residents need to support their children. In 2018, *The New Dawn* reported he had told, "residents that his plan was to transform the community into a modern environment in which every resident would enjoy the comfort of life through the provision of basic social services" and that he, "wished the house of his late grandma could be left out of the re-roofing plan so as to reflect the true picture of the poverty he experienced before transitioning into an icon."[759] Before that visit in the 1990s, the George Manneh Weah Foundation School was built by the football star and had provided schooling for many years with some children going on to universities in Liberia. It was also reported that he had, "reminded the residents that he lobbied for the school to be renamed Gibraltar Community Academy when he got elected as Senator of Montserrado County in 2014", and that they should "see themselves as the symbol of sustainable reconciliation and unification in Liberia."[760] Despite the slumping economy, hardships in every community and criticisms that the economic woes worsened under his leadership due to administration lapses, perceived incompetence and failure to tackle corruption, Weah's message resonated in his stronghold where he grew up.

The broken economy rhetoric was prominent in his Annual Message delivered in January 2019 when the President declared, "The state of the economy that my administration inherited leaves a lot to do and to be decided. Our economy is broken; our government is broke. Our currency is in free fall; inflation is rising. Unemployment is at an unprecedented high and our foreign reserves are at an all-time low".[761]

Riding on the wave of a populist cry, Gibraltar residents had no problem cosying up to the President's pronouncement that he would slice his salary. "Weah is doing well. When you go to Duala, Old Road and Duport Road Markets, Weah has built those markets. If I was to grade Weah, I would grade him 500% and add my own percentage to it and if he wins the second six years, we will name him king because he will be there for life."[762] Under Liberia's constitution, a President is only allowed to serve two six-year terms. But not for residents in Gibraltar.

Theresa M. Foday of Gibraltar Loan Empowerment club says there's no need for an election in 2023. "George Weah has already won. If we vote, Weah will surely win. He will stay another 24 years in power. So those who say George Weah's popularity has gone low, they are sleeping because Weah is even more popular since he started development in Liberia. He has given us scholarships, he is fixing our roads and market buildings, and he has re-roofed our homes. So, we are not experiencing leakage when it rains. So, he will win elections for the second term."[763]

Nevertheless, Theresa still sees lingering issues with the economy. "We want Weah to work on the economy, most especially the U.S. exchange rate in the country, so that prices can reduce on the market. If Liberia can be like Sierra Leone, Ghana and Nigeria that value their currencies more than the U.S. dollars, it will help our economy. Because when you carry US$5 in the market, you can't buy anything good to cook because prices are too high for the poor people."[764]

Where critics and opponents of Weah see doom, some of his supporters see a shining light, a beacon of hope even amid despair. "I hear people are saying Weah's popularity is decreasing, but I can say that is false,"[765] laments Oldalfo, a high-school graduate. In contrast he says, Weah's popularity is increasing on a daily basis. "Even though I am not working presently; but George Weah has given jobs [to] some of our community people, and I hope when he wins elections again in 2023, he pays attention to the rest of us that he left behind when he gave our friends jobs. And I know he will think of us when he wins the election next year. As for the economy being hard, I would say, things are difficult everywhere and not Liberia alone. A bag of rice is sold at US$50, and Liberia is selling a bag of rice at US$13, so the buying rate between Liberia and Ghana, Liberia is far better than Ghana. Nevertheless, I want Weah to address the economic issues."[766]

But not everyone in Gibraltar lives comfortable with any such delusions of grandeur. Harriet Nyeneh of the Gibraltar Loan Empowerment Club, says while she likes Weah personally, a lot of the people in his inner circle are not doing well for him. Feeling abandoned, Harriet says since putting a lot of his people in government, they shut the door on Gibraltar and many parts of the country. "They do not care about the other people again. I do not think they are giving Weah good advice, or they are only pretending in front of him and behind him, they do their own thing."[767]

Harriet's lament puts a lot into perspective. The issue of the government being outsourced by the President to his trusted lieutenant, McGill, is reminiscent of the views amongst the folks in Gibraltar. For many, the popular footballer had lost touch with his roots, perhaps not by his own doing but mostly owing to the trappings of power.

Like Odalfo, Harriet agrees that President Weah cannot give everybody a job, but those given jobs should look at the bottom of the ladder, to those less fortunate, those unable to catch a break. "When Weah [gave] me [a] job, it means I should help take care of the other people. But his under people (subordinates) are not doing it. Even at the job sites, some people who are doing the same jobs as others are making higher money, while others are making a low amount for the same job. Many of the Opposition are working in the government, while we who have been suffering behind Weah since 2005, are the ones left out."[768]

Harriet and her entire family voted for Weah, but no one is reaping the benefits of the victory. "We are not enjoying [it]. For speaking to George Weah during [the] Claratown tournament, my brother Tee Nyeneh was nearly attacked by two strange men, just because Weah met my oldest brother organising the program and talked with [him] for 25 minutes. Weah told my brother [that] he wanted them to talk and asked one of his SSS officers to take down his phone number, but that was the end of the story; because since December last year, nobody has called my brother. He went to Weah's church first Sunday in January, but the protocol did not allow him to enter the church."[769]

The church is Forky Klon Jlaleh Family Fellowship Church, constructed by Weah who is also the lead pastor, another one of his side attractions to the Presidency that also includes recording music and playing sports at every chance he gets.

The challenges facing Weah are endless.

It is the very reason Weah chose the Samuel Doe football stadium in Monrovia for his inauguration. Football was and is his passion. It had served him well and he wanted those in slums like Gibraltar to know he would not turn his back on them. Weah recalled in his 2019 *New York Times* Op-Ed that, "Growing up as a poor child, I intimately saw and experienced the hardships an ordinary Liberian faced. I know the difficulties and horrors our people suffered before and during the crippling conflicts that tore Liberia apart from 1989 to 2003."[770] This is why in the mid- and late-'90s, Weah often returned home as a goodwill ambassador for the United Nations Children's Emergency Fund to help draw attention to the people's plight and to work to disarm child soldiers.

Now as Head of State, overseeing an entire nation, the burden rested on his shoulders.

Betty Wesseh, a prominent elder in the Gibraltar Community who claims to be Weah's aunt, is hoping that he keeps his promise to the people of Gibraltar, as well as to the people of Liberia. "I want Weah not to forget about his family and find a job for our children in Gibraltar because when they finish with school they cannot go forward. My two boys finished high school but [there's] no money for them to go to college. In every community when you are a big person, there will be some people who will like you and there will be some people will not like you, so, it's the same with George Weah here."[771]

These days Gibraltar is nowhere close to what it used to be. Old Lady Margaret Nah says the reason is simple. "These days our children like too much confusion, and when we advise them, they say that we are in the Third World – and [it's] not like the old days [anymore]. This is why they are drinking, smoking and taking drugs, because they can't listen to the advice from the old people."[772]

Although he's now President, Old Lady Margaret Nah says President Weah knows all the corners of Gibraltar. "When George Weah was here, he and his friends played football and gambled on Ludo boards, where everybody used to put their shirt on their shoulders and roll the dice, but he never used to fight, because there was no confusion. These days, things are different. If you play and win, your friend will want to kill you because you win. Even over common football game, you can take a knife and stab another human being."[773]

For many of the residents in Gibraltar, having one of their own become not just a world best footballer, but President, is quite a feat. However, some, like Abraham Sieh Sonpon, a long strain of disappointment lingers. "I am angry with Weah, and the next time he comes here, I will chastise him, because he lied to me. After struggling with this political party all these years, I am living like a destitute. He promised us, that if the party was going to win, our lives were going to change. Now it is four years, since [he] got in power, but things are yet to turn around. He is picking and choosing, and those around him usually say [that] not everybody will work in the government, but do they know the kind of role we played in Weah's life?" [774]

Sonpon says he does not have anything against Weah, but really hopes that he resets his mind and revisits things he promised to the people he left behind.

Coming from the slums of Gibraltar, Weah's rise out of poverty to football stardom to the Presidency defied expectations but the gap between Liberia's rich and poor remains. The Dalai Lama once said, "Efforts must be made to reduce the gap, else it will make the poor feel inferior and frustrate them leading to jealousy and violence. In order to reduce this gap, the poor must develop confidence that they can also do things and the rich must help in whatever way they can."[775]

For Sonpon, one of the few Weah left behind, the disappointment is grave. "I have given up. My daughter just graduated, and I did not have the first cent to buy food for our guests, things are tough on me. Those Weah promises yesterday have not happened because of hidden agenda and being selective. He has forgotten what he promised, forgotten those who stood by him, when nobody knew who George Weah was."[776]

Like his predecessors, Weah fell prey to the charm of sycophancy. It is the driving force that led the late President Samuel Kanyon Doe to his tragic demise. Doe took power on April 12, 1980, and was soon surrounded by a number of prominent figures in the Progressive era such as Togba Nah Tipoteh, Gabriel Baccus Matthews, George Boley, Samuel P. Jackson and a lot of others.

Doe seized power in order to liberate Liberia from the Tolbert-led True Whig Party and the Progressives who were among Tolbert's strongest critics. He found the perfect alibi with which to demonise the centuries-old American-Liberian rule and move Liberia towards prosperity and the end of corruption, nepotism and greed.

For more than a century, Liberia has survived several leaders who often surrounded themselves with many people. Some people meant well, and others did not. Then there are those who many see as the blasphemous surrogates that are infamous. They sang their way to the feet of the leaders, hoping to consolidate access and enjoy the ears of the Presidency.

Charles Taylor, the former warlord who formed a rebel group and invaded Liberia to rid the country of Doe, succeeded in becoming President. During his reign he also had his followers. Today, many of those who sang Mr. Taylor's songs of praise are still roaming around Monrovia, occasionally telling peers that they tried to advise Taylor but that he wouldn't listen. Others often find the courage to defend him when they can. The same could easily be said of former President Ellen Johnson Sirleaf who led Liberia from 2006 to 2017. Her rule was dominated by flattering supporters, many of whom reinvented themselves for the new political dispensation and quickly gained uncontrollable access to power.

The wheel has turned to George Weah, the leader of the grassroots Coalition for Democratic Change, who seems to enjoy and tolerate the glorification of his Presidency by many who are only fortunate to have a job or feel happy being a stone's throw away to the helm of power.

Some historians have drawn distinct similarities between former President William V. S. Tubman, who led Liberia for 27 consecutive years, and Weah. On the day Tubman died, the late A. Doris D. Grimes, wife of former Foreign Minister, J. Rudolph Grimes, wrote, "The area from Roberts International Airport to Monrovia was lined with people, with drums and other musical instruments on both sides of the street, and also traditional dancers, devils, etc. However, it was very scary – you could hear a pin drop – a tribute paid to a President by Liberia, 'slavishly grateful – dynamic, far-sighted, godly, astute leaders – a leader whose policy is the blind saw, the lame go and hear the doves'. Typical Liberians speak … "a leader who was tempted by water, by fire …"[777]

The Liberian Studies Journal, edited by Dr. D. Elwood Dunn, opines, "The present normally contains features of the past and is pregnant with them for the future, so to acknowledge these memories, we can recognise the leitmotiv of the emerging opposition to the TWPs in the Tolbert years 1971–1980."[778]

Heading into the 2023 Presidential and legislative elections, George Weah and his ruling CDC find themselves in a precarious situation that, if not carefully monitored, could contribute to another dictatorship.

Ironically, in statements and on paper, the Office of the Presidency often presents an attitude that the administration is tolerant of criticism, while at the same time allowing important members of the government to openly approach critics who have a different view.

Critics of President Weah believe that he simply cannot and should not allow power to go to his head and to stop believing that everything is good when the realities on the ground point to something else. The government must say what it means, and the supporters, surrogates, and sycophants of the President must strive to be on the same side or fail the government.

Warren Buffet, the American business magnate, investor and philanthropist, once said, "It's more important to look out of the windshield than in the rearview mirror." Oftentimes, leaders forget their past and ever-so-often are too content with the present to safeguard the future. This may be the case with George Weah, the boy from Gibraltar who grew up in the slums kicking plastic bottles as substitute for football, most of the time without decent shoes. The likes of Sonpon and Old Lady Margaret paint contrasting portraits and impressions of perhaps the greatest son to ever grace the shores of Gibraltar.

While some in Gibraltar are now feeling regret, the fears expressed by the likes of Jerome Verdier in the aftermath of that fateful meeting in Florida when Weah first put forward his interest in politics, still resonate. Looking back, Verdier says he does hold some regret that George Weah's leadership has turned out to be what it is. "I am so sorry for the young people who trusted him as an icon from the slums who would make life different in Liberia. What I did with the Congress for Democratic Change was part of my vision, that was thwarted by what became of the eventual CDC. I decry what's happening in Liberia under his watch, but my membership in the CDC was part of my contribution to nation building; to that, I have no regrets."[779]

Weah's most important contribution to Liberia remains unblemished; he rose to the occasion when it mattered to put Liberia on the football map. While doing the same for his Presidency could even surpass that, the unlearned lessons of history are likely to lower any expectations, especially when Weah has done very little to prove that he is more than an emperor without clothes, allowing his surrogates to run the affairs of state while he engages in his favourite pastimes like singing, dancing and playing his favourite sports.

Winston Churchill, the late British Prime Minister, famously claimed that, of all human qualities, courage was the most esteemed, because it guaranteed all others. On the football field, George Weah had the courage to bulldoze his way through defenders at will, gaining the pride and admiration of the world.

As President, that courage appears to be lacking.

Riding on the mantra of a grassroots movement, George Weah was expected to use his base to push an agenda for change, an agenda for political and economic empowerment for those still languishing at the bottom of the economic ladder. George Weah was expected to effect change for those in the slums like Gibraltar, New Kru Town, Slipway, Waterside and all those areas he rose from to defy the odds en route to the Presidency.

In reality, the mantra of hope and change resulted in pleadings from the people for a leader who would reduce their suffering. Liberians have become restless and disenchanted and while public distrust remains high, Africa's oldest republic is still widely divided on tribal lines as the gap between the rich and the poor widens in the wake of massive corruption and while the rape and abuse of children becomes even more prevalent.

The fact of the matter is, Weah successfully made the transition from footballer to President. Now, he finds himself engulfed in a state of uncertainty regarding his ability to lead and deliver for his grassroots base which include victims of various forms of injustices like domestic violence, police brutality, corruption, greed, nepotism, hunger, income inequality, sexual harassment, land conflict, death, betrayal, homelessness and a host of others.

For the grass rooters, Weah was one of them. He had experienced the pain and suffering and heard the cries growing up in the slums of Gibraltar. He is now at the helm of power, overseeing all these different personalities, sharing various experiences and somehow finding them connected to one another.

George Weah was supposed to be the glue that could hold it all together. Amid the turmoil of a nation emerging out of the ashes of war and nurturing a successful democratic transition, lay the ugly Shakespearean truth that, 'uneasy lies the head that wears a crown'. The line from *Henry IV Part 2,* spoke to Weah's dilemma and clearly underscored the major responsibility facing the football icon. Even he acknowledged that much when he assumed the mantle of authority on his inauguration day in January 2018, when he said, "It will be my task, my duty, and my honour, to lead this nation from division to national unity, and toward a future of hope and prosperity. I have here taken an oath before you, and before the Almighty God, to uphold our constitution and to preside over this government and this country to the best of my abilities. Rest assured; I will not let you down."[780]

While the jury is still out over whether President Weah is on course to achieving much of what he set out to do, the man of many names – King George Oppong Ousman Forky Klon Jlaleh Gbeh-ku gbeh Tarpeh Manneh Weah – appears to be conflicted about his political identity.

After all is said and done, how will he be remembered? Which legacy will most likely stand the test of time or bring him the most pride? His domineering displays on the football pitch or transforming the lives of the Liberian people?

Many of Weah's critics will point to rising poverty and unemployment levels and high-level corruption which have become even more entrenched under his watch as issues likely to raise the most eyebrows. In the same vein, many of Weah's followers and lovers of the beautiful game of football see him as an iconic figure who will forever be remembered for putting Liberia on the global stage in a positive light.

To his own detriment, Weah had set the bar high for himself. "We cannot remain spectators in our own economy. My government will prioritise the interests of Liberian-owned businesses and offer programs to help them become more competitive and offer services that international investors seek as partners,"[781] he said on Inauguration Day, 2018.

In reality, many believe that Liberians became spectators of their own economy under President Weah, under whose watch the votes of millions of Liberians were outsourced to his trusted lieutenant and Minister of State, Nathaniel McGill, leaving Liberians by the wayside as bystanders to the affairs of their own country.

27

'FORGIVE ME'

───────

George Weah would be the first to admit that football for him, is an inborn tendency. From the moment he started kicking the ball as a kid to the moment in 1995 when he conquered the world by winning Africa Best, European Best and World Best in the same year, becoming the first player in the game's history to achieve the feat, Weah has never shied away from his love of the game.

The beautiful game has been his solace, a haven that keeps him content when everything around him has gone awry. Whether it is criticisms about the poor state of the country's economy, abject poverty, bad governance, or corruption, it really doesn't matter when President George Oppong Manneh Weah is on the football pitch.

"This is an inborn tendency and can never go away,"[782] he would tell bystanders and government officials who came by on Thursday, April 8, 2021, to dedicate the new Tusa football pitch in the township of Barnersville. "So, please forgive me whenever you see me on a sports pitch, please forgive me – that doesn't change who I am. It's where I came from, it is the pitch that brought me to this honourable office and we can't forsake where we came from, this is why you see me with you all the time."[783]

President Weah's plea for forgiveness in a nation of nearly five million people stricken by lingering pains and suffering, and still grappling with the realities of political transitions from war to peace while trying to restore its economic sanity, could almost be mistaken as a blip considering criticism that he often reduces the Liberian Presidency to a football pitch.

No African professional footballer has ever been elected President. It is often a tricky line between love and hate for footballers venturing into the rugged jungle of African politics.

Emmanuel Adebayor, the former English Premier League side striker, found out the hard way in November 2017 when he attracted fury from anti-government protesters after a comment on the political crisis in the country. The former captain of the Togolese national team said in an interview that the protesters should first think of contributing to the country. "If the President leaves, will the people without jobs find one more easily? Not sure. We have Libya as an example with Gaddafi. We saw this country with and without him. Libyans are regretting it! The Togolese diaspora in Paris who talk about marching, fly back to the country if you want to march,"[784] he told French media *So Foot* after some hesitation.

Adebayor's comment came as thousands of people protested across Togo amid an unprecedented political crisis, brought about by calls for the introduction of Presidential term limits.

Faure Gnassingbé has been head of state since 2005 when he took over from his father Gnassingbé Eyadema, who seized power in a coup in 1967, seven years after independence. The anti-government protests began in August and had spread across the entire country.

Adebayor's comment attracted a lot of criticisms from opposition supporters on social media who also said they weren't surprised because the player had supported President Faure Gnassingbé in 2015 during the Presidential election. Perhaps this is why retired Ivory Coast international and Chelsea/Marseille striker, Didier Drogba, brushed off the issue when his friend, Weah, encouraged him to follow in his political footsteps after the Ivorian sent words of congratulation to him in December 2020, after Weah clinched the Presidency.

Subtly resisting the overtures from Weah, Drogba dismissed talk of entering politics and possibly rising to become President of the Ivory Coast. For Drogba, there were different ways a person could impact on their society. He stressed that, despite politics being one of those ways, he had other ideas.

One of them was his quest to head Ivory Coast's Football Federation. That quest was heavily rejected after the electoral committee in charge of the association election announced in August 2021 that the former striker did not have enough nominations.

Ironically, Weah sought the Presidency of the Liberia Football Association in November 2003.

Despite his pledge to bring much-needed development to football in the country, his quest was nipped in the bud.

Dismissing speculations that he could follow in the footsteps of Weah and run for the Presidency in the Ivory Coast, Drogba said: "It's not necessarily the case that all footballers will [now] want to become President. George [Weah] has opened the way for him to make an impact in his own way, and others can make an impact on their communities in other ways. He has been a model for me for a long time. He has been a big brother also for a long time and what he has done today shows that in the labour force, with perseverance, we can achieve our objectives and to realise our dreams for the good of the community."[785]

In 2018, President Weah organised a friendly match between Liberia and Nigeria at the Samuel K. Doe Sports Complex to mark the occasion of the retirement of the iconic number 14 jersey which he donned during his active footballing days. But the President has never ceased to wear the jersey, especially for his Weah All Stars (WAS) and during the inter-ministerial games.

On the day he opened the Tusa field, President Weah scored four goals for his Weah All Stars, illustrating that even at age 54, he still possessed the knack for scoring goals – and the wizardry to drive by opposing defenders. "I'm the best dribbler and if they try, they will dislocate some of their body. I'm very fancy,"[786] Weah told the BBC's Mike Thomson in 2019 when asked about whether opposing players are allowed to tackle the President.

Only time will tell whether the George Weah's Presidency will, in the not-too distant future, open a floodgate of retired African – or even popular global – stars venturing into politics.

Over the course of the first term of his Presidency, Weah has also showcased his singing skills with the release of several tracks and occasionally conducts service at a private family church, the Forky Klon Jlaleh Family Fellowship Church, which he constructed in 2018.

At the ushering of 2020, Weah preached a suitable sermon for those raising questions about his choice of pastime: "God has given each and every person talent that they can use for their own benefit."[787]

Weah's talent for bringing attention to Liberia is indisputable. It is however a complex balance when governing a country of five million people.

President Weah is still widely popular amongst the youth and remains a role model for many young Liberians who, like him, grew up in the slums in the capital, Monrovia.

His story is one of hope and determination that anyone can rise from the bottomless pit to conquer the world in whatever they put their mind to – and work hard towards it.

For now, President Weah is not only overseeing a nation rich in rubber, forestry, and mining, but one which, for the last 175 years, has been lingering in a state of recurring economic and political uncertainty – a political uncertainty that has continued for Weah since he won the Liberian Presidency in 2017, a political uncertainty brought on, perhaps, by Weah's own insecurities about himself. Liberia had never elected a president as popular as George Weah. For many, football has always been a pastime which is why many Liberians throng to video clubs, even in the remotest parts of the country, to catch a glimpse of today's legends: Ronaldo, Messi, and a new generation of football greats, as they did for Weah in his prime. For George Weah, football, has and will always be a way of life. The beautiful game had brought him from obscurity to greatness, from a relatively unknown to a jewel of the world – beloved, marvelled, hailed and even worshipped.

As President, George Weah had finally came face to face with the reality that even football heroes have their off-days, days when those who once showered them with praises will suddenly reject them for not scoring a goal or going into a slump for several games without scoring. It's the same in politics where voters tend to hold on to promissory notes guaranteeing that their lives would change for the better, that all of their troubles would be over and that the grass will always be greener on the other side.

For Weah, it was becoming increasingly clear that the Presidency he sought and coveted for years was not as easy as it set out to be. Heading into the crucial 2023 elections, shades from his predecessor, Ellen Johnson

Sirleaf, were evidence that the writing was on the wall. Speaking at the funeral of the fallen former head of the Interim Government of National Unity, Dr. Amos Sawyer, Sirleaf raised questions about the Liberia she left behind, particularly the governance commission she had set up to help institute reforms and codes of conducts for government officials. Sawyer, as head of that commission for the two-terms of the Sirleaf administration, helped raise the bar. For Sirleaf, "the essence of this effort was to give it more scope, more authority and more independence. I am forever grateful that he remained in that position until my administration ended. And, then I ask, where is the Governance Commission in addressing current national issues?"[788]

For Sirleaf, the Governance Commission went AWOL under the Weah administration and was basically a non-entity and one of the most ineffective government institutions.

The lack of governance under Weah was trumpeted by Dr. Linda Thomas-Greenfield, U.S. Ambassador to the United Nations, who, while addressing a virtual event at the Wilson Center on March 31, 2022, in New York, indicted the Weah-led government for corruption.

Dr. Thomas-Greenfield lamented, "I say this as a true friend of Liberia and Liberians know me for being that friend. Liberia has a serious problem right now and that's taking on a number of issues, foremost among them is the issue of corruption. And for me, corruption is an act of robbery, plain and simple. It is government stealing from the people of Liberia, from the mouths of children. It takes away access to health care. It denies citizens their right to public safety. It stops young people from getting the education they deserve. It takes away the future from them. It prevents the country from having the healthy business environment that it needs to lift Liberians out of poverty. It has denied Liberia its place in history. Corruption is a democracy killer, and we cannot have that in a place like Liberia. I want you to underline this, 'Liberia has a serious problem right now... foremost among them is the issue of corruption.'"[789]

Dr. Thomas-Greenfield's comments at the Wilson Centre were preceded by a stinging Op-Ed from U.S. Ambassador to Liberia, Michael A. McCarthy, on the 213th anniversary of the birth of Liberia's first president Joseph

Jenkins Roberts entitled, "What Would J.J. Roberts Have to Say about Liberia Today?"

Ambassador McCarthy wrote, "Troublingly, Embassy investigations indicate that not only are some citizens diverting public medical resources and low-cost drugs for personal gain, but that babies, young children, and birthing mothers are dying needlessly as a result."[790]

On February 4, 2022, the U.S. House of Representatives introduced Resolution 907 calling on the U.S. Treasury and State Departments to continue to impose targeted sanctions against those responsible for undermining the rule of law and trust of the Liberian people through corruption, gross violations of human rights, and other acts that threaten the peace and security of Liberia.

For McCarthy, comments from former Ambassador Thomas-Greenfield and Dana Banks, Special Assistant to U.S. President Joe Biden, indicate that the U.S. Government is sufficiently concerned about corruption in Liberia to sanction individuals. "Corruption leads to citizen frustration and has had destabilising effects on countries in the region. It poses significant risks to peace and democracy."[791]

Perhaps, this was Weah's intent when he sought forgiveness regarding that "inborn tendency" that "can never go away". His plea was perhaps an acknowledgement that his love for the beautiful game was partly responsible for his governance lapses and suddenly eclipsing his quest to transform Liberia and now drawing condemnations from not just his predecessor, but key international stakeholders as well.

Lewis Benedictus Smedes, a renowned Christian author, ethicist and theologian wrote in his best-selling book, *Forgive and Forget: Healing the Hurts We Don't Deserve*, "To forgive is to set a prisoner free and discover that the prisoner was you." [792]

George Weah often was accused of holding on to the past, of not forgiving people who crossed his path. But here he was, in the biggest game of his political life, with the lives of so many people at stake, asking to be forgiven. Was he finally acknowledging the errors of his ways? What did it all mean for those yet to be forgiven by him? More importantly, what did it all mean for those Liberians languishing at the bottom of the economic ladder?

Politics can be cruel toward the naivety of those at the helm of power. For George Weah, the realisation of the inevitable has meant that nothing and no one will change his perspective on life- and that no one will take away his love for the beautiful game, even to his own detriment or political survival.

Over the course of the past five years, George Weah has been unapologetic about his choices. For the football icon-turned politician, his entire life has been defined by characteristics which have been embedded in him from sports, particularly football.

In April 2022, at the dedication of a modern sports park at the centre of the Airfield sports ground where Coach Sithole first laid eyes on him at the start of his football career, George asked, "What are these character traits to which I am referring? They are Perseverance, Respect, Discipline, and Teamwork. These are core values from sports that must be drilled into our young people for them to succeed in whatever they choose to do in life. For this reason, the concept of sport as a national development tool is one that I hold very dear to my heart."[793]

The characteristics may be dear to George's heart but in reality, his leadership and governance of Liberia had been eclipsed by his lack of willingness to realise the dangers of his failure to make the necessary changes that could cement his political legacy. These include major adjustment to his government that would see poorly performing officials being shown the door. All this supplies the backdrop of his repeated caution that there would be zero tolerance for non-performing officials.

In reality, the irony of Weah's lapses of judgement has seen him lose focus amid shifted priorities that came at a cost to his Presidential legacy.

This was evident on March 28, 2022, when he and other government officials were greeted with darkness upon their arrival at the country's major entry point, the Roberts International Airport, from the United Arab Emirates (UAE) where they went to participate in an exposition in Dubai. Similarly, on March 29, 2022, travellers were compelled to use the torch of their phones to provide light in the terminals at the airport. A video, which went viral on the social media, showed the travellers complaining and expressing frustration over the "disgraceful" situation.

Under President Weah, basic necessities like consistent electricity and water have suddenly became a nagging headache for Liberians and a lingering issue for the government. Food and fuel prices have skyrocketed, and many are struggling to get by.

At the end of Weah's first year in office, the opposition People's Unification Party, aptly summed up the dilemma many Liberians had found themselves in, saying, "Our people, your people are hungry; the bread-and-butter issue keeps getting worse. A poorly performed economy is not a good sign for peace and security; when people are hungry, they are most definitely angry; Liberia is angry because its people are hungry."[794]

All this has been compounded by the fact that the Confederation of African Football (CAF) has failed to approve the country's main football stadium, the Samuel Kanyon Doe Stadium for the World Cup and Africa Cup of Nations qualifying matches, dealing a major blow to Weah's football legacy. The stadium's facilities were condemned by the sport's governing body as "unfit" to host international games due to poor bathroom, pitch and seating facilities.

The stadium was commissioned by late President William R. Tolbert, who did not start the construction and was removed from power in a 1980 coup d'état. Doe, who toppled Tolbert in that coup, completed the stadium in the 1980s and named the facility after himself.

The stadium has had frequent problems with overcrowding due to, on at least one occasion, illegal ticket sales. In 2008, eight people died of suffocation following a football match, and in 2014, spectators were reported to have fainted. These days, the stadium which has been the site of international concerts, national political events, and multiple World Cup qualifying matches is now a shadow of its former self, from the glory days when football brought united Liberia.

Many remember the famous Reggae Sunsplash concert held at the stadium in 1988, just a year before the Civil War started, that featured reggae greats, Burning Spear, Yellowman and other well-known roots and dancehall reggae artists flown in from Jamaica. It was here that George Weah scored some great goals as the target man for the Lone Star and it was here that he was inaugurated as President.

All this was not lost on George Weah when he was inaugurated into office in January 2018. The newly-minted President declared: "I have spent many years of my life in stadiums, but today is a feeling like no other. I am overwhelmed with the crowd and the energy here today, and I guarantee you, when we finish, there will not be a winning or a losing side. Today, we all wear the jersey of Liberia, and the victory belongs to the people, to peace, and to democracy."[795]

In becoming President, George Weah had scored a Pyrrhic victory, his success had come with unacceptable costs to not just his life, but his Presidency. Football and politics have defined the life of George Weah and for the latter part of the past few years, have gone hand in hand. Football has been George Weah's life, his reluctance to let go of the game and put more emphasis on governance and his legacy, has somewhat complicated his Presidential legacy to the extent that it has affected his expressed vision and love for Liberia.

How will George Weah be remembered? How does he want to be remembered? How will he be judged in the court of public opinion, long after the dust has settled on his Presidency? In football, the icon will always be revered as one of the game's greatest, in politics, the jury is still out with Weah holding his destiny in his own hands.

David Richmond Gergen, an American political commentator and former presidential adviser who served during the administrations of Richard Nixon, Gerald Ford, Ronald Reagan and Bill Clinton and regularly offers political analysis for the Cable News Network (CNN), once said, "Politics is like watching football. Yes, you can see it directly on your screen, but I think a lot of people want to have some understanding of what's happening, why the play is unfolding the way it is, and I think that's where it can help them, not to render judgments but to help people make their own judgments in a more informed way."[796]

AFTERWORD

Warning messages, stark utterances amid concerns from Washington on corruption in Liberia were unmistakable and clear writings on the wall to the Weah Administration in Monrovia but they were either ignored or taken for granted. Corruption in Liberia had become not only a bane to real progress in the country but was also a source of deep embarrassment to U.S. officials including the new American ambassador to Liberia, Michael McCarthy, who arrived in the country in January of 2021.

McCarthy is an old hand in the U.S. foreign service, a graduate of Tulane University who had several diplomatic stints in Africa, including South Africa, South Sudan and Eritrea; and served as a Country Desk Officer in the Bureau of African Affairs at the U.S. State Department. McCarthy and other American officials were faced with a difficult choice: remain silent on the magnitude of corruption and the outward show of wealth by key Weah lieutenants or do something dramatic, even if it would appear as tilting the scales of the October 2023 elections. President Weah had resisted numerous warning signs and private discussions with other international stakeholders to reorganise his government, by removing corrupt and inept officials, particularly those on the radar and targeted for sanctions under the Global Magnitsky Act of 2016. The Act was enacted by the United States Congress and signed into law in December 2016 by President Barack Obama with the aim to punish corrupt foreign officials and human rights violators by freezing their assets and barring them from entering the United

States of America. The Act targets foreign officials, whose transgressions reach such "scope and gravity as to threaten the stability of international political and economic systems".

The Magnitsky Act was thus an option to send an unmistakable warning to the Weah Administration. But before sanctioning corrupt Liberian officials, the Biden Administration laid out a strategic plan to force the hand of Weah to change course on corruption, graft and bad governance but those messages went unheeded, especially those on strengthening integrity institutions and curbing the egregious corruption that was on display in Liberia.

Thus, key U.S. officials were tipped to up the ante by publicly shaming the Weah Administration with the hope that outward pressure would force the Liberian leader to change course. One of the first opportunities came during the celebration of Liberia's Bicentennial in February 2022. On February 6, 1820, more than 200 years earlier, the first group of formerly enslaved people from the United States settled on an island on the West Coast of Africa in the land mass which eventually became Liberia. They departed from New York in February 1820 on the ship *Elizabeth*, dubbed the *Mayflower* of Liberia with an initial detour to the British colony of Sierra Leone.

An association named and styled the American Colonization Society (ACS) had been established in 1816 and subsequently received funding from the U.S. Congress with the controversial goal of returning freed slaves to a place in Africa. Although the U.S. abolished the Trans-Atlantic Slave Trade in 1808, domestic slavery was not abolished until the Emancipation Proclamation on June 19, 1865, with a national holiday Juneteenth, established in the United States now to commemorate that event.

With the new U.S. policy on corruption in the Weah Administration in full swing, official utterances had to be harsh and undiplomatic. Thus, Dana Banks, a senior aide to United States President Joe Biden sent out the first salvo when she was in Liberia to commemorate the country's bicentennial, a year-long event.

Here was Dana Banks, an African-American, descendant of slaves and now a senior Biden Administration official, two hundred years later, warning that corruption was "an act of robbery" – robbing Liberians of access to "health care, public safety, and education", robbing the country of a "healthy business environment"[797], which would keep millions in poverty and decrease economic opportunities and thereby exacerbating inequality, further eroding stability and emaciating the integrity of the state.

Much had been done by the international system, especially the United States of America to push Liberia along the road to democracy and good governance since the country's fourteen year Civil Wars ended in 2003, but the Weah Administration was failing to sustain the course and legitimate fears were being expressed that business as usual in Liberia could impede democracy and the country's stability, returning Liberia to its dark days of war and strife.

In essence, the country's forebears, who had fought for independence and freedom were turning in their graves, as Liberia continued to be mired in governance lapses threatening the core of Liberia's survival and existence. It was within this backdrop that Ambassador McCarthy lamented in a March 15, 2022, Op-Ed entitled, "What Would J.J. Roberts Have to Say About Liberia Today", about how the country was on the verge of collapse because the vices of yesteryears were still hurting those languishing at the bottom of the economic ladder.[798]

McCarthy was particularly troubled that the U.S. government was sufficiently concerned about corruption to the extent that sanctions were on the horizon, declaring that corruption leads to citizens' frustration and has destabilising effects on countries in the region and posed significant risks to peace and security.[799]

Dr. Linda Thomas-Greenfield, a former U.S. Ambassador to Liberia, now serving as her country's ambassador to the U.N. also added her voice to the issue of graft, declaring while addressing a panel marking the 200-year commemoration of U.S.-Liberia ties that Liberia had a serious problem regarding the issue of corruption, a cancer she lamented was taking food from the mouths of children and taking away access to affordable health care while denying citizens their rights to public safety and stopping young people of Liberia from getting the education they deserve. She warned that corruption was a "democracy killer."[800]

In essence, the warning signs were not only directed at the Weah Administration but the people of Liberia and their past leaders. Liberia was no longer progressing. Past and former leaders were choosing their short-term gains over the long-term benefits of the country. America had to act and do so swiftly to send an unmistakable message to President Weah and prod Liberians to take actions to push the administration in a totally different direction.

So, when Ambassador McCarthy took the podium to address the press on August 15, 2022, it was clear that the first list of sanctioned officials was about to be hit.

Chief amongst them was Nathaniel McGill, the President's key advisor and one considered the unofficial President, due to the massive influence he wielded and the open fact that McGill was the one, in whom, President Weah had totally outsourced running the affairs of the state. McGill was arguably the most powerful Minister of State and Chief of Staff in the country's history or recent memory.

In the build-up to Ambassador Michael McCarthy's Monday, August 15, 2022, news conference, the U.S. Embassy in Monrovia had notified a select group of media owners that it had a message to deliver to the press.

Ambassador McCarthy announced that the U.S. Department of the Treasury's Office of Foreign Assets Control (OFAC) had, "designated Nathaniel McGill, Sayma Syrenius Cephus, and Bill Twehway for their involvement in ongoing public corruption in Liberia. The officials were designated pursuant to Executive Order (E.O.) 13818, which builds upon and implements the Global Magnitsky Human Rights Accountability Act and targets perpetrators of serious human rights abuse and corruption around the world."[801]

Regarding McGill, the Treasury Department said the minister had "bribed business owners, received bribes from potential investors, and accepted kickbacks for steering contracts to companies in which he has an interest."[802] The Treasury department also stated that the minister had "manipulated public procurement processes in order to award multi-million-dollar contracts to companies in which he has ownership, including by abusing emergency procurement processes to rig contract bids."[803] McGill their text continues was "credibly accused of involvement in a wide range of other corrupt schemes including soliciting bribes from government office seekers and misappropriating government assets for his personal gain. He used government funds allocated to other Liberian government institutions to run his own projects, made off-the-books payments in cash to senior government leaders, and organized warlords to threaten political rivals. McGill received an unjustified stipend from various Liberian government institutions and used his position to prevent his misappropriation from being discovered. McGill regularly distributes thousands of dollars in undocumented cash to other government officials for government and non-government activities."[804] Using the very formal language it deploys for such cases, the Treasury Department concluded: "McGill is being designated for being a foreign person who is a current government official who is responsible for or complicit in, or who has directly or indirectly engaged in, corruption, including the misappropriation of state assets, the expropriation of private assets for personal gain, corruption related to government contracts or the extraction of natural resources, or bribery." The clarity and gravity of the U.S. verdict were unmistakeable. They were not pulling any punches.

At the same time, Sayma Syrenius Cephus, the Solicitor General and Chief Prosecutor of Liberia, was accused by the U.S. of having developed "close relationships with suspects of criminal investigations and had received bribes from individuals in exchange for having their cases dropped. Cephus has worked behind the scenes to establish arrangements with subjects of money laundering investigations to cease investigations in order to personally benefit financially. He shields money launderers and helps clear them through the court system and has intimidated other prosecutors to quash investigations. Cephus has also utilized his position to hinder investigations and block the prosecution of corruption cases involving members of the government. Cephus has been accused of tampering with and purposefully withholding evidence in cases involving members of opposition political parties to ensure conviction."[805] Cephus was also according to credible sources involved in obstructing the execution of a warrant to get the call log of a suspected money launderer.[806]

Cephus was likewise designated by the Treasury Department– in the exact same words as used for McGill – as being a foreign person and perpetrator of corruption under the Global Magnitsky Human Rights Accountability Act.

The third individual sanctioned was Bill Twehway. Twehway was the former Managing Director of the National Port Authority (NPA). According to the U.S. Treasury, Twehway "orchestrated the diversion of $1.5 million in vessel storage fee funds from the NPA into a private account. Twehway secretly formed a private company to which, through his position at the NPA, he later unilaterally awarded a contract for loading and unloading cargo at the Port of Buchanan. The contract was awarded to the company less than a month after its founding. Twehway and others used family members to obfuscate their involvement in the company while still bene-fitting financially from the company."[807]

Twehway was also likewise designated by the Treasury Department– in the exact same words as used for McGill and Cephus – as being a foreign person and perpetrator of corruption under the Global Magnitsky Human Rights Accountability Act.

The sanctions meant that all property and interests in property of the three listed in the "United States or in the possession or control of U.S. persons must be blocked and reported to OFAC [Office of Foreign Assets Control]."[808] Entities owned, by the three, to 50% or more were also blocked. The OFAC's regulations enacted a general prohibition against dealings with designated persons that involved property or interest in property. The ruling makes it clear that other persons engaged in transactions with the three might themselves be sanctioned and also foreign financial institutions like-wise. U.S. motives are also spelt out plainly: "The ultimate goal of sanctions is not to punish, but to bring about a positive change in behavior." And if that was not clear and sobering enough for the Weah administration, the action by the U.S. was a chilling reminder of the implications of the sanc-tions: "the values that form an essential foundation of stable, secure, and functioning societies; have devastating impacts on individuals; weaken democratic institutions; degrade the rule of law; perpetuate violent conflicts; facilitate the activities of dangerous persons; and undermine economic markets."[809] Thus the U.S. was seeking "to impose tangible and significant consequences on those who commit serious human rights abuse or engage in corruption, as well as to protect the financial system of the United States from abuse by these same persons."[810] The sanctions were by no means just aimed at protecting the U.S. financial systems from abuses by the targeted individuals, but was intended to serve as a deterrent against corruption.

In some way, greed had perhaps gotten the best of some of those in the President's inner circle. The sanctions sought to put the brakes on a government, spiralling out of control and failing to address the concerns from its international partners and stakeholders. What was needed was a breather, an opportunity perhaps for President Weah to put his house in order and reset the button on governance.

As a footballer, George Weah made a lot of sacrifices to reach the pinnacle of the beautiful game but somehow as President, many of Weah's critics were unsure he was willing to do the same to salvage the ruins of his presidency.

Even after the U.S. announced sanctions, President Weah struggled to force the resignation of the targeted officials.

It wasn't until more than a month later, that McGill, Twehway and Cephus bowed to pressure and finally tendered in their resignations.[811] McGill had been particularly reluctant, amid chatters or rumours that he would break ranks and spill the beans on the President and take everyone in the government down with him. Both McGill and Cephus denied the allegations contained in the U.S. Treasury sanctions report.

Acknowledging that the sanctions had ruined his reputation, McGill says he believes that someone may have told the Americans something when they were genuinely trying to find facts. McGill, in a statement announcing his resignation, insisted that he had never been involved with any form of corruption.

In fact, rumours appeared saying that aides close to McGill had floated an alleged plot on social media alleging that a plan was being hatched to eliminate McGill because he knew too much and could leak out the source of the money the President allegedly used to build his multi-unit apartments. The killing of the auditors, the murder of EPS officer in Nimba and on whose instructions as well as the disappearance of the US$25 million of COVID-19 money, the pocketing of fees paid for COVID examinations at the Roberts International Airport and a host of other issues dogging the Weah-led government.

The alleged plot suggested that McGill had become a very dangerous threat to the President, and he needed to be taken out.

There were even rumours that McGill was reaching out to the U.S. Embassy in a bid to strike a deal and turn the tables on the President.

The fallout from the sanctions also triggered other economic maladies, exacerbating effects of the Ukraine war on rising prices of commodities on the market and the fears of the resurrection of the April 14, 1979, rice riots, as shortage of the country's staple food became rampant in the latter part of 2022.

Once again, the blame fell on one of Weah's appointees, Commerce Minister Marwine Diggs, a long-time friend of the President, and allegedly one of the many paramours of the Liberian leader.

Callers to various radio talk shows pointed fingers at the minister, who also faced mounting pressure from rice importers who complained of losses as a result of keeping the price of rice stable on the Liberian market in fulfillment of a request made by the government.

The President surprised many upon his return from the 77th United Nations General Assembly in September 2022 when he downplayed reports of a rice shortage, describing these as "mere street gossip" as he declared that there was sufficient food in the country to serve Liberians. "We need not always listen to the street gossip. This is not the first time it has happened. Those responsible for importing rice say we have rice up to next year. I don't believe there's rice scarcity there is rice. We will verify it again. Don't listen to the noise in the street."[812]

But subsequently it was learned that several factors were contributing to the lack of rice on the market including bad faith from the government in paying subsidy payments to importers. In one instance it was alleged that the Deputy Minister of Finance Samora Wolokollie indicated that out of 11 million dollars owed importers in the current fiscal period, 5 million dollars had been paid. But that was subsequently rejected by an official at the Ministry of Commerce and Industry (MOCI) who reported that only $US3.5 million dollars had been transmitted to the MOCI. Another factor contributing to the impending rice crisis as of late September 2022 was that regular dredging at the port had been delayed by incompetence and bureaucratic snafus, thus making it impossible for large tonnage vessels with huge quantities of rice to berth at the Freeport of Monrovia.

What President Weah alluded to as "noise in the streets" was resonating across the country as the president's inability to know what was truly obtaining in the country regarding the shortage of rice, evoking spectre and memories of the events of April 14, 1979, leading to Samuel Kanyon Doe's coup and decades of instability in Liberia. Weah's reluctance to take such a pressing and threatening matter seriously, once again raised questions about his ability to lead.

Weah appears lost without McGill steering the affairs of state. The disgraced former Minister had been his rock, his unofficial Prime Minister, the man in whose hands he had placed his presidency at the expense of his legacy. With McGill out of the picture, it was time to regroup, time to take stock of the past five years.

It suddenly became clear why the President was reluctant to part ways with McGill. With the 2023 presidential elections nearing, who will put the pieces together? Who will put the plans in motion to secure the president's second term? More importantly, critics of the President remained in a state of bewilderment, pondering why he allowed McGill to amass so much power and what would it mean for his own future, his own legacy and place in the annals of history. Such is the dilemma that President Weah faces as the country moved toward a pivotal election in October 2023

ACKNOWLEDGEMENTS

———

Writing this book has been one of the greatest challenges of my life and I owe a debt of gratitude to so many people who guided me along the way. First, I would not have been able to bring this story to life without the urging of my friend, mentor and Arsenal FC fan mate, Helene Cooper, who during an afternoon lunch in a downtown Washington, D.C. restaurant, first gave me the spark and the encouragement to tell the story of one of the greatest footballers to ever live and how he transitioned to the presidency of Liberia.

Until that moment, the thought never occurred to me. Helene's *New York Times* bestsellers, *The House on Sugar Beach* inspired so many people, including me. Her, second book, *Madame President: The Extraordinary Journey of Ellen Johnson Sirleaf,* brought the life journey of Liberia's 24th President.

I owe so much to Helene for the push that has led to what I believe is one of the best accomplishments of my life and a historical revelation that will last for generations to come.

Alhaji Yaya Kamara who helped George Weah fulfill his lifelong dream of playing for his childhood club, Invincible Eleven, accepted my request and invited me into his home to meet his family and took me back in time to share his memory of a young and hungry Weah looking to find his footing in the beautiful game.

Alhaji was patient, composed and full of knowledge and wisdom. His perspective opened my eyes to a part of Weah I never knew and one I'm sure many have come to appreciate after reading this piece of work.

Finding Alhaji would not have been possible without the help of Kaddieyatu Diarra Findley, who was instrumental in pointing me into Alhaji and other notable former friends of Weah who shared the recollections of the Weah they knew, long before he became an iconic world class footballer.

The surviving children of the late Coach Mohammed Fernando Sithole, Georgette and Joe were instrumental in sharing memories of the man who helped to groom George Weah into the footballer he became.

I can't say how appreciative I am to Cameroonian journalist and Voice of America reporter Moki Edwin Kindzeka for his hard work in helping me with interviews of key figures who crossed George Weah's path during his time with Tonnerre Yaoundé in Cameroon. Moki was patient with my inquiries and dedicated to ensuring that nothing was left out of Weah's journey to football stardom in Cameroon.

I also owe a debt of gratitude to my friend, Mr. Kofi Buckman who helped me trace Charles Oppong, the former Ghana Black Stars and Asante Kotoko great after whom George Weah got his nickname, "Oppong". Charles was very instrumental in recalling the rivalry that existed between Kotoko vs. Invincible Eleven and Liberia and Ghana vs. Liberia when he crossed paths with George Weah.

My gratitude to Abraham Kromah for putting me in touch with Musa Massaquoi, one of the few surviving eyewitnesses who was on the scene when Weah's 9th Street home was gutted by fire on April 6, 1996. Musa held nothing back in recalling those dark days when Benjamin Yeaten, one of the most feared warlords of the Civil War, along with Jack the Rebel spearheaded the assault on Weah's home.

Jonathan "Boye Charles" Sogbie welcomed me into his home to share his recollection about the internal rivalry between he and George while playing for both the Invincible Eleven and the Liberian national team the Lone Star. Sogbie's description of some of the key moments of the early days and internal wrangling in the national team that led to Liberia's failure to qualify for the 2002 World Cup and the trappings that led to their poor performances in two Africa Cup of Nations tournaments, in both Mali and South Africa.

To Dionysious Sebwe, my former classmate from Cathedral Catholic High School, your recollection of key events and memories from the Lone Star days and run-ins with Weah brought a new dimension to this story.

I also owe a lot of gratitude to Louis Crayton, the former goalkeeper of the Lone Star who helped share the good, the bad and the ugly side of the Lone Star training camps on the eve of the crucial World Cup qualifier against the Black Stars of Ghana and internal wrangling that hurt the team's chances for qualification.

This book would not have been possible without the insight from James Kollie, one of the pioneers in the formation of the Congress for Democratic Change, who offered depth and a historical perspective about the early squabbles surrounding the formation of the grassroots movement that would later claim state power in Liberia.

Special thanks also to Mr. Jerome Verdier, former head of the Truth and Reconciliation Commission and his brother, James, former chair of the Liberia Anti-Corruption Commission who shared their early memories and interactions with Weah.

I also would like to express great thanks to my lawyer and friend, Cllr. Samuel Kofi Woods who shared with me the backstory to how efforts to form an alliance with Weah fell apart in Miami Beach, Florida. Cllr. H. Varney G. Sherman offered striking insight into his relationship with Weah and the backstory to Weah's failed presidential bid in 2005.

James Salinsa Debbah, regarded as Liberia's most celebrated footballer accepted my request for several days of interviews in which he went to great lengths to describe in long and strenuous detail his relationship with Weah, that is still unsettling in so many ways, beyond the pages of this book.

Special thanks to Idella Cooper for helping me research and access case files in the James Bestman case, an important part of this project.

I am also grateful to Mulbah Morlu who gave some background into the failed attempts to form a political alliance between Charles Brumskine's Liberty Party and Weah's Congress for Democratic Change.

Ambassador Winston Tubman, who ran for the Liberian Presidency with Weah as his running mate in the 2011 presidential elections was reluctant at first to sit and talk about that journey and what it was like working with George, but finally agreed to share his story about what happened behind the scenes. His input was very instrumental in filling out an expansive canvas.

Special thanks to Heidi Blake of the *Sunday Times* for speaking to me about her book, The Ugly Game, which she co-authored with Jonathan Calvert detailing accounts gathered from the FIFA files and the corruption saga surrounding how Qatar won the rights to host the 2022 FIFA World Cup. The book, highlighting how Mohammed Bin Hammam, Qatar's top football official, used his position to help secure the votes also delves into Bin Hammam's ties with Weah, who asked the Qatari official to help him pay his college fees as he sought to polish his credentials in his bid to give his shot at the presidency another go.

Although George Weah did not agree to speak to me for this project, I'm grateful that his Vice President Jewel Howard Taylor did. The oftentimes, controversial VP was open and honest about her experience working with Weah and how she responded when he first approached her to be his running mate. I appreciate her for exhibiting bravery in sharing both the joys and pains in the Weah government at a time when many who were approached were reluctant or in some cases afraid to speak on the record.

I want to express thanks to my friend Orlind Cooper for putting together footages on the 2018 inauguration of Weah which helped me bring colour to this story.

I also owe a debt to former Associate Justice Kabineh Ja'neh and former Defense Minister Brownie Samukai for agreeing to share their ordeals as victims of injustice meted out by the Weah government which led to them losing their respective jobs, Ja'neh, his seat on the Supreme Court bench and Samukai, his elected post, as Senator from Lofa County.

Special thanks to my long-time friend and media colleague, Mae Azango for helping me solicit the views of residents in Gibraltar and Claratown, where Weah grew up.

To my cousin, Reginald Goodridge, who was a Minister of Information during the days of former President Charles Taylor, I owe a debt of gratitude for agreeing to share some behind-the-scenes moments between Weah and former President Taylor as well as the circumstances that led to his fallout with Weah.

I owe so much more to Paul Roberts and the team at Jericho Writers for pushing me beyond the limits to make this book as close to perfection that it could ever be. Paul's inputs on chapter arrangements, style and press for consistency was at times annoying but was in the right place, and I am forever grateful.

I did not stumble on Andrew Lockett at Reedsy by accident, it was destined. Like me, Andrew is an ardent football fan and understands the King's English. His attention to every bit of detail has been a blessing and I really do appreciate every advice and input to making this book complete.

My journalistic life has been full of challenges and one person who has really pushed me is Jenny Horrocks. I owe much of my professional successes to her. As a shy correspondent for the BBC in The Gambia in the early 1990s, Jenny was the producer for the African sports programme "Fast Track" and saw the potential in me I never knew I had, or maybe knew but never really seized upon it. Jenny's push was motivational, exceptional. I believe we all need that one person that crosses our path for a reason, to elevate one's reason for living. Jenny has been that, for me. She changed my life, and I am forever grateful.

I appreciate the help also of business partners, Niahson Kirk Porte and his wife, Kadi, who have been the rock holding the pieces of our wonderful newspaper together.

My uncle Kenneth Yahkpawolo Best inspires me each day. As a young man growing up on the streets of Broad Street Snapper Hill, I saw in him the journalist I want to be.

When I started this project, nearly four years ago, it was necessary to take some time off the daily activities at *FrontPageAfrica*. I would not have had the flexibility had it not been for dedication and hard work of our newsroom chief, Lennart Dodoo and the rest of the team including Selma Lomax, Henry Karmo, Gerald C. Koinyeneh, Willie Tokpah, Obediah Johnson and Edwin Genoway, for going above and beyond.

I am also grateful to my good friends, Samuel Siebu, Agatha Joseph, Sando Karneh, Rodney Richards and my geez partner, Glendy Junius Reeves.

Writing this book was an emotional rollercoaster of ups and downs, met with some disappointments along the way. Despite the challenges, I'm happy to have had the comfort of very close circle of friends and family I could turn to for advice. My sisters Yvonne, Brenda and Maureen and my brother, George.

Family has been my rock and I am forever grateful for everyone who has played a part in the journalist I have become and the man I was destined to be.

NOTES AND SOURCES

———

The book has been researched over a period of years in the midst of day to day journalism which has also mapped unfolding events. Sections of Chapters 7, 11, 12, 16, 17, 18, 21, 22, 23, 24 were first written by the author for *FrontPageAfrica* and published there respectively on February 7, 2019 (two articles), on September 27, 2021 and on May 17, 2018, January 24, 2020, on October 26, 2021, March 7, 2019, September 6, 2017 and November 3 and 4, 2019 and October 15, 2018, June 30, 2020 and July 10, 2018 and November 18, 2021. Additionally, some of the final stretches of Chapter 25 was inspired by and includes echoes of the wording of the *FrontPageAfrica* article, "The Problem with Liberia is the Sycophants and Surrogates Surrounding Pres. Weah", August 20, 2018, *FrontPageAfrica*. Published here with thanks to *FrontPageAfrica* and its staff. Material in Chapter 22 is greatly indebted to Civitas Maxima who assisted with its drafting. Thanks are extended to all the author's professional colleagues, authors and interviewers and to the publishers thereof in respect of quoted material. Keeping a track of Liberian affairs is a difficult undertaking but not a lonely one and thanks to all whose work preceded and helped inform this book.

Most of the book relies on internet sources with all the strengths and weaknesses that implies. The author has endeavoured to provide title and dates for as many of these as possible. The reader may should they chose to look find quotes from news websites even if a simple search though paywalls, broken web links and sites that have closed down are perennial problems.

Short links to websites in other areas than news websites are sometimes provided but due to length and other considerations full weblinks are not provided and in many cases are simply not available online. This applies to several documents and interviews. In respect of any missing or inaccurate details for which advance apologies are extended please contact the Publisher. In the event of further editions any necessary corrections would be made.

List of *FPA* Articles

February 7, 2019. Kofi Woods Details Behind the Scenes Discussion That Spurred 2005 Speculations. February 7, 2019. Liberia 'Heading In Wrong Direction' – Kofi Woods.. June 11, 2020. Liberia: History of Fraudulent Elections Resurrecting Concerns as President Closes in on NEC Appointment. September 27, 2021. Liberia: Exit Dilemma for Opposition Alliance –Why It may Be Too Late for Feuding Parties to Party Ways. May 17, 2018. Liberia: Jewel's Apology – A Sign of Deeper Feud with Pres. Weah? January 24, 2020. Liberia: VP Jewel Howard Taylor: "I Am Definitely Not A Race Car Parked In A Garage; In Fact …" (FULL INTERVIEW). October 26, 2021. Liberia: Opposition Bruhaha Draws Similarities That Triggered 2017 Alliance's Demise. March 7, 2019. Liberia: Foul-Play or Accident? Death of Another Central Bank Staffer Triggers Fears in Missing Billions Saga. November 3, 2019. Liberia Flunks Half of Millennium Challenge Scorecard, First Time Since "09", November 3, 2019. November 4, 2019. ANALYSIS: What Liberia Must Do to Maintain the Millennium Challenge Compact After Dismal Scorecard. October 15, 2018. Liberia: 1st Lady Eyeing US$10M for Foundation Amid Code of Conduct, Conflict of Interest Breach. June 30, 2020. Liberia: 1st Lady's Brother Trying to Revive Marcus Garvey's Unfulfilled Vision; Dismisses Mining Claims. July 10, 2018. Meet Angela List of Ghana: The Most Powerful "Investor" In Weah-Led Liberia. November 18, 2021. Liberia: By-Election Results Suggest Voters Rejected Politics of Ego, Numbers Boast. Additionally, some of the final stretches of Chapter 25 was inspired by and includes echoes of the wording of the *FrontPageAfrica* article, "The Problem with Liberia is the Sycophants and Surrogates Surrounding Pres. Weah", August 20, 2018, *FrontPageAfrica*. Published here with thanks to *FrontPageAfrica* and its staff.

ABOUT THE AUTHOR

——

Rodney Dean Sieh is an award-winning journalist, editor, and publisher of Liberia's largest independent print and online daily, *FrontPageAfrica*, a ground-breaking publication that has brought down senior government figures and exposed political corruption.

Jailed twice for publishing dissenting articles about the powerful Liberian government and its Supreme Court, Rodney, a former Correspondent for the BBC, faced final sentencing of 5,000 years in prison in 2013. The ruling sparked an international outcry and prompted support from numerous high-profile journalist-rights organizations, inspiring Sieh's now-infamous op-ed in "*The New York Times*" entitled *Jailed for Journalism* and leading to his eventual release.

Fearless in his quest to speak truth to power and push the bounds of investigative journalism, Rodney is the recipient of multiple journalism and press-freedom awards across the world, including Journalist of the Year. In 2014, he was named one of Reporters Without Borders top 100 "Information Heroes" and is the bestselling author of *Journalist on Trial: Fighting Corruption, Media Muzzling and a 5,000-Year Prison Sentence in Liberia*.

INDEX

NOTES

1 Alhaji Yaya Kamara, Interview with Author, October 7, 2021

2 Ibid

3 Ibid

4 Ibid

5 Ibid

6 Ibid

7 Ibid

8 Ibid

9 Ibid

10 Ibid

11 Ibid

12 Ibid

13 Ibid

14 Ibid

15 James Salinsa Debbah, Interview with Author, September 12, 2021

16 Alhaji Yaya Kamara, Interview with Author, October 7, 2021

17 Ibid

18 Ibid

19 Ibid

20 Ibid

21 Ibid

22 Ibid

23 Ibid

24 Ibid

25 Ibid

26 Ibid

27 Ibid

28 Ibid

29 Ibid

30 Ibid

31 Ibid

32 Ibid

33 Ibid

34 Ibid

35 Ibid

36 Ibid

37 Ibid

38 George Telewoda, Interview with Author, September 21, 2021

39 Joe Sithole, Interview with Author, August 21, 2021

40 Georgette Sithole, Interview with Author, August 21, 2021

41 Joe Sithole, Interview with Author, August 21, 2021

42 Ibid

43 Ibid

44 Georgette Sithole, Interview with Author, August 21, 2021

45 George Telewoda, Interview with Author, September 21, 2021

46 Ibid

47 Ibid

48 Ibid

49 Georgette Sithole, Interview with Author, August 21, 2021

50 Joe Sithole, Interview with Author, August 21, 2021

51 Jonathan "Boye Charles" Sogbie, Interview with Author, September 25, 2021

52 Georgette Sithole, Interview with Author, August 21, 2021

53 George Telewoda, Interview with Author, September 21, 2021

54 Ibid

55 George Telewoda, Interview with Author, September 21, 2021

56 Charles Oppong, Interview with Author, November 11, 2021

57 Ibid

58 Ibid1

59 Ibid

60 Ibid

61 Ibid

62 Ibid

63 Ibid

64 Ibid

65 Ibid

66 Ibid

67 Ibid

68 Ibid

69 Ibid

70 Bessala Henriette, Interview with Author, October 12, 2021,

71 Ibid

72 Dieudonné Nke, Interview with Author, October 14, 2021

73 Ibid

74 Pierre Semengue, Interview with Author, October 14, 2021

75 "Cameroun/Liberia: George Weah - Souvenirs de Yaoundé", Josiane R. Matia, *Cameroon Tribune,* January 2, 2018

76 Kangsen Wakai, "A Secret History of Mr. George Weah", Chimurenga, 23 January, 2018. Chimurengachronic.co.za

77 Ibid

78 Ibid

79 Ibid

80 Ibid

81 Ibid

82 Ibid

83 Ibid

84 Pierre Semengue, Interview with Author, October 14, 2021

85 Ibid

86 Dr Achille Essomba Many, Interview with Author, October 14, 2021

87 Hugo Bossokeng, Interview with Author, October 14, 2021

88 Jean Paul Akono, Interview with Author, October 14, 2021

89 Bessala Henriette, Interview with Author, October 12, 2021

90 Arsène Wenger, *My Life and Lessons in Red & White*, Orion, May 2021

91 Arsène Wenger, Arsenal Football Club Website, February 7, 2018

92 Ibid

93 Ibid

94 Ibid

95 Ibid

96 James Salinsa Debbah, Interview with Author September 12, 2021

97 Arsène Wenger, Arsenal Football Club Website, February 7 2018

98 Ibid

99 Arsène Wenger, Arsenal Football Club Website, February 2018

100 Ibid

101 "Football: Porto to Report Weah Over `Clash' with Costa", November 22, 1996, *The Independent.*

102 Francois Massaquoi quoted by *The New York Times*, December 18, 1996, in "Weah's Ban Puts Soccer Fairness Rule on The Line"

103 Rene Eberle quoted by *The New York Times*, December 18, 1996, in "Weah's Ban Puts Soccer Fairness Rule on The Line"

104 "Porto to Report Weah Over `Clash' with Costa", November 22, 1996, *The Independent.*

105 Joao Havelange, former FIFA's President, December 1996

106 "Weah Snubs Golden Handshake", August 19, 2000, BBC website.

107 Alberto Zaccheroni, Interview with coachesvoice.com, November 2016

108 Ibid

109 "I Didn't Sacrifice $2m for Somebody to Tell Me to Shut up and F**k Off: The George Weah and Man City Disaster", Eoin O'Callaghan, the42.ie, September 19, 2018

110 Joe Royle, quoted by Eoin O'Callaghan,
    the42.ie, September 19, 2018, as above

111 George Weah, quoted by Eoin O'Callaghan,
    the42.ie, September 19, 2018, as above

112 Brazilian football legend, Pelé, interview
    clip used in the Netflix documentary film,
    Pelé (2021)

113 Musa Massaquoi, Interview with Author,
    October 10, 2021

114 Ibid

115 Ibid

116 Ibid

117 Ibid

118 Ibid

119 Musa Massaquoi, Interview with Author,
    October 10, 2021

120 Ibid

121 Reginald Goodridge, Interview with Author,
    October 30, 2021

122 Ibid

123 Ibid

124 Ibid

125 Ibid

126 Ibid

127 Ibid

128 Musa Massaquoi, Interview with Author,
    October 10, 2021

129 Ibid

130 Ibid

131 Ibid

132 Ibid

133 Lewis Brown, Interview with Author,
    November 25, 2021

134 Dionysius Sebwe, Interview with
    Author, May 2021

135 Ibid

136 Ibid

137 Ibid

138 Louis Crayton, Interview with the Author,
    August 19, 2021

139 Ibid

140 Ibid

141 Ibid

142 Ibid

143 Ibid

144 Ibid

145 Ibid

146 Ibid

147 Ibid

148 Ibid

149 Ibid

150 Ibid

151 Ibid

152 Ibid

153 Jonathan "Boye Charles" Sogbie, Interview
    with Author, September 25, 2021

154 George Weah, speaking to local radio
    station DC101, 2002

155 Dionysius Sebwe, Interview with
    Author, May 2021

156 Ibid

157 Ibid

158 Ibid

159 Ibid

160 Ibid

161 Ibid

162 James "Salinsa" Debbah, Interview with
    Author, September 12, 2021

163 Ibid

164 Ibid

165 George Weah, Interview with journalist,
    January 19, 2002. BBC 'Focus on Africa'.

166 Ibid

167 Ibid

168 Jonathan "Boye Charles" Sogbie, Interview
    with Author, September 25, 2021

169 Ibid

170 Ibid

171 Ibid

172 Ibid

173 Ibid

174 Ibid

175 Ibid

176 Ibid

177 Ibid

178 Ibid

179 Ibid

180 Ibid

181 Ibid

182 Ibid

183 Ibid

184 Ibid

185 Ibid

186 Ibid

187 Ibid

188 Ibid

189 Ibid

190 Ibid

191 Ibid

192 Ibid

193 Ibid

194 Ibid

195 Ibid

196 Ibid

197 Ibid

198 Ibid

199 Ibid

200 Ibid

201 Ibid

202 Ibid

203 Ibid

204 Ibid

205 "George Oppong Manneh Weah – The Patriot I Know", Zeogar Wilson, October 20, 2017, *FrontPageAfrica*

206 Ibid

207 Jonathan "Boye Charles" Sogbie, Interview with Author, September 25, 2021

208 Ibid

209 Ibid

210 Ibid

211 Ibid

212 Ibid

213 Ibid

214 Ibid

215 Ibid

216 Ibid

217 Ibid

218 Ibid

219 Ibid

220 Ibid

221 Ibid

222 Ibid

223 Ibid

224 Ibid

225 Ibid

226 Jonathan "Boye Charles" Sogbie, Interview with Author, September 25, 2021

227 Ibid

228 Ibid

229 Ibid

230 James "Salinsa" Debbah, Interview with Author September 12, 2021

231 Ibid

232 Ibid

233 Ibid

234 George Weah Interview with BBC, January 24, 2002

235 Ibid

236 Ibid

237 Samuel Kofi Woods, Interview with Author September 19, 2020

238 Ibid

239 Ibid

240 Ibid

241 Ibid

242 Ibid

243 Samuel Kofi Woods, Interview with Author September 19, 2020

244 James Kollie blog, "October 2004 – Part 1: The Dangerous Tactics That Significantly Undermined the Grassroots Organizing", April 9, 2017. jameskollie.net

245 Ibid

246 Ibid

247 Ibid

248 Ibid

249 Ibid

250 Ibid

251 Ibid

252 Ibid

253 Ibid

254 Ibid

255 Ibid

256 Ibid

257 Ibid

258 Ibid

259 James Verdier, Interview with Author, March 3, 2022

260 Ibid

261 Ibid

262 Ibid

263 James Kollie, Interview with Author, September 10, 2021

264 Ibid

265 Jerome Verdier, Interview with Author, March 3, 2022

266 Ibid

267 Ibid

268 Ibid

269 Ibid

270 Ibid

271 Ibid

272 Ibid

273 James Kollie, Interview with Author, September 10, 2021

274 ESPYs Press Release, 2004

275 Denzel Washington, speech presenting George Weah with Arthur Ashe Award, July 18, 2004

276 Ron Semiao, Senior Vice President of ESPN Original Entertainment

277 George Weah, in a featured package preceding his award from Denzel Washington, July 18, 2004

278 Ibid

279 Ibid

280 George Weah, speaking to local radio station DC101, November 18, 2004

281 George Weah, Interview with *Daily Observer* newspaper, 2005

282 Ibid

283 Ibid

284 Ibid

285 George Weah, Interview with *Daily Observer*, 2005

286 Ibid

287 NEC ruling on George Weah dual citizenship, 2005

288 "Liberia Footballer Set for Poll", August 13, 2005, BBC. news.bbc.co.uk

289 James Salinsa Debbah, Interview with Author September 12, 2021

290 George Weah, Interview with *Daily Observer*, 2005

291 George Weah, Interview with *Daily Observer* , 2005

292 Michelle Obama, Former US First Lady, May 12, 2019

293 George Weah, Interview with the *Daily Observer*, 2005

294 Varney Sherman, Interview with Author, June 16, 2021

295 James Kollie, Interview with Author, April 6, 2022

296 Ibid

297 Ibid

298 Ibid

299 James Kollie, Interview with Author, April 6, 2022

300 "USAID/OFDA Fiscal Year (FY) 1996 Situation Report # 1 Liberia", June 5, 1996, U.S. Agency for International Development/Office of Foreign Disaster Assistance. usaid.gov

301 Varney Sherman, Interview with Author, June 16, 2021

302 Ibid

303 Ibid

304 Ibid

305 Ibid

306 Ibid

307 Ibid

308 Ibid

309 Ibid

310 Ibid

311 Ibid

312 Ibid

313 Ibid

314 Ibid

315 "Statement on Second Round of the
Presidential Election 8th November 2005",
African Union Observer Mission in Liberia,
November 9, 2005. aceprject.org

316 "*United States v. Christian*", 111 F. Supp.
3d 287 (E.D.N.Y. 2015), June 24, 2015.
https://casetext.com; "*People v. Bestman*",
262 A.D.2d 567, 692 N.Y.S.2d 422 (N.Y.
App. Div. 1999), June 21, 1999. https://
casetext.com. See also "'Drug Lord Brothers
'turned Park Hill into a War Zone"
Prosecutor Says in Closing Remarks at
Federal Trial', October 22, 2014, John M.
Annese, *Staten Island Advance*.
silive.com/news

317 "Notorious Staten Island Criminals
Helping Feds Win Cases for Possible Cut in
Prison Time", January 23, 2015, John M.
Annese, *Staten Island Advance*.
silive.com/news

318 Ellen Johnson Sirleaf, Speaking at the
funeral of Hannah Brent, August 21, 2009

319 James Bestman, Statement to Federal
Bureau of Investigation, June 6, 2010

320 George Weah, Interview with James Butty
of the Voice of America, Daybreak Africa,
June 11, 2010

321 Ibid

322 Ibid

323 Ibid

324 FBI, Baltimore Division, US Attorney's
Office, District of Maryland, "Marijuana
Dealer Sentenced to Over 21 Years in
Prison on Drug and Money Laundering
Charges", April 6, 2012. https://
archives.fbi.gov

325 Ibid

326 "25 Years of The Carter Center, Annual
Report, 2005-2006". The Carter Center,
Atlanta, GA; National Democratic
Institute/Carter Center Issue
Preliminary Statement on 2005 Liberia
Elections, 12 October 2005.www.
cartercenter.org

327 "Observing Presidential and Legislative
Elections In Liberia Final Report on the
International Observation Delegations
October–November 2005". The National
Democratic Institute and The Carter Center.
October 11 and November 8, 2005. ndi.org

328 J. Fonati Koffa, Interview with Author,
August 17, 2021

329 George Weah, Letter leaked to
FrontPageAfrica, November 14, 2010

330 Israel Akinsanya, Interview with Author,
October 12, 2021

331 "Liberia: Opposition Bruhaha Draws
Similarities That Triggered 2017 Alliance's
Demise", October 26, 2021, Rodney Sieh,
FrontPageAfrica, 2021

332 George Weah, Speaking on the campaign
trail during 2005 elections quoted in
"Profile: George Weah", BBC, November 11,
2005. news.bbc.co.uk

333 Slogan used by Liberians, 1997

334 Ellen Johnson Sirleaf, Interview with
FrontPageAfrica, September 27, 2021

335 Mulbah K. Morlu Jr, Letter to the National
Executive Committee, November 2, 2010

336 Winston Tubman, Interview with Author,
December 4, 2021

337 Ibid

338 Ibid

339 Ibid

340 Ibid

341 Ibid

342 Ibid

343 Ibid

344 Ibid

345 Ibid

346 Ibid

347 Ibid

348 Ibid

349 Ibid

350 Ibid

351 Ibid

352 Ibid

353 Ibid

354 Winston Tubman, Interview with *Daily Observer*, 2005

355 Ibid

356 Winston Tubman, Interview with Author, December 4, 2021

357 Ibid

358 Winston Tubman, Interview with Author, December 4, 2021

359 Ellen Johnson Sirleaf, Speech, US Congress, March 15, 2006. https://awpc.cattcenter. iastate.edu

360 Winston Tubman, Interview with Author, December 4, 2021

361 Ibid

362 Ibid

363 Ibid

364 George Badue, Spokesperson for Liberian National Police, November 8, 2011

365 Speciosa Wadira Kazibwe, Election observer, November 8, 1011

366 Ellen Johnson Sirleaf, November 8, 2011, quoted in, "Liberia: Run-off election campaign ends", November 7, 2011. News24.com.

367 George Weah, message to his partisans and supporters, November 26, 2011

368 Acarous Moses Gray, statement announcing Tubman's dismissal from the party, 2011

369 Winston Tubman, Interview with Author, December 4, 2021

370 Ibid

371 Ibid

372 Ibid

373 Ibid

374 Ibid

375 Ibid

376 Ibid

377 Ibid

378 George Weah, Interview with *Daily Observer* newspaper, 2005

379 Ibid

380 George Solo, Interview with Author, January 17, 2022

381 Ibid

382 George Solo, Interview with Author, January 17, 2022

383 "Koijee Arrest and Detention Is Political Machination Concocted by Robert Sirleaf and His Mother President Sirleaf", John S. Morlu, November 10, 2014, John S. Morlu, *The Perspective*. theperespective.org.

384 Dionysius Sebwe, Interview with Author, May 2021

385 James "Salinsa" Debbah, Interview with Author September 12, 2021

386 Ibid

387 Jonathan "Boye Charles" Sogbie, Interview with Author September 25, 2021

388 Ibid

389 Ibid

390 Ibid

391 "Weah Reveals Why He Resigned As Peace Ambassador – 'I Gave Their Money Back'", August 15, 2017, *FrontPageAfrica*

392 "Liberia: President Weah Issues Reconciliation Plea", February 15, Tina S. Mehnpaine, Allafrica.com.

393 George Weah, Speech, Bicentennial Celebration, February 14, 2022

394 Ibid

395 Ibid

396 Nelson Mandela, quote from film *Invictus*, released December 11, 2009

397 Nelson Mandela, Inaugural address, May 10, 1994. www.sanews.gov.za

398 Ellen Johnson Sirleaf, Inaugural Speech, January 2012. www.emansion.gov.lr

399 George Weah, Inaugural Speech, January 22, 2018. www.emansion.gov.lr

400 Ibid

401 "FIFA ethics judges ban Bb aide for life for bribery", January 20, 2017, apnews.com

402 Ibid

403 Najeeb Chirakal, Email published in
　　Sunday Times (of London), 2014

404 George Weah, Email, published by, *Sunday
　　Times*, 2014

405 Lenn Eugene Nagbe, Email, published by,
　　Sunday Times, 2014

406 George Weah, "FIFA Panel Questions
　　Ex-Milan Player Weah on World Cup",
　　interview with Bloomberg News, Alex Duff,
　　June 3, 2014.

407 Assets Declaration of George Weah, to the
　　National Elections Commission, 2014

408 Section 10.1 of the revised Code of
　　Conduct of Liberia, 2014. emansion.gov.lr

409 George Weah, Inaugural Speech, January 22,
　　2018. emansion.gov.lr

410 Records quoted from Broward County,
　　cited in: "Liberia: George Weah's Property
　　Empire Fuels Distrust Over Asset
　　Declaration", January 23, 2021, Radio
　　France International, rfi.fr.

411 Ibid

412 Ibid

413 Ibid

414 Ibid

415 Ibid

416 Remarks by Special Assistant to U.S.
　　President Dana Banks at Liberia
　　Bicentennial Launch, February 14, 2022

417 Ibid

418 Ibid

419 Ibid

420 Ellen Johnson Sirleaf, statement to the
　　press, 2005

421 Companies Run by Ex-cricketer Phil
　　Edmonds 'Paid Bribes to Officials'" Simon
　　Godley, *The Guardian*. 11 May 2016.

422 Jewel Howard Taylor, Interview with
　　Author, May 15, 2021

423 Ibid

424 Ibid

425 Ibid

426 Ibid

427 Ibid

428 Human Rights Watch, 2005

429 Jewel Howard Taylor, Interview with
　　Author, May 15, 2021

430 Ibid

431 Ibid

432 Ibid

433 Ibid

434 Ibid

435 Ibid

436 Article 51 of the Liberian Constitution.
　　https://judiciary.gov.lr

437 Jewel Howard Taylor, Interview with
　　Author, May 15, 2021

438 Ibid

439 Ibid

440 Ibid

441 Ibid

442 Ibid

443 George Weah, statement to Journalist,
　　October 2017

444 Kebbeh Mongar, statement of intervention,
　　December 2018

445 Ibid

446 "Liberia: Consider Me Your 'Son'; Not An
　　Outsider: President Weah Tells Lofians",
　　June 4, 2021, Selma Lomax,

　　FrontPageAfrica. https://
　　frontpageafricaonline.com

447 Ibid

448 "Liberia: Pres. Weah Hints Picking Jewel
　　Howard-Taylor Again As 2023 Running
　　Mate", June 4, 2021, Selma Lomax,

　　FrontPageAfrica. https://
　　frontpageafricaonline.com

449 Ellen Johnson Sirleaf, Interview with
　　Author, September 22, 2021

450 Excerpt from Ganta Resolution, 2016

451 "Liberia: Opposition Bruhaha Draws
　　Similarities That Triggered 2017 Alliance's
　　Demise.", October 26, 2021, Rodney Sieh,

FrontPageAfrica. https://frontpageafricaonline.com

452 World Bank report, 2016, reported in "Rise to Uplift Social Disaster", July 19, 2021, bringchange88.com

453 George Weah, Inaugural Speech, January 22, 2018. www.emansion.gov.lr

454 Ibid

455 Ibid

456 Ibid

457 Ibid

458 Ibid

459 Ibid

460 Ibid

461 Muhammadu Buhari, Inaugural Speech, June 1, 2020, "Full text of President Muhammadu Buhari's Speech", October 22, 2020. vanguardngr.com

462 Henry Costa, Interview with Author, June 16, 2021

463 Ibid. [Matthews had been the leader of the April 14, 1979 rice riots and many later blamed him for the subsequent riots and looting]

464 "Liberia: 'Extremists Responsible for 1979 Rice Riot'", April 18, 2022, Robin Dopoe, *Daily Observer*

465 Patrick Honnah, owner of Punch FM TV in a statement, June 16, 2018

466 Jonathan Paylayleh, Interview with Author, May 22, 2021

467 Ibid

468 Ibid

469 Ibid

470 Ibid

471 Ibid

472 Ibid

473 Ibid

474 Sayma Syrenius Cephus, Interview with journalist, 2019, quoted in "Liberia: Political Parties Condemn Shutdown After Government Clamps Down on Roots FM",

October 11, 2019, Alline Dunbar and Augustine T. Tweah, *FrontPageAfrica*

475 The Press Union of Liberia, Open letter to the UN, 2018, quoted in "Liberia Stakeholder Report for the United Nations Universal Periodic Review Regarding Impunity for Past Human Rights Violations", October 3, 2019, Human Rights Watch. hrw.org.

476 George Weah, Inaugural Speech, January 22, 2018. www.emansion.gov.lr

477 Kroll Associates Inc, Report, February 2019. https://www.usaid.gov

478 "Statement on the release of the Independent Review Report by Kroll Associates Inc" USA Embassy, Monrovia, February 28, 2019. usaid.gov

479 Ibid

480 See "Liberia: $25 Mil Mop Up Exercise Audit Report 'Indicts' Govt Officials", May 16, 2019, Emmanuel Abelo, *African Star* and link, "AG Report of Factual Findings on Applying the Agreed-Upon Procedures of the US$ 25 Million Mop-Up Exercise".

481 Kroll Associates Inc, Report, February 2019. www.usaid.gov

482 General Auditing Commission (GAC), Report, 2019. See 480 above. gac.gov.lr

483 Family member source quoted by *FrontPageAfrica*: see: "Family of Late Central Bank Senior Staff Rebuts Early Accounts of His Death", March 5, 2019, Alaskai Moore Johnson.

484 Statement, The Bethel Cathedral of Hope Church, March 8, 2019

485 Ibid

486 Philip A. Z. Banks III, Ruling of the Supreme Court of Liberia, 2017

487 Ibid

488 Ibid

489 Joseph N. Boakai, news conference, December 2017

490 Charles Walker Brumskine, news conference, 30 December, 2017. Facebookcom/cwbrumskine2017/posts

491 Alexander B. Cummings, news conference, October, 2017

492 Benoni Urey, news conference, October, 2017

493 Kabineh Ja'neh, statement, 2017

494 Kabineh Ja'neh, statement on the election ruling, 2017

495 Ibid

496 Ibid

497 Ibid

498 Supreme Court of Liberia (Decided November 30, 2018) Opinion of the Court, delivered by Justice Korkpor.

499 "Ja'neh Entangles in US$27m road fund?", *The New Dawn* March 19, 2019

500 Ibid

501 Ibid

502 Kabineh Ja'neh, Interview with Author, March 1, 2022

503 Ibid

504 Ibid

505 Ibid

506 Ibid

507 Ibid

508 Ibid

509 Arthur Johnson quoted in "Ja'neh's Lawyer Detests Foul Play in Ongoing Impeachment Proceedings", March 4, 2019, Emmanuel Weedee-Conway, Heritage. heritageneeslib.com

510 Ibid

511 "About Us", Community Court of Justice. www.courtecowas.org (n.d.)

512 "West Africa: Ja'neh Wins At ECOWAS Court, But..." Abednego Davis for *Daily Observer*, November 11, 2020.

513 Sayma Syrenius Cephus, responding to ECOWAS Court ruling, November 17, 2020

514 ECOWAS Court, responding to Liberian Government, 2020

515 *Counsellor K. M. Jan'Neh v. Republic of Liberia and Judge Y. D. Kaba,* November 10, 2020. courtecowas.org

516 Ibid

517 Kabineh Ja'neh, Interview with Author, March 1, 2022

518 Ibid

519 Ibid

520 Kabineh Ja'neh, Interview with Author, March 1, 2022

521 Ibid

522 Ibid

523523 Ibid

524 "Open Letter To The Liberian Senate On The Removal Proceedings Against Associate Justice Kabineh Mohammed Ja'neh", J. Aloysious Toe from *FrontPageAfrica* Op-Ed 15 February 2019. https://frontpageafricaonline.com

525 Ibid

526 Ibid

527 Ibid

528 "The Removal Of Justice Kabineh M. Ja'neh Was Unconstitutional", Cllr. Tiawan S. Gongloe, 21 May 2019, *The Perspective.* www.theperepective.org

529 Ibid

530 "A Free Press and Personal Rule", Theodore Roosevelt, in *Kansas City Star*, May 7, 1918.

531 "MPC Files Writ Of Prohibition Against Brownie Samukai's Certification", *Hot Pepper Liberia* March 3, 2021. hotpepperliberia.com

532 Ibid

533 John D. Barlone, Case File to Halt Samukai's Certification by the National Elections Commission (NEC), March 2, 2021

534 "Full Text of Supreme Ruling in Brownie Samukai Case", August 20, 2021, *FrontPageAfrica.*
https://frontpageafricaonline.com

535 Samora P.Z. Wolokollie, confirmation in court, March 13, 2020

536 Presidential Proclamation Concerning Brownie Samukai, 22 February 2022. Statement by Nathaniel McGill.

537 "No Clemency for Samukai, But Jail Sentence Suspended" – Minister McGill Clarifies", February 23, *The Analyst.* Analystliberiaonline.com

538 John Brownell, Interview with Author, March 2, 2022

539 Ibid

540 Ibid

541 James Verdier, Interview with Author, March 4, 2022

542 Nathaniel F. McGill, letter to another Commissioner at the LACC, February 26, 2019

543 James Verdier, interview with Radio France International, February 14, 2019

544 Lenn Eugene Nagbe, interview with Radio France International, February 19, 2019

545 George Weah, response to critics October 31, 2018 in Gbarnga, quoted in "Liberia: President Weah Labels Loan Critics As 'Enemies' Of State'", June 12, 2018, *FrontPageAfrica* https:// frontpageafricaonline.com

546 George Weah, Inaugural Speech, January 22, 2018. www.emansion.gov.lr

547 Harry Truman, America's 33rd President

548 "Oppong Open It; Salinsa Close It", *The Sports Chronicle,* 1988

549 "VICTORY: Lone Star Smashes Black Stars 2-0, Qualifies for World Cup Round Two", *Daily Observer,* 1988

550 Kadala Kromah, Lone Star coach, Interview with BBC Sport, July 5, 2004. news. bbc.co.uk

551 James "Salinsa" Debbah, Interview with Author, September 12, 2021

552 Ibid

553 Ibid

554 Ibid

555 Ibid

556 James "Salinsa" Debbah, Interview with BBC Sports, August 10, 2005

557 James "Salinsa" Debbah, Interview with Author September 12, 2021

558 George Weah, Interview with BBC Sports, August 10, 2005

559 James "Salinsa" Debbah, Interview with Author, September 12, 2021

560 Ibid

561 Ibid

562 Ibid

563 Ibid

564 Ibid

565 Ibid

566 Ibid

567 Ibid

568 Ibid

569 Ibid

570 Ibid

571 Ibid

572 Ibid

573 Ibid

574 Ibid

575 Ibid

576 Ibid

577 Ibid

578 Ibid

579 Ibid

580 Ibid

581 Ibid

582 Ibid

583 Ibid

584 Ibid

585 George Weah, Interview with *Daily Observer*, 2004

586 Mahatma Gandhi, Letter to Rajkumari, August 29, 1947

587 Reginald Goodridge, Interview with Author, October 30, 2021

588 Ibid

589 Ibid

590 Ibid

591 Ibid

592 Ibid

593 Ibid

594 Ibid

595 Ibid

596 Ibid

597 Ibid

598 Ibid

599 Ibid

600 Ibid

601 Ibid

602 Ibid

603 Ibid

604 Ibid

605 Ibid

606 Ibid

607 Ibid

608 Lewis Brown, Interview with Author, November 25, 2021

609 Reginald Goodridge, Interview with Author, October 30, 2021

610 Ibid

611 Ibid

612 Ibid

613 Ibid

614 Ibid

615 Ibid

616 Ibid

617 Reginald Goodridge quoted in "Court Awards E. J. Roye Building Ownership to Government of Liberia", September 6, 2017, Bettie K. Johnson Mbayo, *FrontPageAfrica*. https:// frontpageafricaonline.com

618 Ibid

619 Ibid

620 Ibid

621 Ibid

622 Ibid

623 Reginald Goodridge, Interview with Author, October 30, 2021

624 Ibid

625 Winston Tubman, Interview with Author, December 4, 2021

626 Ibid

627 Ibid

628 Ibid

629 "Liberia: President Weah Proposes Several Bills To Support PAPD", January 31, 2019, *FrontPageAfrica*. https:// frontpageafricaonline.com

630 Ibid

631 Ibid

632 Ibid

633 Ibid

634 "Annual Message To the Second Session of the Fifty-Fourth National Legislature of the Republic of Liberia", George Weah, January 28, 2019. www.emansion.gov.lr

635 Ibid

636 Liberia: Background and U.S. Relations", February 14, 2020. EveryCRSReport.com.

637 "Agnes Taylor Sues War Crimes Court Advocates for Wrongful Prosecution Despite 'Evidence of Torture' against Her", May 13, 2022, Lennart Dodoo, *FrontPageAfrica*. https:// frontpageafricaonline.com

638 Civitas Maxima (n.d.), "Michel Desaedeleer". https://civitas-maxima.org

639 Civitas Maxima (n.d.), "Mohammed Jabbateh". https://civitas-maxima.org

640 "Reasonable Doubt: Gibril Massaquoi Acquitted", April 29, 2022, Civitas Maxima. civitas-maxima.org

641 "Liberia's President Should Showcase Justice on International Stage", September 17,

2020, Elise Keppler, Human Rights Watch. https://www.hrw.org/news

642 Beth Van Schaak quoted in, "Liberia: US Ambassador on War Crimes to Seek Clarity from Liberian Legislature on Stalled Draft War Crimes Court Statutes", October 7, 2022, Gerald C. Koinyeneh,

FrontPageAfrica. https:// frontpageafricaonline.com

643 Ibid

644 "Pres. George Weah's Speech at the 74th United Nations General Assembly (Full Text)", September 25, 2019,

FrontPageAfrica. https:// frontpageafricaonline.com

645 "Liberia's President Should Showcase Justice on International Stage", September 17, 2020, Elise Keppler, Human Rights Watch. https://www.hrw.org/news

646 Ibid

647 Joseph R. Biden, Memorandum Establishing The Fight Against Corruption as a Core National Security Interest, June 3, 2021, The White House. https://www. whitehouse.gov

648 U.S. Mission in Liberia, Response Statement, 2021

649 "A Conflicted Leader: George Weah's First Year in Liberia", Elizabeth Donnelly/ Geraldine O'Mahony, January 28, 2019, Chatham House. https://www. chathamhouse.org

650 Ibid

651 See "FPA Under Attack; Attempt to Shut Newspaper Down Fails", April 10, 2021, Lennart Doddoo, *FrontPage Africa;*
"LETTER FROM THE EDITOR: A Bounty on My Head- Exposing the Ills Come with Risks, I'm Ready for the Fight", July 16, 2021, Rodney Sieh,

FrontPageAfrica. https:// frontpageafricaonline.com

652 Ibid

653 "New Millennium Challenge Compact Scorecard Shows Improvement in Rule of Law in Liberia", November 9, 2020,

Lennart Dodoo, *FrontPageAfrica.* https:// frontpageafricaonline.com

654 Jonathan Nash, Statement in Monrovia, June 2018

655 Michael McCarthy, from "Ambassador McCarthy Makes a Call-to-Action to Stop Power Theft in Liberia"

August 26, 2021, U.S. Embassy in Liberia. lr.usembassy.gov

656 Ibid

657 Ibid

658 Ibid

659 Ibid

660 Ibid

661 Ibid

662 Winston Tubman, Interview with Author, December 4, 2021

663 Ibid

664 Naymote Report, January 2021 .naymote.com

665 Clar Marie Weah, Interview with Rabin Nickens on Cultural Caribbean TV, 2018. Youtube.com.

666 Ibid

667 Ibid

668 Ibid

669 Ibid

670 Ibid

671 Ibid

672 Ibid

673 Ibid

674 "Model MacDella Cooper Gives Birth to Third Child", Richard Johnson, October 20, 2014, *The New York Post.*

675 Ibid

676 Clar Marie Weah, Interview with Rabin Nickens on Cultural Caribbean TV, 2018. Youtube.com

677 Sam Mannah, Statement about Weah's warrant, 2017.

678 "Liberian Presidential Candidate Weah's Lawyers to Go to U.S. Over Warrant", May 3, 2016, reuters.com

679 Eugene M. Benton, Newton County Court, Statement on Weah's request, 2017

680 "U.S. Court Denies Weah Attorney Fees in Child Support Case", January 24, 2017, *FrontPageAfrica*. https://frontpageafricaonline.com

681 MacDella Cooper, Interview [and report] with Radio France International, August 12, 2020.

682 Ibid

683 Leymah Gbowee, Speech, Liberia's 172 Independence Celebrations, July 26, 2019. See full text *at New Republic Liberia*, July 27, 2019. newrepublicliberia.com

684 Clar Marie Weah, Interview with Rabin Nickens on Cultural Caribbean TV, 2018. Youtube.cm

685 Ibid

686 Ibid

687 Ibid

688 Ibid

689 Ibid

690 Clar Marie Weah, Interview with Rabin Nickens on Cultural Caribbean TV, 2018. Youtube.cm

691 Section 9.6 of Liberia's Code of Conduct. Emansion.gov.lr

692 Clar Marie Weah, Interview with Rabin Nickens on Cultural Caribbean TV, 2018. Youtube.cm

693 Ibid

694 Ibid

695 Ibid

696 Ibid

697 Michael Duncan, Interview, "Liberia: 1st Lady's Brother Trying to Revive Marcus Garvey's Unfulfilled Vision; Dismisses Mining Claims", June 30, 2020, Rodney Sieh, *FrontPageAfrica*. https://frontpageafricaonline.com

698 Ibid

699 Ibid

700 Ibid

701 Ibid

702 Ibid

703 George Weah, Inaugural Speech, January 22, 2018. www.emansion.gov.lr

704 Honor Ford-Smith, p. 18, *Interventions: International Journal of Postcolonial Studies*, 6:1, 2004

705 J.J. Dossen, Response letter to UNIA, 1926

706 A source quoted in, "Liberia: 1st Lady's Brother Trying to Revive Marcus Garvey's Unfulfilled Vision; Dismisses Mining Claims", June 30, 2020, Rodney Sieh, *FrontPageAfrica*. https://frontpageafricaonline.com

707 Michael Duncan, Interview, "Liberia: 1st Lady's Brother Trying to Revive Marcus Garvey's Unfulfilled Vision; Dismisses Mining Claims", June 30, 2020, Rodney Sieh, *FrontPageAfrica*. https://frontpageafricaonline.com

708 Ibid

709 George Weah, Statement, Forkay Klon Jlateh Family Fellowship Church, October 4, 2020

710 Ibid

711 "Why Leaders Cheat: 4 Reasons (And) 1 Solution", Tomas Chamorro-Premuzic, *Huffington Post,* January 16, 2013. huffpost.com

712 Dionysius Sebwe, Interview *FrontPageAfrica*, March 2019.

713 Article 35 of the Liberian Constitution. judiciary.gov.lr

714 George Weah, statement to lawmakers, July 6, 2018.

715 Ibid

716 Ibid

717 Patrick Sendolo, statement during an appearance before a Senate committee,

March 2017, quoted in "Lands & Mines Minister Confirms Putu Mining Exit From Liberia", March 13, 2017, *FrontPageAfrica*. https://frontpageafricaonline.com

718 John Maxwell, *The 21 Irrefutable Laws of Leadership: Follow Them and People Will Follow You*, HarperColllins, 1998

719 Samuel K. Doe, on air, April 12, 1980

720 Samuel K. Doe, quoted in "The Rule of Samuel K. Doe", August 19, 1982, Carla Hall, *The Washington Post*. Washingtonpost.com

721 "The Rule of Samuel K. Doe", August 19, 1982, Carla Hall, *The Washington Post*. Washingtonpost.com

722 "Liberia: Rice Importers Reportedly Hoarding, Being Selective in Their Sales; Retailers Protest", March 30, 2022, Obediah Johnson, *FrontPageAfrica*. https://frontpageafricaonline.com

723 The Liberian Economy", A. Qureshi, Yoshio Mizoe and Francis d'A. Collings, January 1, 1964, International Monetary Fund. www.elibrary.imf.org

724 George Weah, Inaugural Speech, January 22, 2018. www.emansion.gov.lr

725 Ibid

726 Gloria Shalom, comment on YouTube

727 Randgt, comment on YouTube

728 Isaac Dikenah, comment on YouTube

729 Mark Reeves, comment on YouTube

730 "Mr Liar Man", KMTV Liberia Official Channel, YouTube

731 Solomon Joah, on air, Liberia Broadcasting System, May 2019

732 Ibid

733 "Liberia: Minister of State Nathaniel McGill Assuming Role of Civil Service Agency Director?" September 5, 2018, *FrontPageAfrica*. https://frontpageafricaonline.com

734 Ibid

735 Deborah Flomo, quoted in "Liberia: By-Election Results Suggest Voters Rejected Politics of Ego, Numbers Boast", November, 18, 2021, Rodney Sieh, *FrontPageAfrica*. https://frontpageafricaonline.com

736 Mulbah K. Morlu Jr, Interview with Author, November 13, 2021

737 George Wisner, Interview with Author, October 13, 2021

738 The US State Department, stating challenges of the FIU, 2021

739 Financial Intelligence Unit (FIU), Indictment report. December 2021, quoted in ""Liberia: Justice Minister Laments Cllr. Syrennius Cephus' Insubordination", January 14, 2022, Lennart Dodoo, *FrontPageAfrica*. https://frontpageafricaonline.com

740 Ibid

741 Liberia: Solicitor General, City Court Judge Believed to Be in Deal with Main Suspected Criminal in Major Money Laundering Case", 13 January, 2022, *FrontPageAfrica* https://frontpageafricaonline.com

742 Bill Clinton, video nterview with Jane Wales, July 2008

743 Wilson Tarpeh, news conference, 2008

744 Wilson Tarpeh, news conference, 2008

745 Bill Clinton, interview with Jane Wales, July 2008

746 Denzel Washington, presenting Weah with the 2004 ESPY's award, 2004.

747 George Solo, Interview with Author, January 17, 2022

748 Ibid

749 Ibid

750 Ibid

751 Ibid

752 Old Lady Margaret Nah, Interview with Author, December 2021

753 George Weah, *New York Times* Op-Ed, 2018

754 J. Odalfus Wesseh, Interview with Author, December 2021

755 Ibid

756 George Weah, Visit to the Gibraltar Community, April 23, 2018, reported in "President Weah to Re-Roof All Homes in Gibraltar Community", April 24, 2018. www.emansion.gov.lr

757 "Liberia: Weah's Gibraltar Re-Roofing Project Under Scrutiny; Approved Vouchers Show over US$1 Million Spent", December 24, 2018, Lennart Dodoo for *FrontPageAfrica*. https://frontpageafricaonline.com

758 George Weah, Inaugural Speech, January 22, 2018. www.emansion.gov.lr

759 "Weah Gives Hope to Gibraltar Residents", April 25, 2008, *The New Dawn*. thenewdawnliberia.com

760 Ibid

761 "Annual Message To the Second Session of the Fifty-Fourth National Legislature of the Republic of Liberia", George Weah, January 28, 2019. emansion.gov.lr

762 Theresa M. Foday, Interview with Author, December 2021

763 Ibid

764 Ibid

765 J. Odalfus Wesseh, Interview with Author, December 2021

766 J. Odalfus Wesseh, Interview with Author, December 2021

767 Harriet Nyeneh, Interview with Author, December 2021

768 Ibid

769 Ibid

770 George Weah, "Don't Forget About Liberia, *New York Times*, April 19, 2018

771 Betty Wesseh, Interview with Author, December 2021

772 Old Lady Margaret Nah, Interview with Author, December 2021

773 Ibid

774 Abraham Sieh Sonpon, Interview with Author, December 2021

775 "Reduce the Gap Between Rich and Poor: Dalai Lama", February 14, 2011.

776 Abraham Sieh Sonpon, Interview with Author, December 2021

777 A. Doris D. Grimes, July 23, 1971

778 D. Elwood Dunn, *Liberian Studies Journal,* 2019

779 Jerome Verdier, Interview with Author, March 3, 2022

780 George Weah, Inaugural Speech, January 22, 2018. www.emansion.gov.lr

781 Ibid

782 George Weah, April 8, 2021, in "Liberia: Pres. Weah Asks Liberians to Forgive Him Each Time They See Him Playing Football; Says It's an Inborn Tendency", April 8, 2021, Lennart Dodoo, *FrontPageAfrica*. https://frontpageafricaonline.com

783 Ibid

784 Emmanuel Adebayor, Interview with *So Foot,* November 8, 2017. sofoot.com

785 Didier Drogba, Africanews.com, January 18, 2018

786 George Weah, "Liberia - Where No-One Dares to Tackle President George Weah", interview with Mike Thomson, BBC, February 19, 2019. bbc.co.uk.

787 George Weah, Watch Night Sermon, December 31, 2019.

788 Ellen Johnson Sirleaf, Speaking at funeral of Dr. Amos Sawyer, April 2, 2022, in "Liberia: 'Where Is the Governance Commission Now?, April 4, 2022, David S. Menjor, *Liberian Observer*. www.liberianobserver.com

789 "Remarks by Ambassador Thomas-Greenfield at the Wilson Center's Virtual Event 'Commemorating 200 Years of U.S.-Liberia Ties: Moving Forward Together'", March 31, 2022, United States

Mission to the United Nations. https://usun.usmission.gov

790 Michael McCarthy, Op-ed, "What Would J.J. Roberts Say About Liberia Today", March 15, 2022, U.S. Embassy in Liberia. lr.usembassy.gov

791 Ibid

792 Lewis Benedictus Smedes, *Forgive and Forget: Healing the Hurts We Don't Deserve*, 1984

793 President George Weah, Invincible Sports Park, Monrovia, April 15, 2022. Text, "President Weah Dedicates Invincible Sports Park". emansion.gov.lr

794 Statement by the opposition People's Unification Party, July 2021

795 President George Weah, Inaugural Speech, January 22, 2018. www.emansion.gov.lr

796 David Richmond Gergen (n.d.), AZ Quotes. azquotes.com

797 Remarks by Special Assistant to U.S. President Dana Banks at Liberia Bicentennial Launch", February 14, 2022, *African Star*. africanstar.org

798 Michael McCarthy, Op-ed, "What Would J.J. Roberts Say About Liberia Today", March 15, 2022, U.S. Embassy in Liberia. lr.usembassy.gov

799 Ibid

800 "Remarks by Ambassador Thomas-Greenfield at the Wilson Center's Virtual Event 'Commemorating 200 Years of U.S.-Liberia Ties: Moving Forward Together'", March 31, 2022, United States Mission to the United Nations. https://usun.usmission.gov

801 "Press Release: Treasury Sanctions Senior Liberian Government Officials for Public Corruption", 15 August, 2022, U.S. Department of the Treasury. hometreasury.gov

802 Ibid

803 Ibid

804 Ibid

805 Ibid

806 "Liberia: Solicitor General, City Court Judge Believed to Be in Deal with Main Suspected Criminal in Major Money Laundering Case", January 13, 2022, *FrontPageAfrica*. https://frontpageafricaonline.com

807 "Press Release: Treasury Sanctions Senior Liberian Government Officials for Public Corruption", 15 August, 2022, U.S. Department of the Treasury. hometreasury.gov

808 Ibid

809 Press Release: Treasury Sanctions Senior Liberian Government Officials for Public Corruption", 15 August, 2022, U.S. Department of the Treasury. hometreasury.gov

810 Ibid

811 "Liberia: Sanctioned Officials of Govt Resign", September 13, 2022, *FrontPage Africa*. https://frontpageafricaonline.com

812 "On Rice Saga", September 30, 2022, Obediah Johnson, *FrontPageAfrica*. https://frontpageafricaonline.com